Man and Nature

Man
and
Nature
Studies in the Evolution
of the Human Species

EDITED BY

Frederick S. Hulse
UNIVERSITY OF ARIZONA

RANDOM HOUSE
NEW YORK

First Edition

9 8 7 6 5 4 3 2 1

Copyright © 1975 by Frederick S. Hulse

Library of Congress Cataloging in Publication Data

Hulse, Frederick Seymour, 1906–   comp.
    Man and nature.

    Includes bibliographies.
        1. Human evolution—Addresses, essays, lectures.
2. Human ecology—Addresses, essays, lectures.
I. Title.
GN281.H84   573.2   74–23791
ISBN 0–394–31828–5

Cover: Lawrence Daniels & Friends, Inc.
Text Design: Meryl Sussman Levavi

Manufactured in the United States of America. Composed by American Book–Stratford Press, Brattleboro, Vt.
Printed and bound by Halliday Litho., West Hanover, Mass.

Acknowledgments

SIR GAVIN DE BEER, "Mosaic Evolution" from *Streams of Culture*. Copyright © 1969 by Sir Gavin de Beer. Reprinted by permission of the author and J. B. Lippincott Company.

JEAN BENOIST, "Saint-Barthélemy: Physical Anthropology of an Isolate" from *American Journal of Physical Anthropology*, 22 (1964): 473–488. Reprinted by permission of the author and Johnson Reprint Corporation.

BATSHEVA BONNÉ, "Are There Hebrews Left?" from *American Journal of Physical Anthropology*, 24 (1966): 135–146. Reprinted by permission of the author and Johnson Reprint Corporation.

RACHEL CARSON, "The Obligation to Endure" from *Silent Spring*. Copyright © 1962 by Rachel Carson. Reprinted by permission of Houghton Mifflin Company.

NAPOLEON A. CHAGNON, JAMES V. NEEL, LOWELL WEITKAMP, HENRY GERSHOWITZ, and MANUEL AYRES, "The Influence of Cultural Factors on the Demography and Pattern of Gene Flow from the Makiritare to the Yanomama Indians" from *American Journal of Physical Anthropology*, 32 (1970): 339–350. Reprinted by permission of the authors and Johnson Reprint Corporation.

RAYMOND A. DART, "Australopithecus africanus: The Man-Ape of South Africa" from *Nature*, 115 (1925): 195–199. Reprinted by permission of the author and Macmillan (Journals) Ltd.

CHARLES DARWIN, "On the Variation of Organic Beings in a State of Nature" and an extract from his unpublished "Essay of 1844" from *Evolution by Natural Selection* (1958), edited by Sir Gavin de Beer. Reprinted by courtesy of Cambridge University Press.

JEAN HIERNAUX, "Heredity and Environment: Their Influence on Human Morphology" from *American Journal of Physical Anthropology*, 21 (1963): 575–590. Reprinted by permission of the author and Johnson Reprint Corporation.

F. CLARK HOWELL, "Upper Pleistocene Men of the Southwest Asian Mousterian" from *Hundert Jahre Neanderthaler, 1856–1956*, G. H. R. von Koenigswald (ed.). Copyright 1958 by the Wenner-Gren Foundation for Anthropological Research, Inc., New York. Reprinted by permission of the author and the Wenner-Gren Foundation.

FREDERICK S. HULSE, "Has Mankind a Future?" from *Dyn*. Copyright © 1972 by Durham University Anthropological Society. Reprinted by permission of the author and publisher.

G. E. HUTCHINSON, "Homage to Santa Rosalia, or Why are there so many kinds of animals?" from *The American Naturalist*, 93 (1959): 145–159. Copyright © 1959 by the University of Chicago. All rights reserved. Reprinted by permission of the author and the publisher.

JUNICHIRO ITANI, "The Society of Japanese Monkeys" from *The Japan Quarterly*, Vol. VIII, No. 4, 1961, pp. 1–14. Reprinted by permission of the author and Asahi Shimbun Publishing Company.

TEUKU JACOB, "The Sixth Skull Cap of *Pithecanthropus erectus*" from *American Journal of Physical Anthropology*, 25 (1966): 243–253. Reprinted by permission of the author and Johnson Reprint Corporation.

ARTHUR J. JELINEK, "Man's Role in the Extinction of Pleistocene Faunas" in *Pleistocene Extinctions*, P. S. Martin and H. E. Wright (eds.), pp. 193–200. Copyright © 1967 by Yale University. Reprinted by permission of the author and Yale University Press.

TERESA LASKA-MIERZEJEWSKA, "Effect of Ecological and Socio-economic Factors on the Age at Menarche, Body Height and Weight of Rural Girls in Poland" from *Human Biology*, 42.2 (1970): 284–292. Copyright © 1970 by Wayne State University Press. Reprinted by permission of the author and the publisher.

W. FARNSWORTH LOOMIS, "Skin Pigment Regulation of Vitamin-D Biosynthesis in Man" from *Science*, 157: 501–506. Copyright © 1967 by the American Association for the Advancement of Science. Reprinted by permission of the author and the publisher.

RUSSELL W. NEWMAN, "Why Man Is Such a Sweaty and Thirsty Naked Animal: A Speculative Review" from *Human Biology*, 42.1 (1970): 12–27. Copyright © 1970 by Wayne State University Press. Reprinted by permission of the author and the publisher.

WILLIAM S. POLLITZER, "The Negroes of Charleston (S.C.): A Study of Hemoglobin Types, Serology, and Morphology" from *American Journal of Physical Anthropology*, 16 (1958): 241–263. Reprinted by permission of the author and Johnson Reprint Corporation.

D. F. ROBERTS, "Basal Metabolism, Race and Climate" from *Journal of the Royal Anthropological Institute,* 82 (1952): 169–183. Reprinted by permission of the author and the Royal Anthropological Institute of Great Britain and Ireland.

EUGÈNE SCHREIDER, "Body-height and Inbreeding in France" from *American Journal of Physical Anthropology,* 26 (1967): 1–4, and "Inbreeding, Biological and Mental Variations in France" from *American Journal of Physical Anthropology,* 30 (1969): 215–220. Reprinted by permission of the author and Johnson Reprint Corporation.

J. C. SHARMA, "Convergent Evolution in the Tribes of Bastar" from *American Journal of Physical Anthropology,* 28 (1968): 113–118. Reprinted by permission of the author and Johnson Reprint Corporation.

A. T. STEEGMAN, JR., "Cold Adaptation and the Human Face" from *American Journal of Physical Anthropology,* 32 (1970): 243–250. Reprinted by permission of the author and Johnson Reprint Corporation.

Preface

SINCE FIRST READING *The Origin of Species* IN MY GRAND-father's library one summer long ago, I've had the opportunity to enjoy and appreciate the published works of many scientists who contributed to increasing our knowledge of man's place in nature. There are many excellent books dealing with human evolution and other aspects of anthropology. Yet original findings are more usually published as articles of varying length in scientific journals. Such articles report discoveries and experiments, summarize a body of existing knowledge, present viewpoints with respect to controversies, and advance hypotheses concerning problems. It is from such material that the information contained in most textbooks is derived. Consequently it seems only fair to give students the chance to read such primary sources, and many collections of readings have been published in order to present the varied viewpoints and interests of anthropologists. Naturally, each of them also represents the viewpoint and interests of the collector.

This volume represents my viewpoint and interests. It is organized around the theme of the evolution of our unique ecological position in the world of life. No attempt is made to present only the most recently published articles or the most sensational. A number of them are undoubtedly quite technical, and some of them are certainly speculative. All of them, however, are selections which excited my interest as soon as they came to my attention and which still stimulate me whenever I read them again. They reveal the great range of interests to be found among anthropologists. Each makes a solid contribution to the advancement of knowledge in the field of human biology. The first part of this selection of readings deals with evolution in general and the past evolution of the human species. The second part demonstrates the way in which our species is still evolving. I hope that the reader will enjoy these articles as much as I have.

FREDERICK S. HULSE

Tucson, Arizona
June 1974

Contents

Man and Nature

The Ecological Balance: What Is Man's Place in Nature?

F OR HUNDREDS OF MILLIONS OF YEARS THE WORLD WHICH WE now call ours was the home of many forms of life, but not of human beings. Our species is one of the most recent to have evolved. As time passed, conditions changed, and the sorts of animals and plants living in the world changed too. But, as a rule, the changes were so slow and gradual as to be imperceptible. At any given place, and during any given period of time, the different kinds of creatures appeared to constitute a well-balanced community. This was the sort of world in which our ancestors lived and evolved into the human species. The environmental conditions surrounding them were not, at first, modified very much by their efforts.

But among the most interesting characteristics of our species has been its growing power to modify the surrounding environment a very great deal. One of the first things that a student of anthropology needs to learn is the extent to which human activities have altered both the physical and the biological world. All animals seek greater comfort, of course, and some, such as beavers, may alter their surroundings quite a bit as a result of their efforts. This is perfectly natural and innocent. Human beings have simply been very much more effective in their efforts. Consequently, the so-called side effects (by which we mean the unintended and unanticipated results) of our attempts to make the environment more comfortable have often been disastrous. Until recently, almost no attention was paid to this fact. In 1962, however, the distinguished biologist Rachel Carson published *Silent Spring*, a book which could not be overlooked because of the thorough documentation which it provided for the thesis that we are rapidly approaching an ecological disaster. This book has been hysterically attacked, but it tells the truth.

So I have picked its second chapter, "The Obligation to Endure," as the first of the readings in this volume.

1. Rachel Carson

The Obligation to Endure

The history of life on earth has been a history of interaction between living things and their surroundings. To a large extent, the physical form and the habits of the earth's vegetation and its animal life have been molded by the environment. Considering the whole span of earthly time, the opposite effect, in which life actually modifies its surroundings, has been relatively slight. Only within the moment of time represented by the present century has one species—man—acquired significant power to alter the nature of his world.

During the past quarter century this power has not only increased to one of disturbing magnitude but it has changed in character. The most alarming of all man's assaults upon the environment is the contamination of air, earth, rivers, and sea with dangerous and even lethal materials. This pollution is for the most part irrecoverable; the chain of evil it initiates not only in the world that must support life but in living tissues is for the most part irreversible. In this now universal contamination of the environment, chemicals are the sinister and little-recognized partners of radiation in changing the very nature of the world—the very nature of its life. Strontium 90, released through nuclear explosions into the air, comes to earth in rain or drifts down as fallout, lodges in soil, enters into the grass or corn or wheat grown there, and in time takes up its abode in the bones of a human being, there to remain until his death. Similarly, chemicals sprayed on croplands or forests or gardens lie long in soil, entering into living organisms, passing from one to another in a chain of poisoning and death. Or they pass mysteriously by underground streams until they emerge and, through the alchemy of air and sunlight, combine into new forms that kill vegetation, sicken cattle, and work unknown harm on those who drink from once-pure wells. As Albert Schweitzer has said, "Man can hardly even recognize the devils of his own creation."

It took hundreds of millions of years to produce the life that now inhabits the earth—eons of time in which that developing and evolving and diversifying life reached a state of adjustment and balance with its surroundings. The environment, rigorously shaping and directing the life it supported, contained elements that were hostile as well as supporting. Certain rocks gave out dangerous radiation; even within the light of the sun, from which all life draws its energy, there were short-wave radiations with power to injure. Given time—time not in years but in millennia—life adjusts, and a balance has been reached. For time is the essential ingredient; but in the modern world there is no time.

The rapidity of change and the speed with which new situations are created follow the impetuous and heedless pace of man rather than the deliberate pace of nature. Radiation is no longer merely the background radiation of rocks, the bombardment of cosmic rays, the ultraviolet of the sun that have existed before there was any life on earth; radiation is now the unnatural creation of man's tampering with the atom. The chemicals to which life is asked to make its adjustment are no longer merely the calcium and silica and copper and all the rest of the minerals washed out of the rocks and carried in rivers to the sea; they are the synthetic creations of man's inventive mind, brewed in his laboratories, and having no counterparts in nature.

To adjust to these chemicals would require time on the scale that is nature's; it would require not merely the years of a man's life but the life of generations. And even this, were it by some miracle possible, would be futile, for the new chemicals come from our laboratories in an endless stream; almost five hundred annually find their way into actual use in the United States alone. The figure is staggering and its implications are not easily grasped—500 new chemicals to which the bodies of men and animals are required somehow to adapt each year, chemicals totally outside the limits of biologic experience.

Among them are many that are used in man's war against nature. Since the mid-1940's over 200 basic chemicals have been created for use in killing insects, weeds, rodents, and other organisms described in the modern vernacular as "pests"; and they are sold under several thousand different brand names.

These sprays, dusts, and aerosols are now applied almost universally to farms, gardens, forests, and homes—nonselective chemicals that have the power to kill every insect, the "good" and the "bad," to still the song of birds and the leaping of fish in the streams, to coat the leaves with a deadly film, and to linger on in soil—all this though the intended target may be only a few weeds or insects. Can anyone believe it is possible to lay down such a barrage of poisons on the surface of the earth without making it unfit for all life? They should not be called "insecticides," but "biocides."

The whole process of spraying seems caught up in an endless spiral. Since DDT was released for civilian use, a process of escalation has been going on in which ever more toxic materials must be found. This has happened because insects, in a triumphant vindication of Darwin's principle of the survival of the fittest, have evolved super races immune to the particular insecticide used, hence a deadlier one has always to be developed—and then a deadlier one than that. It has happened also because, for reasons to be described later, destructive insects often undergo a "flareback," or resurgence, after spraying, in numbers greater than before. Thus the chemical war is never won, and all life is caught in its violent crossfire.

Along with the possibility of the extinction of mankind by nuclear war, the central problem of our age has therefore become the contamination of man's total environment with such substances of incredible potential for harm—substances that accumulate in the tissues of plants and animals and even penetrate the germ cells to shatter or alter the very material of heredity upon which the shape of the future depends.

Some would-be architects of our future look toward a time when it will be possible to alter the human germ plasm by design. But we may easily be doing so now by inadvertence, for many chemicals, like radiation, bring about gene mutations. It is ironic to think that man might determine his own future by something so seemingly trivial as the choice of an insect spray.

All this has been risked—for what? Future historians may well be amazed by our distorted sense of proportion. How could intelligent beings seek to control a few unwanted species by a method that contaminated the entire environment and brought the threat of disease and death even to their own kind? Yet this is precisely what we have done. We have done it, moreover, for reasons that collapse the moment we examine them. We are told that the enormous and expanding use of pesticides is necessary to maintain farm production. Yet is our real problem not one of *overproduction*? Our farms, despite measures to remove acreages from production and to pay farmers *not* to produce, have yielded such a staggering excess of crops that the American taxpayer in 1962 is paying out more than one billion dollars a year as the total carrying cost of the surplus-food storage program. And is the situation helped when one branch of the Agriculture Department tries to reduce production while another states, as it did in 1958, "It is believed generally that reduction of crop acreages under provisions of the Soil Bank will stimulate interest in use of chemicals to obtain maximum production on the land retained in crops."

All this is not to say there is no insect problem and no need of control. I am saying, rather, that control must be geared to realities, not to mythical situations, and that the methods employed must be such that they do not destroy us along with the insects.

The problem whose attempted solution has brought such a train of disaster in its wake is an accompaniment of our modern way of life. Long before the age of man, insects inhabited the earth—a group of extraordinarily varied and adaptable beings. Over the course of time since man's advent, a small percentage of the more than half a million species of insects have come into conflict with human welfare in two principal ways: as competitors for the food supply and as carriers of human disease.

Disease-carrying insects become important where human beings are crowded together, especially under conditions where sanitation is poor, as in time of natural disaster or war or in situations of extreme poverty and deprivation. Then control of some sort becomes necessary. It is a sobering fact, however, as we shall presently see, that the method of massive chemical control has had only limited success, and also threatens to worsen the very conditions it is intended to curb.

Under primitive agricultural conditions the farmer had few insect problems.

These arose with the intensification of agriculture—the devotion of immense acreages to a single crop. Such a system set the stage for explosive increases in specific insect populations. Single-crop farming does not take advantage of the principles by which nature works; it is agriculture as an engineer might conceive it to be. Nature has introduced great variety into the landscape, but man has displayed a passion for simplifying it. Thus he undoes the built-in checks and balances by which nature holds the species within bounds. One important natural check is a limit on the amount of suitable habitat for each species. Obviously then, an insect that lives on wheat can build up its population to much higher levels on a farm devoted to wheat than on one in which wheat is intermingled with other crops to which the insect is not adapted.

The same thing happens in other situations. A generation or more ago, the towns of large areas of the United States lined their streets with the noble elm tree. Now the beauty they hopefully created is threatened with complete destruction as disease sweeps through the elms, carried by a beetle that would have only limited chance to build up large populations and to spread from tree to tree if the elms were only occasional trees in a richly diversified planting.

Another factor in the modern insect problem is one that must be viewed against a background of geologic and human history: the spreading of thousands of different kinds of organisms from their native homes to invade new territories. This worldwide migration has been studied and graphically described by the British ecologist Charles Elton in his recent book *The Ecology of Invasions*. During the Cretaceous Period, some hundred million years ago, flooding seas cut many land bridges between continents and living things found themselves confined in what Elton calls "colossal separate nature reserves." There, isolated from others of their kind, they developed many new species. When some of the land masses were joined again, about 15 million years ago, these species began to move out into new territories—a movement that is not only still in progress but is now receiving considerable assistance from man.

The importation of plants is the primary agent in the modern spread of species, for animals have almost invariably gone along with the plants, quarantine being a comparatively recent and not completely effective innovation. The United States Office of Plant Introduction alone has introduced almost 200,000 species and varieties of plants from all over the world. Nearly half of the 180 or so major insect enemies of plants in the United States are accidental imports from abroad, and most of them have come as hitchhikers on plants.

In new territory, out of reach of the restraining hand of the natural enemies that kept down its numbers in its native land, an invading plant or animal is able to become enormously abundant. Thus it is no accident that our most troublesome insects are introduced species.

These invasions, both the naturally occurring and those dependent on human assistance, are likely to continue indefinitely. Quarantine and massive chemical campaigns are only extremely expensive ways of buying time. We are faced, according to Dr. Elton, "with a life-and-death need not just to find new technological means of suppressing this plant or that animal"; instead we need the basic knowledge of animal populations and their relations to their surroundings that will "promote an even balance and damp down the explosive power of outbreaks and new invasions."

Much of the necessary knowledge is now available but we do not use it. We train ecologists in our universities and even employ them in our governmental agencies but we seldom take their advice. We allow the chemical death rain to fall as though there were no alternative, whereas in fact there are many, and our ingenuity could soon discover many more if given opportunity.

Have we fallen into a mesmerized state that makes us accept as inevitable that which is inferior or detrimental, as though having lost the will or the vision to demand that which is good? Such thinking, in the words of the ecologist Paul Shepard, "idealizes life with only its head out of water, inches above the limits of toleration of the corruption of its own environment . . . Why should we tolerate a diet of weak poisons, a home in insipid surroundings, a circle of acquaintances who are not quite our enemies, the noise of motors with just enough relief to prevent insanity? Who would want to live in a world which is just not quite fatal?"

Yet such a world is pressed upon us. The crusade to create a chemically sterile, insect-free world seems to have engendered a fanatic zeal on the part of many specialists and most of the so-called control agencies. On every hand there is evidence that those engaged in spraying operations exercise a ruthless power. "The regulatory entomologists . . . function as prosecutor, judge and jury, tax assessor and collector and sheriff to enforce their own orders," said Connecticut entomologist Neely Turner. The most flagrant abuses go unchecked in both state and federal agencies.

It is not my contention that chemical insecticides must never be used. I do contend that we have put poisonous and biologically potent chemicals indiscriminately into the hands of persons largely or wholly ignorant of their potentials for harm. We have subjected enormous numbers of people to contact with these poisons, without their consent and often without their knowledge. If the Bill of Rights contains no guarantee that a citizen shall be secure against lethal poisons distributed either by private individuals or by public officials, it is surely only because our forefathers, despite their considerable wisdom and foresight, could conceive of no such problem.

I contend, furthermore, that we have allowed these chemicals to be used with little or no advance investigation of their effect on soil, water, wildlife, and man himself. Future generations are unlikely to condone our lack of prudent concern for the integrity of the natural world that supports all life.

There is still very limited awareness of the nature of the threat. This is an era of specialists, each of whom sees his own problem and is unaware of or intolerant of the larger frame into which it fits. It is also an era dominated by industry, in which the right to make a dollar at whatever cost is seldom challenged. When the public protests, confronted with some obvious evidence of damaging results of pesticide applications, it is fed little tranquilizing pills of half truth. We urgently need an end to these false assurances, to the sugar coating of unpalatable facts. It is the public that is being asked to assume the risks that the insect controllers calculate. The public must decide whether it wishes to continue on the present road, and it can do so only when in full possession of the facts. In the words of Jean Rostand, "The obligation to endure gives us the right to know."

The Origin of Species: Creation or Natural Selection

W

HEN CHARLES DARWIN SAILED AROUND THE WORLD ON H.M.S. *Beagle* during the 1830s, the idea of biological evolution, though far from new, was most unpopular among naturalists. No one had been able to give a satisfactory explanation of how one species could be transformed into another. Under the influence of Platonic dogma concerning the primacy of ideal types, all variation within a species was assumed to be a sign of imperfection, or pathology. Each species had its proper place in the great chain of being. Nor, in European mythology, was the idea that everything changes regarded as very relevant, even though changes could be observed everywhere.

What Darwin saw and studied during this long voyage, and the time which it gave him for undisturbed reflection, led him to the conclusion that variation in nature is by no means a mistake, but rather the raw material from which natural selection can, and does, work to produce changes within a species in response to changes in its conditions of life. Not many years later, before Darwin had made his views public, another wandering naturalist, Alfred R. Wallace, reached the same conclusion as a result of all that he had seen and studied. Early in 1858 he sent Darwin a sketch of his theory: that new species originate by means of natural selection.

On July 1, 1858, this paper, together with excerpts from Darwin's still unpublished work, was read at a meeting of the Linnean Society of London, and the intellectual world of Europe was turned upside down. Or, rather, it was turned right side up for the first time, since once this hypothesis had been clearly stated, and the mass of supporting evidence revealed, its power as an explanatory tool was very clear. As another scientist of the time observed: "How extremely stupid of me not to have realized this before!" Therefore, as the second selection in this volume, I have picked Darwin's original paper, as read in 1858, together with the final section of his "Essay of 1844" on the same topic.

2. Charles Darwin

On the Variation of Organic Beings in a State of Nature

On the Natural Means of Selection; On the Comparison of Domestic Races and True Species

De Candolle, in an eloquent passage, has declared that all nature is at war, one organism with another, or with external nature. Seeing the contented face of nature, this may at first well be doubted: but reflection will inevitably prove it to be true. The war, however, is not constant, but recurrent in a slight degree at short periods, and more severely at occasional more distant periods; and hence its effects are easily overlooked. It is the doctrine of Malthus applied in most cases with tenfold force. As in every climate there are seasons, for each of its inhabitants, of greater and less abundance, so all annually breed; and the moral restraint which in some small degree checks the increase of mankind is entirely lost. Even slow-breeding mankind has doubled in twenty-five years; and if he could increase his food with greater ease, he would double in less time. But for animals without artificial means, the amount of food for each species must, *on an average,* be constant, whereas the increase of all organisms tends to be geometrical, and in a vast majority of cases at an enormous ratio. Suppose in a certain spot there are eight pairs of birds, and that *only* four pairs of them annually (including double hatches) rear only four young, and that these go on rearing their young at the same rate, then at the end of seven years (a short life, excluding violent deaths, for any bird) there will be 2048 birds, instead of the original sixteen. As this increase is quite impossible, we must conclude either that birds do not rear nearly half their young, or that the average life of a bird is, from accident, not nearly seven years. Both checks probably concur. The same kind of calculation applied to all plants and animals affords results more or less striking, but in very few instances more striking than in man.

Many practical illustrations of this rapid tendency to increase are on record, among which, during peculiar seasons, are the extraordinary numbers of certain animals; for instance, during the years 1826 to 1828, in La Plata, when from drought some millions of cattle perished, the whole country actually *swarmed* with mice. Now I think it cannot be doubted that during the breeding season all the mice (with the exception of a few males or females in excess) ordinarily pair, and therefore that this astounding increase during three years must be attributed to a greater number than usual surviving the first year, and then breeding, and so on till the third year, when their numbers were brought down to their usual limits on the return of wet weather. Where man has introduced plants and animals into a new and favourable country, there are many accounts in how surprisingly few years the whole country has become stocked with them. This increase would necessarily stop as soon as the country was fully stocked; and yet we have every reason to believe, from what is known of wild animals, that *all* would pair in the spring. In the majority of cases it is most difficult to imagine where the check falls—though generally, no doubt, on the seeds, eggs, and young; but when we remember how impossible, even in mankind (so much better known than any other animal), it is to infer from repeated casual observations what the average duration of life is, or to discover the different percentage of deaths to births in different countries, we ought to feel no surprise at our being unable to discover where the check falls in any animal or plant. It should always be remembered, that in most cases the checks are recurrent yearly in a small, regular degree, and in an extreme degree during unusually cold, hot, dry, or wet years, according to the constitution of the being in question. Lighten any check in the least degree, and the geometrical powers of increase in every organism will almost instantly increase the average number of the favoured species. Nature may be compared to a surface on which rest ten thousand sharp wedges touching each other and driven inwards by incessant blows. Fully to realize these views much reflection is requisite. Malthus on man should be studied; and all such cases as those of the mice in La Plata, of the cattle and horses when first turned out in South America, of the birds by our calculation, etc., should be well considered. Reflect on the enormous multiplying power *inherent and annually in action* in all animals; reflect on the countless seeds scattered by a hundred ingenious contrivances, year after year, over the whole face of the land; and yet we have every reason to suppose that the average percentage of each of the inhabitants of a country usually remains constant. Finally, let it be borne in mind that this average number of individuals (the external conditions remaining the same) in each country is kept up by recurrent struggles against other species or against external nature (as on the borders of the arctic regions, where the cold checks life), and that ordinarily each individual of every species holds its place, either by its own struggle and capacity of acquiring nourishment in some period of its life, from the egg upwards; or by the struggle of its parents (in short-lived organisms, when the main check occurs at longer intervals) with other individuals of the *same* or *different* species.

But let the external conditions of a country alter. If in a small degree, the relative proportions of the inhabitants will in most cases simply be slightly changed; but let the number of inhabitants be small, as on an island, and free access to it from other countries be circumscribed, and let the change of conditions continue progressing (forming new stations), in such a case the original inhabitants must cease to be as perfectly adapted to the changed conditions as they were originally. It has been shown in a former part of this work, that such changes of external conditions would, from their acting on the reproductive system, probably cause the organization of those beings which were most affected to become, as under domestication, plastic. Now, can it be doubted, from the struggle each individual has to obtain subsistence, that any minute variation in structure, habits, or instincts, adapting that individual better to the new conditions, would tell upon its vigour and health? In the struggle it would have a better *chance* of surviving; and those of its offspring which inherited the variation, be it ever so slight, would also have a better *chance*. Yearly more are bred than can survive; the smallest grain in the balance, in the long run, must tell on which death shall fall, and which shall survive. Let this work of selection on the one hand, and death on the other, go on for a thousand generations, who will pretend to affirm that it would produce no effect, when we remember what, in a few years, Bakewell effected in cattle, and Western in sheep, by this identical principle of selection?

To give an imaginary example from changes in progress on an island: let the organization of a canine animal which preyed chiefly on rabbits, but sometimes on hares, become slightly plastic; let these same changes cause the number of rabbits very slowly to decrease, and the number of hares to increase; the effect of this would be that the fox or dog would be driven to try to catch more hares: his organization, however, being slightly plastic, those individuals with the lightest forms, longest limbs, and best eyesight, let the difference be ever so small, would be slightly favoured, and would tend to live longer, and to survive during that time of the year when food was scarcest; they would also rear more young, which would tend to inherit these slight peculiarities. The less fleet ones would be rigidly destroyed. I can see no more reason to doubt that these causes in a thousand generations would produce a marked effect, and adapt the form of the fox or dog to the catching of hares instead of rabbits, than that greyhounds can be improved by selection and careful breeding. So would it be with plants under similar circumstances. If the number of individuals of a species with plumed seeds could be increased by greater powers of dissemination within its own area (that is, if the check to increase fell chiefly on the seeds), those seeds which were provided with ever so little more down, would in the long run be most disseminated; hence a greater number of seeds thus formed would germinate, and would tend to produce plants inheriting the slightly better-adapted down.[1]

Besides this natural means of selection, by which those individuals are preserved, whether in their egg, or larval, or mature state, which are best adapted to the place they fill in nature, there is a second agency at work in most unisexual animals, tending to produce the same effect, namely the struggle of the males for the females. These struggles are generally decided by the law of battle, but in the case of birds, apparently, by the charms of their song, by their beauty or their power of courtship, as in the dancing rock-thrush of Guiana. The most vigorous and healthy males, implying perfect adaptation, must generally gain the victory in their contests. This kind of selection, however, is less rigorous than the other; it does not require the death of the less successful, but gives to them fewer descendants. The struggle falls, moreover, at a time of year when food is generally

---

[1] I can see no more difficulty in this, than in the planter improving his varieties of the cotton plant. C. D. 1858.

abundant, and perhaps the effect chiefly produced would be the modification of the secondary sexual characters, which are not related to the power of obtaining food, or to defence from enemies, but to fighting with or rivalling other males. The result of this struggle amongst the males may be compared in some respects to that produced by those agriculturists, who pay less attention to the careful selection of all their young animals, and more to the occasional use of a choice male.

. . .

Why Do We Wish to Reject the Theory of Common Descent?

Thus have many general facts, or laws, been included under one explanation; and the difficulties encountered are those which would naturally result from our acknowledged ignorance. And why should we not admit this theory of descent? Can it be shown that organic beings in a natural state are *all absolutely invariable*? Can it be said that the *limit of variation* or the number of varieties capable of being formed under domestication are known? Can any distinct line be drawn *between a race and a species*? To these three questions we may certainly answer in the negative. As long as species were thought to be divided and defined by an impassable barrier of *sterility,* whilst we were ignorant of geology, and imagined that the *world was of short duration,* and the number of its past inhabitants few, we were justified in assuming individual creations, or in saying with Whewell that the beginnings of all things are hidden from man. Why then do we feel so strong an inclination to reject this theory—especially when the actual case of any two species, or even of any two races, is adduced—and one is asked, have these two originally descended from the same parent womb? I believe it is because we are always slow in admitting any great change of which we do not see the intermediate steps. The mind cannot grasp the full meaning of the term of a million or hundred million years, and cannot consequently add up and perceive the full effects of small successive variations accumulated during almost infinitely many generations. The difficulty is the same with that which, with most geologists, it has taken long years to remove, as when Lyell propounded that great valleys were hollowed out [and long lines of inland cliffs had been formed] by the slow action of the waves of the sea. A man may long view a grand precipice without actually believing, though he may not deny it, that thousands of feet in thickness of solid rock once extended over many square miles where the open sea now rolls; without fully believing that the same sea which he sees beating the rock at his feet has been the sole removing power.

Shall we then allow that the three distinct species of *Rhinoceros* which separately inhabit Java and Sumatra and the neighbouring mainland of Malacca were created, male and female, out of the inorganic materials of these countries? Without any adequate cause, as far as our reason serves, shall we say that they were merely, from living near each other, created very like each other, so as to form a section of the genus dissimilar from the African section, some of the species of which sections inhabit very similar and some very dissimilar stations?

Shall we say that without any apparent cause they were created on the same generic type with the ancient woolly rhinoceros of Siberia and of the other species which formerly inhabited the same main division of the world: that they were created, less and less closely related, but still with interbranching affinities, with all the other living and extinct mammalia? That without any apparent adequate cause their short necks should contain the same number of vertebrae with the giraffe; that their thick legs should be built on the same plan with those of the antelope, of the mouse, of the hand of the monkey, of the wing of the bat, and of the fin of the porpoise. That in each of these species the second bone of their leg should show clear traces of two bones having been soldered and united into one, that the complicated bones of their head should become intelligible on the supposition of their having been formed of three expanded vertebrae; that in the jaws of each when dissected young there should exist small teeth which never come to the surface. That in possessing these useless abortive teeth, and in other characters, these three rhinoceroses in their embryonic state should much more closely resemble other mammalia than they do when mature. And lastly, that in a still earlier period of life, their arteries should run and branch as in a fish, to carry the blood to gills which do not exist. Now these three species of rhinoceros closely resemble each other; more closely than many generally acknowledged races of our domestic animals; these three species if domesticated would almost certainly vary, and races adapted to different ends might be selected out of such variations. In this state they would probably breed together, and their offspring would possibly be quite, and probably in some degree, fertile; and in either case, by continued crossing, one of these specific forms might be absorbed and lost in another. I repeat, shall we then say that a pair, or a gravid female, of each of these three species of rhinoceros, were separately created with deceptive appearances of true relationship, with the stamp of inutility on some parts, and of conversion in other parts, out of the inorganic elements of Java, Sumatra and Malacca? or have they descended, like our domestic races, from the same parent-stock? For my own part I could no more admit the former proposition than I could admit that the planets move in their courses, and that a stone falls to the ground, not through the intervention of the secondary and appointed law of gravity, but from the direct volition of the Creator.

Before concluding it will be well to show, although this has incidentally appeared, how far the theory of common descent can legitimately be extended. If we once admit that two true species of the same genus can have descended from the same parent, it will not be possible to deny that two species of two genera may also have descended from a common stock. For in some families the genera approach almost as closely as species of the same genus; and in some orders, for instance in the monocotyledonous plants, the families run closely into each other. We do not hesitate to assign a common origin to dogs or cabbages, because they are divided into groups analogous to the groups in nature. Many naturalists indeed admit that all groups are artificial; and that they depend entirely on the extinction of intermediate species. Some naturalists, however, affirm that though driven from considering sterility as the characteristic of species, an entire incapacity to propagate together is the best evidence of the existence of natural genera. Even if we put on one side the undoubted fact that some species of the same genus will not breed together, we cannot possibly admit the above rule, seeing that the grouse and pheasant (considered by some good ornithologists as forming two families), the bull-finch and canary-bird have bred together.

No doubt the more remote two species are from each other, the weaker the arguments become in favour of their common descent. In species of two distinct families the analogy, from the variation of domestic organisms and from the manner of their intermarrying, fails; and the arguments from their geographical distribution quite or almost quite fails. But if we once admit the general principles of this work, as far as a clear unity of type can be made out in groups of species, adapted to play diversified parts in the economy of nature, whether shown in the structure of the embryonic or mature being, and especially if shown by a community of abortive parts, we are legitimately led to admit their community of descent. Naturalists dispute how widely this unity of type extends: most, however, admit that the vertebrata are built on one type; the articulata on another; the mollusca on a third; and the radiata on probably more than one. Plants also appear to fall under three or four great types. On this theory, therefore, all the organisms *yet discovered* are descendants of probably less than ten parent-forms.

Conclusion

My reasons have now been assigned for believing that specific forms are not immutable creations. The terms used by naturalists of affinity, unity of type, adaptive characters, the metamorphosis and abortion of organs, cease to be metaphorical expressions and become intelligible facts. We no longer look at an organic being as a savage does at a ship or other great work of art, as at a thing wholly beyond his comprehension, but as a production that has a history which we may search into. How interesting do all instincts become when we speculate on their origin as hereditary habits, or as slight congenital modifications of former instincts perpetuated by the individuals so characterized having been preserved. When we look at every complex instinct and mechanism as the summing up of a long history of contrivances, each most useful to its possessor, nearly in the same way as when we look at a great mechanical invention as the summing up of the labour, the experience, the reason, and even the blunders of numerous workmen. How interesting does the geographical distribution of all organic beings, past and present, become as throwing light on the ancient geography of the world. Geology loses glory from the imperfection of its archives, but it gains in the immensity of its subject. There is much grandeur in looking at every existing organic being either as the lineal successor of some form now buried under thousands of feet of solid rock, or as being the co-descendant of that buried form of some more ancient and utterly lost inhabitant of this world. It accords with what we know of the laws impressed by the Creator on matter that the production and extinction of forms should, like the birth and death of individuals, be the result of secondary means. It is derogatory that the Creator of countless

Universes should have made by individual acts of His will the myriads of creeping parasites and worms, which since the earliest dawn of life have swarmed over the land and in the depths of the ocean. We cease to be astonished that a group of animals should have been formed to lay their eggs in the bowels and flesh of other sensitive beings; that some animals should live by and even delight in cruelty; that animals should be led away by false instincts; that annually there should be an incalculable waste of the pollen, eggs and immature beings; for we see in all this the inevitable consequences of one great law, of the multiplication of organic beings not created immutable. From death, famine, and the struggle for existence, we see that the most exalted end which we are capable of conceiving, namely, the creation of the higher animals, has directly proceeded. Doubtless, our first impression is to disbelieve that any secondary law could produce infinitely numerous organic beings, each characterized by the most exquisite workmanship and widely extended adaptations: it at first accords better with our faculties to suppose that each required the fiat of a Creator. There is a [simple] grandeur in this view of life with its several powers of growth, reproduction and of sensation, having been originally breathed into matter under a few forms, perhaps into only one, and that whilst this planet has gone cycling onwards according to the fixed laws of gravity and whilst land and water have gone on replacing each other— that from so simple an origin, through the selection of infinitesimal varieties, endless forms most beautiful and most wonderful have been evolved.

Variety, Evolution, and Ecological Niches

HOW MANY DIFFERENT SORTS OF ANIMALS AND PLANTS have you seen during the last week? Does it occur to you to wonder how such a variety of living things can all support themselves in the same locality? Ecologists not only wonder about this but attempt to find out. After Darwin's work had demonstrated that evolution, by means of natural selection, had led to the diversification of the forms of life, it remained for later generations of biologists to explore the ramifications of his discovery. Natural selection affects not only single organisms but whole populations of such organisms; and not only populations but communities composed of many different species. Within such communities, different sorts of creatures—young and old, male and female, as well as different species—have to adapt to each other's presence. Thus the study of the mutual relationships between the forms of life inhabiting a locality is one of the major aspects of ecology.

If we are to understand how our species fits into the community, we need to learn how other sorts of creatures fit together. If we are to understand how our genus, during its evolution, came to shift its means of livelihood so drastically, we need to learn how other varieties of animals have been able to exploit new ways of making a living, as did some of Darwin's finches in the Galápagos. We need to learn the rules by which the evolutionary game is played. Among these rules those which regulate the number of different kinds of creatures for which ecological niches are available within a community are really basic. In the following article, a scholar with a very subtle mind, Dr. G. E. Hutchinson, discusses the question "Why are there so many kinds of animals?"

3. G. E. Hutchinson

Homage to Santa Rosalia, or Why Are There So Many Kinds of Animals?*

When you did me the honor of asking me to fill your presidential chair, I accepted perhaps without duly considering the duties of the president of a society, founded largely to further the study of evolution, at the close of the year that marks the centenary of Darwin and Wallace's initial presentation of the theory of natural selection. It seemed to me that most of the significant aspects of modern evolutionary theory have come either from geneticists, or from those heroic museum workers who suffering through years of neglect, were able to establish about 20 years ago what has come to be called the "new systematics." You had, however, chosen an ecologist as your president and one of that school at times supposed to study the environment without any relation to the organism.

A few months later I happened to be in Sicily. An early interest in zoogeography and in aquatic insects led me to attempt to collect near Palermo, certain species of water-bugs, of the genus Corixa, described a century ago by Fieber and supposed to occur in the region, but never fully reinvestigated. It is hard to find suitable localities in so highly cultivated a landscape as the Concha d'Oro. Fortunately, I was driven up Monte Pellegrino, the hill that rises to the west of the city, to admire the view. A little below the summit, a church with a simple baroque facade stands in front of a cave in the limestone of the hill. Here in the 16th century a stalactite encrusted skeleton associated with a cross and twelve beads was discovered. Of this skeleton nothing is certainly known save that it is that of Santa Rosalia, a saint of whom little is reliably reported save that she seems to have lived in the 12th century, that her skeleton was found in this cave, and that she has been the chief patroness of Palermo ever since. Other limestone caverns on Monte Pellegrino had yielded bones of extinct pleistocene Equus, and on the walls of one of the rock shelters at the bottom of the hill there are beautiful Gravettian engravings. Moreover, a small relic of the saint that I saw in the treasury of the Cathedral of Monreale has a venerable and petrified appearance, as might be expected. Nothing in her history being known to the contrary, perhaps for the

---

* Address of the President, American Society of Naturalists, delivered at the annual meeting, Washington, D.C., December 30, 1958.

moment we may take Santa Rosalia as the patroness of evolutionary studies, for just below the sanctuary, fed no doubt by the water that percolates through the limestone cracks of the mountain, and which formed the sacred cave, lies a small artificial pond, and when I could get to the pond a few weeks later, I got from it a hint of what I was looking for.

Vast numbers of Corixidae were living in the water. At first I was rather disappointed because every specimen of the larger of the two species present was a female, and so lacking in most critical diagnostic features, while both sexes of the second slightly smaller species were present in about equal number. Examination of the material at leisure, and of the relevant literature, has convinced me that the two species are the common European *C. punctata* and *C. affinis,* and that the peculiar Mediterranean species are illusionary. The larger *C. punctata* was clearly at the end of its breeding season, the smaller *C. affinis* was probably just beginning to breed. This is the sort of observation that any naturalist can and does make all the time. It was not until I asked myself why the larger species should breed first, and then the more general question as to why there should be two and not 20 or 200 species of the genus in the pond, that ideas suitable to present to you began to emerge. These ideas finally prompted the very general question as to why there are such an enormous number of animal species.

There are at the present time supposed to be (Muller and Campbell, 1954; Hyman, 1955) about one million described species of animals. Of these about three-quarters are insects, of which a quite disproportionately large number are members of a single order, the Coleoptera.[1] The marine fauna although it has at its disposal a much greater area than has the terrestrial, lacks this astonishing diversity (Thorson, 1958). If the insects are excluded, it would seem to be more diverse. The proper answer to my initial question would be to develop a theory at least predicting an order of magnitude for the number of species of 10^6 rather than 10^8 or 10^4. This I certainly cannot do. At most it is merely possible to point out some of the factors which would have to be considered if such a theory was ever to be constructed.

Before developing my ideas I should like to say that I subscribe to the view that the process of natural selection, coupled with isolation and later mutual invasion of ranges leads to the evolution of sympatric species, which at equilibrium occupy distinct niches, according to the Volterra-Gause principle. The empirical reasons for adopting this view and the correlative view that the boundaries of realized niches are set by competition are mainly indirect. So far as niches may be defined in terms of food, the subject has been carefully considered by Lack (1954). In general all the indirect evidence is in accord with the view, which has the advantage of confirming theoretical expectation. Most of the opinions that have been held to the contrary appear to be due to misunderstandings and to loose formulation of the problem (Hutchinson, 1958).

[1] There is a story, possibly apocryphal, of the distinguished British biologist, J. B. S. Haldane, who found himself in the company of a group of theologians. On being asked what one could conclude as to the nature of the Creator from a study of his creation, Haldane is said to have answered, "An inordinate fondness for beetles."

In any study of evolutionary ecology, food relations appear as one of the most important aspects of the system of animate nature. There is quite obviously much more to living communities than the raw dictum "eat or be eaten," but in order to understand the higher intricacies of any ecological system, it is most easy to start from this crudely simple point of view.

FOOD CHAINS

Animal ecologists frequently think in terms of food chains, of the form *individuals of species S_1 are eaten by those of S_2, of S_2 by S_3, of S_3 by S_4*, etc. In such a food chain S_1 will ordinarily be some holophylic organism or material derived from such organisms. The simplest case is that in which we have a true *predator chain* in Odum's (1953) convenient terminology, in which the lowest link is a green plant, the next a herbivorous animal, the next a primary carnivore, the next a secondary carnivore, etc. A specially important type of predator chain may be designated Eltonian, because in recent years C. S. Elton (1927) has emphasized its widespread significance, in which the predator at each level is larger and rarer than its prey. This phenomenon was recognized much earlier, notably by A. R. Wallace in his contribution to the 1858 communication to the Linnean Society of London.

In such a system we can make a theoretical guess of the order of magnitude of the diversity that a single food chain can introduce into a community. If we assume that in general 20 per cent of the energy passing through one link can enter the next link in the chain, which is overgenerous (cf. Lindeman, 1942; Slobodkin in an unpublished study finds 13 per cent as a reasonable upper limit) and if we suppose that each predator has twice the mass (or 1.26 the linear dimensions) of its prey, which is a very low estimate of the size difference between links, the fifth animal link will have a population of one ten thousandth (10^{-4}) of the first, and the fiftieth animal link, if there was one, a population of 10^{-49} the size of the first. Five animal links are certainly possible, a few fairly clear cut cases having been in fact recorded. If, however, we wanted 50 links, starting with a protozoan or rotifer feeding an algae with a density of 10^6 cells per ml, we should need a volume of 10^{26} cubic kilometers to accommodate on an average one specimen of the ultimate predator, and this is vastly greater than the volume of the world ocean. Clearly the Eltonian food chain of itself cannot give any great diversity, and the same is almost certainly true of the other types of food chain, based on detritus feeding or on parasitism.

Natural Selection

Before proceeding to a further consideration of diversity, it is, however, desirable to consider the kinds of selective force that may operate on a food chain, for this may limit the possible diversity.

It is reasonably certain that natural selection will tend to maintain the efficiency of transfer from one level to another at a maximum. Any increase in the predatory efficiency of the nth link of a simple food chain will however always increase the possibility of the extermination of the $(n-1)^{th}$ link. If this occurs either the species constituting the nth link must adapt itself to eating the $(n-2)^{th}$ link or itself become extinct. This process will in fact tend to shortening of food chains. A lengthening can presumably occur most simply by the development of a new terminal carnivore link, as its niche is by definition previously empty. In most cases this is not likely to be easy. The evolution of the whale-bone whales, which, at least in the case of *Balaenoptera borealis,* can feed largely on copepods and so rank on occasions as primary carnivores (Bigelow, 1926), presumably constitutes the most dramatic example of the shortening of a food chain. Mechanical considerations would have prevented the evolution of a larger rarer predator, until man developed essentially non-Eltonian methods of hunting whales.

Effect of Size

A second important limitation of the length of a food chain is due to the fact that ordinarily animals change their size during free life. If the terminal member of a chain were a fish that grew from say one cm to 150 cms in the course of an ordinary life, this size change would set a limit by competition to the possible number of otherwise conceivable links in the 1–150 cm range. At least in fishes this type of process (metaphoetesis) may involve the smaller specimens belonging to links below the larger and the chain length is thus lengthened, though under strong limitations, by cannibalism.

We may next enquire into what determines the number of food chains in a community. In part the answer is clear, though if we cease to be zoologists and become biologists, the answer begs the question. Within certain limits, the number of kinds of primary producers is certainly involved, because many herbivorous animals are somewhat eclectic in their tastes and many more limited by their size or by such structural adaptations for feeding that they have been able to develop.

Effects of Terrestrial Plants

The extraordinary diversity of the terrestrial fauna, which is much greater than that of the marine fauna, is clearly due largely to the diversity provided by terrestrial plants. This diversity is actually two-fold. Firstly, since terrestrial plants compete for light, they have tended to evolve into structures growing into a gaseous medium of negligible buoyancy. This has led to the formation of specialized supporting, photosynthetic, and reproductive structures which inevitably differ in chemical and physical properties. The ancient Danes and Irish are supposed to have eaten elm-bark; and sometimes sawdust, in periods of stress, has been hydrolyzed to produce edible carbohydrate; but usually man, the most omnivorous of all animals, has avoided almost all parts of trees except fruits as sources of food, though various individual species of animals can deal with practically every tissue of many arboreal species. A major source of terrestrial diversity was thus introduced by the evolution of almost 200,000 species of flowering plants, and the three quarters of a million insects supposedly known today are in part a product of that diversity. But of itself merely providing five or ten kinds of food of different consistencies and compositions does not get us much further than the five or ten links of an Eltonian pyramid. On the whole the problem still remains, but in the new form: why are there so many kinds of plants? As a zoologist I do not want to attack that question directly, I want to stick with animals, but also to get the answer. Since, however, the plants are part of the general system of communities, any sufficiently abstract properties of such communities are likely to be relevant to plants as well as to herbivores and carnivores. It is, therefore, by being somewhat abstract, though with concrete zoological details as examples, that I intend to proceed.

INTERRELATIONS OF FOOD CHAINS

Biological communities do not consist of independent food chains, but of food webs, of such a kind that an individual at any level (corresponding to a link in a single chain) can use some but not all of the food provided by species in the levels below it.

It has long been realized that the presence of two species at any level, either of which can be eaten by a predator at a level above, but which may differ in palatability, ease of capture or seasonal and local abundance, may provide alternative foods for the predator. The predator, therefore, will neither become extinct itself nor exterminate its usual prey, when for any reason, not dependent on prey-predator relationships, the usual prey happens to be abnormally scarce. This aspect of complicated food webs has been stressed by many ecologists, of whom the Chicago school as represented by Allee, Emerson, Park, Park and Schmidt (1949), Odum (1953) and Elton (1958), may in particular be mentioned. Recently MacArthur (1955) using an ingenious but simple application of information theory has generalized the points of view of earlier workers by providing a formal proof of the increase in stability of a community as the number of links in its food web increases.

MacArthur concludes that in the evolution of a natural community two partly antagonistic processes are occurring. More efficient species will replace less efficient species, but more stable communities will outlast less stable communities. In the process of community formation, the entry of a new species may involve one of three possibilities. It may completely displace an old species. This of itself does not necessarily change the stability, though it may do so if the new species inherently has a more stable population (cf. Slobodkin, 1956) than the old. Secondly, it may occupy an unfilled niche, which may, by providing new partially independent links, increase stability. Thirdly, it may partition a niche with a pre-existing species. Elton (1958) in a fascinating work largely devoted to the fate of species accidentally or purposefully introduced by man, concludes that in very diverse communities such introductions are difficult. Early in the history of a community we may suppose many niches will be empty and invasion will proceed easily; as the community becomes more diversified, the process will be progressively more difficult. Sometimes an extremely successful invader may oust a species but add little or nothing to stability, at other times the invader by some specialization will be able to compete successfully for the marginal parts of a niche. In all cases it is probable that invasion is most likely when one or more species happen to be fluctuating and are underrepresented at a given moment. As the communities build up, these opportunities will get progressively rarer. In this way a complex community containing some highly specialized species is constructed asymptotically.

Modern ecological theory therefore appears to answer our initial question at least partially by saying that there is a great diversity of organisms because communities of many diversified organisms are better able to persist than are communities of fewer less diversified organisms. Even though the entry of an invader which takes over part of a niche will lead to the reduction in the *average* population of the species originally present, it will also lead to an increase in stability reducing the risk of the original population being at times underrepresented to a dangerous degree. In this way loss of some niche space may be compensated by reduction in the amplitude of fluctuations in a way that can be advantageous to both species. The process however appears likely to be asymptotic and we have now to consider what sets the asymptote, or in simpler words why are there not more different kinds of animals?

LIMITATION OF DIVERSITY

It is first obvious that the processes of evolution of communities must be under various sorts of external control, and that in some cases such control limits the possible diversity. Several investigators, notably Odum (1953) and MacArthur (1955), have pointed out that the more or less cyclical oscillations observed in arctic and boreal fauna may be due in part to the communities not being sufficiently complex to damp out oscillations. It is certain that the fauna of any such region is qualitatively poorer than that of warm temperate and tropical areas of comparable effective precipitation. It is probably considered to be intuitively obvious that this should be so, but on analysis the obviousness tends to disappear. If we can have one or two species of a large family adapted to the rigors of Arctic existence, why can we not have more? It is reasonable to suppose that the total biomass may be involved. If the fundamental productivity of an area is limited by a short growing season to such a degree that the total biomass is less than under more favorable conditions, then the rarer species in a community may be so rare that they do not exist. It is also probable that certain absolute limitations on growth-forms of plants, such as those that make the development of forest impossible above a certain latitude, may in so acting, severely limit the number of niches. Dr. Robert MacArthur points out that the development of high tropical rain forest increases the bird fauna more than that of mammals, and Thorson (1957) likewise has shown that the so-called infauna show no increase of species toward the tropics while the marine epifauna become more diversified. The importance of this aspect of the plant or animal substratum, which depends largely on the length of the growing season and other aspects of productivity is related to that of the environmental mosaic discussed later.

We may also inquire, but at present cannot obtain any likely answer, whether the arctic fauna is not itself too young to have achieved its maximum diversity. Finally, the continual occurrence of catastrophes, as Wynne-Edwards (1952) has emphasized, may keep the arctic terrestrial community in a state of perennial though stunted youth.

Closely related to the problems of environmental rigor and stability, is the question of the absolute size of the habitat that can be colonized. Over much of western Europe there are three common species of small voles, namely *Microtus arvalis*, *M. agrestis* and *Clethrionomys glareolus*. These are sympatric but with somewhat different ecological preferences.

In the smaller islands off Britain and in the English channel, there is only one case of two species co-occurring on an island, namely *M. agrestis* and Clethrionomys on the island of Mull in the Inner Hebrides (Barrett-Hamilton and Hinton, 1911–1921). On the Orkneys the single species is *M. orcadensis,* which in morphology and cytology is a well-differentiated ally of *M. arvalis;* a comparable animal (*M. sarnius*) occurs on Guernsey. On most of the Scottish Islands only subspecies of *M. agrestis* occur, but on Mull and Raasay, on the Welsh island of Skomer, as well as on Jersey, races of Clethrionomys of somewhat uncertain status are found. No voles have reached Ireland, presumably for paleogeographic reasons, but they are also absent from a number of small islands, notably Alderney and Sark. The last named island must have been as well placed as Guernsey to receive *Microtus arvalis*. Still stranger is the fact that although it could not have got to the Orkneys without entering the mainland of Britain, no vole of the *arvalis* type now occurs in the latter country. Cases of this sort may be perhaps explained by the lack of favorable refuges in randomly distributed very unfavorable seasons or under special kinds of competition. This explanation is very reasonable as an explanation of the lack of Microtus on Sark, where it may have had difficulty in competing with *Rattus rattus* in a small area. It would be stretching one's credulity to suppose that the area of Great Britain is too small to permit the existence of two sympatric species of Microtus, but no other explanation seems to have been proposed.

It is a matter of considerable interest that Lack (1942) studying the populations of birds on some of these small British islands concluded that such populations are often unstable, and that the few species present often occupied larger niches than on the mainland in the presence of competitors. Such faunas provide examples of communities held at an early stage in development because there is not enough space for the evolution of a fuller and more stable community.

NICHE REQUIREMENTS

The various evolutionary tendencies, notably metaphoetesis, which operate on single food chains must operate equally on the food web, but we also have a new, if comparable, problem as to how much difference between two species at the same level is needed to prevent them from occupying the same niche. Where metric characters are involved we can gain some insight into this extremely important problem by the study of what Brown and Wilson (1956) have called *character displacement* or the divergence shown when two partly allopatric species of comparable niche requirements become sympatric in part of their range.

I have collected together a number of cases of mammals and birds which appear to exhibit the phenomenon (Table 1). These cases involve metric characters related to the trophic apparatus, the length of the culmen in birds and of the skull in mammals appearing to provide appropriate measures. Where the species co-occur, the ratio of the larger to the small form varies from 1.1 to 1.4, the mean ratio being 1.28 or roughly 1.3. This latter figure may tentatively be used as an indication of the kind of difference necessary to permit two species to co-occur in different niches but at the same level of a food web. In the case of the aquatic insects with which I began my address, we have over most of Europe three very closely allied species of Corixa, the largest *punctata,* being about 116 per cent longer than the middle sized species *macrocephala,* and 146 per cent longer than the small species *affinis.* In northwestern Europe there is a fourth species, *C. dentipes,* as large as *C. punctata* and very similar in appearance. A single observation (Brown, 1948) suggests that this is what I have elsewhere (Hutchinson, 1951) termed a fugitive species, maintaining itself in the face of competition mainly on account of greater mobility. According to Macan (1954) while both *affinis* and *macrocephala* may occur with *punctata* they never are found with each other, so that all three species never occur together. In the eastern part of the range, *macrocephala* drops out, and *punctata* appears to have a discontinuous distribution, being recorded as far east as Simla, but not in southern Persia or Kashmir, where *affinis* occurs. In these eastern localities, where it occurs by itself, *affinis* is larger and darker than in the west, and superficially looks like *macrocephala* (Hutchinson, 1940).

This case is very interesting because it looks as though character displacement is occurring, but that the size differences between the three species are just not great enough to allow them all to co-occur. Other characters than size are in fact clearly involved in the separation, *macrocephala* preferring deeper water than *affinis* and the latter being more tolerant of brackish conditions. It is also interesting because it calls attention to a marked difference that must occur between hemimetabolous insects with annual life cycles involving relatively long growth periods, and birds or mammals in which the period of growth in length is short

TABLE 1

Mean character displacement in measurable trophic structures in mammals (skull) and birds (culmen); data for Mustela from Miller (1912); Apodemus from Cranbrook (1957); Sitta from Brown and Wilson (1956) after Vaurie; Galapagos finches from Lack (1947)

	Locality and measurement when sympatric	Locality and measurement when allopatric	Ratio when sympatric
Mustela nivalis	Britain; skull ♂ 39.3 ♀ 33.6 mm.	(boccamela) S. France, Italy ♂ 42.9 ♀ 34.7 mm. (iberica) Spain, Portugal ♂ 40.4 ♀ 36.0	♂ 100:128 ♀ 100:134
M. erminea	Britain; " ♂ 50.4 ♀ 45.0	(hibernica) Ireland ♂ 46.0 ♀ 41.9	
Apodemus sylvaticus	Britain; " 24.8	unnamed races on Channel Islands 25.6–26.7	100:109
A. flavicollis	Britain; " 27.0		
Sitta tephronota	Iran; culmen 29.0	races east of overlap 25.5	100:124
S. neumayer	Iran; " 23.5	races west of overlap 26.0	
Geospiza fortis	Indefatigable Isl.; culmen 12.0	Daphne Isl. 10.5	100:143
G. fuliginosa	Indefatigable Isl.; " 8.4	Crossman Isl. 9.3	
Camarhynchus parvulus	James Isl.; " 7.0	N. Albemarle Isl. 7.0	James 100:140:180
	Indefatigable Isl.; " 7.5	Chatham Isl. 8.0	100:129
	S. Albemarle Isl.; " 7.3		
C. psittacula	James Isl.; " 9.8	Abington Isl. 10.1	Indefatigable 100:128:162
	Indefatigable Isl.; " 9.6	Bindloe Isl. 10.5	100:127
	S. Albemarle Isl.; " 8.5		
C. pallidus	James Isl.; " 12.6	N. Albemarle Isl. 11.7	S. Albemarle 100:116:153
	Indefatigable Isl.; " 12.1	Chatham Isl. 10.8	100:132
	S. Albemarle Isl.; " 11.2		

Mean ratio 100:128

and of a very special nature compared with the total life span. In the latter, niche separation may be possible merely through genetic size differences, while in a pair of animals like *C. punctata* and *C. affinis* we need not only a size difference but a seasonal one in reproduction; this is likely to be a rather complicated matter. For the larger of two species always to be larger, it must never breed later than the smaller one. I do not doubt that this is what was happening in the pond on Monte Pellegrino, but have no idea how the difference is achieved.

I want to emphasize the complexity of the adaptation necessary on the part of two species inhabiting adjacent niches in a given biotope, as it probably underlies a phenomenon which to some has appeared rather puzzling. MacArthur (1957) has shown that in a sufficiently large bird fauna, in a uniform undisturbed habitat, areas occupied by the different species appear to correspond to the random non-overlapping fractionation of a plane or volume. Kohn (1959) has found the same thing for the cone-shells (Conus) on the Hawaiian reefs. This type of arrangement almost certainly implies such individual and unpredictable complexities in the determination of the niche boundaries, and so of the actual areas colonized, that in any overall view, the process would appear random. It is fairly obvious that in different types of community the divisibility of niches will differ and so the degree of diversity that can be achieved. The fine details of the process have not been adequately investigated, though many data must already exist that could be organized to throw light on the problem.

MOSAIC NATURE OF THE ENVIRONMENT

A final aspect of the limitation of possible diversity, and one that perhaps is of greatest importance, concerns what may be called the mosaic nature of the environment. Except perhaps in open water when only uniform quasi-horizontal surfaces are considered, every area colonized by organisms has some local diversity. The significance of such local diversity depends very largely on the size of the organisms under consideration. In another paper MacArthur and I (Hutchinson and MacArthur, 1959) have attempted a theoretical formulation of this property of living communities and have pointed out that even if we consider only the herbivorous level or only one of the carnivorous levels, there are likely, above a certain lower limit of size, to be more species of small or medium sized organisms than of large organisms. It is difficult to go much beyond crude qualitative impressions in testing this hypothesis, but we find that for mammal faunas, which contain such diverse organisms that they may well be regarded as models of whole faunas, there is a definite hint of the kind of theoretical distribution that we deduce. In qualitative terms the phenomenon can be exemplified by any of the larger species of ungulates which may require a number of different kinds of terrain within their home ranges, any one of which types of terrain might be the habitat of some small species. Most of the genera or even subfamilies of very large terrestrial animals contain only one or two sympatric species. In this connection I cannot refrain from pointing out the immense scientific importance of obtaining a really full insight into the ecology of the large mammals of Africa while they can still be studied under natural conditions. It is indeed quite possible that the results of studies on these wonderful animals would in long-range though purely practical terms pay for the establishment of greater reservations and National Parks than at present exist.

In the passerine birds the occurrence of five or six closely related sympatric species is a commonplace. In the mammal fauna of western Europe no genus appears to contain more than four strictly sympatric species. In Britain this number is not reached even by Mustela with three species, on the adjacent parts of the continent there may be three sympatric shrews of the genus Crocidura and in parts of Holland three of Microtus. In the same general region there are genera of insects containing hundreds of species, as in Athela in the Coleoptera and Dasyhelea in the Diptera Nematocera. The same phenomenon will be encountered whenever any well-studied fauna is considered. Irrespective of their position in a food chain, small size, by permitting animals to become specialized to the conditions offered by small diversified elements of the environmental mosaic, clearly makes possible a degree of diversity quite unknown among groups of larger organisms.

We may, therefore, conclude that the reason why there are so many species of animals is at least partly because a complex trophic organization of a community is more stable than a simple one, but that limits are set by the tendency of food chains to shorten or become blurred, by unfavorable physical factors, by space, by the fineness of possible subdivision of niches, and by those characters of the environmental mosaic which permit a greater diversity of small than of large allied species.

CONCLUDING DISCUSSION

In conclusion I should like to point out three very general aspects of the sort of process I have described. One speculative approach to evolutionary theory arises from some of these conclusions. Just as adaptive evolution by natural selection is less easy in a small population of a species than in a larger one, because the total pool of genetic variability is inevitably less, so it is probable that a group containing many diversified species will be able to seize new evolutionary opportunities more easily than an undiversified group. There will be some limits to this process. Where large size permits the development of a brain capable of much new learnt behavior, the greater plasticity acquired by the individual species will offset the disadvantage of the small number of allied species characteristic of groups of large animals. Early during evolution the main process from the standpoint of community structure was the filling of all the niche space potentially available for producer and decomposer organisms and for herbivorous animals. As the latter, and still more as carnivorous animals began to appear, the persistence of more stable communities would imply splitting of niches previously occupied by single species as the communities became more diverse. As this process continued one would expect the overall rate of evolution to have increased, as the increasing diversity increased the probability of the existence of species preadapted to new and unusual niches. It is reasonable to suppose that strong predation among macroscopic metazoa did not begin until the late Precambrian, and that the appearance of powerful predators led to the appearance of fossilizable skeletons. This seems the only reasonable hypothesis, of those so far advanced, to account for the relatively sudden appearance of several fossilizable groups in the Lower Cambrian. The process of diversification would, according to this argument, be somewhat autocatakinetic even without the increased stability that it would produce; with the increase in stability it would be still more a self inducing process, but one, as we have seen, with an upper limit. Part of this upper limit is set by the impossibility of having many sympatric allied species of large animals. These however are the animals that can pass from primarily innate to highly modifiable behavior. From an evolutionary point of view, once they have appeared, there is perhaps less need for diversity, though from other points of view, as Elton (1958) has stressed in dealing with human activities, the stability provided by diversity can be valuable even to the most adaptable of all large animals. We may perhaps therefore see in the process of evolution an increase in diversity at an increasing rate till the early Paleozoic, by which time the familiar types of community structure were established. There followed then a long period in which various large and finally large-brained species became dominant, and then a period in which man has been reducing diversity by a rapidly increasing tendency to cause extinction of supposedly unwanted species, often in an indiscriminate manner. Finally, we may hope for a limited reversal of this process when man becomes aware of the value of diversity no less in an economic than in an esthetic and scientific sense.

A second and much more metaphysical general point is perhaps worth a moment's discussion. The evolution of biological communities, though each species appears to fend for itself alone, produces integrated aggregates which increase in stability. There is nothing mysterious about this; it follows from mathematical theory and appears to be confirmed to some extent empirically. It is however a phenomenon which also finds analogies in other fields in which a more complex type of behavior, that we intuitively regard as higher, emerges as the result of the interaction of less complex types of behavior, that we call lower. The emergence of love as an antidote to aggression, as Lorenz pictures the process, or the development of cooperation from various forms of more or less inevitable group behavior that Allee (1931) has stressed are examples of this from the more complex types of biological systems.

In the ordinary sense of explanation in science, such phenomena are explicable. The types of holistic philosophy which import *ad hoc* mysteries into science whenever such a situation is met are obviously unnecessary. Yet perhaps we may wonder whether the empirical fact that it is the nature of things for this type of explicable emergence to occur is not something that itself requires an explanation. Many objections can be raised to such a view; a friendly organization of biologists could not occur in a universe in which cooperative behavior was impossible and without your cooperation I could not raise the problem. The question may in fact appear to certain types of philosophers not to be a real one, though I suspect such philosophers in their desire to demonstrate how often people talk nonsense, may sometimes show less ingenuity than would be desirable in finding some sense in such questions. Even if the answer to such a question were positive, it might not get us very far; to an existentialist, life would have merely provided yet one more problem; students of Whitehead might be made happier, though on the whole the obscurities of that great writer do not seem to generate unhappiness; the religious philosophers would welcome a positive answer but note that it told them nothing that they did not know before; Marxists might merely say, "I told you so." In spite of this I suspect that the question is worth raising, and that it could be phrased so as to provide some sort of real dichotomy between alternatives; I therefore raise it knowing that I cannot, and suspecting that at present others cannot, provide an intellectually satisfying answer.

My third general point is less metaphysical, but not without interest. If I am right that it is easier to have a greater diversity of small than of large organisms, then the evolutionary process in small organisms will differ somewhat from that of large ones. Wherever we have a great array of allied sympatric species there must be an emphasis on very accurate interspecific mating barriers which is unnecessary where virtually no sympatric allies occur. We ourselves are large animals in this sense; it would seem very unlikely that the peculiar lability that seems to exist in man, in which even the direction of normal sexual behavior must be learnt, could have developed to quite the existing extent if species recognition, involving closely related sympatric congeners, had been necessary. Elsewhere (Hutchinson, 1959) I have attempted to show that the difficulties that *Homo sapiens* has to face in this regard may imply various unsuspected processes in human evolutionary selection. But perhaps Santa Rosalia would find at this point that we are speculating too freely, so for the moment, while under her patronage, I will say no more.

ACKNOWLEDGMENTS

Dr. A. Minganti of the University of Palermo enabled me to collect on Monte Pellegrino. Professor B. M. Knox of the Department of Classics of Yale University gave me a rare and elegant word from the Greek to express the blurring of a food chain. Dr. L. B. Slobodkin of the University of Michigan and Dr. R. H. MacArthur of the University of Pennsylvania provided me with their customary kinds of intellectual stimulation. To all these friends I am most grateful.

LITERATURE CITED

Allee, W. C., 1931, Animal aggregations: a study in general sociology. vii, 431 pp. University of Chicago Press, Chicago, Illinois.
Allee, W. C., A. E. Emerson, O. Park, T. Park and K. P. Schmidt, 1949, Principles of animal ecology. xii, 837 pp. W. B. Saunders Co., Philadelphia, Pennsylvania.

Barrett-Hamilton, G. E. H., and M. A. C. Hinton, 1911–1921, A history of British mammals. Vol. 2. 748 pp. Gurney and Jackson, London, England.

Bigelow, H. B., 1926, Plankton of the offshore waters of the Gulf of Maine. Bull. U.S. Bur. Fisheries 40: 1–509.

Brown, E. S., 1958, A contribution towards an ecological survey of the aquatic and semi-aquatic Hemiptera-Heteroptera (water-bugs) of the British Isles etc. Trans. Soc. British Entom. 9: 151–195.

Brown, W. L., and E. O. Wilson, 1956, Character displacement. Systematic Zoology 5: 49–64.

Cranbrook, Lord, 1957, Long-tailed field mice (Apodemus) from the Channel Islands. Proc. Zool. Soc. London 128: 597–600.

Elton, C. S., 1958, The ecology of invasions by animals and plants. 159 pp. Methuen Ltd., London, England.

Hutchinson, G. E., 1951, Copepodology for the ornithologist. Ecology 32: 571–577.

———, 1958, Concluding remarks. Cold Spring Harbor Symp. Quant. Biol 22: 415–427.

———, 1959, A speculative consideration of certain possible forms of sexual selection in man. Amer. Nat. 93: 81–92.

Hutchinson, G. E., and R. MacArthur, 1959, A theoretical ecological model of size distributions among species of animals. Amer. Nat. 93: 117–126.

Hyman, L. H., 1955, How many species? Systematic Zoology 4: 142–143.

Kohn, A. J., 1959, The ecology of Conus in Hawaii. Ecol. Monogr. (in press).

Lack, D., 1942, Ecological features of the bird faunas of British small islands. J. Animal Ecol. London 11: 9–36.

———, 1947, Darwin's Finches. x, 208 pp. Cambridge University Press, Cambridge, England.

———, 1954, The natural regulation of animal numbers. viii, 347 pp. Clarendon Press, Oxford, England.

Lindeman, R. L., 1942, The trophic-dynamic aspect of ecology. Ecology 23: 399–408.

Macan, T. T., 1954, A contribution to the study of the ecology of Corixidae (Hempit). J. Animal Ecol. 23: 115–141.

MacArthur, R. H., 1955, Fluctuations of animal populations and a measure of community stability. Ecology 35: 533–536.

———, 1957, On the relative abundance of bird species. Proc. Nat. Acad. Sci. Wash. 43: 293–295.

Miller, G. S., Catalogue of the mammals of Western Europe. xv, 1019 pp. British Museum, London, England.

Muller, S. W., and A. Campbell, 1954, The relative number of living and fossil species of animals. Systematic Zoology 3: 168–170.

Odum, E. P., 1953, Fundamentals of ecology. xii, 387 pp. W. B. Saunders Co., Philadelphia, Pennsylvania, and London, England.

Slobodkin, L. B., 1955, Condition for population equilibrium. Ecology 35: 530–533.

Thorson, G., 1957, Bottom communities. Chap. 17 in Treatise on marine ecology and paleoecology. Vol. 1. Geol. Soc. Amer. Memoir 67: 461–534.

Wallace, A. R., 1858, On the tendency of varieties to depart indefinitely from the original type. In C. Darwin and A. R. Wallace, On the tendency of species to form varieties; and on the perpetuation of varieties and species by natural means of selection. J. Linn. Soc. (Zool.) 3: 45–62.

Wynne-Edwards, V. C., 1952, Zoology of the Baird Expedition (1950). I. The birds observed in central and southeast Baffin Island. Auk 69: 353–391.

What Did Natural Selection Select? The Tales Which Old Bones Tell

IN DARWIN'S YOUTH THE FOSSIL EVIDENCE FOR EVOLUTION WAS rather meager, but during his lifetime more and more remains of ancient forms of life were discovered. Nevertheless, he had to depend, for the most part, upon the evidence derived from comparing living creatures, in developing and defending his ideas about natural selection and evolution. The paleontological record was spotty; there were many missing links; indeed, transitional forms were embarrassingly rare. Nor was the interpretation of the fossil evidence at all easy. Eminent anatomists, such as Virchow in the case of the original Neanderthal find and Keith in the case of the Piltdown hoax, came to inexcusably false conclusions.

However, as time has gone on we have learned much more, both about the functional anatomy and physiology of living animals and about the life of the past. We have better methods of dating, we have a continually growing number of fossil remains from a greater number of areas, and we have learned to interpret what the fossils tell us in a more sophisticated manner. Thus, when living fishes of the order Coelacanthini, thought to have been extinct since the Cretaceous, were caught in the Indian Ocean during the 1950s, they looked very much indeed as had been expected. Thus many gaps in the ancestral lines of various animals, including *Homo sapiens*, have now been filled by the discovery of appropriate fossils.

We have a better appreciation of the significance of morphological patterns; a deeper understanding of the rules of the evolutionary game; a fuller appreciation of how major transitions in adaptations took place. The following article, "Mosaic Evolution" by Sir Gavin de Beer, is a very clear exposition of these facts.

4. Sir Gavin de Beer

Mosaic Evolution*

No man who has the honour to preside over the Zoological Section of the British Association meeting in Oxford can be unmindful of two facts. The first is the memorable meeting of 1860, when T. H. Huxley championed Darwin's recently propounded theory of evolution by means of natural selection, and blazed for it a trail which has now become one of the greatest ornaments of intellectual endeavour. The other is the fact that this meeting is being held in the Department which was presided over for many fruitful years by that great master of zoology, Edwin Stephen Goodrich. For half a century he devoted himself to the study of comparative anatomy and embryology with the object of providing evidence of the course which evolution has taken. Those of us who had the privilege to know him have reason to be proud.

In searching for a subject on which to address you today, it is therefore not unfitting that I should select one bearing on the subject of evolution.

I have a certain apprehension in speaking on any scientific subject, particularly that of evolution, without having some solid object to talk about so as to anchor my words to a firm sea-bed of evidence, and the material which I have selected for this purpose is the specimen of the fossil *Archaeopteryx lithographica* preserved in the British Museum (Natural History), probably the most precious, the most beautiful, and the most interesting fossil hitherto discovered in the world.

It is over ninety years since it was described by my predecessor, Sir Richard Owen, and since then a few contributions have been made to our knowledge of it; but when I came to examine it, and applied to it modern methods of research such as photography under ultra-violet illumination, I considered that it was worthy of a complete reinvestigation. It is some of the results of this work which I am putting forward before you today for the first time, with the object not only of describing the new facts which have come to light, but also of providing evidence

* Presidential Address to the Zoology Section of the British Association for the Advancement of Science, delivered on September 2, 1954, at Oxford. From *The Advancement of Science*, No. 42, September, 1954.

on which I hope to demonstrate a principle of evolution which deserves further attention.

Archaeopteryx and the Transition from Reptiles to Birds

The fossil is preserved in a slab and corresponding counter-slab of a block of limestone from the Solnhofen deposit of the Jurassic, about 150 million years old. At the very first glance its most important features become apparent, for while some of them are thoroughly characteristic of reptiles, others are no less completely characteristic of birds. It is this intermediate position which *Archaeopteryx* occupies that makes it an object of such enormous interest.

First the reptilian features:

1. the long tail of twenty vertebrae, all of them free up to the tip as would be found in a reptile;
2. the simple articulation between the vertebrae without any of the complications found in birds;
3. the short sacrum, involving no more than six vertebrae by means of which the vertebral column is attached to the pelvic girdle;
4. the free metacarpal bones in the hand, and the presence of claws on all three fingers;
5. the free metatarsal bones in the foot;
6. the simple ribs and gastralia in the ventral body wall;
7. the simple brain with elongated, slender cerebral hemispheres, optic lobes, and a small cerebellum.

All these are characters which would not be in the least out of place if found in any reptile. On the other hand, there are a number of features in *Archaeopteryx* which are absolutely characteristic of birds:

1. First the feathers, the impressions of which show that they were composed of rachis and barbs forming the vanes, identical in structure with those in modern birds.
2. Next comes the fact that these feathers are arranged on the forearm to form a wing, in a manner again precisely similar to that which is found in modern birds. There is a group of flight-feathers called the primaries, inserted on the hand and wrist, and another group called the secondaries, inserted on the forearm; covering the bases of these flight-feathers are coverts.
3. Then there is the fact that the two collar-bones are joined to form a merry-thought, a character found only in birds.
4. In the pelvic girdle the pubes are directed backwards, again as in other birds.
5. Lastly, the foot shows that the big toe was opposed to the other three toes, which is the characteristic adaptation by means of which birds perch on twigs of trees.

From the evidence already presented, it is clear that *Archaeopteryx* was an arboreal animal, and that it had the power of gliding through the air supported by the flight-feathers on its wings and those of its long tail.

For many years a search has been made for the sternum. The determination of this structure is of the greatest importance, since the absence or presence on the sternum of a keel is the evidence on which to conclude that the bird had weak or strong pectoral muscles, and either was not or was able to carry out vigorous and active flight. The sternum has now been revealed and shows no sign of any keel, so it must be concluded that *Archaeopteryx* glided rather than flew.

It may be of interest to show how the sternum was discovered. For this purpose it is necessary to look at a photograph of the counter-slab taken with ultra-violet illumination under which conditions bones are fluorescent while the matrix is not. Where with ordinary light there was little to be seen, under ultra-violet light it was at once clear that a hitherto unrecognized element was there in the form of a thin bony shell torn away from the main body of the bone on the main slab. The corresponding place was then examined on the main slab. Between the left humerus and the left scapula a structure immediately became apparent and attracted attention. Having once been found, the structure was further revealed on the main slab by scratching away the matrix with fine chisels and needles. The sternum, for that is the only thing that it could be, was poorly ossified and must have been largely cartilaginous during life. Indeed, its spongy structure implies this. There remained to be supplied the proof that the structure in question is in fact bony, and this can fortunately be done by means of X-rays. There is a sufficient difference in density between the phosphate in the bones and the carbonates of the limestone matrix for it to be possible to reveal it by X-rays with suitable dosage, and the sternum throws its shadow just like the other bones of the skeleton.

Turning now to the brain: when photographed under ordinary light on the slab, it shows the natural cast as seen from the right side. The right cerebral hemisphere and the right optic lobe are beautifully revealed because the right frontal and parietal bones are detached and lie on the counter-slab. When photographed under ultra-violet light, the brain-cast is seen to be surrounded by a number of bones, among which can be identified the left frontal and parietal, the auditory capsule, and the occipital region. On the counter-slab the right frontal and parietal are beautifully preserved, and the hollow which they form fits perfectly over the shape of the right cerebral hemisphere and optic lobe on the main slab. Ultra-violet light confirms the bony nature of these structures.

The most interesting feature in the brain is the small size of the cerebellum, which did not as in modern birds encroach on the space occupied by the optic lobes. In this respect the recent investigations confirm the observations of T. Edinger (1926). There is an important correlation between the absence of a keel on the sternum, poor power of flight, and the small size of the cerebellum. It is the acrobatic power of flight of modern birds, made possible by the insertion of the powerful pectoral muscles on the keel of the sternum, that necessitates the development of a large cerebellum to co-ordinate the motor activities. None of this had yet happened at the level of evolution represented by *Archaeopteryx*.

Other anatomical details may be illustrated briefly. Among the new structures discovered on the counter-slab is a vertebra which for the first time reveals the concave and simple articular surface of the centrum.

Sir John Evans discovered in 1862 that *Archaeopteryx* possessed teeth on the premaxilla and maxilla. Ultra-violet light shows the details of these structures, and the way in which the teeth are fitted into their sockets and have a little pediment, like the base of a column. The presence of teeth in *Archaeopteryx* is, of course, not unique among birds, since the Cretaceous fossils *Hesperornis* and *Ichthyornis* possessed them.

Transition: Conversion or Mosaic?

From what has already been said, it is clear that *Archaeopteryx* provides a magnificent example of an animal intermediate between two classes, the reptiles and the birds, with each of which it shares a number of well-marked characters. It is, however, worth-while spending a little more time in considering what precisely is meant by the statement that an animal is intermediate between two classes.

If we look at almost any part of a living vertebrate animal, we can tell at once which class the animal belongs to: skin, skeleton, brain, heart, kidneys, are all stamped with the identity of their class. This shows that in the evolution of the classes of vertebrates as we know them alive today, all the parts of their bodies have undergone modification. This might suggest that in the evolutionary process which converted animals of one class into the next, there was a gradual and general transformation of the whole animal. If the evolution of the vertebrate classes involved processes of this nature, and an animal was caught in the transitional stage, the parts of such an animal would be intermediate in structure between the two classes.

On the other hand, the statement that an animal was intermediate might mean that it was a mixture and that the transition affected some parts of the animal and not others, with the result that some parts were similar to those of one type, other parts similar to the other type, and few or no parts intermediate in structure. In such a case the animal might be regarded as a mosaic in which the pieces could be replaced independently one by one, so that the transitional stages were a jumble of characters, some of them similar to those of the class from which the animal evolved, others similar to those of the class into which the animal was evolving.

If now it be asked which kind of transition is shown by *Archaeopteryx,* the answer is perfectly clear. It is a mosaic in which some characters are perfectly reptilian, and others no less perfectly avian. In its evolution from its reptilian ancestors, therefore, the modifications which it has undergone have affected some structures to produce their complete transformation, while other structures have not yet been affected at all. In the subsequent evolution from *Archaeopteryx* to the conditions found in modern birds, the latter structures, in their turn, have been affected, with the result that in the brain, vertebrae, sacrum, and carinated sternum, modern birds have got even further away from the condition of their original reptilian ancestors than was *Archaeopteryx*.

The condition in *Archaeopteryx* may most conveniently be shown in tabular form:

ARCHAEOPTERYX

Reptilian characters	Avian characters
simple brain with small cerebellum	feathers
long tail of separate vertebrae	arrangement of feathers
simple articulation of vertebrae	fused clavicles
short sacrum	pubes directed backwards
free metacarpals	opposable hallux
free metatarsal	
simple ribs	
gastralia	

If the transition from reptiles to birds was characterized by what I propose to call "mosaic evolution," it becomes of interest to enquire whether the same mode was followed in the transition between other classes of vertebrates, and to make a general investigaton into the evolution of the classes of jawed vertebrates alive today.

Vertebrate animals present themselves to the eye and to the mind as disposed along five great levels, or shelves extending one above the other along the walls of time. The lowest shelf is for the fishes, the second for amphibia, the third for reptiles, and the fourth and fifth for birds and mammals. In each case, except for the last, the definition of the contents of the shelf is based on the fundamental structural and functional requirements of adaptation in a broad way to the medium or media in which the animals live. A life wholly spent in water is the governing factor for the fish; early life in water followed by life on land for the amphibia (although some may secondarily return to an aquatic existence); complete emancipation from early larval life in water for the reptiles (although some may become secondarily adapted to an aquatic medium); ability to fly in the air by means of feathers for the birds. The mammals are exposed to the same ecological problems as the reptiles, and if they are placed on a shelf above them, it is because their basic adaptation to their problems is on a level so much more efficient that an arbitrary but accepted convention has sanctioned this practice and used mammary glands and hair as diagnostic features in living forms, although it may well be that these structures were also present in the ancestors of the mammals while they were still undoubted reptiles.

In each case, only one passage from a shelf to the next has been successful and has given rise to forms which have survived as the classes of vertebrates alive today. As G. G. Simpson (1951) has stressed, it is because they have successfully survived and radiated in their newly conquered environments that these groups have become classes. If they had failed to "break-through" onto a higher shelf, like the numerous other unsuccessful competitors, they would not have given rise to a class. If the pterodactyls had established themselves in the mastery of the air, they would no doubt be regarded as a class, but they went extinct.

So firmly are the differences between the various grades of vertebrate animals impressed on the student that there is a tendency to imagine that the "hard work" of evolution consists in the transition from one shelf to that above it. There is here the possibility of error, for if evolution is measured by the quantity of change observed between the starting and ending points of a given line of descent, "more" evolution may take place on and within each shelf than in the passage from one shelf to the next. Within each shelf, evolution involves adaptive radiation which diversifies the animals to a very great extent as the different lines become more and more closely adjusted to special environments. The reptiles show this well with their astonishing diversity of form and size. Quite apart from the transitions from one shelf to the next, there is a very wide tolerance for the amount of change of size, shape, proportions, accretion or loss, which a strain of evolving animals may show.

In the case of the transitional passages from one shelf to the next, the starting and ending points of the evolutionary progress are known and definable. From one known condition the animals must have arrived at another, not very different from it but possessing a few fundamentally important characters which define the level of the next shelf.

If the method of transition from reptiles to birds, as is shown in *Archaeopteryx,* be of general applicability, it should be possible by direct appeal to the facts of observation to demonstrate its occurrence in the case of other great transitions, from fish to amphibia, from amphibia to reptiles, and from reptiles to mammals. In each case fossils are known which, although not themselves the direct ancestors of the remainder of the animals in the shelf to which the evolution is progressing, were nevertheless so closely related to them that they can be taken as examples of animals in transition. It will be of interest to consider them in a little more detail.

The Transition from Fish to Amphibian

Bony fish are alike in the possession of the following structures which not only enable them to live in their watery medium but are characteristic of them: paired fins in the form of paddles, median fins supported by cartilaginous radials and dermal fin-rays (lepidotrichia), lateral-line canals protected in tubes in the dermal bones, opercular bones protecting the branchial cavity, and a bony connexion between the hind part of the skull and the pectoral girdle. The amphibia, on the other hand, are characterized by the pentadactyl limbs; the median fins, which are found only in their aquatic forms, have no supporting radials or rays, and the lateral-line organs lie in grooves in the bones or simply in the skin, not in tubes in the bones; the bony operculum has vanished, as has the chain of bones connecting the skull with the pectoral girdle.

It is therefore remarkable that, as E. Jarvik (1952) has shown, the Ichthyostegalia present an intermediate and mixed condition in which median fins are present, supported by radials and lepidotrichia, and the lateral-line organs perforate the bones in tubes. These structures are absolutely characteristic of fish. On the other hand, the Ichthyostegalia have pentadactyl limbs, absolutely characteristic of amphibia. Less sensational than these, but nevertheless characteristic of one or the other of the two types between which the transition is made, are the following structures of Ichthyostegalia: presence of a pre-opercular bone, a (small) subopercular bone, and an ethmosphenoid bone, all of which are found in bony fish but not in amphibia; the presence of bicipital ribs, and the shortening of the hinder part of the skull which is unjointed and free from the pectoral girdle, all of which are characteristic of amphibia but not of fish.

If it were not for the pentadactyl limbs, the Ichthyostegalia would have to be regarded as fish instead of amphibia; and the fact that a single piece of the mosaic pattern marks the passage of the frontier between one class of vertebrates and another suggests that such a transition can be achieved by a moderate quantity of evolutionary change.

In his Croonian Lecture, D. M. S. Watson (1925) has already shown that the physiological and mechanical problems that required to be solved by the ancestors of the amphibia in their passage from life in water to life on land necessitated no new neurological or muscular machinery. The system of myotomes (muscle-plates) segmentally arranged on each side of the body which enables a fish to swim also enables an amphibian to crawl; the muscles of the floor of the mouth, which, by raising it when the mouth is closed, force water back into the pharynx and out through the gill-slits in the fish, also force air down into the lungs in the amphibian; the hyomandibula, which is applied to the imperforate side of the ear-capsule in fish and helps to support the upper jaw, also enables vibrations to be transmitted to the inner ear, even without the perforation of the fenestra ovalis which the most primitive amphibia have not yet achieved. In brief, the passage from class Pisces to class Amphibia involved no upheaval or sensational reconstruction of the body. This is what would be expected if the transition took place by mosaic evolution, one piece at a time.

The Ichthyostegalia present another feature of interest and general applicability, which arises out of the fact that they cannot themselves be taken as lying on the direct line of transition from the fish to the amphibia. The reason why they cannot be so regarded is that they possess some characters which are too specialized for it to have been possible for the remainder of the amphibia to have been evolved from them. Among these characters are the structure of the occipital region, and the anterior position of the articulation between the quadrate and the lower jaw. These are characters which other amphibia show at a later period of evolution, and in which the Ichthyostegalia are precociously advanced. But the fact that an animal can at one and the same time show so many features which would make it an ideal transitional form, and also spoil this picture by possessing one or two characters which rule it out as a direct ancestor, is itself an argument in support of the principle of mosaic evolution, with the different pieces evolving separately, and some of them too fast. This phenomenon is found again and again in the study of transitions from one type of animal to another, and appears to be of general applicability. It would be more difficult to understand if the transitions took place by a gradual and simultaneous conversion of all the parts of the animal.

Conversely, there are animals which in some of their features have failed to keep pace with the general progress of the group to which they belong. A case is provided by the amphibian *Eogyrinus* which is more advanced than the Ichthyostegalia in general structure and yet retains the connexion between the bones of the skull and those of the shoulder girdle which the Ichthyostegalia had already lost.

It may be of interest to have the analysis of certain characters during the transition from fish to amphibia in tabular form:

ICHTHYOSTEGA

Fish characters	Amphibian characters
median fin	pentadactyl limbs
radials	bicipital ribs
lepidotrichia	long forepart of skull, short hind part
pre-opercular bone	skull free from pectoral girdle
subopercular bone (vestigial)	no joint in skull
tubes for lateral line	
ethmosphenoid ossification	**Specialized characters**
short parasphenoid	structure of occipital region
	quadrate articulation too far forward

The Transition from Amphibian to Reptile

In the transition from amphibian to reptile the essential difference between them is that whereas the amphibia[1] never emancipated themselves completely from water, which is necessary for the sperm to find the egg (in the absence of internal fertilization), for the egg and larva to develop in, and for the skin to breathe, the reptiles succeeded in getting completely free from water. This they did by the evolution of copulatory organs allowing internal fertilization, the evolution of embryonic membranes (chorion, amnion, and allantois) which made it possible for the embryo to develop within a fluid medium (in the amniotic cavity) as a closed system (the cleidoic egg) inside a shell on dry land or in the oviduct; and by the acquisition of an efficient mechanism of pulmonary respiration with the ribs and intercostal muscles expanding the lungs.

The reptilian emancipation from water is reflected anatomically in the fact that

[1] An exception must be made of the caecilians which, although still amphibians, have acquired independence from water by means of internal fertilization, and many of which are viviparous. They are, however, so highly specialized that they cannot be said to have made a new "shelf."

the reptilian skull shows no grooves for lateral-line canals. The other structural characters diagnostic of reptiles are hard to define and involve minute details. Some of them are given in the table below

SEYMOURIA

Amphibian characters	Reptilian characters
reticulate ornamentation of skull	foramen ovale large, low down, bordered by basipterygoid process
lateral-line canal grooves present	
no supra-occipital bone	lachrymal extends from orbit to nostril
large opening from braincase to inner ear	choanae near midline
	articular separate from supra-angular
massive paroccipital process directed upwards	basioccipital largely exposed ventrally
	large tubera basisphenoidales
tubular flange covering paroccipital	lower jaw hinges by articular, an independent ossification
palatine with tooth in pit	
ectopterygoid with very weak flange facing lower jaw	odontoid process a single ossification
	neural arches wide and swollen
shape of large pterygoid	articular surface of zygapophyses horizontal
maxillary teeth with alternate replacement, with fluted roots, fused to their base and to a labial wall of bone	digital formula 2–3–4–5–4
deep otic notch	humerus with entepicondylar foramen
intertemporal bone present	
quadrate inclined backwards	
mandible with postsplenial and three coronoids	
axis vertebra resembling one behind it	
intercentra with process for head of rib	
single sacral vertebra	
separate intermedium in tarsus	

Pre-Amphibian characters

large tooth on third coronoid
procoracoid but no coracoid

One of them is remarkable: the lower jaw hinges by means of the articular bone, an independent ossification, characteristic of no amphibian and all reptiles. *Seymouria*, which is an intermediate form long regarded as the most primitive known reptile, possesses the articular bone, but it has now been shown to have lateral-line canal grooves, and was an amphibian. It has just not got onto the new shelf. Nevertheless, D. M. S. Watson's remarks (1919, p. 291) apply with no less force than when he wrote them (before it was recognized that *Seymouria* was an amphibian): "In every part of its skeleton," he wrote, "it shows a mixture of Temnospondyl [amphibian] and Reptilian characters, each recognizable, in general showing little evidence of an intermediate condition. The whole effect of its structure is that of a mosaic of separate details, some completely amphibian, some completely reptilian, and very few, if any, showing a passage leading from one to the other."

It is clear, therefore, that the evidence from the study of the transition from amphibia to reptilia is in favour of the mosaic mode of evolution.

Seymouria also illustrates a further consequence of this type of evolution. Just as in some cases (e.g., *Ichthyostega*) an animal may show characters which have evolved too fast relative to the other characters, in other cases certain characters may have been left in a profoundly archaic condition. An example is provided in *Seymouria* by the presence of a procoracoid without a coracoid, and a large tooth on the third coronoid. These characters are those of osteolepid fish.

The Transition from Reptile to Mammal

The transition from the reptilian to the mammalian shelf of evolution is in many ways the most difficult to study. This is partly because fossils which might be regarded as ancestral to the existing mammals have not yet been found; partly because the mesozoic mammalian fossils that are known belong to unrelated groups which left no descendants; and partly because many of the features commonly accepted as characteristic of mammals were present in the group of theromorph reptiles that evolved parallel with the mammals. For example, the advanced therapsid reptiles show the following features: in the skull two occipital condyles, a bony false palate, disappearance of the pineal foramen and of the postorbital bar, appearance of turbinal bones, and a large dentary with an ascending ramus; teeth differentiated into incisors, canines, and molars, with single replacement; in the skeleton of the limbs and girdles, the loss of the cleithrum, the forward rotation of the ilium, the presence of the olecranon process of the ulna, the tuber calcis in the foot, and the reduction of the digital formula to 2-3-3-3-3; in the brain a cerebellum with vermis, flocculi, and pons Varolii.

Thanks to the work of R. Broom (1932), C.-C. Young (1947) and W. G. Kuehne, it is known that in the Triassic therapsid group of Ictidosauria, *Tritylodon* from South Africa, *Bienotherium* from China, and *Oligokyphus* from England show still closer resemblance to mammals in that their skull has lost the pre-frontal, postfrontal, and postorbital bones, the molar teeth have two roots, and the acromion process on the scapula is present. The only feature left which shows that the Therapsida, including the Ictidosauria, were still reptiles, according to the current definition, is the articulation of the lower jaw by means of the articular and quadrate bones, with the correlated condition that the columella auris was the only auditory ossicle and the angular remained in the lower jaw and had not been transformed into a tympanic bone.

The designation of the above-mentioned characters as mammalian is therefore true only when consideration is restricted to existing and living reptiles and mammals. They are not diagnostic characters and should be called mammal-like. When all the fossil forms are considered, as they must be, the only diagnostic feature of the mammals as currently accepted is the articulation of the lower jaw by means of the dentary and squamosal, and the conversion of the quadrate and articular into the incus and malleus and of the columella auris into the stapes.

Living mammals are warm-blooded and have hair which enables them to minimize the loss of heat; it is almost certain that this was also true of the higher theromorph reptiles, because of the agility which their structure argues and the presence of turbinals whose function it is to warm the air in its passage through the nose to the lungs. It is probable that these reptiles also had two ventricles, non-nucleated red blood-corpuscles, and a diaphragm, all of which are features which raise the efficiency of the circulatory and respiratory systems. What cannot be inferred from the fossilized parts, however, is whether they were viviparous, and had mammary glands, and a single left aortic arch. Judging from the monotremes, the ancestors of the mammals lacked the first of these characters but possessed the last two.

In the evolution of the other classes of vertebrates, there has in each case been a clean-cut and sudden adaptation to a new medium: the partial and total conquest of dry land, and the mastery of the air. Each of these shelves of vertebrate evolution can be characterized, therefore, not only by the diagnostic structural features, but also by a habitat. In the case of the evolution of the mammals this was not so. In the production of the mammals, there was no conquest of a new medium; primitive reptiles and mammals alike inhabited the land. Mammals are only perfected reptiles, more efficient, better adapted, and possessed of a greater degree of independence of their environment.

It follows that mammals were able to evolve slowly and gradually by progressive modifications here and there all over the body; and the point at which the distinction between reptiles and mammals is placed is purely arbitrary. In any case the diagnostic feature commonly accepted, the squamoso-dentary articulation of the lower jaw, cannot be correlated with the solution of any major problem of adaptation as was the case with the pentadactyl limb, the absence of lateral-line canal grooves, and the feathers. What this change did was to enable the mammals to chew and to hear more efficiently.

If the possession of hair were taken as the mammalian criterion, indicating a homoeothermous condition, and if it could be demonstrated in fossils, most of the higher therapsid reptiles would almost certainly be included in the mammals. The selection as a criterion of a feature which evolved late (the squamoso-dentary articulation) has had the result of relegating the important phases of mammalian evolution to the pre-mammalian stage. It follows that the reptiles among which the ancestors of mammals must be sought were already almost full of mammal-like characters. These reptiles were the Ictidosauria, and it is largely because they were Triassic and therefore too late that they cannot be regarded as directly ancestral to the mammals. The Ictidosauria must, however, have resembled these ancestral forms, and when their characters are tabulated it is seen that a few of

them are fairly ancestral or reptilian while most are equally definitely progressive
or mammal-like:

ICTIDOSAURIA

Ancestral reptilian characters	Progressive mammal-like characters
quadrate-articular articulation	two occipital condyles
columella auris simple	bony false palate
postdentary bones in lower jaw	no pineal foramen
interclavicle present	no postorbital bar
coracoid present	no pre-frontal bone
procoracoid present	no postorbital bone
	dentary large with ascending ramus
	turbinal bones
	teeth heterodont, diphyodont, molars with two roots
	no cleithrum
	olecranon process present
	acromion process present
	tuber calcis present
	ilium rotated forward
	digital formula 2–3–3–3–3
	cerebellum with vermis, flocculi, and pons Varolii

Instead, therefore, of presenting a picture in which a small number of pieces
conform to the new type showing a striking mosaic, most of the pieces belong to
the new type and only a few reflect the old: the mosaic has almost been converted
into a self-coloured pattern.

There is another possibility of studying the transition from reptiles to mammals
because there are mammals alive today which, although so highly specialized that
they cannot be regarded as ancestral to any other mammals, also show a number
of features which they must have inherited from the earliest mammals. These are
the monotremes, and it is remarkable that they also show a mosaic of reptilian
and mammalian characters, all the more interesting because they include soft
parts.

Thoroughly reptilian are the oviparous type of reproduction with yolk in the
egg and a shell; the presence of the egg-tooth and caruncle used for hatching; the
presence of coracoids, procoracoids and interclavicle; and the absence of a corpus
callosum from the brain.

On the other hand, the presence of hair, mammary glands, non-nucleated red
blood-corpuscles, the diaphragm, single left aortic arch, squamoso-dentary articulation of the lower jaw, three auditory ossicles, and seven cervical vertebrae shows
equally definite mammalian and mammal-like characters.

In other words, the monotremes have been produced from their reptilian ancestors by mosaic evolution and have remained in a condition in which some of the oldest reptilian pieces of the mosaic are preserved:

ORNITHORHYNCHUS

Reptilian characters	Mammalian characters
oviparous reproduction with shell and yolk	hair
egg-tooth and caruncle	mammary glands
squamosal canal	non-nucleated red blood-cells
coracoid, procoracoid, interclavicle present	diaphragm
no corpus callosum	single left aorta
no pinna to ear	squamoso-dentary articulation
no cribriform plate	three auditory ossicles
taenia clino-orbitalis present	seven cervical vertebrae

The Transition from Ape to Man

The transition from the subhuman to the human level is not only the most interesting, but perhaps the clearest, example of mosaic evolution. The starting point is the australopithecines, fossil forms that flourished in East Africa about one million years ago. A number of different specimens have been found, but unfortunately a Linnaean Latin name for a new genus or species has been given to many of them, such as *Paranthropus, Plesianthropus, Zinjanthropus, Homo habilis.* These names, and the distinctions which they are intended to convey, are not acceptable to evolutionists who know from genetics, population-studies, and comparative anatomy that in populations evolving rapidly and increasing greatly in numbers, which was the case with the australopithecines, variability is very wide, and there is no justification for ascribing the variant forms to separate genera or species, when they were only varieties of australopithecines. This is why, following Sir Wilfrid Le Gros Clark, evolutionists prefer to speak of levels: australopithecine, pithecanthropine (who was already *Homo,* many believe), and modern man. In the following table, a primitive, unspecialized form of australopithecine has been taken as a term of comparison.

A reasoned estimate of the number of individuals in the population of australopithecines one million years ago, when these man-like apes were turning into ape-like men, worked out by E. S. Deevey, is 125,000. Thereafter, it must have increased very rapidly. This is the place to remind the reader of Darwin's warning: modern man is not descended from any existing living ape, but if man's ancestor were alive today he would unquestionably be classified among the apes.

If the limb-bones of australopithecines had been found alone, they would have been regarded as human; if the molar teeth had been found alone, they would have been ascribed to an ape. Nor is this all: these ape-like creatures stood erect, as is proved by their hip-girdles and thigh-bones; and they carried their heads erect, as is shown by the forward position of the foramen magnum at the base of the skull. The evolution of man in the different parts of his body was not synchronous, and this is another definition of mosaic evolution.

AUSTRALOPITHECINE

Ape-like characters	Man-like characters
brain-volume small (600 c.c.)	nuchal crest low
jaws massive	small rounded forehead
jaws projecting	brain-case set high in the head
molar teeth large	foramen magnum well forward
ankle-bone head curved	teeth arranged in curved arch
	canine teeth spade-shaped
	first lower premolar small with two cusps
	type of wear in molar teeth (human method of chewing)
	form of milk-teeth
	forelimbs delicately built
	shape of hip-girdle and thigh-bone indicating vertical stance

Conclusion

It has now been seen that in the transitions between classes of living vertebrates, there is evidence that morphological evolution has progressed by means of the mode here described as mosaic. The alternative type of change, involving gradual and general conversion of the whole organism, must have occurred in regard to such characters as the chemical constitution of the body-fluids; it does not seem to have occurred in the evolutionary changes which lifted animals from one class of vertebrates to the next.

It is possible that this is connected in some way with what, following C. H. Waddington, we can call the epigenetic climate of a developing organism. Owing to the genetic make-up and the internal conditions of development in an organism, there may be only a limited number of changes possible, and it is legitimate to think that changes restricted to single organ-systems are more likely to have occurred than progressive changes affecting the entire organism. It is further probable that changes restricted to single organ-systems at a time were more viable and less likely to succumb to selection. Organisms are delicately balanced and adjusted mechanisms, and on the average, changes are more likely to upset than to strengthen them. Selection may therefore be expected to have acted with greater rigour against organisms varying in more than one direction at a time, unless the directions were correlated, as was the case with the evolution of limbs and teeth in some horses, for example.

It has long been held by palaeontologists that the different parts of organisms are capable of independent evolution, proceeding at different rates. This emerges very clearly from studies of rates of evolution as presented by G. G. Simpson (1953), and may appear to be so well known as to make this paper redundant. Perhaps it is, but it may be worth stressing that the principle of the independence of characters, shown, for example, in tooth-length and tooth-height in the evolution of the horses, also applies to the evolution of the classes of vertebrates.

A necessary consequence of mosaic evolution and of the independence of characters evolving at different rates is the production of animals showing mixtures of primitive and specialized characters.

It is a commonplace of palaeontology that in the search for ancestral forms of groups, the fossils which very nearly fill the bill usually show one or more characters that rule them out from the direct ancestry of the descendants, either because they have already lost some structure which the early members of the descendant group still have, or because they possess some structure which the early members of the group in question have not yet evolved. An example of the latter is *Ichthyostega,* where the position of the articulation of the lower jaw is more advanced than in the earliest amphibia.

In each case the fossil gives a very good approximation of the conditions that must have obtained in the real ancestor, but the picture has been spoiled by the precocious evolution of a single character or two, in which the animal anticipated the condition found in the later stages of the evolution of the group in question. A useful term to denote characters of this sort has been coined by K. P. Oakley. Following him, we may call a character in which an animal anticipates a later stage of the evolution of a group (with which it must therefore be evolving in parallel) ecgonomorphic (resembling the descendant).

Conversely, there are cases where characters have survived little-modified from the ancestral state through later stages of evolution. An example is provided by the tooth on the third coronoid of the lower jaw in *Seymouria,* in which it resembles no other known amphibian but reflects the conditions in osteolepid fish. Following E. I. White, we may call such a character progenomorphic (resembling the ancestor). The Ictidosauria as a group may be regarded as progenomorphs, for no structural features of theirs would rule them out from the ancestry of mammals if they occurred earlier in the fossil record. It must be concluded that they have preserved those ancestral features almost without change. The same may be true of *Seymouria,* which was too late to be ancestral to the reptiles.

Only in the case of *Archaeopteryx* is it permissible to say that no time-relations or structural features have yet been found to disqualify it from being regarded as ancestral to a class, viz., birds.

Finally there is the fact that one and the same animal may show primitive and specialized characters in different parts of its body. This was recognized by W. D. Matthew, who applied the term "compensation" to this condition which is, of course, only another case of mosaic evolution, in which the organism shows both ecgonomorphic and progenomorphic characters. An example is that of the Permian labyrinthodont *Trimerorhachis,* in which the condition of the occipital condyle is extremely primitive (like the Carboniferous forms), but the flattening of the skull very specialized (like the Triassic forms).

The significance and possible wide application of mosaic evolution as a general principle was suggested by D. M. S. Watson when he wrote (1919, p. 300): "The curious way in which the structure of *Seymouria* is built up of perfectly well developed amphibian characters and equally decisive reptilian features, those of intermediate type being very rare, affords a magnificent example of the way in which the evolution of great groups may have taken place." I believe that it has, and therefore propose to give to the mosaic mode of evolution the name of Watson's Rule.

BIBLIOGRAPHY

Broom, R. *The Mammal-like Reptiles of South Africa and the Origin of Mammals.* London, 1932.

Clark, Sir W. E. Le Gros. *Man-Apes or Ape-Men?* New York, 1967.

Deevey, E. S. "The Human Population" *Scientific American,* 203, 1960, 195.

Edinger, T. "The Brain of Archaeopteryx" *Ann. Mag. Nat. Hist.,* Ser. 9, Vol. xviii, 1926, 151.

Jarvik, E. "On the Fish-like Tail in the Ichthyostegid Stegocephalians with Descriptions of a New Stegocephalian and a New Crossopterygian from the Upper Devonian of East Greenland" *Meddel. Grönland,* Bd. 114, No. 12, Copenhagen, 1952.

Oakley, K. P. "Swanscombe Man" *Proc. Geol. Soc. Lond.,* 63, 1952, 271.

Simpson, G. G. *The Major Features of Evolution.* New York, 1953.

————. "The Principles of Classification and a Classification of Mammals" *Bull. Amer. Mus. Nat. Hist.,* 85, New York, 1945.

Watson, D. M. S. "The Evolution and Origin of the Amphibia" *Philos. Trans. Roy. Soc.,* Ser. B 214, 1925, 189.

————. "On Seymouria, The Most Primitive Known Reptile" *Proc. Zool. Soc. Lond.,* 1919, 267.

White, E. I. "Australian Arthrodires" *Bull. Brit. Mus. (Nat. Hist.),* 1, 1952, 251.

Young, C.-C. "Mammal-like Reptiles from Lufeng, Yunan, China" *Proc. Zool. Soc. Lond.,* 117, 1947, 537.

Ethology and Evolution: The Study of Primate Societies

E VEN BEFORE EVOLUTION OR NATURAL SELECTION HAD BEEN seriously suggested in the scientific community, the anatomical similarity of *Homo sapiens* to apes and monkeys was unescapably obvious. Galen, the Greek physician, studied and wrote about the anatomy of a monkey, the so-called Barbary ape, and dissected them in order to improve his skill as a surgeon. Linnaeus, two centuries ago, who invented the taxonomical system that we use today, classified our species as a member of the Primate order. Accepting the idea that human behavior resembles that of the primates has proved more difficult, even after the acceptance of the Darwinian explanation of human origins. Culture is still widely supposed to be the exclusive property of humankind. Is it possible to learn anything about ourselves by observing the naturalistic behavior of apes and monkeys?

During the last fifty years, and particularly since about 1950, more and more anthropologists have been trying to find out. Work by psychologists in laboratories had already revealed surprising mental abilities among primates, and the earliest field studies provided tantalizing suggestions of almost human social behavior. By now, there are scores of alert, mostly young, anthropologists engaged in the study of primate ethology, and the literature is expanding at an almost explosive rate. How much new light is being cast, or will be cast, upon the origins of human behavior patterns and cultural characteristics is still debatable and is being vigorously debated. Many early misconceptions have been disposed of, which is a blessing. But many simplistic explanations of human nature have been propounded and gained unwarranted popularity too. We all have culturally-determined preconceptions, and these can easily misguide anyone.

Consequently it is particularly gratifying that Japanese scientific observers, whose cultural biases are so different from those of Americans, have been among the most numerous, the most observant, and the most sophisticated primate ethologists. They are fortunate in being able to watch the activities of monkeys within a few miles of their own universities and they have exploited their good fortune industriously. The following article, "The Society of Japanese Monkeys," by an outstanding Japanese scholar, Professor Junichiro Itani, well illustrates the high quality of research accomplished in Japan.

5. Junichiro Itani

The Society of Japanese Monkeys

Provisionizing

It is thirteen years since, at Toi-misaki at the southeastern extremity of Kyushu, I first saw a wild Japanese monkey. We were observing the wild horses which live on the cape when, one day, on a sunny ridge with a clear view down to the Pacific Ocean below, we came across a troop of monkeys. They crossed to the ridge beyond the one where we were, chattering to each other in an astonishing variety of voices, and eventually disappeared from sight behind it. They made an indelible impression on our minds as they passed before us: monkeys with bright red faces, mother monkeys with babies on their backs, great males marching proudly with their short tails held erect—the very essence, one felt, of wild life.

In 1950 we formed a study group in Kyoto University called the Primates Research Group. Our less than ten members, led by Professors Miyaji Denzaburō and Imanishi Kinji, ranged in search of monkeys from the Shimokita Peninsula, known as the most northerly point in the world at which monkeys are found, all the way down to Yakushima, which is the most southerly habitat of the Japanese monkey. We visited with particular frequency Toi-misaki, Kō-shima and Takasaki-yama in Kyushu, as well as Mino'o, near Osaka, and Arashi-yama in the outskirts of Kyoto. We traveled light, with nothing but a pair of binoculars slung over our shoulders and a field notebook in our pockets. Our search for monkeys took us over pathless mountains, and our short list of equipment was later supplemented with a small sickle, an extremely useful implement for cutting through dense tangles of thorns and creepers on the track of monkeys.

Nevertheless, though we went in search of monkeys every day, our "bag" for the day—the number of monkeys we got close to, and the number we were able to get within range of our binoculars—was, like the hunter's daily bag, extremely variable. At times, by clearing a way with our sickles through the undergrowth down some valley and hiding ourselves behind rocks, we were able to observe a troop of monkeys go down the valley in a well-formed procession. Or, by jumping into the midst of a troop when it was spread out searching for food, and throwing it into utter confusion by running hither and thither among its members, we were able to watch how it restored order in its ranks and what it did to avert the crisis.

But we were not so lucky every day. Free as they were to run and leap wherever they chose on the ground or in the trees, their appearances and disappearances were as bewilderingly sudden as though they were forest sprites. On some days, even, they would outmaneuver us so successfully that we would walk from dawn to dusk without catching so much as a glimpse of them; on such days, we had to be content to take back with us our notes of cries faintly heard in the distance, of footprints, of fragments of food they had left scattered about, or of their droppings.

We carried on in this fashion for more than two years. We managed in this way to get a general outline of what a troop of Japanese monkeys was like, but there we seemed to stick, unable to achieve a breakthrough. Something must obviously be done. So, early in the summer of 1952, we tried setting out sweet potatoes and barley on rocks in a deep forest on Kō-shima through which the monkeys were accustomed to pass, and we confirmed that they ate the potatoes.

In August we visited Kō-shima again, and this time set out larger quantities of sweet potatoes and barley at a larger number of points. In time, we ascertained that the troop's wanderings were clearly influenced by the food we set out, and also that all the food we set out was cleared up by the monkeys within the same day. We next gradually reduced the number of these "provisionizing" points, till finally we had reduced them to one spot, Otomari Bay, the only sandy beach on that small island. On the rocks on this beach we would set out large quantities of sweet potatoes and barley.

On the beach, there was a fisherman's house of which the monkeys were at first wary, refusing to come down to where the food was. However, the suspicion and fear they felt toward human beings was eventually no match for their greed. Hitherto, we had only snatched glimpses of them through dense bushes or trees, but now we had a completely unobstructed view of them on the other side of the beach, right before our very eyes. Once they realized that we would do them no harm, they gradually grew bolder. Thus the provisionizing had been a success, and we had achieved our breakthrough.

For us, it was something like the transfer from a hunting life to an agricultural life. Every day so far we had been, unmistakably, hunters. Now, however, we sowed our sweet potatoes and barley in one set spot, and at that same spot we reaped our harvest: we were farmers, and our harvests were certainly great.

Our first task was to distinguish between individual monkeys. Having done so, we gave each of them names. This told us the membership of the group, as well as relationships between individuals and the social status of each individual, so that eventually we were able to grasp the social structure of the troop as a whole.

At the end of same year, the troop at Takasaki-yama was provisionized. At present, more than twenty troops have been provisionized at various points throughout the country (see Fig. 1). We have most of them under study at the moment, and they have provided us with a remarkably rich source of material for

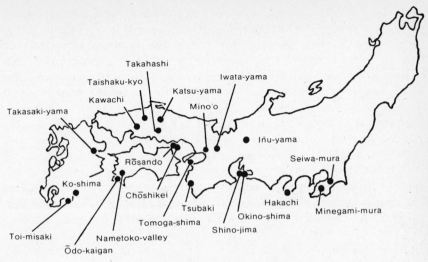

Fig. 1.   Troops so far provisionized.

making a comparative study of the troops. A number of these troops have now been subjected to continuous observation over a period of nine years. When it was first provisionized, the Takasaki-yama troop had about 220 members; this number has now swelled to over 800. Everything that happened to the troop in the meantime, as well as the growth of each individual, the births and the deaths, were all put down in our field notes, and their analysis is still in progress. The object of these studies, of course, is to throw light on the society of the non-human primates close to man, and by so doing to trace the course that man himself has followed.

Jupiter

Dr. C. R. Carpenter, a pioneer of field research on monkeys, tattooed identification numbers on each of the Rhesus monkeys he had roaming free on Santiago Island, near Puerto Rico. We, however, decided to get to know each of them by sight, and gave them names instead of numbers. "Is such a thing really possible?" we are often asked; yet in fact, each of us knew the faces of at least two hundred monkeys. At first, of course, one uses small individual characteristics—a white spot below the left eye, a tuft on the tip of the tail, a torn right ear—as aids in identification, but eventually one can distinguish a monkey even from his back view. Recognition is possible not through such slight peculiarities but through the over-all appearance or individuality. With monkeys, the individual character is quite clearly marked, and such individuality is better represented by a name than a number.

We were responsible for christening more than 1,000 wild monkeys in all. Some of them we shall probably never forget as long as we live. One of them in particular—a monkey on Takasaki-yama called Jupiter—will always be remembered by all of us. He was a monkey of great spirit and valor. Always on the alert, he was strict at times to the point of cruelty. He retained these qualities all through the eight years that we knew him. When he died, on January 16 this year, he must have been over 30. His incisors and canines were worn down to the gums, and his skull showed far more aging than any of the many skulls of Japanese monkeys in our research rooms.

Nevertheless, throughout the eight years that we knew him, Jupiter was the number one leader of the Takasaki-yama troop. To his dying day, he remained king of this especially large troop. Though we missed him, his death gave us a chance to study a number of exceedingly interesting problems involved in understanding the way troops of Japanese monkeys behave. The first of these concerns the life-span of the Japanese monkey; another the stability of the leader's position in the troop. It would not be possible for a single individual to retain the position of most dominant leader for as long as eight years if the troop did not have a firm framework.

Yet Jupiter in his last years was quite feeble. Physically, he was no match for the younger and more energetic males in the classes known as sub-leaders and peripheral males. He could hardly have maintained his position without something other than the strength of his teeth and arms. Our numerous records convinced us that it had some connection with the individual's influence and achievements, and particularly with the confidence of the females who make up the center of the troop. Jupiter's life and death afforded valuable evidence in support of this view.

After Jupiter's death Titan, the troop's second leader, took over quite smoothly without any chaos in the troop. Where Jupiter had been intrepid and adventurous, Titan was a sedate, dignified monkey. It will be interesting to study the effect on the troop as a whole of such a difference in the personality of the leader.

From 1953 to 1956, the troop's affairs were managed jointly by six leaders, including Jupiter and Titan. The finest specimens of male to be found in the troop, they were always at the center, leading the troop and controlling it. Subsequently Pan, who had been third in rank, and Monk, who was fourth, disappeared, no one knew where. In all likelihood they had not died but left the troop, though we are still in the dark as to the reason.

Dominance Rank and Class

Probably no other animal society has the same well-marked dominance rank system as that of the Japanese monkey. Suppose, for example, that two males of about the same size are sitting a few meters apart and that an orange is rolled in between them. One of the two will get up unhurriedly and help himself to the orange with a complete composure that seems to say, "this is mine." The other monkey's behavior is most interesting, and can only be described as "seeing and not seeing." In fact, no trouble at all occurs between the two. However many times one repeats this simple "orange test," the result is the same: the same individual always takes the orange, while the other, despite a great interest in the proceedings, pretends to be totally unaware of what is happening and makes no attempt to take the orange. The former male is technically referred to as the dominant and the latter as the subordinate.

In 1956 the ranks in the Takasaki-yama troop could be arranged in a straight line of descent from the first place to about the thirtieth. In chickens and mice one can observe a circular system of ranks—A is stronger than B, B is stronger than C, C is stronger than A. The linear ranking referred to here, however, implies a complete absence of the contradictions inherent in such a system. Judging only from this, the society of Japanese monkeys might seem to be based on power. However, this dominance rank order is in fact an extremely important means of keeping social order, dictated by the presence together in the same troop of large numbers of males. The division of food, their sexual activities, the control of the troop as a whole and their readiness to defend themselves against enemies from without all have this system of ranks as their main prop. The dominance rank order among its adult males is, in fact, one of the pillars on which the very existence of the troop depends.

It is quite easy to determine which of two individuals has the ascendancy even without relying on the orange test, since the behavior of the monkeys among themselves itself shows inferiority and superiority. The tail, for instance—in the Japanese monkey less than 10 cm. in length—is an extremely sensitive indicator of rank. Let us imagine we are at the center of a troop of monkeys eating at one of the provisionizing places. One, and one only of the males will have his short tail straight up in the air. It means that he is the highest-ranking male in the group. Let us imagine now, though, that another, different male comes ambling up to the group. His tail is up as he comes, and the other male, whose tail was up until now, gently drops it. The newcomer is the higher in rank.

Expressions of inferiority are equally well defined. They involve a grimace as if the monkey were crying, and are sometimes accompanied by a defensive cry. Another admission of inferiority is the action known as "presenting," which is identical with that of the female during copulation. Before a superior, a male will go on all fours and present his buttocks, and the dominant individual will sometimes mount him. Though both are males, this is not a case of homosexual behavior, but an affirmation by the two monkeys of the superior-inferior relationship existing between them. Suppose, for example, one male in a careless moment picks up in front of a dominant male an orange that has come rolling his way. The dominant male will immediately attack him. The attacked male will flee a certain distance, then stop in his tracks and present himself, buttocks foremost, to his attacker. The attacker mounts him in a leisurely fashion, as though to say "you see, I'm the stronger," and everything is forgotten and forgiven.

This provides one way of escape from the strict system of ranks and smooths out social relationships among the males. It does not mean, however, that the same behavior is to be observed between any combination of two males. Particularly among large troops such as that on Takasaki-yama, it is observable only between males of about the same age and close to each other in rank. If an incident of the kind just described had taken place between a male well up in the hierarchy and a young adult male, the only alternative for the latter would have been to run away. The young adult male cannot get out of anything by "presenting."

Any one section of the troop among the male members of which presenting and mounting are effective can be looked on as a "class." To take the Takasaki-yama troop as an example, the class structure of the males consists of leaders, sub-leaders and peripheral males, the peripheral males further having upper, middle, and lower sub-divisions. In the troop as it was in 1955, the classes more or less corresponded to the monkeys' ages. The leader class had six members, the sub-leader class ten, and the peripheral male class a total of twenty-eight. The leaders occupy the position in the center of the group, together with all the females and infants. The sub-leaders form a ring about them, while the peripheral males range about the outer circumference (see Fig. 2). The males of the leader class control and lead the troop; the sub-leaders aid them in this, while the peripheral males act as lookouts and scouts, walk in the van and at the rear when the troop moves from one place to another in procession, and give warning and defend the troop in times of attack from without. It should be mentioned in passing that the females also have ranks, but that these are constantly changing and are very unstable compared with those of the males.

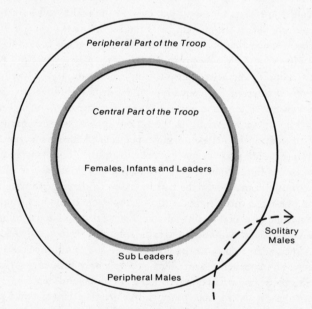

Fig. 2. Social structure of the troop.

Infants playing in a puddle after a rainy night. Such play among baby monkeys of the same age serves automatically to decide their future rank.

Bacchus "proposing." He advances toward the female with a dancing gait, lips protruding, opening and closing rhythmically.

Bacchus keeping control in the troop. He hastens to the scene of a quarrel among the females, emitting a cry of "ga, ga, ga . . ." as he goes.

A leader biting a female. Though his movements are exaggerated, he is not in fact biting very hard, nor are the female's shrieks justified.

Two sub-leaders. As their expressions quite clearly reveal, the monkey on the left is the higher in rank.

Young adult male giving the warning call "kuwan," at which a hush falls over the whole troop. If the situation gets still more dangerous, a larger male comes forward and takes over the call.

The Japanese monkey is equally at home on the ground and up in the trees.

An adult female "calling." This call of "uyaa," signifying "arrival," is the least emotionally charged of all the troop's vocalizations.

Relaxation after a meal in the center of the troop. On the right, Bacchus, one of the leaders. On the left, a female infant grooms her mother while her younger sister plays on the mother's head.

Paternal care. A sub-leader, Syaraku, is grooming a female infant of one year.

On such occasions it is very important, it seems, that the stronger male's new dominance should be backed up by recognition from the other monkeys in the troop. Paternal care is one sign of the desire to impress the center of the troop, and Uzen showed the tendency particularly strongly. It is a mystery, then, why Uzen, in the autumn of 1960, should quite summarily have abandoned his position as first among the sub-leaders and left the troop. Events in the society of monkeys still hold many riddles for us.

Besides paternal care, there are quite a number of other troop-centered activities which, though "social" behavior, conceal a machinery whereby the accumulation of the action eventually affects the individual's position. The activity of the leaders, particularly toward the females, known as "control attack" is an example, and so is an action in which the individual shakes a tree as hard as he can, crying "ga-ga-ga-ga-ga" in the meantime as though to arouse a kind of tension in the troop. In this respect, the reconnoitering and look-out activities of the peripheral males are similar. However, although these activities seem to be common to every troop, paternal care has been observed only in the troops at Takasaki-yama and at Takahashi in Okayama Prefecture.

Culture and Communication

Paternal care is not the only difference of custom existing between troop and troop. Our studies of the kind of food eaten by different troops have revealed all kinds of variations. The monkeys of Takasaki-yama are very fond of the fruit of the *muku* (*Aphananthe aspera*) tree; the hard stone inside they either throw away or swallow whole to be excreted later. The monkeys on Arashiyama, however, break the stone with their teeth and eat the albuminous matter inside. The monkeys at Mino'o dig up the roots of the yam to eat, and also eat snails. The monkeys at Taishaku-kyō eat the bark of pine trees. Monkeys on Mount Ryōzen in the Suzuka range are known to catch and eat the flesh of hares while the snow is on the ground in the winter. Some of the monkeys in troops living on the coasts of Wakasa and two or three other places eat shellfish. These are all habits which cannot ordinarily be observed in other troops.

One troop, thus, will eat things which other troops will not. This means that Japanese monkeys do not, simply, eat anything that seems likely as food but that the troop has its own fixed ideas of what is edible and what inedible. Obviously these ideas are handed down within the troop. Such behavior and customs are referred to as "protoculture." Other characteristics besides food habits that are looked on as cultural phenomena include sexual behavior and social organization. For instance, males in the Taishaku-kyō troop do not practice masturbation. Again, the monkeys on Yakushima have a habit called "testing," in which the male lifts up the female's tail to inspect her external genitals. The most conspicuous indication of the compactness of a troop is the density of individuals. In one of the Shōdo-shima troops, individuals are almost touching, something which is not found in other troops.

We were able to observe the process whereby a number of activities gradually formed themselves into elements in the culture of that troop. In 1953, a young female in the Kō-shima troop began to wash in the sea the potatoes that we set out on the beach. Little by little, the habit spread to other monkeys in the troop, until today a full two-thirds of all the individuals in the group invariably wash their potatoes before eating them, and the practice is more or less completely established as an element in the troop's cultural life. The washing of the sweet potatoes spread gradually, to the first young female's playmates, to her brothers and sisters, then to their particularly intimate associates.

We once experimented to see how the habit of eating caramels—an entirely unfamiliar food—would spread among the Takasaki-yama troop. The trial, conducted over a period of more than one year with one hundred individuals whom we recognized by sight, produced the following conclusions: Infants of under three were extremely positive in their attitude toward new things, and were quick to start eating the caramels. The acquisition rate dropped considerably with age, however, and elderly individuals proved most conservative of all. As in the case of washing the sweet potatoes, the habit spread from the individual to those particularly close to him; the acquisition rate of female monkeys with infants was quicker, thus, than that of adult males, while that of leaders and sub-leaders who practiced paternal care was quicker than that of the peripheral males who did not. The channels for the spread of new cultural elements which were thus revealed were probably also followed in the first place by the old-established elements, being transmitted from senior to junior members of the troop.

However, this spreading and handing-down of customs is a completely one-sided form of communication. The individual learns by observing another individual, with whom it has an extremely close relationship, performing some unfamiliar action; the latter never tells him "this tastes good," or "you should try this," or "the sand comes off if you wash it." The faculty of communication which would make such directions or explanations possible is not developed in the Japanese monkey. They have over thirty different kinds of vocalization, but these are used for other purposes.

These different kinds of vocalization can as a whole be divided into "calling" and "crying." Calling is usually used for communication between the individual and the group, and is not accompanied by any violent emotion. Most of the varieties consist of exchanges such as those used when the troop sets out or calls a halt, signals en route, calls from the vanguard or the rear of the procession, and so on. This extremely varied calling helps in the maintenance of control over the troop in its relentlessly nomadic life, since in the dense forest or bush they have to rely principally on their ears rather than their eyes.

Unlike "calling," "crying" is usually backed up by some strong emotion. It might be better in fact, to say that the sound produced is itself part of a violent emotional outburst. Mostly the basic emotion is anger or sorrow, and the occasion is usually social contact between individual and individual, the function being the adjustment of the social relationship between the two.

A characteristic feature of the vocalizations produced by the Japanese monkey is the greater variety to be found in calling as opposed to crying. There is also another, warning cry which, though used for communication between the individual and the group, has a particular type of urgency and violence. A shrill cry of "kuan" is emitted, always by a single monkey, whereupon the whole troop falls silent and switches to swift preparations for avoiding the enemy from without. The whole transition is a very clear indication of the splendid teamwork existing in the troop.

The cries emitted during those activities occurring between individuals which have a clear-cut social function—such as the presenting and mounting already mentioned—seem so far to be unconnected with any form of speech. There do exist cries, suggesting coaxing or compliance, which are extremely expressive, but only one or two examples have been observed. Even so, it is interesting that such cries should be developing in connection with relationships involving such things as rank and sex.

We intend to pursue our studies of the Japanese monkey still further yet. We are hoping, for example, that provisionization will yield many further harvests. This is obviously a heresy viewed in the light of natural history's traditional prohibition against disturbing the objects of study in any way. How otherwise, though, could we have peered into the innermost workings of their society? With a number of troops, we have worked out blood relationships between the members, and are carrying out research on this basis. Using such methods of study, we have so far observed no instances of sexual relationships between mother and son; discoveries such as this are undoubtedly of the greatest importance in considering the evolution of our own human society.

The Descent of Man: Some Fossil Evidence

D
ARWIN HAD ASSUMED THAT OUR ANCESTORS DIFFERENTI-
ated from those of the apes somewhere in Africa, but in his day there
was no fossil evidence available to support or deny his assumption.
After his death, and particularly during the first quarter of the present
century, paleontologists busied themselves by searching elsewhere for
the remains of early man and of the "missing link" between man and
ape. Dubois, in Java, dug up a fossil skullcap and mandible which did
indeed seem somewhat apish, but also somewhat human, and a femur
which was perfectly human. Many human fossils, including the huge
Heidelberg jaw, had been found in Europe, and the Piltdown hoax had
been perpetrated. Many fossils of Miocene apes had been dug up in
India, but no "Ape-men." A primitive human tooth was found in northern China and labeled "Sinanthropus."

No one expected that South Africa would produce evidence concerning the earliest stages of human evolution. So when Professor Raymond
Dart published the account of his discovery of the fossil skull which he
named *Australopithecus africanus,* his conclusions concerning the significance of this specimen evoked incredulity. Later, as more and more
and still more remains of this variety of "ape-men" were excavated and
carefully studied, it became obvious that his analysis had been correct.
Darwin's assumption was indeed upheld. It is very interesting, therefore,
to read Dart's own account of this remarkable discovery, which changed
the entire course of scientific thinking about the problem of human
origins.

6. Raymond A. Dart

Australopithecus africanus:
The Man-Ape of South Africa

Towards the close of 1924, Miss Josephine Salmons, student demonstrator of anatomy in the University of the Witwatersrand, brought to me the fossilised skull of a cercopithecid monkey which, through her instrumentality, was very generously loaned to the Department for description by its owner, Mr. E. G. Izod, of the Rand Mines Limited. I learned that this valuable fossil had been blasted out of the limestone cliff formation—at a vertical depth of 50 feet and a horizontal depth of 200 feet—at Taungs, which lies 80 miles north of Kimberley on the main line to Rhodesia, in Bechuanaland, by operatives of the Northern Lime Company. Important stratigraphical evidence has been forthcoming recently from this district concerning the succession of stone ages in South Africa (Neville Jones, Jour. Roy. Anthrop. Inst., 1920), and the feeling was entertained that this lime deposit, like that of Broken Hill in Rhodesia, might contain fossil remains of primitive man.

I immediately consulted Dr. R. B. Young, professor of geology in the University of the Witwatersrand, about the discovery, and he, by a fortunate coincidence, was called down to Taungs almost synchronously to investigate geologically the lime deposits of an adjacent farm. During his visit to Taungs, Prof. Young was enabled, through the courtesy of Mr. A. F. Campbell, general manager of the Northern Lime Company, to inspect the site of the discovery and to select further samples of fossil material for me from the same formation. These included a natural cercopithecid endocranial cast, a second and larger cast, and some rock fragments disclosing portions of bone. Finally, Dr. Gordon D. Laing, senior lecturer in anatomy, obtained news, through his friend Mr. Ridley Hendry, of another primate skull from the same cliff. This cercopithecid skull, the possession of Mr. De Wet, of the Langlaagte Deep Mine, has also been liberally entrusted by him to the Department for scientific investigation.

The cercopithecid remains placed at our disposal certainly represent more than one species of catarrhine ape. The discovery of Cercopithecidæ in this area is not novel, for I have been informed that Mr. S. Haughton has in the press a paper discussing at least one species of baboon from this same spot (Royal Society of

Fig. 1.   Norma facialis of *Australopithecus africanus* aligned on the Frankfort horizontal.

South Africa). It is of importance that, outside of the famous Fayüm area, primate deposits have been found on the African mainland at Oldaway (Hans Reck, *Sitzungsbericht der Gesellsch. Naturforsch. Freunde,* 1914), on the shores of Victoria Nyanza (C. W. Andrews, *Ann. Mag. Nat. Hist.,* 1916), and in Bechuanaland, for these discoveries lend promise to the expectation that a tolerably complete story of higher primate evolution in Africa will yet be wrested from our rocks.

In manipulating the pieces of rock brought back by Prof. Young, I found that the larger natural endocranial cast articulated exactly by its fractured frontal extremity with another piece of rock in which the broken lower and posterior margin of the left side of a mandible was visible. After cleaning the rock mass, the outline of the hinder and lower part of the facial skeleton came into view. Careful development of the solid limestone in which it was embedded finally revealed the almost entire face depicted in the accompanying photographs.

It was apparent when the larger endocranial cast was first observed that it was specially important, for its size and sulcal pattern revealed sufficient similarity with those of the chimpanzee and gorilla to demonstrate that one was handling in this instance an anthropoid and not a cercopithecid ape. Fossil anthropoids have not hitherto been recorded south of the Fayüm in Egypt, and living anthropoids have not been discovered in recent times south of Lake Kivu region in Belgian Congo, nearly 2000 miles to the north, as the crow flies.

All fossil anthropoids found hitherto have been known only from mandibular or maxillary fragments, so far as crania are concerned, and so the general appearance of the types they represented has been unknown; consequently, a condition of affairs where virtually the whole face and lower jaw, replete with teeth, together with the major portion of the brain pattern, have been preserved, constitutes a specimen of unusual value in fossil anthropoid discovery. Here, as in *Homo rhodesiensis,* Southern Africa has provided documents of higher primate evolution that are amongst the most complete extant.

Apart from this evidential completeness, the specimen is of importance because it exhibits an extinct race of apes *intermediate between living anthropoids and man.*

In the first place, the whole cranium displays *humanoid* rather than anthropoid lineaments. It is markedly dolichocephalic and leptoprosopic, and manifests in a striking degree the *harmonious relation* of calvaria to face emphasised by Pruner-Bey. As Topinard says, "A cranium elongated from before backwards, and at the same time elevated, is already in harmony by itself; but if the face, on the other hand, is elongated from above downwards, and narrows, the harmony is complete." I have assessed roughly the difference in the relationship of the glabella-gnathion facial length to the glabella-inion calvarial length in recent African anthropoids of an age comparable with that of this specimen (depicted in Duckworth's "Anthropology and Morphology," second edition, vol. i.), and find that, if the glabella-inion length be regarded in all three as 100, then the glabella-gnathion length in the young chimpanzee is approximately 88, in the young gorilla 80, and in this fossil 70, which proportion suitably demonstrates the enhanced relationship of cerebral length to facial length in the fossil (Fig. 2).

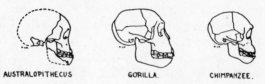

AUSTRALOPITHECUS   GORILLA.   CHIMPANZEE.

Fig. 2. Cranial form in living anthropoids of similar age (after Duckworth) and in the new fossil. For this comparison, the fossil is regarded as having the same calvarial length as the gorilla.

The glabella is tolerably pronounced, but any traces of the salient supra-orbital ridges, which are present even in immature living anthropoids, are here entirely absent. Thus the relatively increased glabella-inion measurement is due to brain and not to bone. Allowing 4 mm. for the bone thickness in the inion region, that measurement in the fossil is 127 mm.; *i.e.* 4 mm. less than the same measurement in an adult chimpanzee in the Anatomy Museum at the University of the Witwatersrand. The orbits are not in any sense detached from the forehead, which rises steadily from their margins in a fashion amazingly human. The interorbital width is very small (13 mm.) and the ethmoids are not blown out laterally as in modern African anthropoids. This lack of ethmoidal expansion causes the lacrimal fossæ to face posteriorly and to lie relatively far back in the orbits, as in man. The orbits, instead of being subquadrate as in anthropoids, are almost circular, furnishing an orbital index of 100, which is well within the range of human variation (Topinard, "Anthropology"). The malars, zygomatic arches, maxillæ, and mandible all betray a delicate and humanoid character. The facial prognathism is relatively slight, the gnathic index of Flower giving a value of 109, which is scarcely greater than that of certain Bushmen (Strandloopers) examined by Shrubsall. The nasal bones are not prolonged below the level of the lower orbital margins, as in anthropoids, but end above these, as in man, and are incompletely fused together in their lower half. Their maximum length (17 mm.) is not so great as that of the nasals in *Eoanthropus dawsoni*. They are depressed in the median line, as in the chimpanzee, in their lower half, but it seems probable that this depression has occurred post-mortem, for the upper half of each bone is arched forwards (Fig. 1). The nasal aperture is small and is just wider than it is high (17 mm. × 16 mm.). There is no nasal spine, the floor of the nasal cavity being continuous with the anterior aspect of the alveolar portions of the maxillæ, after the fashion of the chimpanzee and of certain New Caledonians and negroes (Topinard, *loc. cit.*).

In the second place, the dentition is *humanoid* rather than anthropoid. The specimen is juvenile, for the first permanent molar tooth only has erupted in both jaws on both sides of the face; *i.e.* it corresponds anatomically with a human child of six years of age. Observations upon the milk dentition of living primates are few, and only one molar tooth of the deciduous dentition in one fossil anthropoid is known (Gregory, "The Origin and Evolution of the Human Dentition," 1920). Hence the data for the necessary comparisons are meagre, but certain striking features of the milk dentition of this creature may be mentioned. The tips of the canine teeth transgress very slightly (0.5–0.75 mm.) the general margin of the teeth in each jaw, *i.e.* very little more than does the human milk canine. There is no diastema whatever between the premolars and canines on either side of the lower jaw, such as is present in the deciduous dentition of living anthropoids; but the canines in this jaw come, as in the human jaw, into alignment with the incisors (Gregory, *loc. cit.*). There is a diastema (2 mm. on the right side, and 3 mm. on the left side) between the canines and lateral incisors of the upper jaw;

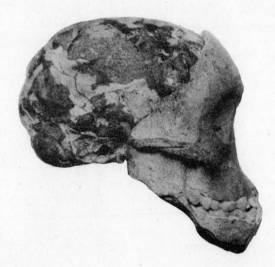

Fig. 3. Norma lateralis of *Australopithecus africanus* aligned on the Frankfort horizontal.

but seeing, first, that the incisors are narrow, and, secondly, that diastemata (1 mm.–1.5 mm.) occur between the central incisors of the upper jaw and between the medial and lateral incisors of both sides in the lower jaw, and, thirdly, that some separation of the milk teeth takes place even in mankind (Tomes, "Dental Anatomy," seventh edition) during the establishment of the permanent dentition, it is evident that the diastemata which occur in the upper jaw are small. The lower canines, nevertheless, show wearing facets both for the upper canines and for the upper lateral incisors.

The incisors as a group are irregular in size, tend to overlap one another, and are almost vertical, as in man; they are not symmetrical and well spaced, and do not project forwards markedly, as in anthropoids. The upper lateral incisors do project forwards to some extent and perhaps also do the upper central incisors very slightly, but the lateral lower incisors betray no evidence of forward projection, and the central lower incisors are not even vertical as in most races of mankind, but are directed slightly backwards, as *sometimes* occurs in man. Owing to these remarkably human characters displayed by the deciduous dentition, when contour tracings of the upper jaw are made, it is found that the jaw and the teeth, as a whole, take up a parabolic arrangement comparable only with that presented by mankind amongst the higher primates. These facts, together with the more minute anatomy of the teeth, will be illustrated and discussed in the memoir which is in the process of elaboration concerning the fossil remains.

In the third place, the mandible itself is *humanoid* rather than anthropoid. Its ramus is, on the whole, short and slender as compared with that of anthropoids, but the bone itself is more massive than that of a human being of the same age. Its symphyseal region is virtually complete and reveals anteriorly a more vertical outline than is found in anthropoids or even in the jaw of Piltdown man. The anterior symphyseal surface is scarcely less vertical than that of Heidelberg man. The posterior symphyseal surface in living anthropoids differs from that of modern man in possessing a pronounced posterior prolongation of the lower border, which joins together the two halves of the mandible, and so forms the well-known *simian shelf* and above it a deep genial impression for the attachment of the tongue musculature. In this character, *Eoanthropus dawsoni* scarcely differs from the anthropoids, especially the chimpanzee; but this new fossil betrays no evidence of such a shelf, the lower border of the mandible having been massive and rounded after the fashion of the mandible of *Homo heidelbergensis*.

That hominid characters were not restricted to the face in this extinct primate group is borne out by the relatively forward situation of the foramen magnum. The position of the basion can be assessed within a few millimetres of error, because a portion of the right exoccipital is present alongside the cast of the basal aspect of the cerebellum. Its position is such that the basi-prosthion measurement is 89 mm., while the basi-inion measurement is at least 54 mm. This relationship may be expressed in the form of a "head-balancing" index of 60.7. The same index in a baboon provides a value of 41.3, in an adult chimpanzee 50.7, in Rhodesian man 83.7, in a dolichocephalic European 90.9, and in a brachycephalic

Fig. 4. Norma basalis of *Australopithecus africanus* aligned on the Frankfort horizontal.

European 105.8. It is significant that this index, which indicates in a measure the poise of the skull upon the vertebral column, points to the assumption by this fossil group of an attitude appreciably more erect than that of modern anthropoids. The improved poise of the head, and the better posture of the whole body framework which accompanied this alteration in the angle at which its dominant member was supported, is of great significance. It means that a greater reliance was being placed by this group upon the feet as organs of progression, and that the hands were being freed from their more primitive function of accessory organs of locomotion. Bipedal animals, their hands were assuming a higher evolutionary rôle not only as delicate tactual, examining organs which were adding copiously to the animal's knowledge of its physical environment, but also as instruments of the growing intelligence in carrying out more elaborate, purposeful, and skilled movements, and as organs of offence and defence. The latter is rendered the more probable, in view, first, of their failure to develop massive canines and hideous features, and, secondly, of the fact that even living baboons and anthropoid apes can and do use sticks and stones as implements and as weapons of offence ("Descent of Man," p. 81 *et seq.*).

Lastly, there remains a consideration of the endocranial cast which was responsible for the discovery of the face. The cast comprises the right cerebral and cerebellar hemispheres (both of which fortunately meet the median line throughout their entire dorsal length) and the anterior portion of the left cerebral hemisphere. The remainder of the cranial cavity seems to have been empty, for the left face of the cast is clothed with a picturesque lime crystal deposit; the vacuity in the left half of the cranial cavity was probably responsible for the fragmentation of the specimen during the blasting. The cranial capacity of the specimen may best be appreciated by the statement that the length of the cavity could not have been less than 114 mm., which is 3 mm. greater than that of an adult chimpanzee in the Museum of the Anatomy Department in the University of the Witwatersrand, and only 14 mm. less than the greatest length of the cast of the endocranium of a gorilla chosen for casting on account of its great size. Few data are available concerning the expansion of brain matter which takes place in the living anthropoid brain between the time of eruption of the first permanent molars and the time of their becoming adult. So far as man is concerned, Owen ("Anatomy of Vertebrates," vol. iii.) tells us that "The brain has advanced to near its term of size at about ten years, but it does not usually obtain its full development till between twenty and thirty years of age." R. Boyd (1860) discovered an increase in weight of nearly 250 grams in the brains of male human beings after they had reached the age of seven years. It is therefore reasonable to believe that the adult forms typified by our present specimen possessed brains which were larger than that of this juvenile specimen, and equalled, if they did not actually supersede, that of the gorilla in absolute size.

Whatever the total dimensions of the adult brain may have been, there are not lacking evidences that the brain in this group of fossil forms was distinctive in type and was an instrument of greater intelligence that that of living anthropoids. The face of the endocranial cast is scarred unfortunately in several places (cross-hatched in the dioptographic tracing—see Fig. 5). It is evident that the relative

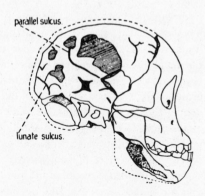

Fig. 5. Dioptographic tracing of *Australopithecus africanus* (right side), × ⅓.

proportion of cerebral to cerebellar matter in this brain was greater than in the gorilla's. The brain does not show that general pre- and post-Rolandic flattening characteristic of the living anthropoids, but presents a rounded and well-filled-out contour, which points to a symmetrical and balanced development of the faculties of associative memory and intelligent activity. The pithecoid type of parallel sulcus is preserved, but the sulcus lunatus has been thrust backwards towards the occipital pole by a pronounced general bulging of the parieto-temporo-occipital association areas.

To emphasise this matter, I have reproduced (Fig. 6) superimposed coronal contour tracings taken at the widest part of the parietal region in the gorilla endocranial cast and in this fossil. Nothing could illustrate better the mental gap

Fig. 6. Contour tracings of coronal sections through the widest part of the parietal region of the endocranial casts in Australopithecus ..... and in a gorilla ----.

that exists between living anthropoid apes and the group of creatures which the fossil represents than the flattened atrophic appearance of the parietal region of the brain (which lies between the visual field on one hand, and the tactile and auditory fields on the other) in the former and its surgent vertical and dorso-lateral expansion in the latter. The expansion in this area of the brain is the more significant in that it explains the posterior *humanoid* situation of the sulcus lunatus. It indicates (together with the narrow interorbital interval and human characters of the orbit) the fact that this group of beings, having acquired the faculty of stereoscopic vision, had profited beyond living anthropoids by setting aside a relatively much larger area of the cerebral cortex to serve as a storehouse of information concerning their objective environment as its details were simul-taneously revealed to the senses of vision and touch, and also of hearing. They possessed to a degree unappreciated by living anthropoids the use of their hands and ears and the consequent faculty of associating with the colour, form, and general appearance of objects, their weight, texture, resilience, and flexibility, as well as the significance of sounds emitted by them. In other words, their eyes saw, their ears heard, and their hands handled objects with greater meaning and to fuller purpose than the corresponding organs in recent apes. They had laid down the foundations of that discriminative knowledge of the appearance, feeling, and sound of things that was a necessary milestone in the acquisition of articulate speech.

There is, therefore, an ultra-simian quality of the brain depicted in this immature endocranial cast which harmonises with the ultra-simian features revealed by the entire cranial topography and corroborates the various inferences drawn therefrom. The two thousand miles of territory which separate this crea-ture from its nearest living anthropoid cousins is indirect testimony to its in-creased intelligence and mastery of its environment. It is manifest that we are in the presence here of a pre-human stock, neither chimpanzee nor gorilla, which possesses a series of differential characters not encountered hitherto in any anthropoid stock. This complex of characters exhibited is such that it cannot be interpreted as belonging to a form ancestral to any living anthropoid. For this reason, we may be equally confident that there can be no question here of a primitive anthropoid stock such as has been recovered from the Egyptian Fayüm. Fossil anthropoids, varieties of Dryopithecus, have been retrieved in many parts of

Europe, Northern Africa, and Northern India, but the present specimen, despite its youth, cannot be confused with anthropoids having the dryopithecid dentition. Other fossil anthropoids from the Siwalik hills in India (Miocene and Pliocene) are known which, according to certain observers, may be ancestral to modern anthropoids and even to man.

Whether our present fossil is to be correlated with the discoveries made in India is not yet apparent; that question can only be solved by a careful comparison of the permanent molar teeth from both localities. It is obvious, meanwhile, that it represents a fossil group distinctly advanced beyond living anthropoids in those two dominantly human characters of facial and dental recession on one hand, and improved quality of the brain on the other. Unlike Pithecanthropus, it does not represent an ape-like man, a caricature of precocious hominid failure, but a creature well advanced beyond modern anthropoids in just those characters, facial and cerebral, which are to be anticipated in an extinct link between man and his simian ancestor. At the same time, it is equally evident that a creature with anthropoid brain capacity, and lacking the distinctive, localised temporal expansions which appear to be concomitant with and necessary to articulate man, is no true man. It is therefore logically regarded as a man-like ape. I propose tentatively, then, that a new family of *Homo-simiadæ* be created for the reception of the group of individuals which it represents, and that the first known species of the group be designated *Australopithecus africanus,* in commemoration, first, of the extreme southern and unexpected horizon of its discovery, and secondly, of the continent in which so many new and important discoveries connected with the early history of man have recently been made, thus vindicating the Darwinian claim that Africa would prove to be the cradle of mankind.

It will appear to many a remarkable fact that an ultra-simian and pre-human stock should be discovered, in the first place, at this extreme southern point in Africa, and, secondly, in Bechuanaland, for one does not associate with the present climatic conditions obtaining on the eastern fringe of the Kalahari desert an environment favourable to higher primate life. It is generally believed by geologists (*vide* A. W. Rogers, "Post-Cretaceous Climates of South Africa," *South African Journal of Science,* vol. xix., 1922) that the climate has fluctuated within exceedingly narrow limits in this country since Cretaceous times. We must therefore conclude that it was only the enhanced cerebral powers possessed by this group which made their existence possible in this untoward environment.

In anticipating the discovery of the true links between the apes and man in tropical countries, there has been a tendency to overlook the fact that, in the luxuriant forests of the tropical belts, Nature was supplying with profligate and lavish hand an easy and sluggish solution, by adaptive specialisation, of the problem of existence in creatures so well equipped mentally as living anthropoids are. For the production of man a different apprenticeship was needed to sharpen the wits and quicken the higher manifestations of intellect—a more open veldt country where competition was keener between swiftness and stealth, and where adroitness of thinking and movement played a preponderating rôle in the preservation of the species. Darwin has said, "no country in the world abounds in a greater degree with dangerous beasts than Southern Africa," and, in my opinion, Southern Africa, by providing a vast open country with occasional wooded belts and a relative scarcity of water, together with a fierce and bitter mammalian competition, furnished a laboratory such as was essential to this penultimate phase of human evolution.

In Southern Africa, where climatic conditions appear to have fluctuated little since Cretaceous times, and where ample dolomitic formations have provided innumerable refuges during life, and burial-places after death, for our troglodytic forefathers, we may confidently anticipate many complementary discoveries concerning this period in our evolution.

In conclusion, I desire to place on record my indebtedness to Miss Salmons, Prof. Young, and Mr. Campbell, without whose aid the discovery would not have been made; to Mr. Len Richardson for providing the photographs; to Dr. Laing and my laboratory staff for their willing assistance; and particularly to Mr. H. Le Helloco, student demonstrator in the Anatomy Department, who has prepared the illustrations for this preliminary statement.

By the Sweat of Thy Brow Shalt Thou Earn Thy Bread

ONE NOTABLE CHARACTERISTIC WHICH SETS OUR SPECIES apart from all other primates is the peculiar distribution of hair on the human body, a fact which has led one popular writer to call us "The Naked Ape." Fossil evidence, of course, can never tell us how long ago our ancestors lost the coat of long hair which covers the bodies of all our close relatives. In all human races today, hair is concentrated on the head, at the pubes, and under the arms, while adult males have more hair on their faces, chests, and limbs than do children or adult females. Hair seems to function as an aspect of sexual dimorphism rather than for climatic protection in our species. We cannot help but wonder how this came to be, and how long ago the change took place.

Lacking direct evidence, we must depend upon what archaeology has revealed concerning the conditions of life to which our ancestors were exposed and the activities in which they were engaged. It now seems clear that from the time of *Australopithecus,* or even earlier, the ecological niche occupied by the human stock differed from that exploited by the apes. In fact, our ancestors entered a new adaptive zone, which subjected them to new selective pressures and provided them with new opportunities. Their diet changed: more meat was eaten. Their life style changed: food was commonly shared. It has been said, not too facetiously, that they were apes trying to be wolves. Among the most stimulating and provocative suggestions about how the activities of our early ancestors affected their physiology and appearance is the following article by Dr. Russell W. Newman.

7. Russell W. Newman

Why Man Is Such a Sweaty and Thirsty Naked Animal: A Speculative Review

Our present view of the earliest differentiation of man's ancestors from the primate stock assumes a gradual shift in habitat from forest to open grasslands in the tropics and sub-tropics of the Old World during the Pliocene epoch. This period encompassed some critical innovations in: morphology (complete upright posture and gait, increased cranial capacity, etc.), economy (increasingly carnivorous), behavior (tool making, speech), and probably others not integrated into the central theory of evolution. This paper presents the argument that this shift from forest to grassland resulted in certain physiological adaptations to environmental heat loads that still characterize our species; Barnicot (1959) suggested just such a relationship a decade ago.

Specifically, the physical avenues of heat exchange between an animal and its environment will be reiterated to establish a common vocabulary; the interplay between these avenues and selected tropical environments will then be examined with reference to human responses to point up the specializations which characterize our species. Water requirements and the associated patterns of thirst and drinking habits are reviewed since they may have influenced the daily regimen. Finally, the experimental data now available on non-human primates under heat stress will be presented to see whether the human response is characteristic of the primate order.

Avenues of Heat Exchange

There are four channels of energy exchange between the animal and its environment: conduction, convection, radiation, and evaporation. Modern man uses all of them in varying combinations and proportions, as did his ancestors. The first three channels operate toward either a net loss or gain of heat for the organism. The fourth channel, evaporation, is generally considered to result only in heat loss.

Conduction is the flow of heat without displacement of the material and can occur in gases, liquids, or solids. The most familiar example of conduction occurs when touching an object which is either hot or cold; in the first instance we conduct heat towards us, in the second we lose heat. The importance of conduction is tied to the habits of a given species; in man it is not a major source of heat exchange. Conduction is often considered simultaneously with convection as a dual avenue of heat exchange, and this combination will be used here.

Convection is a flow of heat by the physical movement of the gas or liquid in contact. The best example is the increase in cooling (or heating) produced by wind. This convective air current cools by carrying away the heat conducted from the skin and by presenting a steady supply of air which is cooler than the skin surface. Convective exchange thus occurs at the outer boundary of a thin layer of still air which surrounds the body. It acts in the absence of wind because of the air movement produced by the expansion of the warmed air *per se,* but convective exchange increases dramatically with movement of either the air or the body.

Radiation is an exchange of heat from a warmer to a cooler object which is independent of the intervening medium. It includes the direct acquisition of heat from the sun as ultra-violet, visible, and infra-red energy and the more subtle exchanges by which we radiate heat to, or receive it from our surroundings. This is an exceedingly important channel for heat exchange in man, and some of its complexities will be examined later.

The fourth method, evaporation, results in the loss of "latent" heat required to vaporize water from the skin and from the membranes of the respiratory tract. The total evaporative heat loss, comprised of three parts, includes respiratory loss—which is relatively constant in man since he does not generally pant, diffusional skin loss—which is also rather constant, and sensible perspiration, i.e. active thermal sweating, which supplements the diffusional phase when either the environment imposes a sufficient heat load (at rest at about $30°$ C) or when exercise increases body heat production.

Environmental Conditions of the Forest and Savanna

Man's ancestors probably did not step from tropical forest to sunbaked grasslands in one short bound. However, these two extremes will be contrasted, with the understanding that there are many intermediate conditions. Except for periods of storms and rain, tropical forests at ground level in the daytime are typified by warm temperatures averaging $28-32°$ C as the daily maximum, very little air movement, a very high humidity (the air almost saturated with moisture), and little radiant heat from the sun (Richards 1957, Read 1968). This is only marginally stressful to an inactive animal because this combination of an air temperature slightly below skin temperature with a high ambient humidity and low air movement makes it just physically possible for the animal to lose the heat generated by metabolism. An active animal has increased difficulty because it will produce two or three times as much heat and, although the higher skin temperature accompanying the physical activity of an exercising animal increases the heat transferred by radiation slightly, little real increase from convection or evaporation is possible because of the relatively small temperature and vapor pressure differences between the skin and air. We can characterize a forest-dwelling animal as being almost solely dependent on radiational heat loss for thermoregulation with a minor contribution from conductance when lying or sitting on the forest floor.

Open country (savanna or steppe) at comparable latitudes presents a different set of meteorological conditions for mammals. The most obvious difference is that solar radiation becomes an important element since it can impinge directly on the animal and its immediate surroundings. If an animal is not in shade, it will receive radiation directly from the sun; that energy which is not reflected (50–60%) will be absorbed as heat. Even in the shade, air temperature rises, usually about 5° C, primarily from the heat re-radiated by the ground and all nearby objects which are in sunlight. The radiant heat load absorbed cannot be simply described in terms of surface temperatures since animals have defensive mechanisms which modify this load. Under high radiant heat loads, exposed sand or rock may reach surface temperatures of 60° C, a level painful to touch; the tips of the wool in Merino sheep can reach 85° C in desert sun (MacFarlane 1964), but their skins never reach this level for various reasons. The effect of solar insolation in mammals is best described either in terms of the energy received and absorbed or by some measure of the resulting strain (reaction to the stress). A nude man sitting in the sun in the desert may absorb 200 kcal/m^2/hr (Adolph 1947), while Lee (1963) equates desert solar radiation to a rise of 7° C in air temperature. In the tropical savanna, direct radiation is reduced below that in the desert by the increased amount of water vapor in the air which absorbs some of the ultra-violet and visible portions of the light spectrum; a figure of about 100 kcal/m^2/hr has been estimated for such an area (Roller and Goldman 1967). This reduces the 7° C equivalent air temperature increase, but nevertheless still represents a stressful condition for a quiet animal. The other two meteorological factors mentioned for the forest environment, air movement and humidity, also change. Air movement increases many-fold outside the forest although it obviously varies from time to time; in fact, the term "wind-speed" is only appropriate outside the forest proper. Humidity in the tropics is always higher than that which we associate with higher latitudes, but relative humidities of less than 50% are common outside the forest. These humidities provide much greater potential for evaporative heat loss than the saturated air under the forest canopy.

This "open country" combination of meteorological conditions imposes a higher stress on the animal than did the tropical forest. Both conductive and radiant heat exchanges now flow from the environment to the animal; they have become avenues of heat gain. The only way to re-establish a heat-loss relationship (except by retreating to caves or burrows) is for peripheral vasodilation to raise skin temperature to levels above ambient temperature and, indeed, above the surface temperatures of everything nearby. There are definite limits to this approach since skin temperature must remain below deeper body temperature for metabolic heat to be dissipated from its sites of origin and since the upper tolerable level of skin (as well as deep body) temperature is relatively low. Convective heat loss is now more important, because of increased air movement, but can only assist heat transfer from the skin if the air temperature is lower than skin temperature; if the reverse is true, the warmer air simply increases the heat load as it moves over the skin. Fortunately, the fourth avenue of heat transfer, evaporative heat loss, is much greater in the relatively dry open country than it was under the higher humidities of the forest, if sufficient moisture can be made available at the surface of the animal by panting or sweating or the spreading of saliva or urine on the skin. Finally, it is noteworthy that under conditions where heat storage from radiant insolation is a problem, as in open country, larger body size becomes advantageous since it minimizes the surface area (cm^2) per unit of body volume (cm^3) and thus spreads the radiant heat load throughout a greater mass, sparing the critical centers.

Adaptations of Heat Stress

Many specific adaptations to environmental stresses have been observed in mammals. Only a few appear relevant to human evolution, and these are observed primarily in ungulates and carnivores. Almost all of these findings are from domestic animals although many of the principles must also apply to related wild species.

Some small animals in hot environments (especially desert forms) have become nocturnal and spend the day underground; this was not man's adaptation. Many of the larger carnivores (especially the cats) kill and feed at intervals of as much as 2–3 days, resting between kills in the shadiest and coolest locations in their territory. On the other hand, man seems to have followed the general primate pattern of frequent feeding, and our ancestors must have spent many of their waking hours in pursuit of food even under conditions of high heat stresses. There may have been some behavioral adaptations in daily activity and feeding habits, but it does not appear that major changes in food acquisition patterns took place specifically to avoid stressful environmental conditions. There is one peculiarity of man that needs to be mentioned although it is not a true heat adaptation. Being erect *per se*, in open grassland, substantially reduces the solar heat load by minimizing the amount of surface area exposed to direct sunlight. For example, a standing man receives only two-thirds as much direct solar radiation as a standing sheep of equivalent size on a daily average and less than one-quarter as much at the noontime peak loads (Lee 1950). However, the assumption of an upright posture was so fundamental to human evolution that this thermal advantage can only be considered as a minor and fortuitous by-product.

One of the most important mammalian defenses against radiant heat loads is a dense and highly reflective coat of body hair. This serves multiple purposes: reflecting up to half of the solar energy, absorbing some of the unreflected portion at a distance from the skin for dissipation by convection and re-radiation, and providing an insulative space against the conductance of the absorbed heat toward the skin. A dense coat may be a dual purpose thermal protective system since it is most conspicuous in large desert mammals who face a high radiant heat input during the day and an equally impressive radiant heat loss at night. Man's evolution obviously did not include this specialization; in fact, man has gone in the opposite direction, toward virtual absence of body hair.

Keeping a body surface covered with a film of moisture, thus insuring a relatively high heat loss, is the only alternative to reducing a high radiant heat load by means of insulative fur or wool. Man's most important thermal adaptation is increased evaporative heat loss through thermal sweating. Of course, not all mammals sweat to regulate their body temperature; the dog dissipates body heat by panting. Even well adapted tropical animals such as goats may depend primarily on respiratory heat losses for cooling. However, respiratory heat loss offers much less effective surface area and is not as efficient as sweating. Animals which depend on panting usually show other defensive adaptations and, unlike man, have developed tolerance to hyperventilatory sequelae. Sweat glands have been observed in many animals which do not appear to use this type of evaporative heat loss as their principal defensive mechanism. Man is noted among the mammals not for either the number or size of his sweat glands (Weiner and Hellmann 1960), but only for the very high secretory level at which they operate. Man has been observed to sweat at the rate of three liters per hour for short periods of heavy work in high heat (Eichna et al. 1945). Two liters per hour is quite common for the combination of exercise and heat and about the human limit for sustained sweating (Ladell 1964). One liter per hour is a reasonable figure for many hot conditions. No other mammal is known to sweat as much per unit surface area as man. The nearest competitors on a surface area basis are the donkey and the camel (Schmidt-Nielson 1964). Some breeds of cattle are heavy sweat producers but also simultaneously utilize panting (MacFarlane 1968). None of these can produce more than half of the sweat per unit of surface area (500 gm vs. 1000 $gm/m^2/hr$) that can be achieved by man. Sweating and panting are in general complementary, and for a sweating animal such as man panting is a secondary line of defence, used only when sweating is inadequate (Bianca 1968). Panting in man is apt to produce physiological problems of respiratory instead of thermal nature (Goldman et al. 1965).

Since all other primates have considerable hair covering, it has always been accepted that our ancestors must once have had a respectable amount of body hair. The question has been when and why did they lose it. Most of the explanations offered have implied that nakedness was an advantage in hot conditions. For example, Coon (1955) states: ". . . the absence of this covering . . . must be considered adaptive, on the one hand to hot dry conditions in which the surface of the skin must be free to permit the breezes to evaporate sweat, . . ." La Barre (1964) links nakedness with a need for "diffusion of metabolic heat from the rapid spurts of energy required in hunting"; Montagu (1964) postulates a loss of hair with increased sweating capacity as a mechanism for avoidance of overheating from a hunting way of life. This concept has been perpetuated in recent textbooks (Campbell 1967) and in a much more qualified format in a recent work for the lay audience (Morris 1967). One of the purposes of this review is to point out that this explanation does not fit the available data from man and other mammals. Unless we postulate an ancestral condition of dense, long fleece such as in wool-bearing sheep or the winter coat of camels, body hair is no bar to convective heat loss and has nothing to do with the radiation of long-wave infrared heat to cooler objects. There is no evidence that a hair coat interferes with the evaporation of sweat; what can be said is that exposure to the sun after the removal of the body hair increases sweating in cattle (Berman 1957) and panting in sheep (MacFarlane 1968), because the total heat load has been increased. Many men have been studied in heat with a solar load while nude and wearing light clothing which is roughly equivalent to body hair. At rest or light work the clothed man gained about two-thirds as much heat as the nude man and sweated commensurately less, and this is roughly the same savings in heat gain that one gets from going out of the sunshine into shade (Adolph 1947, Lee 1964). It seems obvious that man's present glabrous state is a marked disadvantage under high radiant heat loads rather than the other way around, and that man's specialization for and great dependence on thermal sweating stems from his increased heat load in the sun.

It is much more difficult to evaluate the "metabolic-heat-generated-from-hunting" suggestion with comparative data since there is no other predatory species which seems to have had to lose its hair to be able to catch its prey. This might indicate that our ancestors either pushed their prey to exhaustion in what Krantz (1968) has termed persistence hunting, or that they were woefully inefficient hunters. Sweat rate is not a very good measure of physiological strain under conditions of short and uneven bursts of exercise although it is an excellent indicator for long-term, moderate work in the heat. This is because sweating is a somewhat delayed response, usually requiring at least 20 minutes to reach peak production. There certainly are no data on the energy requirements of our hypothetical early ancestors, but there are well established limits on modern man which place a work limit of approximately 300 kcal/hr of heat production for 8 hours per day if the level is to be maintained day after day without a problem of accumulated fatigue (Passmore and Durnin 1955). This is only about one half the limit of man's capacity for evaporative heat loss by sweating.

Water Requirements and Thirst

Any discussion of evaporative heat losses must include a consideration of the replacement of the lost body fluid. Man is the most dependent on thermal sweating among the mammals thus far investigated and may well be the most dependent on a continuing source of water; his principal competitor would be the horse. The only two aspects of this problem to be considered will be man's drinking requirements and the effects of dehydration.

Every liter of water that an average 70 kg man loses represents nearly a $1\frac{1}{2}\%$ loss in body weight. Sweating in the heat can reach the level of 2 liters per hour under conditions of sustained work; respiratory water loss in man is small, seldom over 15 grams per hour; and diffusional water loss through the skin probably never exceeds $1\frac{1}{2}\%$ of weight per day (Ladell 1965). These losses must be replaced to avoid progressive dehydration. A man who has accumulated a 2%

weight loss from sweating is thirsty, by 10% he is helpless, and death occurs at 18–20% (Folk 1966). There is much less information on other species, but the cat and dog die at about this same level of dehydration while camels, sheep, and donkeys can survive over a 30% weight loss of water (Whittow 1968). The mechanisms by which species tolerate dehydration vary and lie outside the scope of this survey, but it is interesting that man does not diminish sweating in the heat to fit his state of hydration until he is dangerously dehydrated (Adolph 1947).

Total daily water requirements for an animal in the heat is a complicated problem and many of its facets are not particularly relevant to our consideration of evolutionary forces. Assuming no marked seasonal differences in the water content of the vegetable foods consumed, and that the animal portion of the diet is very constant in water content, then body water losses from increased requirements for evaporative heat loss have to be replaced by additional drinking. In theory, this could be accomplished by either more at one time or by frequent watering. All domestic animals and probably most wild forms increase the frequency of drinking under heat stress provided water is available. Many have a remarkable ability to rehydrate themselves each time they drink. This may involve large quantities in remarkably short periods; camels ingest up to 100 liters within 10 minutes (Schmidt-Nielson et al. 1956), donkeys, 20 liters in 3 minutes (Schmidt-Nielson 1964), guanacos, 9 liters in 8 minutes (Rosenmann and Morrison 1963), and sheep, 9 liters in 10 minutes (MacFarlane 1964). Carnivores generally cannot ingest as large a quantity of water as the ruminants for anatomical reasons, although the dog can hold almost 2 liters (Adolph 1947), and the cat has been reported to drink over 7% of its body weight in 10 minutes (Wolf 1958). Except for some small rodents and lagomorphs, man must be the least capable of rapidly ingesting water among all the mammals. Man reaches satiety after rapidly consuming 1 liter of water and cannot imbibe over 2 liters in a 10 minute period (Folk 1966). It is obvious, therefore, that man must resort to frequent rather than copious drinking to prevent even moderate dehydration. It is strange to find, in the same animal, both the least capacity to ingest water and the greatest dependence on thermal sweating. Its occurrence in a species which has in modern times been so successful in the tropics represents a triumph of technology (the ability to carry and store water outside the body) over biological limitations.

Not only is man unable to consume more than a small amount of water at one time, but he does not generally replace his water loss during the heat of the day. This "voluntary dehydration" in man can exceed 2 liters, but such a temporary negative water balance is not unique to man, probably occurring in all species. Presumably, in voluntary dehydration the free circulating water of the gut is being withdrawn and tissue dehydration does not start until the gut water has been largely utilized. This provides an initial buffer against dehydration which may be quite important in ruminants (12–15% of body weight) but of more limited potential in non-ruminants (5% of weight or less) (Chew 1965). The significant point in man is that any voluntary dehydration incurred during the day is routinely replaced at night, with and following his evening meal.

Problems of Changing Patterns of Thirst

Thirst in humans is a personal imperative which is only satisfied by individual drinking. The term "thirst" is difficult to use with the same connotations for other species because our subjective sensations cannot be verified in non-humans. Many gregarious species have group watering periods, widely spaced in time and probably related to both the water content of the diet and the ambient daytime temperature. Individual members of such groups rarely wander off alone in search of a drink. In domestic animals this may be an ancient trait, carried over and perhaps even intensified by breeding selection. In many wild species including the terrestrial primates it must stem from the increased vulnerability of individuals (cf. Washburn and Devore 1961 on baboons). Even the time of day for group drinking is quite consistent. This implies either that the members do not normally develop marked individual differences in thirst or that these are subordinated to the daily regimen of the group. Both alternatives appear to be the antithesis of human thirst behavioral patterns. In our species the young have a propensity for becoming thirsty at inopportune times and are vociferous about satisfying this thirst. In fairness, it must be admitted that daily water requirements for the young are higher than adults per unit of body weight (Wolf 1958), while their capacity per drink is commensurately smaller. A gradual shift from group patterns to individual drinking in accordance with physiological needs would appear first in sub-adults and lactating females, the two most vulnerable portions of a mammalian group. Perhaps this shift could have occurred when, with sufficient economic specialization, part of the group did not wander with the adult male or males but remained relatively sedentary and near the water source. Even adult hominoid males might have been under similar constraints until they developed defensive weaponry to inhibit predators.

Cattle which are normally daytime drinkers increase the frequency and volume of night drinking under hot conditions (Yousef et al. 1968), but cattle are protected domestic animals. It was pointed out earlier that modern man rehydrates by drinking during the evening when evaporative heat loss is minimal. Modern day, terrestrial, non-human primates have not been reported as nocturnal drinkers in the wild. Before water containers were invented this might have posed quite a problem for our ancestors and been just as important as security in dictating the location of campsites.

Heat Responses in Non-Human Primates

Human reaction to various levels of heat stress is by far the best known of all animals, but the rest of the primate order are among the least studied. From what little is known, it is obvious that we cannot safely extrapolate what we have learned about man to his primate relatives. Some data are available on the cebus, rhesus, baboon, and chimpanzee. A pertinent question raised by this review is do non-human primates utilize thermal sweating as their important avenue of heat loss under hot conditions? This cannot be answered from the available information; it is not even certain from laboratory experiments whether monkeys can tolerate heat stresses well within the capability of many animals.

A series of cebus monkeys (Hardy 1954) and chimps (Dale et al. 1965) have been measured in calorimeters which distinguish between evaporation, conduction-convection, and radiation as sources of heat loss. Unfortunately for this discussion the chimps were only exposed to one temperature, 24° C. A comparison of these two primates with man is given in Table 1.

TABLE 1

Relative mechanisms of heat loss utilized in three primate species

	Temp.	Radiation	Conduction and Convection	Evaporation
Man[1]	24° C	66%	15%	19%
	34° C	0	45%	55%
Cebus[1]	24° C	40%	25%	35%
	34° C	0	35%	65%
Chimp[2]	24° C	30%	35%	35%

[1] From Hardy 1954.
[2] From Dale et al. 1965.

Obviously if the percentage for one avenue of heat loss rises the others must decrease. At 24° C, both the cebus and chimp showed greater conductive-convective losses than man, but the cebus were in a metal chair and the chimps in a metal cage; these provided abnormal surface areas for conduction-convection losses. This plus the hair covering on the cebus and chimp and the relatively high evaporative loss explain why the radiant exchange was so much less than that of a naked man. The evaporative heat losses at 24° C were absolutely as well as relatively high in the non-human subjects. This temperature is too low for us to expect thermal sweating in any of the species so the high values must have been caused by higher diffusional skin water losses or increased respiratory exchange. Man and cebus were losing more heat than they were producing at 24° C, but the chimp's were very close to thermal balance.

At 34° C, radiation exchange was virtually eliminated since skin and wall temperatures in the calorimeters were practically identical. Evaporative loss increased three-fold in man from sweating. The two-fold increase in evaporative loss in the cebus has been ascribed to sweating because skin temperature remained relatively cool as calorimeter temperature rose, and this requires a moist skin surface. On the other hand the total evaporative cooling in the monkeys was not sufficient to prevent rectal temperature from rising rapidly to 40° C when the experiments were terminated to avoid heat stroke.

Experiments with macaques and baboons in heat present a very ·confused picture. One young rhesus was exposed to 40° C, 55% RH presumably in a cage and with water (Robinson and Morrison 1957). This monkey's rectal temperature rose very slightly, and the animal showed no evidence of panting. The investigators did not check for sweating but inferred that it must have been present. A group of rhesus were exposed to two temperatures, 29° C and 38° C, with comparable humidity, and two different positions of arm restraint while the animals were prone (Frankel et al. 1958). At 29° C, the type of restraint did not make any difference, and the animals maintained a steady, slightly depressed rectal temperature for over 4 hours. At 38° C, those with arms held back along the sides had slightly elevated but steady rectal temperatures while a position with the arms extended resulted in an almost explosive rise in rectal temperature which required premature termination of exposure. As if this were not confusing enough, no evidence of sweat production could be observed on these rhesus during the heat exposures (Folk 1965). Four young male savanna baboons exposed to 45° C, 50% RH (Funkhauser et al. 1967) in a primate restraint chair showed both sweating and panting but with insufficient total evaporative heat loss to prevent a dangerous elevation of body temperature. This combination of heat and humidity was very stressful and would have caused some panting in man (Goldman et al. 1965). The baboons increased their respiratory rate very rapidly, a response expected from a panting species. Unfortunately, these subjects were deprived of water for 24 hours prior to the heat exposure, and most animal species show effect of dehydration in their responses; the oryx, which is primarily a sweating species, shifts entirely to panting for heat loss when dehydrated (Taylor 1969).

Our knowledge of the non-human primates' reaction to heat is obviously fragmentary and contradictory. Whether the contradictions arise from problems in techniques, e.g. the resistance of primates to physical restraint, or for other reasons is as yet unknown.

Conclusions

Man's specialized dependence on thermal sweating appears to be an evolutionary adaptation to the tropics. The marked limitations on the amount of water which man can consume at one time, and the lack of any of the water conserving adaptations observed in desert mammals argues for a well-watered tropical habitat, or, at least certainly not a tropical desert. On the other hand profuse sweating does not in itself provide efficient evaporative heat loss under the high humidity and lack of air movement which characterizes the tropical forest. An environmental niche of tropical parklands and grasslands best corresponds to the observed thermoregulatory responses.

It has been argued here that man's propensity for sweating came about because his nakedness increased the total radiant heat load received and not because loss of hair somehow enhanced the efficiency of sweat evaporation. Therefore, either the two processes developed simultaneously or the decline in body hair preceded the increase in sweating. If nakedness was a disadvantage in a savanna environment which required a compensatory adaptation (sweating), loss of hair must have stemmed from other causes or preceded the occupation of the habitat in question, at least for its inception. Our traditional ideas of what our ancestors looked like has included far more body hair than our own species until forms very similar and closely related to Homo sapiens appear. The illustrations (with one exception) for as recent a work as Howell's "Early Man" (1968) show hirsutism as a rather conservative trait over millions of years. If one had to select times and habitats when progressive denudation was not a distinct environmental disadvantage, the choices would seem to be between a very early period when our ancestors were primarily forest dwellers or a very recent period when primitive clothing could provide the same protection against either solar heat or cold.

The primary difficulty in arguing for the recent loss of body hair is that there seems to be no single and powerful environmental driving force other than recurrent cold that is obvious after the Pliocene epoch. Furthermore, the developing complexity and efficiency of even primitive man's technology would have decreased the probability of a straightforward biological adaptation. Finally, since all modern men lack an effective sun-screen of body hair and all sweat profusely in the heat, this specialization either must have occurred at a time and place when the evolving species was geographically compact, or at least contiguous, or represents a highly improbable parallel evolution in a variety of noncomparable environments.

The obvious time and place where progressive denudation would have been least disadvantageous is the ancient forest habitat. Radiant energy does penetrate the forest canopy in limited amounts, and that portion of the spectrum which is primarily transmitted through vegetation, the near infra-red wavelengths of 0.75 to 0.93 microns, is exactly the energy best reflected by human skin (Gates 1968). This may be purely coincidental, but it lends a little support to this suggestion that loss of body hair in man was somehow stimulated much earlier in time than our present estimates.

In conclusion, man suffers from a unique trio of conditions: hypotrichosis corpus, hyperhydrosis, and polydipsia. The appearance and development of this combination must have been the result of some of the habits of our ancestors, or in more popular phraseology, of the ecological niche of the survivors who gave rise to our evolving ancestors. There is little hope that the osseous remains in the fossil record will provide much in the way of clues to the time of initiation and rate of change in these characteristics. There is hope that judicious speculation based on comparative studies which focus on the problems can help us to define the possible limits within which one may safely theorize.

Abstract and Summary

A shift in habitat from forest to tropical grasslands by man's early ancestors in Tertiary times resulted in a rather distinctive reaction to external heat loads. If our ancestors had already lost most of their body hair or were in the process of doing so, the combination of increased solar exposure in open country and greater absorption of solar energy by the naked skin magnified the total heat load. This must have constituted a disadvantage which required some compensation; in man it has taken the form of dependence on thermal sweating for heat dissipation to the point where Homo sapiens has the greatest sweating capacity for a given surface area of any known animal. Heavy sweating without simultaneous drinking inevitably leads to tissue dehydration. Man is very intolerant of dehydration and has limited capacity to rehydrate rapidly. He is dependent on frequent and relatively small drinks of water under hot conditions. This must have influenced species behavior, at least until water containers were invented. Unfortunately, our present knowledge of how our non-human primate relatives react to heat stress is fragmentary and contradictory. We can't be sure that our modern specializations are uniquely human or are part of a general primate pattern.

LITERATURE CITED

ADOLPH, E. F. 1947 Physiology of man in the desert. Interscience, New York.

BARNICOT, N. A. 1959 Climatic factors in the evolution of human populations. Cold Spring Harbor Symposia on Quantitative Biology, 24: 115–129.

BERMAN, A. 1957 Influence of some factors on the relative evaporation rate from the skin of cattle. Nature, 179: 1256.

BIANCA, W. 1968 Thermoregulation. In, Adaptation of Domestic Animals, ed. by E. S. E. Hafez, pp. 97–118. Lea and Febiger, Philadelphia.

CAMPBELL, B. G. 1967 Human Evolution. An Introduction to Man's Adaptations. Aldine, Chicago.

CHEW, R. M. 1965 Water metabolism of mammals. In, Physiological Mammalogy, vol. II, Mammalian reactions to stressful environments, ed. by W. V. Mayer and R. G. Van Gelder, pp. 43–148. Academic Press, New York.

COON, C. S. 1955 Some problems of human variability and natural selection in climate and culture. Amer. Naturalist, 89: 257–280.

DALE, H. E., M. D. SHANKLINE, H. D. JOHNSON AND W. H. BROWN 1965 Energy metabolism of the chimpanzee. A comparison of direct and indirect calorimetry. Tech. Report ARL-TR-65-17, 6571st Aeromed. Res. Lab., Holloman AFB, New Mexico.

EICHNA, L. W., W. F. BEAN, W. B. BEAN AND W. B. SHELLEY 1945 The upper limits of heat and humidity tolerated by acclimatized men working in hot environments. J. Indust. Hygiene and Toxicol., 27: 59–84.

FOLK, G. E., JR. 1966 Introduction to Environmental Physiology. Lea and Febiger, Philadelphia.

FRANKEL, H. M., G. E. FOLK, JR. AND F. N. CRAIG 1958 Effects of type of restraint upon heat tolerance in monkeys. Proc. Exp. Biol. Med., 97: 339–341.

FUNKHAUSER, G. E., E. A. HIGGINS, T. ADAMS AND C. C. SNOW 1967 The response of the savannah baboon (Papio cynocephalus) to thermal stress. Life Sciences, 6: 1615–1620.

GATES, D. M. 1968 Physical environment. In, Adaptation of Domestic Animals, ed. by E. S. E. Hafez, pp. 46–60. Lea and Febiger, Philadelphia.

GOLDMAN, R. F., E. B. GREEN AND P. F. IAMPIETRO 1965 Tolerance of hot, wet environments by resting men. J. Appl. Physiol., 20: 271–277.

HARDY, J. D. 1955 Control of heat loss and heat production in physiologic temperature regulation. Harvey Lectures, 49: 242–270. Academic Press, New York.

HOWELL, F. C. 1968 Early Man. Time-Life, New York.

KRANTZ, G. 1968 Brain size and hunting ability in earliest man. Current Anthropology, 9: 450–451.

LA BARRE, W. 1964 Comments on The Human Revolution by C. F. Hockett and R. Ascher. Current Anthropology, 5: 147–150.

LADELL, W. S. S. 1964 Terrestrial animals in humid heat: man. In, Hdbk. of Physiology, 4, Adaptation to the Environment, ed. by D. B. Dill, pp. 625–659. Williams and Wilkins, Baltimore.

——— 1965 Water and salt intakes. In, The Physiology of Human Survival, ed. by O. G. Edholm and A. L. Bacharach, pp. 235–299. Academic Press, London.

LEE, D. H. K. 1950 Studies of heat regulation in the sheep with special reference to the Merino. Aust. J. Agric. Res., 1: 200–216.

——— 1963 Physiology and the arid zone. In, Environmental Physiology and Psychology in Arid Conditions, Reviews of Research, 22, pp. 15–36. UNESCO, Paris.

——— 1964 Terrestrial animals in dry heat: man in the desert. In, Hdbk. of Physiology, 4, Adaptation to the Environment, ed. by D. B. Dill, pp. 551–582. Williams and Wilkins, Baltimore.

MACFARLANE, W. V. 1964 Terrestrial animals in dry heat: ungulates. In, Hdbk. of Physiology, 4, Adaptation to the Environment, ed. by D. B. Dill, pp. 509–539. Williams and Wilkins, Baltimore.

——— 1968 Comparative functions of ruminants in hot environments. In, Adaptation of Domestic Animals, ed. by E. S. E. Hafez, pp. 264–276. Lea and Febiger, Philadelphia.

MONTAGU, A. 1964 Comments on The Human Revolution by C. F. Hockett and R. Ascher. Current Anthropology, 5: 160–161.

MORRIS, D. 1967 The Naked Ape. McGraw-Hill, New York.

PASSMORE, R. AND J. V. G. A. DURNIN 1955 Human energy expenditure. Physiol. Rev., 35: 801–840.

READ, R. G. 1968 Evaporative power in the tropical forest of the Panama canal zone. J. Appl. Meteor., 7: 417–424.

RICHARDS, P. W. 1952 The Tropical Rain Forest, an Ecological Study. Cambridge Univ. Press, London.

ROBINSON, K. W. AND P. R. MORRISON 1957 The reactions to hot atmospheres of various species of Australian marsupial and placental animals. J. Cellular Comp. Physiol., 49: 455–478.

ROLLER, W. L. AND R. F. GOLDMAN 1967 Estimation of solar radiation environment. Int. J. Biometeor., 11: 329–336.

ROSENMANN, M. AND P. R. MORRISON 1963 The physiological response to heat and dehydration in the guanaco. Physiol. Zool., 36: 45–51.

SCHMIDT-NIELSON, K. 1964 Desert Animals. Physiological Problems in Heat and Water. Clarendon Press, Oxford.

SCHMIDT-NIELSON, K., B. SCHMIDT-NIELSON, T. R. HOUPT AND S. A. JARNUM 1956 The question of water storage in the stomach of the camel. Mammalia, 20: 1–15.

TAYLOR, C. R. 1969 The eland and the oryx. Sci. Amer., 220: 88–95.

WASHBURN, S. L. AND I. DEVORE 1961 Social behavior of baboons and early man. In, Social Life of Early Man, ed. by S. L. Washburn, pp. 91–105. Aldine, Chicago.

WEINER, J. S. AND K. HELLMANN 1960 The sweat glands. Biol. Rev., 25: 141–186.

WHITTOW, G. C. 1968 Body fluid regulation. In, Adaptation of Domestic Animals, ed. by E. S. E. Hafez, pp. 119–126. Lea and Febiger, Philadelphia.

WOLF, A. V. 1958 Thirst. Physiology of the Urge to Drink and Problems of Water Lack. C. C. Thomas, Springfield.

YOUSFE, M. K., L. HAHN AND H. D. JOHNSON 1968 Adaptation of cattle. In, Adaptation of Domestic Animals, ed. by E. S. E. Hafez, pp. 233–245. Lea and Febiger, Philadelphia.

The Descent of Man: More Fossil Evidence

IT IS SOMEWHAT EMBARRASSING TO HAVE TO REPORT THAT, FOR many decades, all the accounts of discoveries of the fossil evidence for human evolution were written by European or American scientists. Much of the evidence itself—especially that pertaining to the later phases of human evolution—was derived from Europe, and this too is unfortunate, because this small continent is at the periphery of the vast land mass where most of our early ancestors lived. Anthropologists may well have overestimated the importance, to the general course of human evolution, of what took place near their own universities and museums. And even the data derived from diggings in Egypt and Kenya, India and China, Java and the Near East have, until recently, been published, for the most part, by scholars from the Western world.

But it is pleasant to report that this situation has been changing. Chinese paleoanthropologists have been busy finding and analyzing human fossil remains ever since the discovery of "Sinanthropus" during the 1920s and 1930s. Indian scientists are active in seeking for evidence concerning our early ancestors. In Java, during the past two decades, Indonesian paleoanthropologists have been looking for, and finding, more and more specimens of the "ape-men" first discovered by Dubois not very long after Darwin's death. This variety, now known as *Homo erectus*, appears to have evolved from *Australopithecus* and to have been distributed over a much wider range, extending from Morocco to South Africa and from Germany to China and Java. A skullcap of this species from Java is excellently described and analyzed by Professor Teuku Jacob in the following article.

8. Teuku Jacob

The Sixth Skull Cap of
Pithecanthropus erectus

Abstract. The sixth skull cap of *Pithecanthropus erectus* (or skull V, since the Modjokerto skull has not been given a number) was found in the upper layers of the Trinil beds of Sangiran (Central Java) in 1963, associated with fossils of the Sino-Malayan fauna. No stone tools were discovered in direct association with the find.

The specimen consists of the occipital, both parietals, both temporals, sphenoid fragments, the frontal and the left zygomatic bone. We consider the skull to be a male in his early twenties. The occipital, parietal, frontal and temporal bones demonstrate definite pithecanthropine characteristics, and the cranial capacity is estimated to be 975 cm³.

Of the superstructures, the supraorbital torus is extraordinarily thick, approaching the condition in *Australopithecus boisei* and Rhodesian man. And the sagittal torus is certainly higher than in skulls I and II, but lower than in skull IV. In addition, the angle between the occipital and nuchal planes is larger than in the previous finds. As revealed by various features, the gap between the robustness of skull IV on one hand, and skulls I, II and III on the other, is bridged by the present find. There is no reasonable taxonomic need to ascribe this specimen to a new species, because it seems to be merely an intrapopulational variant of the same species.

Other skulls of *P. erectus* suggest that the bregmatic eminence, and hence the vertex, is invariably situated at bregma, but this new skull cap deviates from the pattern. Its pteric regions disclose the anthropoid X and I types. The middle meningeal groove pattern is similar to other *Pithecanthropus* skulls; however, it betrays a known anomaly in that the main stem is covered for a short distance by a bony plate. The mastoid process is fairly well developed, and is also well pneumatized as in *P. pekinensis,* with its air cells invading the pronounced supramastoid crest.

The zygomatic bone, the first one recovered of *P. erectus,* does not show characters of particular importance. In fact, its thickness is in the range of modern man.

We would like to stress that the absence of the cranial base does not necessarily indicate that the specimen must be a poor victim of cannibalism, since the morphology of the base renders it more susceptible to post-mortem natural traumata.

Five other skulls of *Pithecanthropus erectus* have been found in Indonesia since the famous discovery of the first skull by Dubois at Trinil (East Java) in 1891, which became the holotype of the species and is known as skull I. The second skull was found near Djetis, Modjokerto (East Java), in 1936, and belongs to a *Pithecanthropus* child, but at first was recognized as *Homo modjokertensis*. Although later its taxonomic name is changed to *Pithecanthropus modjokertensis*, the skull is not referred to by a code number.

The third skull which is frequently called skull II, like subsequent skulls, was discovered in the Sangiran dome area (Central Java) in 1937 in the village of Bapang near the Tjemoro River, a tributary of the Solo River. The next one, designated as skull III, was found the following year in the village of Tandjung, and the fifth in 1938–39 and is known as *Pithecanthropus robustus* or skull IV. Though this latter was given a different specific name, it was also provided with a number, in contradistinction to the Modjokerto specimen. Skulls I, II and III came from the Trinil beds, while the child skull and skull IV are from the underlying Djetis beds.

All these discoveries were made before the second world war. In the postwar period several paleoanthropological finds have been reported. A Meganthropus mandible was described by Marks ('53) and a *Pithecanthropus* mandible by Sartono ('62). Marks wrote in his concluding remarks (p. 33):

> Only by extensive and systematic research in the Sangiran deposits, as well as in other places on Java where Pleistocene deposits are present, may we hope to come to an eventual solution of . . . problems pertaining to the ancestry of *Homo sapiens*. It would be a pity, nay, unforgivable, if it would be impossible, for lack of funds or otherwise, to continue and extend the search for Fossil man, especially where conditions on Java are so much more favorable in this respect than anywhere else in the world.

These remarks constitute one of the small factors leading to the setup of a paleoanthropological research project in 1962. The following year a skull was discovered with the aid of the local population in the village of Tandjung in the Sangiran area; the discovery took place in two successive months. The first group of fossil fragments was found in July and is announced by Sartono ('64), and the second group in August and reported by the author (Jacob, '64a). The author thought that both groups of bone fragments belong to the same individual, which turned out to be the case. Consequently, the fragments have been assembled, and it is the purpose of this paper to report on the whole skull cap (Project catalogue no. SC II).

Although lately Java man is often referred to as *Homo erectus erectus,* in this paper we maintain the binomen *Pithecanthropus erectus.*

DESCRIPTION

The Site

The sixth skull cap of *Pithecanthropus erectus* was discovered in the village of Tandjung in the Sangiran area near a tributary of the Tjemoro River on the opposite bank of which skull III was found in 1937. The actual site of the find is an upper layer of the Trinil beds consisting of "cross-bedded yellowish white tuffaceous sandstone" (Sartono, '64). In the surrounding area surface finds include bone fragments and skulls of *Bibos palaesondaicus.* Excavations carried out in 1963–64 resulted in many fossil fragments of bovids, stegodonts, *Sus sp., Hippopotamus sp.,* and *Rusa sp.,* and complete skulls of *Bubalus palaeokerabau* and *Bibos palaesondaicus.* Thus, the find was extracted from the Trinil beds associated with the Sino-Malayan fauna of Middle Pleistocene age. No stone artifacts were found in association with the skull cap.

The Find

The first group of fossil fragments consists of the right parietal, the frontal and the left zygomatic bones, the right mastoid, and small fragments of the left parietal, the right temporal and the right half of the sphenoid bones. The second group comprises the left parietal, the occipital and the left temporal bones, and minor pieces of the right parietal, the right temporal, the right half of the sphenoid and the frontal bones. Both groups consist of 12 fragments, each with various tiny pieces. The bones are completely fossilized and remarkably thick, having a specific gravity of 2.2. While the color is basically whitish, typical of fossils found in the Trinil beds of Sangiran, the bones show patches of redbrown and black coloration, both on the external and cerebral surfaces. Brown sandstone constitutes the endocast of the skull cap. The margins of bone fragments not covered by the endocast have a lighter color than the covered parts, and by observing the presence of sharp demarcation thus made we can easily distinguish fresh fractures from old ones.

It is apparent that the thickness of the bone is not only attributable to the internal and external tables, but also to the diploë. Its maximum thickness is at the center of the occipital torus, if the supraorbital torus is not taken into account, and its minimum thickness in the lateral part of the nuchal plane medial to the retromastoid process (or the floor of the cerebellar fossa), and in the lateral portion of the frontal bone. The variations in thickness are tabulated in table 1.

Twenty-eight large and small pieces of bone have contact lines or points and are assembled to form the skull cap. The right orbital portion of the frontal bone and the left zygomatic bone present no contact line with the rest of the skull. A

TABLE 1

Variation in bone thickness in various Pithecanthropus skulls [1]

Bone	Measured at	P.e. II	P.e. III	P.e. V	P.p.
Parietal	bregma	(6)	10.5	9	9 – 9.6
	lambda	7.5	7	9	
	asterion	(9)	10	13	14.5–17.4
	pterion	(6)		6	
	eminence: anterior	(10)		8	
	middle	12	7	11	10.8
	posterior	(10)		9	
	Squamous margin	9		7	
Frontal	bregma	9		8	9.3
	supraorbital torus	12.5		19	
	minimum	(2)		2	
Occipital	lambda	13	7	10	
	inion	(19)	9	15	
	internal occipital protuberance	21		14	
	minimum	(2)		2	

[1] Compiled from von Koenigswald (40) and Weidenreich (45, 51). Figures in parentheses are measured from cast. Measurements in mm. P.e. — *Pithecanthropus erectus*; P.p. — *Pithecanthropus pekinensis*.

complete reconstruction must therefore await the eventual recovery of missing portions.

General Appearance

On the whole, the skull is small in size, and the calculated cranial capacity is 975 cm³ according to Pearson's formula for males, taking into consideration the thickness of the bones involved (table 2).

In vertical view the shape of the skull is rather sphenoid, accentuated by the marked postorbital constriction. The occipital torus and the supramastoid crest form a projecting frame, and thus, they present points of greatest cranial dimensions. All the sutures of the vault are open, which contributed to the easy postmortem separation of individual bones. Only the stephanic and pteric portions of the coronal suture show sign of closure (grade 2). The sutures are simple and no sutural bones are encountered. There is also no distinct asymmetry observed.

In norma occipitalis the skull is gable-shaped due to the pronounced sagittal torus and parietal eminences. The greatest breadth is clearly close to the base of the skull. Well marked parasagittal depressions run bilateral to the sagittal torus, emphasizing the pithecanthropine trait. There is no evidence of Inca or interparietal bones.

In frontal view the forehead appears to be very narrow. There is no metopic suture, but a fairly well developed frontal torus is present.

The sagittal torus stands out more prominently in norma frontalis. No knob-like structures, however, are present as in the case of skull IV. What is regarded as the bregmatic eminence is not situated at bregma, but a short distance posterior to it. There is no obelionic protuberance or postobelionic depression. The forehead is low and retreating, while posteriorly, the occipital bone displays a marked angulation. Table 3 summarizes the values of the sagittal curvatures.

TABLE 2

Cranial dimensions in Pithecanthropus [1]

Pithecanthropus	I	II	III	IV	V	Modjokerto	Peking
Sex	Male	Female		Male	Male		
Specific gravity	2.5				2.2	2.572	
Cranial capacity	900	775		900	975	700	1075
Cranial module	135	133.5		141	141.7		
Cranial length	183	176.5	177	199	184	138	193.6
Cranial breadth	130	135		156	139	115	141
Auricular height	92	89		90	102	62	98.4
Length-breadth index	68.8	74.2		62.8	75.5	83.4	72.2
Length-height index	50.3	50.4		45.2	55.4		50.9
Breadth-height index	73.0	67.9		72.0	73.4		
Biparietal breadth	126	131	128	125	128		136.2
Minimum frontal breadth	85	79		78	82		
Biauricular breadth	135	129		156	115		145.5
Distance between temporal lines	92	69		78	91		93.5
Biasteriac breadth	92	125			121		
Bimastoid breadth		102			114		
Bipteric breadth		(100)			93		
Transverse fronto-parietal index	67.4	60.3		62.4	63.1		
Lower parietal breadth index	94.3	101.5		80.2	88.5		94.5
Transverse curvature index	52.3	47.7			42.6		
Transverse parieto-occipital index	72.9	95.5			93.1		
Transverse arc	258	262			270		
Lambda-inion arc	61	56			44		
Lambda-inion chord	53	53		50	43		
Occipital angulation	108°	103°		91°	115°		103.2°
Parietal angulation:							
right		(118°)			120°		
left		(116°)			115°		
Lambda angle		(139°)	120°		129°		

[1] After von Koenigswald ('40), Weidenreich ('45) and Coon ('62). Measurements in mm or cm³.

On the left side the pteric region is of type X, whereas on the right it is of I or frontotemporal type. No epipteric bones are found on either side. The supramastoid crest, in right lateral view, is very well developed and runs obliquely upward and backward. The thin, overlapping part of the temporal squama (which lacks the inner table) is broken, facilitated by the non-fusion of the squamous suture.

The basal view has not much to offer, since the base of the skull is only rudimentarily preserved. To avoid unnecessary repetition, the few basal features present will be dealt with in the description of individual bones. The cerebral surface of the skull cap, however, deserves some general comments. The stages of closure of the endocranial sutures are more advanced than the ectocranial ones as can be clearly seen on the natural margins of the bones. In the middle, the sagittal groove is shallow, deviating to the left at the internal occipital protuberance with the result that the transverse groove is higher on the left side than on the right. Laterally, the sigmoid sulcus is wide but shallow; the superior petrous groove is also distinct.

TABLE 3

Sagittal curvatures in Pithecanthropus skulls [1]

Skull	Frontal			Parietal			Occipital		
	Arc	Chord	Index	Arc	Chord	Index	Arc	Chord	Index
P.e. I	100	98	98.0	91	87.5	96.0	103	78	75.7
II	90	88	97.7	94	91	95.8	101	75	74.2
III				94	88.5	94.1			
IV	116	99	85.4	89?	90?	96.8?	117	78	66.2
V		89		95	92	96.8		81?	
P.p.	120.3	109.8	89.9	102.5	96.2	94.1	114	84	73.8

[1] After Weidenreich ('45) and Coon ('62). Absolute measurements in mm.

The Individual Bones

The occipital bone shows a fresh fracture which separates the left from the right part. A small insignificant part of the occipital plane is broken off fairly recently. Unfortunately, the basilar and lateral portions are missing without leaving a clue of opisthion and the more anterior features.

Regarding the occipital plane, it is conspicuously low and broad, with the angle at lambda of 129° and the biasteriac diameter of 121 mm. The lambdoid suture runs in an anteriorly direct curve. Very remarkable is the occipital torus which extends transversely almost to asterion. Superiorly, there is a fairly well developed supratoral groove. The superior border of the torus is convex, but the inferior border is convex in the median region and concave laterally. Consequently, the middle portion is the widest, corresponding with triangular prominence in *Homo soloensis*. No external occipital crest or external occipital protuberance is evident, so that inion coincides with opisthocranion. Due to the occipital torus and the internal occipital crest the median point of the superstructure is the thickest part of the occipital bone. Extension of the parietal eminence is observed in the occipital plane bilaterally.

In contrast to the plane just described, the nuchal plane is larger, and its lateral part is as thin as in modern man. On the right side, between the torus and the inferior nuchal line, a rough area is present which is the retromastoid process or tuberosity.

Typical of *Pithecanthropus,* the occipital bone exhibits a strong angulation of 115°. It is unfortunate that opisthion is missing, so that the proper sagittal curvature index cannot be calculated.

The cerebral surface of the occipital bone shows deep cerebral fossae, especially on the left side. On the other hand, the cerebellar fossae are shallow, indicating the lesser development of the cerebellum. Owing to the position of the transverse groove the left cerebral fossa is smaller than the right. The internal occipital protuberance is lower than inion, stressing again the relative underdevelopment of the cerebellum and the extent of the nuchal muscles. A distance of 26 mm separates the two structures (table 4). The transverse legs of the cruciate eminence and the grooves are not well developed.

Of all the bones of this skull cap the parietals are the most completely pre-

TABLE 4

Distance between inion and internal occipital
protuberance — in different hominids [1]

Hominid	Distance in mm
P. erectus II	25
average (I, II, IV)	35.21
V	26
Homo soloensis	21–38
Homo neanderthalensis	17.2

[1] After Weidenreich ('51).

served. The left one consists of nine pieces, presenting one recent fracture. Only its bregmatic angle is absent. The right parietal is constructed from five fragments revealing three fresh fractures. Its coronal margin is partially lacking. As does the occipital bone, the parietals display a characteristic pithecanthropine trait: their strong transverse curvature forms a pronounced parietal eminence in the middle. The angle at the eminence is 120° on the right side and 115° on the left, and the transverse curvature index of the bone is 83.2. The angle at bregma is almost 90°, which is also the case with the angle at lambda of the left parietal. Furthermore, the sphenoidal angle is acute, while the mastoid angle is obtuse.

On the left parietal bone a small parietal foramen is found, located 7 mm from the median line. The lambdoid area is flattened, and thus creates a sharp contrast to the bregmatic eminence in the anterior part of the sagittal margin. No longitudinal grooves, however, are discernible in the vicinity of the lambdoid angle as reported in skull II (von Koenigswald, '40). Temporal lines are fairly distinct, and run from the coronal margin to the parietal eminence and end in the asteriac process, which is well developed, particularly on the right side. It is interesting to note that the pteric regions are of rare types, as described above.

Lateral to the sagittal margin a parasagittal depression is present, which is more distinct anteriorly due to the bregmatic eminence. The lateral part of the parietal bone descends in a very steep fashion, whereas in lateral view the bone is only slightly curved. Both parietals are almost quadrangular in shape and the four margins more or less equal each other in length (table 5).

The inner surface attracts attention by its deep and wide middle meningeal

TABLE 5

Dimensions of the right parietal bone in
P. erectus [1]

Margin	Skull III		Skull V	
	Arc	Chord	Arc	Chord
Sagittal	94	88.5	95	92
Coronal	88	77	95	79
Temporal	95	91	95	91
Lambdoid	84	78	78	74

[1] After von Koenigswald ('40). Measurements in mm.

Left   Right

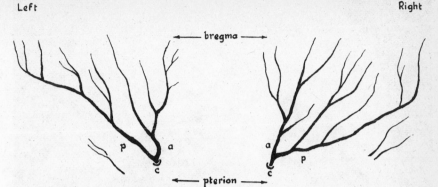

Fig. 1. Middle meningeal groove patterns of the new Pithecanthropus skull on both sides. a, anterior branch; c, meningeal canal; p, posterior branch.

grooves. It is not surprising that the pattern of the grooves reflects bilateral asymmetry, since the arborization of the middle meningeal artery is highly variable. The only similarity of the sulcus on both sides is the large size of the posterior branch which equals the anterior. On the right side the stem of the groove is covered for 8 mm distance by a plate of bone at the sphenoidal angle, a variation which is also encountered in *Homo sapiens*. On the left, the so-called meningeal canal is about 16 mm long. No Pacchionian granulations are observed on either side.

Neither temporal bone is complete. On the left side we have only a part of the squama and the petrous portion (of which the external table is absent) and a small piece of the mastoid portion. Altogether there are three bone fragments. On the right side there are ten pieces consisting of an anterior part of the squamous portion, the mandibular fossa, the supramastoid crest and the mastoid process.

The squamous suture is low and relatively straight. As previously mentioned, the articulating part is broken on the left temporal. A remnant of the supramastoid crest is present, showing extensive air cells, and running obliquely dorsocranially. A small part of the mandibular fossa is preserved with a fairly well developed articular tubercle.

Furthermore, the petrous bone is low and of medium size. The petrous crest, grooved by the superior petrous sinus, runs in an undulating fashion; the axes of its medial and lateral parts form an angle of 135°. In addition, the subarcuate fossa is shallow but distinct, and the arcuate eminence is well developed.

The right temporal squama, like the left one, curves strongly inward anteriorly. The squamous suture forms the superior border of the triangular squama, and the sphenotemporal suture, which is almost vertical, constitutes the anterior border. The inferior border is formed by the supramastoid crest. The three borders are respectively 76 mm, 37 mm and 72 mm in length. The right mastoid, constructed from four pieces of bone betrays a marked mastoid crest, but the apex is broken off. It points downward, forward and slightly medianward.

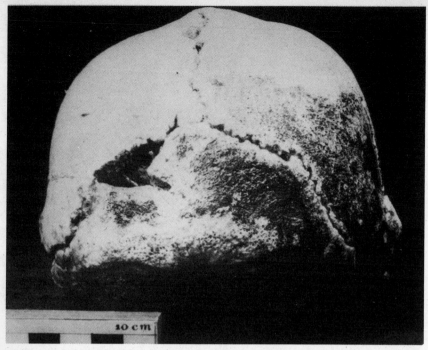

Fig. 2. Occipital view. Note the prominent sagittal torus, the right supra-mastoid crest, and the contour of the occipital torus.

Fig. 3. Vertical view. The breadth of the occipital plane and the thickness of the bone can be clearly observed.

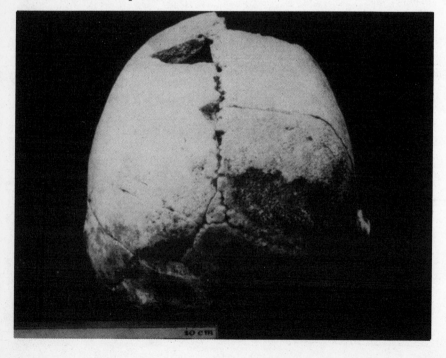

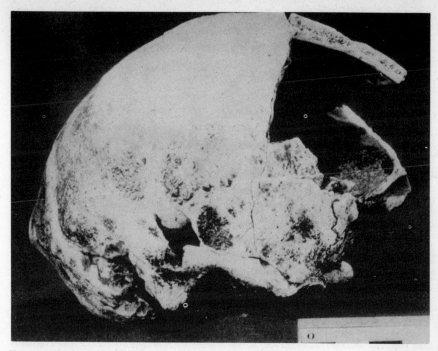

Fig. 4. Right lateral view. This displays the occipital angulation, the temporal squama, the mastoid process and the supramastoid crest with its air cells, as well as the thickness of the bone.

Fig. 5. Frontal view. Note the transverse contour in the anterior region of the skull, especially the parasagittal depression and the bregmatic eminence.

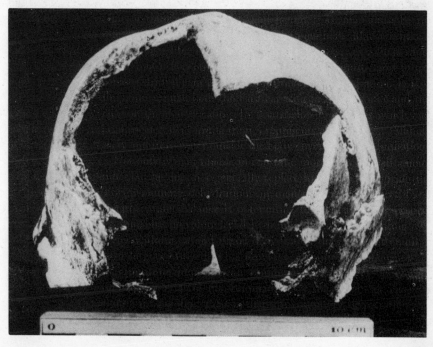

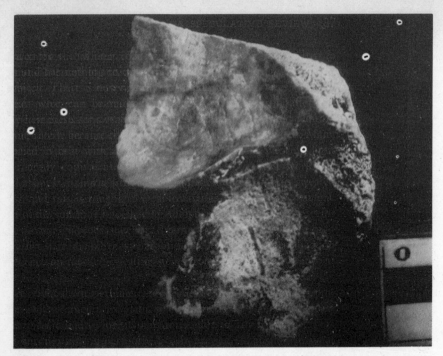

Fig. 6.   The right orbital portion of the frontal bone, in basal view.

Fig. 7.   The left zygomatic bone. Observe the zygomaticofacial foramen and the malomaxillary tuberosity.

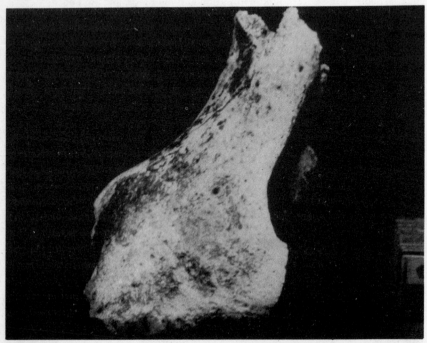

An enormous supramastoid crest (5 mm in breadth) follows an oblique course and accentuates the supramastoid fossa. It creates an angle of 34° with the squamous suture. Neither an anterior nor a posterior supramastoid tubercle is observable. The mastoid process itself is well pneumatized, having large cells in an irregular arrangement. The masoposterior group, particularly, consists of large air cells, while the superior and anteroinferior groups have respectively medium sized and small air cells. Moreover, a large cell is present near the tip of the mastoid.

As far as the mandibular fossa is concerned, the right side of the skull provides more information. The fossa is deep (9 mm), its transverse dimension is 29 mm, and its sagittal dimension 15 mm. The anterior wall is concave with well developed ectoglenoidal and entoglenoidal processes. The deepest part of the fossa is posteriorly located. On its posterior aspect a prominent postglenoidal crest is present, but the tympanic plate and the external acoustic meatus are missing. The axis of the fossa is posteromedially directed, making an angle of 31° with the transverse porion axis. The axes of the anterior wall and of the posterior wall meet at an angle of 29°. The distance between the articular tubercle and the mastoid process is 38 mm.

Now we come to the frontal bone which consists of three pieces. The left part comprises the medial and lateral portions of the squama which shows remarkable postorbital constriction. On the other hand, on the right side we have the orbital portion with several fresh breaks. As demonstrated in table 6, the supraorbital

TABLE 6

Thickness of the supraorbital torus in
different hominids [1]

Hominid	Nasal	Middle	Temporal
A. boisei		20	
Olduvai LLK		25	
P. erectus II		12.5	(11)
P. erectus V	19	19	9
H. Soloensis	13.5–16.8	11.0–14.2	16.2–22.0
Broken Hill		21	

[1] After von Koenigswald ('40), Weidenreich ('51) and Coon ('62). Measurements in mm.

torus is enormous. The supraorbital margin is convex superiorly. A large supraorbital fissure is present, and medial to it there is a sharply demarcated trochlear fossa. However, the lacrimal fossa is conspicuously absent. There are no air cells in the supraorbital torus proper, but the frontal sinus consists of at least three cells, the anteromedial being the largest and the posterolateral slightly smaller (table 7). The supraorbital torus is, in vertical view, not straight in contour, but displays a moderate posterior convexity. A sulcus is apparent above the torus; it differs, however, from the condition found in *Homo soloensis* where the posterior border of the torus is very distinct. The parietal eminence continues onto the frontal bone. Likewise a frontal torus is present as a continuation of the sagittal

TABLE 7

Dimensions of the frontal sinus in Pithecanthropus erectus and Homo soloensis

Hominid	Width	Length	Height
P. *erectus* skull V			
anteromedial cell		12	
Posterolateral cell	11	9	
H. *soloensis* [1]	19–25	14–18	17

[1] After Weidenreich ('51). Measurements in mm.

torus, but generally the frontal bone has a retreating contour. As recorded in table 1, the thinnest part of the bone is in its lateral portion. On the cerebral surface we notice digitate impressions and cerebral projections.

The sphenoid bone, consisting of portions of the greater wing, is too fragmentary to permit detailed description.

Proceeding to the left zygomatic bone, it should be noted that it is separated from the rest of the skull cap at the frontomalar suture, at the sphenomalar suture, near the maxillomalar suture and at the anterior root of the zygomatic arch. Relative to the breadth it is of considerable height (33 mm). The malar tubercle is prominent, and similarly the malomaxillary tuberosity is well marked at the inferior border. This border is 9 mm thick which does not exceed the condition in modern man. The frontal process is 17 mm wide, and no marginal process or orbital eminence is evident. The posterior border of the frontal process descends in a curve and gradually continues as the upper border of the temporal process. It is interesting that the zygomaticofacial foramen is small.

DISCUSSION

There is no doubt that the skull cap discussed belongs to *Pithecanthropus erectus,* because the tell-tale parts of the skull, i.e., the occipital, the parietal and the frontal bones, each and together exhibit characteristics of that hominid (Jacob, '64a). The occipital angulation, the occipital torus, the sagittal torus, the para-sagittal depression, the parietal eminence, the supraorbital torus, the thickness of the bones and the middle meningeal groove pattern constitute the total morphological pattern typical of a *Pithecanthropus* skull. The fact that the fragments were found in the Trinil beds of Sangiran in association with the Sino-Malayan fauna serves to confirm the diagnosis.

The zygomatic bone is the first one discovered for *P. erectus.* Furthermore, the broken mastoid process and supramastoid crest and frontal bone provide opportunity for gross study of pneumatization.

Some characters deviate from what have been considered "characteristic traits of *P. erectus,*" like the contour of the supraorbital torus, the sagittal torus, the occipital angle etc., and these traits present themselves as a challenge to the typological approach which ignores the fact that "variation is the theme of Nature."

The specific gravity of the completely fossilized bones is 2.2, which is a little lower than that of the Trinil skull cap (2.5). This fact, in addition to the skull being extracted from an upper layer of the Trinil beds, leads us to suppose that the specimen is probably from the later part of Middle Pleistocene, especially if the underlying Djetis beds are considered to belong to Middle Pleistocene too, as argued by Hooijer ('55, '56, '57, '58). Von Koenigswald reported a K/Ar date of a basalt specimen from the Trinil beds of Mt. Muria of approximately half a million years ago (von Koenigswald, '62, '64; Coon, '62; Hooijer, '64); this important date, however, does not refute the former argument, since the base of the Pleistocene is longer than one million years old, and similarly the base of Middle Pleistocene is possibly more than half a million years ago (Oakley, '62). It cannot be overemphasized that K/Ar dating and pollen analysis are imperative to enable us to place the specimen in its proper chronological and paleoclimatological sequence.

It is known that Sangiran is not the original living site of *Pithecanthropus* and that fossils accumulated there due to volcanic and stream actions. It is significant that bovid skulls were found intact during the excavations, implying that they were not brought by streams from remote places. But Carthaus reported a story of a Dutch plantation owner who was "carried away by the lahar and emerged alive to tell the tale of how he floated in a warm muddy paste of sand without ever feeling any hard knocks from floating boulders" (de Terra, '43: 449).

The bones of the skull cap are as thick as in other *Pithecanthropus* remains. The parietal is thicker at lambda in our specimen, probably due to the absence of grooves as reported by von Koenigswald ('40) in skull II. Likewise, at asterion the bone is thicker than in skulls II and III owing to the distinct asteriac process. This process, however, is not developed as well as in *Pithecanthropus pekinensis*, where the thickness in that particular region reaches 17.4 mm (Weidenreich, '51). In the Modjokerto child the corresponding measurement is but 3 mm. The occipital torus is more pronounced than in skull III, but less than in skull II. It is worth noting that the minimum thickness is only 2 mm, rendering the skull more vulnerable to damage in those regions. The supraorbital torus is quite thick: in fact it approaches the condition in *Australopithecus boisei*, *Homo rhodesiensis* and *H. soloensis*, but it is considerably less enormous than in the Olduvai LLK skull (Coon, '62). While in *H. soloensis* the lateral corner is the thickest and the mid-portion of the torus the thinnest—a sign of disintegration—the contrary is true in *P. erectus* (table 6).

The sex of the skull is most likely male as suggested by the pronounced supraorbital and sagittal tori, and the larger mastoid process, relative to skull II which is considered to be female. Insofar as the age is concerned, only the cranial sutures are available. No vault suture is completely fused. As can be seen at the bone margins fusion has commenced endocranially. Ectocranially, only the stephanic and pteric portions of the coronal suture reveal second degree closure. Obliteration of cranial sutures occurs earlier in anthropoids than in hominids.

Consequently we estimate that the age at death of the individual to whom this skull belonged was not much more than 20 years. The projecting parietal eminence suggests a youthful age; and besides, no Pacchionian granulations are present to suggest the contrary.

For *P. erectus,* the skull is large. The cranial module of 141.7 is greater than in skulls I, II and IV. The cranial capacity is estimated to be 975 cm³.

Similarly, the sagittal torus with a height of 11 mm, measured at the bregmatic eminence from the parasagittal depression, is higher than in skull II, but lower than in skull IV. No knob-like structures, however, are found in the posterior part of the torus as is the case in skull IV. Different from the other skulls is the bregmatic eminence which is situated definitely posterior to bregma probably owing to the relative better development of the parietal lobe (Weidenreich, '45).

The angulation of the occipital bone is also less than in other *P. erectus* skulls. It is unfortunate that the sagittal occipital curvature index cannot be determined, but it is certainly less than 84.4 (Jacob, '64a). Moreover, the occipital plane is lower than in other skulls, resulting in a larger angle at lambda, and its curvature is for practical purposes absent. A retromastoid tuberosity is present, although not as prominent as reported by Waldeyer ('10) in the Melanesians.

As in other hominids the internal occipital protuberance is lower than inion, and the distance between these two structures in our specimen resembles that of skull II. Weidenreich ('51) gives an average of 35.4 for the other skulls. This figure is in the range of *H. soloensis* and higher than in European Neanderthals.

The parietal bones of *Pithecanthropus* are characterized by their parietal eminence due to angulation, which in this skull is 120° on the right side and 115° on the left, thus simulating the occipital angulation. The quadrangular bone has more or less equal sides, except for a slightly shorter lambdoid margin. Only the coronal margin is a little longer than in skull III. Its sagittal curvature index is 96.8, resembling skull IV. The temporal lines are on the eminence as in *P. pekinensis.*

The pterion types are rare and primitive ones. In Indonesian crania the X and I types occur only in 9% of the cases (Jacob, unpublished data). In *H. soloensis* the pattern is I, which is the most frequent in extant anthropoids (Weidenreich, '51: 254.) The pattern of the middle meningeal grooves is comparable to other pithecanthropines, including the Ternifine skull; in fact it is similar to the arborization found in *Homo soloensis* and *Australopithecus* in respect to the larger size of the posterior branch (Howell, '60). Not reported in other pithecanthropine skulls is the variation in which the middle meningeal artery enters into a bony canal before branching off into the anterior and posterior rami.

Proceeding to the temporal bone, we notice that the dimensions of the squama are in the range of *Pithecanthropus* (table 8). The pyramid is not large, but the mastoid is larger than in skull II and is well pneumatized as in *P. pekinensis* (Hendleman, '27; Himalstein, '59). The mastoid air cells invade also the supramastoid crest, and reveal no radial arrangement. Furthermore, the frontal sinus consists of three or more chambers which are restricted in the interorbital region. The axes of the medial and lateral parts of the petrous bone make an angle of

TABLE 8

Dimensions of the temporal bone in various
hominid skulls [1]

Hominid	Length	Height	Length-height index
P. erectus V	75	37	49.3
P. pekinensis	69.6	34.5	49.7
H. soloensis	73	46.9	64.2 [2]
H. sapiens			65.2

[1] After Weidenreich ('51). Measurements in mm.
[2] Recalculated by the present author.

135°, which roughly equals the condition in *P. pekinensis* (140°). The angle formed by the axes of the anterior and posterior walls of the mandibular fossa is 29°; in skull IV it is 20°, while in *H. soloensis* it is between 50–60°. The distance between the articular tubercle and the mastoid process approaches the condition in modern man.

Of particular import in this find is the zygomatic bone. Its thickness is not extraordinary, since its lower border is in fact thinner than in the Bronze Age skulls from Bali (Jacob, unpublished data) which reach a maximum of 12 mm. Except for the malar tubercle and malomaxillary tuberosity, no other processes are evident.

The base of the skull is badly preserved in this specimen. It has been a rather widespread custom among paleoanthropologists to explain the absence or the damaged condition of the cranial base or viscerocranium as evidence of cannibalistic behavior (Jacob, '64b). This hypothesis, among others, has been applied to *H. soloensis*—who left the best preserved base in human fossil skulls ever discovered (Weidenreich, '51)—*P. pekinensis* and *Australopithecus*. Coon ('62: 508) doubts that the Krapina people, whom he considered to be Caucasoids, were cannibals but he is quite sure that *P. pekinensis* practiced cannibalism (p. 432). Oakley ('61: 184), on the other hand, noted that "a number of the fragments of human bone found at Krapina had been charred, but apparently this was not the case in the Choukoultien deposits, where only animal bones were in a charred or calcined condition."

As mentioned previously, the portion of the occipital bone around the foramen magnum, the floor of the cerebellar fossae and the sides of the frontal bone are significantly thin in our *Pithecanthropus* skull, so that they are very vulnerable to post-mortem natural damage. It is obvious that the base of the skull which contains so many foramina and fissures presents many spots of least resistance. Areas in the vicinity of the transverse "datum lines" described by Gardner et al. ('63: 717) among others, are areas which are frequently broken. And besides, the difference in its thickness renders it susceptible to physical traumata. As can be observed in protohistoric skulls and reports on them, the basilar portion of the occipital bone is easily broken off, and this applies also to the apex of the petrous pyramid, the pterygoid plates, the vomer and others (for example, see Axmacher and Hjortsjö, '59). It is a well known fact that the orbital walls are very fragile, especially the lamina papyracea. To account for any broken cranial base by itself as the consequence of an effort to extract the brain for cannibalistic diet is just as absurd as to explain fractured orbital walls as a result of the extraction of the eyeball for a special paleolithic dish. It may well be that prehistoric men were cannibals and had a gastronomic preference for brains and eyeballs, but a fractured skull base or face in itself does not constitute a convincing proof of it. It is also true and highly commendable that cultural factors have to be taken into consideration in interpreting anthropological data, but on the other hand, it is equally risky to overstress these factors while simply ignoring the plain anatomical facts. Therefore, the absence of the base in the sixth skull of *P. erectus* is not necessarily due to the sensational practice of cannibalism. The pattern of fracture is quite different from that of the skulls obtained from extant cannibalistic tribes.

ACKNOWLEDGMENTS

This report is a part of an investigation supported by the Ministry for National Research of the Republic of Indonesia. For the accompanying photographs and drawing, the author extends his thanks respectively to Mr. Soejono, and Mr. Basoehi of the National Archaeological Institute. And to various colleagues and friends who have kindly provided bibliographic assistance the author expresses his appreciation.

LITERATURE CITED

Axmacher, B., and C. H. Hjortsjö 1959 Examen Anthropologique des Cranes Constituant le Material Protohistorique Exhume a Bamboula, Kourion, Chypre. Lunds Universitets Arsskrift, *55: 2.*

Broek, A. J. P. van den, J. Boeke and J. A. J. Barge 1942 Leerboek der Beschrijvende Ontleedkunde van den Mensch. N. V. A. Oosthoek's Uitg. Maatij., Utrecht.

Coon, C. S. 1962 The Origin of Races. Alfred A. Knopf, New York.

de Terra, Hellmut 1943 Pleistocene geology and early man in Java. Trans. Amer. Philos. Soc., n.s., *32:* part 5, pp. 437–464.

Gardner, Ernest, Donald J. Gray and Ronan O'Rahilly 1963 Anatomy, 2nd ed. W. B. Saunders Company, Philadelphia.

Hendleman, Solomon 1927 Introduction to an ontogenetic and phylogenetic study of the mastoid and middle ear. Laryngoscope, *37:* 710–718.

Himalstein, M. R. 1959 Mastoidpneumatization: A case with interesting developmental and phylogenetic aspects. Laryngoscope, *69:* 561–570.

Hooijer, D. A. 1955 Fossil Proboscidea from the Malay Archipelago and the Punjab. Zool. Verhandelingen, *28.*

—— 1956 The lower boundary of the pleistocene in Java and the age of pithecanthropus. Quaternaria, *3:* 5–10.

—— 1957 The correlation of fossil mammalian faunas and the pliopleistocene boundary in Java. Proc. Kon. Ned. Akad. Wetensch., ser. B, 60, *1:* 1–10.

—— 1958 Fossil bovidae from the malay archipelago and the punjab. Zool. Verhandelingen, *38.*

—— 1964 New records of mammals from the middle pleistocene of sangiran, central Java. Zool. Mededelingen, 40, *10:* 73–88.

Howell, F. Clark 1960 European and northwest african middle pleistocene hominids. Current Anthrop., 1, *3:* 195–232.

Jacob, T. 1964a A new hominid skull cap from pleistocene sangiran. Anthropologica, n.s. 6, *1:* 97–104.

—— 1964b Fosil-Fosil Manusia dari Indonesia. Universitas Gadjah Mada, Jogjakarta.

Koenigswald, G. H. R. von 1940 Neue Pithecanthropus-Funde 1936–1938 Wetensch. Mede-deeligen, *28.*

—— 1962 Das absolute Alter des Pithecanthropus erectus Dubois. In: Evolution and Hominisation (Gottfried Kurth, ed.), 112–119. Gustav Fischer Verlag, Stuttgart.

—— 1964 Potassium-Argon Dates and Early Man: Trinil Report, 6th Int. Congr. Quaternary, Warsaw, 1961, vol. *4:* 325–327.

Marks, P. 1953 Preliminary note on the discovery of a new jaw of meganthropus von koenigswald in the lower middle pleistocene of sangiran, central Java. Indonesian J. Natural Science, *1–3:* 26–33.

Meltzer, Philip E. 1934 The mastoid cells: Their arrangement in relation to the sigmoid portion of the transverse sinus. Arch. Otolaryngol., *19:* 326–335.

Oakley, Kenneth, P. 1961 On Man's Use of Fire, with Comments on Tool-Making and Hunting. In: Social Life of Early Man (Sherwood L. Washburn, ed.), 176–193. Wenner-Gren Foundation for Anthropological Research, Inc., New York.

—— 1962 Dating the emergence of man. Advancement of science, 18, *75:* 415–426.

Sartono, S. 1962 Penemuan Baru Suatu Rahang Bawah Pithecanthropus. Kongres Ilmu Pengetahuan Nasional II, Jogjakarta.

—— 1964 On a new find of another pithecanthropus skull: An announcement. Bull. Geol. Survey Indonesia, 1, *1:* 2–5.

Waldeyer, W. 1910 Weitere Untersuchungen über den Processus retromastoideus. Zeitschr. Ethnol., *42:* 316–317.

Weidenreich, Franz 1945 Giant early man from Java and south China. Anthrop. Papers Am. Mus. Nat. Hist., *40:* part 1.

—— 1951 Morphology of solo man. Anthrop. Papers Am. Mus. Nat. Hist., *43:* part 3.

The Descent of Man: Much More Fossil Evidence

A T THE PRESENT TIME, ODDLY ENOUGH, THERE SEEMS TO BE A curious gap in the fossil evidence that is relevant to the story of human evolution. Scores of specimens of *Australopithecus* have been found, and dozens of specimens of *Homo erectus*. But for the period between almost half a million and about one hundred thousand years ago, only a few specimens (most of them fragments) are available for study. After that, the data begin to become more plentiful: people began to bury their dead companions, which gave their bones greater protection, and many almost complete skeletons from the Mousterian and Upper Paleolithic periods are known. We know much more about the anatomy of these, our modern recent ancestors, as a result of this, and it is now agreed that they all belonged to the same species that we do, *Homo sapiens*.

We also know that there was considerable variation in anatomical traits among them. The group called Neanderthal, who occupied Europe during Mousterian times, and parts of the Near East too, tends to have such differently shaped skulls and faces that they used to be classified as a separate species. Few anthropologists maintain this position today, but there is, as there always has been, a great deal of perfectly legitimate disagreement concerning precisely where, in the scheme of human evolution, the Neanderthal people should be placed. Some assert that this group represents a world-wide "stage," transitional between *Homo erectus* and *Homo sapiens*. To others, including me, this seems a very dubious proposition because of the lack of Neanderthal remains at any considerable distance from Europe.

Fortunately, as time goes on more and more skeletal data are becoming available from the Near East, so that we no longer are dependent upon evidence of Europe concerning the later phases of human evolution. An excellent review of this evidence, by F. Clark Howell, is presented in the following article, "Upper Pleistocene Men of the Southwest Asian Mousterian."

9. F. Clark Howell

Upper Pleistocene Men of the Southwest Asian Mousterian*

A quarter of a century ago discoveries of human skeletal remains, in association with a Mousterian lithic industry of Levallois facies (Levalloiso-Mousterian) were made at several localities in southwestern Asia. These remains, which differed morphologically from both early and classic Neanderthal men of the European continent, have had a mixed reception by students of human paleontology. At the present time there is still no reasonable consensus of opinion as to their relationships to the Neanderthal peoples of Europe. Nor is there any basic agreement as to their possible phylogenetic significance. This is perhaps due in some part to their categorization as "Neanderthal," a usage which tends to so categorize certain fossil hominids as to preclude posing meaningful inquiries about affinities and evolutionary significance. It is also due to unresolved questions concerning their relative geologic age, both with respect to one another and also with reference to European Neanderthal peoples.

Seven sites in five localities of southwestern Asia have yielded skeletal remains which have been attributed to a variety of 'Neanderthal' man. These sites are: (1) M. ez-Zuttiyeh, a cave on the northern shore of the Sea of Galilee (Turville-Petre, 1927); (2) M. et-Tabūn, a cave; and (3) M. es-Skhūl, a rock shelter in the Wadi el-Mughara, on the western slopes of Mt. Carmel (Garrod and Bate, 1937; McCown and Keith, 1939); (4) Shukbah, a cave in the Wadi en-Natuf, northwest of Jerusalem (Keith, 1931); (5) Djebel Qafzeh, a cave in Galilee, south of Nazareth (Köppel, 1935; Neuville, 1951); (6) Shanidar, a cave in southern

* This study was made possible by financial support from the Wenner-Gren Foundation for Anthropological Research to which the writer is deeply grateful. The writer also wishes to express his appreciation to: (1) Dr. K. P. Oakley for his assistance in making available for study the skeleton from the cave of et-Tabūn, housed in the British Museum (Natural History) (London); (2) the Trustees of the American School of Prehistoric Research for permission to study the skeletal materials from the shelter of es-Skhūl, housed in the Peabody Museum, Harvard University (Cambridge, Mass.); (3) Prof. H. V. Vallois for permission to study the unpublished skeletal material from the cave of Djebel Qafzeh, Galilee, housed in the Institute de Paléontologie humaine (Paris).

Kurdistan (Solecki, 1954); and (7) Bisitun, a cave near Kermanshah in western Iran (Coon, 1951).

Problems of interpretation were posed by the earliest of these discoveries. In his thoughtful description of the cranial fragment from ez-Zuttiyeh, the first to be discovered in 1925, Keith (in Turville-Petre, 1927) noted that while "there can be no hesitation in assigning the person represented by the Galilee skull to the Neanderthal species of man," there were also "details in which the Galilean type differs from the Neanderthal varieties which have been discovered in Europe hitherto." Keith recognized the difficulties in determining whether these differences were of an individual or racial nature; subsequently, however, he positively stated that "the ancient Galilean was not the pure Neanderthal type, but a variant of the type . . ." (Keith, 1931).

With the discoveries in the caves of Mt. Carmel sufficient skeletal material became available to make detailed comparisons with various Neanderthal peoples of Europe. Prior to the publication of their definitive study of these remains, Keith and McCown (1937) offered some preliminary conclusions which are of more than historical interest. They felt that two distinct "types" were separable at Mt. Carmel, "the differences being due neither to sex nor to the variation inherent in all living populations." The skeleton of the 'Skhūl type' they found to be "a mosaic of primitive features, some of them to be met with in the Neanderthal remains from western Europe," but the majority of features "are those which we find in the modern races of man, the native races especially." These workers were then convinced that "in no essential point or complex of features can we exclude the Skhūl people from a position among the ancestors of the modern races."

The 'Tabūn type,' on the other hand, was found to possess "a curious complexity of primitive and of specialized features," most of which were "primitive and not neanthropic." While they recognized an "undoubted kinship with the Skhūl type of humanity" they concluded that the 'Tabūn type' was "Neanderthaloid" and was "more akin to the Krapina Neanderthaloids." Previously McCown (1934) had remarked on the contrast between the remains of Tabūn I (skeleton) and Tabūn II (mandible) and at that time he seems to have suspected the presence of two distinct varieties of man in the Tabūn cave. Keith (note in McCown, 1934), however, had the impression "that we are dealing with individuals of one race."

Since the skeletal materials from the Levalloiso-Mousterian horizons at Mount Carmel were found in separate sites in the valley there was the immediate problem of their relative ages. Keith and McCown (1937) concluded that "the evidence indicates quite clearly that the faunas, the industries and, most important, the people of the Skhūl and Tabūn are pre-Würmian in time" and "lived in the latter half of the Riss-Würm interglacial period." They acknowledged that the similarities of the associated faunas and the stone industries suggested that one may consider "the two groups of human remains to be contemporary"; it was recognized, however, that if certain faunal differences were stressed "the Skhūl people may be considered to be slightly later than the inhabitants of the Tabūn."

They maintained this opinion in their final report in which they stated the remains from es-Skhūl (level B) and et-Tabūn (level C) were "contemporaneous in a moderately narrow sense" (McCown and Keith, 1939) and, according to the evidence Bate (Garrod and Bate, 1937) deduced from the fauna, dated to the latter part of the Third Interglacial stage. This dating placed the Mt. Carmel people roughly contemporaneous with early Neanderthal peoples from south-eastern (Krapina), southern (Saccopastore) and central (Ehringsdorf) Europe.

Subsequently, McCown and Keith (1939) abandoned the idea of two distinc-tive human 'types' in the Levalloiso-Mousterian levels of et-Tabūn and es-Skhūl; they recognized, however, that "the range in form . . . is unexpectedly great." Since the skeletal remains had in common certain basic features of morphology they concluded that these were "remains of a single people, the Skhūl and Tabūn types being but the extremes of the same series, there being intermediates between these extremes." This was due, they believed, "to an evolutionary divergence" since these people "were in the throes of evolutionary change." The people of the es-Skhūl were found to resemble closely the later Cro Magnon people of western Europe; but, in their opinion, the former were not directly ancestral to anatomi-cally modern man ("the Mount Carmel people are not the actual ancestors of the Cromagnons but Neanderthaloid collaterals or cousins of the ancestors of that type"). The exact meaning of this conclusion is made clear by Keith's (1948) statement elsewhere that he and McCown believed "that at the period earlier than that represented by the fossil Carmelites, and farther towards the east, a local group of Neanderthalians began to evolve in a Caucasian direction and that these Carmelites represent a later phase of this movement."

In their careful description of the Mt. Carmel skeletal material the morphologi-cal evidence speaks for itself. Many other workers, however, have expressed reluctance in accepting these conclusions. Ashley-Montagu (1940; also 1951), in reviewing their work, was among the first to offer a detailed criticism. He suggested an explanation which these workers had rejected: "relatively recent crossing or hybridization" with the "introduction of new genes from another group." Montagu believed that "any other theory would have to assume the spontaneous mutation of far too many genes, or far too great a change in gene variability, to render such a theory tenable." Hooton (1946) agreed with this explanation, finding McCown and Keith's interpretation "both ambivalent and ambiguous"; whereas, "the results of a radical race mixture within a small group, as observed in modern studies, are exactly the sort of phenomena that are shown in the skeletal series from the caves of Skhūl and Tabūn in Palestine." This form of interpretation was buttressed by the support of an outstanding geneticist who stated that the population arose "as a result of hybridization of a Neanderthaloid and a modern type, these types having been formed earlier in different geographic regions" (Dobzhansky, 1944). This worker believed that the finds of Mount Carmel provided definite proof that "the Neanderthal and the modern types were not isolated reproductively, and hence, were races of the same species rather than distinct species." This interpretation has lately been framed into a far-reaching explanation of human evolution by Weckler (1954).

Most recently, Le Gros Clark (1955) has rejected both the idea of miscegenation and that of evolutionary divergence as envisioned by McCown and Keith. Instead he has suggested that the Mt. Carmel people "appear to represent a transitional stage leading from pre-Mousterian *Homo sapiens* to the later establishment of the definitive species *H. neanderthalensis.*"

There has been no attempt in recent years to reinvestigate some of the important problems concerning the peoples of the Levalloiso-Mousterian in southwestern Asia. There is, however, much new evidence from paleoanthropological investigations in this region and adjacent areas which has an important bearing on previous interpretations of the Mt. Carmel and related fossil men. This evidence suggests that the problem might be reexamined profitably at this time with a view towards resolving some of the earlier divergent interpretations.

Relative Age of the Human Remains

Most students of human evolution have accepted without question the relative dating of the human remains from the Levalloiso-Mousterian which Garrod and Bate (1937) and McCown and Keith (1939) regarded as correct. This dating was based on the stratigraphic succession revealed in the Mt. Carmel caves of et-Tabūn and el-Wad, the sequences of which were presumed to overlap and represent a continuous Upper Pleistocene succession. A series of damper and drier climatic phases, inferred from fluctuating percentages of gazelle and Persian fallow deer, were keyed to the stadial/interstadial system of the European Upper Pleistocene succession to provide a precise correlation (Zeuner, 1938, 1940, 1945, 1952). The fossil human remains in question were believed to date from a drier phase which preceded a markedly damper phase and, thus, to date from the latter part of an interpluvial, corresponding to the Last Interglacial of the European succession.

While there has been a general tendency to follow this correlation, a few other workers have been more sceptical. Braidwood (1943) stressed that "a reliable geochronological correlation between Palestine and Europe" did not exist and, while "archaeologically, a rough relative chronology may be constructed," this "remains a typological construct alone." Vaufrey (1939a, b; 1944) has been particularly vigorous in rejecting the correlation suggested by the work of Garrod, Bate and Zeuner. He has insisted that the whole of the southwest Asian industrial succession was retarded compared with that of western Europe in the Upper Pleistocene. More recently, Bordes (1956) has written in a similar vein and suggested, on purely *a priori* grounds, a late dating for the Syrian mountain shelters of Yabrud which contained an industrial sequence comparable, in certain respects, to that known from the littoral. If these views are correct then the human skeletal remains from the Levalloiso-Mousterian in this area would date from a time equivalent to the first major interstadial within the Last Glacial stage. They would thus post-date rather than pre-date the well known classic Neanderthal group of western Europe, an occurrence which would alter markedly their place in human phylogeny.

In recent years major advances have been made in the study of the geology and paleoanthropology of the later Pleistocene of the east Mediterranean littoral. A coastal marine succession, independent of the caves, has been established with its base tied to the standard European succession through the Tyrrhenian transgression of the Last Interglacial. This succession indicates that a drier (Last) Interpluvial, coincident with the Tyrrhenian high sea level, was followed by a (Last) Pluvial stage; the latter was represented by several damper (and cooler) stadia and drier interstadia. These were probably comparable to the colder stadia, and more temperate interstadia, of the Last Glacial in Europe. The cultural horizons of the cave successions can now be tied in with this standard local chronology in most cases (aided particularly by the discovery of specific industries in datable geological contexts along the coast). It is also now clear that the Mt. Carmel succession was incomplete and contained several erosional and/or industrial hiatuses. A careful study of the faunal evidence also reveals the gazelle/fallow deer graph is not an accurate guide to the interpretation of Upper Pleistocene climatic conditions. The coastal evidence, as well as that provided by the occupied caves and shelters, is discussed in some detail elsewhere (Howell, *in litt.*). It indicates that the Levalloiso-Mousterian industries (and other Mousterian facies), and the associated human skeletal remains, were not of Last Interpluvial (= Interglacial) age. They date instead from an initial stadial of the Last Pluvial (= Glacial). The first stage (Stage 1 = Emiran) of the local Upper Paleolithic sequence dates from the following interstadial (although at some localities there are indications that its roots are in the preceding Levalloiso-Mousterian). The preceding Last Interpluvial was the time of Final Acheulean or Micoquian industries (however, at et-Tabūn an early blade technique is evident at the top of the Micoquian; and, at Yabrud in Syria, an analogous occurrence is present from levels intercalated between a local variety of Mousterian industry which dates from the early stadial of the Last Pluvial).

As in western Europe (where two recent loesses were accumulated) this early part of the Last Pluvial stage seems to have had a considerable duration. At Djebel Qafzeh human skeletal remains were found in the lowermost (level L) of seven Levalloiso-Mousterian occupation levels; these totalled over three meters in thickness (Köppel, 1935). The climate was already damp and cool when the basal levels were deposited; it subsequently became wetter and colder with a final amelioration towards a warmer, but still moist climate (Neuville, 1951). This succession suggests the buildup toward a pluvial stadial and the gradual decline toward interstadial conditions. Moreover, the first stage of the local Upper Paleolithic is represented here in deposits which are recognizably interstadial.

At Mt. Carmel three Levalloiso-Mousterian levels were recognized in the cave of et-Tabūn (Garrod and Bate, 1937). These totalled more than nine meters in thickness! Contrary to what has usually been assumed, as Neuville (1951) has already noted, the lower levels, level F (Final Acheulean) and level E (Micoquian), were not accumulated during a pluvial stage. The first traces of a moister climate are to be found in the lowermost (level D) horizon of the Levalloiso-Mousterian. The composition of these levels provides some evidence of the climate. There was increasingly damper climate from level D (a hardened calcareous sandy-loam with some breccia and limestone blocks) through level C (a hardened calcareous and ferruginous, somewhat brecciated loam); in level B (a non-calcareous sandy-clay filled with limestone blocks) the climate may have been somewhat less moist and probably also cooler than previously. The human skeleton (Tabūn I) and the isolated mandible (Tabūn II) derived from the middle level (C); a few isolated human skeletal remains were also present in the upper level (B).

Two Levalloiso-Mousterian cultural levels (C-B) were present in the rock shelter of es-Skhūl. The human burials occurred in the upper (B) of these levels. It was regarded by McCown and Keith (1939) as "contemporaneous in a moderately narrow sense" with et-Tabūn level C. In a more recent reappraisal of the problem McCown (1950) has reiterated his conviction that "there is no clear cut evidence to establish a time difference between the two sets of human remains and some evidence in favor of their contemporaneity." He admits, however, that he has "a nagging suspicion that there is a time difference but no evidence to settle my doubt."

Actually there is some evidence in favor of such a time difference. In the longer and more complete section of et-Tabūn there were indications of a 'faunal break' between the two upper Levalloiso-Mousterian levels, C and B. This 'great faunal break,' discussed in detail by Bate (in Garrod and Bate, 1937) represented the disappearance of hippopotamus, rhinoceros, an extinct pig (Sus gadarensis), and a number of small mammals (including two species of white-toothed shrew, a hedgehog, a true mole, a fox, a muscardine rodent, a vole of the nivalis group, and a mole vole). Also, some new species were present afterwards, including a hedgehog, a pig and a hare; and the fauna in general had assumed a modern aspect. The fauna from es-Skhūl level B contained elements which were absent after the faunal break represented at et-Tabūn. Thus, Bate was "inclined to think that the Skhūl fauna may be linked with the very latest phase of that of Level C of Tabūn." There were, however, certain noteworthy differences between the two levels: (1) the great abundance of wild cattle (Bos) in es-Skhūl level B; (2) more numerous Persian fallow deer and fewer gazelles in level B of es-Skhūl than in level C of et-Tabūn. These differences, as well as others to be noted may well reflect somewhat damper conditions during accumulation of the cultural deposits of es-Skhūl level B than during those of et-Tabūn level C; or the differences may have been due only to particular hunting habits.

The deposit of es-Skhūl level B was extremely hard. It varied "from a consistency and solidity approximating that of a plaster wall to a condition very like that of concrete"; also, there were "irregular, thin, laminated sills of sterile stalagmite both in the hardened earth and in the very hard breccia," (McCown in Garrod and Bate, 1937). An analysis of this deposit (Garrod and Bate, 1937; Appendix II) shows it to have been a hardened, highly calcareous sandy-clay and earthy travertine. It contrasted with the et-Tabūn level C deposit, a clayey and sandy loam, which although somewhat calcareous (9.5%) and ferruginized (9.3%), was more friable, less consolidated and less stalagmitic.

All the caves excavated in the Wadi el-Mughara are situated on the southern escarpment of the valley and face north. The es-Skhūl shelter is located a bit east of the et-Tabūn and el-Wad caves and around a bend in the valley. It is difficult to regard the differences in the deposits as being due merely to local circumstances; rather they would seem to represent somewhat different climatic conditions during their respective formations. These distinctions would tend to reinforce the inconclusive faunal evidence which has suggested a rather damper climate during the time of formation of es-Skhūl level B. Unfortunately, it is still impossible to determine the magnitude of this difference which may have been relatively slight (in terms of Upper Pleistocene time). On the other hand even a slight difference, from several hundreds to more likely several thousands of years, could be of great importance in terms of the human populations. Stratigraphically, es-Skhūl level B may still fall somewhere between levels C and B of et-Tabūn, as Bate originally suggested. This would imply, however, that the human remains from the Levalloiso-Mousterian levels of es-Skhūl and et-Tabūn would be best considered, at least initially, as two distinct skeletal series. The question of whether each belongs to the same human group or to different groups, as well as their broader affinities, should be a problem for future investigation.

The Human Skeletal Remains

Human remains associated with a Micoquian industry are still too inadequately known to provide evidence of the morphology of those southwest Asian people of the Last Interpluvial. In the Micoquian level E of et-Tabūn only an incomplete shaft of femur (level Ea) and an isolated, worn lower right molar (level Eb) were found. These show some points of resemblance with the later people of the Levalloiso-Mousterian (level C) from this site (McCown and Keith, 1939). The cranial fragment from ez-Zuttiyeh in Galilee has usually been regarded as associated with the Levalloiso-Mousterian industry from that site; however, it may have represented the remains of an earlier man since it came from the base of the occupation zone where Micoquian-like hand-axes occurred (Garrod and Bate, 1937). If this was the case, and the problem can probably never be definitely settled at this late date, then a human variety closely resembling the people from the Levalloiso-Mousterian was already present during the Last Interpluvial. This variety had its closest affinity with the Krapina (Croatia) people from the southeast of the European continent (Gorjanović-Kramberger, 1906). There were also some general resemblances with other early Neanderthal peoples, such as those from Saccopastore (Sergi, 1944, 1948) and Ehringsdorf (Weidenreich, 1928) in southern and central Europe, respectively.

The earliest remains of people of the Levalloiso-Mousterian were those from et-Tabūn level C. The nearly complete skeleton (I) bore a quite marked resemblance to the people from the Krapina rock shelter. Other features, both of the cranium and the postcranial skeleton, tended to approximate the morphological pattern characteristic of anatomically modern man. An isolated mandible (II) and five other bits of the upper and lower limbs of another skeleton were also present in this level. It is not possible, however, to infer the range of variation even from this additional material. The mandible, regarded as that of a male individual, was distinguished particularly by its size and robustness and some morphological details of the symphyseal region. Certain of its features tended to bridge the gap between the morphology of the presumably female skeleton (I) and that of the skeletal series from the es-Skhūl shelter. Actually, as McCown and Keith (1939) were careful to point out, there was a basic morphological likeness in the jaw and the dentition of both specimens I and II from the et-Tabūn cave. In their opinion, with which the writer would agree, "both male and female are probably of the same race as well as being of the same time." The morphology of these people differed markedly, however, from that characteristic of the classic Neanderthal people who lived at that time in western and southern Europe.

The series from es-Skhūl level B comprised the remains of ten individuals as well as sixteen separate isolated fragments. The enumeration of ten individuals may be misleading, however, unless consideration is given to the degree of preservation of the material (McCown and Keith, 1939). Three individuals were children of which only Sk. I preserved most of the skull and postcranial skeleton; Sk. X preserved only a bit of the mandible and part of the upper arm; Sk. VIII preserved only some parts of each leg. The other seven individuals were adult, but only Sk. IV and V had well preserved skulls and postcranial skeletons. Sk. IX preserved much of the cranial vault, but only bits of the postcranial skeleton; Sk. VII preserved much of the postcranial skeleton, but the cranium and mandible were badly crushed; Sk. VI preserved a crushed part of the cranium and mandible and some of the postcranial skeleton; Sk. II preserved fragments of cranium, mandible and parts of each arm; Sk. III preserved only parts of a lower extremity.

The postcranial morphology of two of these skeletons, Sk. IV and Sk. V, bore a marked resemblance to that characteristic of the Upper Paleolithic Cro Magnon people of western Europe. In these specimens, as well as Sk. II, VI and IX, the structure of the facial skeleton as well as the essential aspects of braincase morphology were that which characterize a primitive form of anatomically modern man. Considering these specimens only, all of which have been regarded as male (except Sk. II whose sex is difficult to ascertain anyway), one finds here all the important morphological requirements of an ancestral, proto-Cro Magnon human group. Judging from the few non-adult specimens which were tolerably well preserved, and in particular Sk. I, the juvenile morphology and pattern of growth approximated very closely that of anatomically modern man. It differed markedly from that of classic Neanderthal man of western Europe.

Some of the other skeletons from es-Skhūl exhibited features of their morphology which resembled that of the somewhat earlier people from the Levalloiso-Mousterian levels of the cave of et-Tabūn. This was particularly true for Sk. VI and VII, regarded as male and female, respectively; the resemblance was confined to the postcranial skeleton. However, this series represented a single human population and these features were an aspect of its normal range of variation. In this respect the range of variation of the people of es-Skhūl also overlapped that of some earlier Neanderthal people of Europe. The closest resemblance was with the Krapina population. The people of et-Tabūn resembled those from Krapina even more closely (a larger series from et-Tabūn might disprove this hypothesis, however). In the es-Skhūl series, as in those from et-Tabūn, there was no trace of the characteristic classic Neanderthal morphology.

The pattern of morphology found in the human remains from es-Skhūl is revealed in other skeletal material from the Levalloiso-Mousterian of the Levant. The fragmentary skeletal remains from the cave of Djebel Qafzeh in Galilee exhibit the same features and, so far as this can be observed, the same sort of range of variation. The best preserved skull was that of Qaf. VI which bore a remarkable resemblance to Sk. IV and V (fig. 2). Other specimens included an adult maxilla and mandible (III), an adult palate (V), another adult maxilla and mandible (VII), as well as an immature palate and mandible (IV) and some poorly preserved limb bones (III). This material was neither sufficiently well preserved nor abundant enough to illustrate fully the range of variation for exact comparison with the es-Skhūl series. Nonetheless it fully confirms the significance of the morphology of the people in the Levalloiso-Mousterian of the cave of es-Skhūl.

Evolutionary Significance

The skeletal remains of man from the Levalloiso-Mousterian of southwestern Asia gain in importance when consideration is given to adjacent regions (Table 1). Although a number of prehistoric sites are known in Transcaucasia and the Abkhasian area adjoining the Black Sea, no human skeletal remains have been found in association with Mousterian industries there. However, two sites in the Crimea, Kiik-Koba and Starosel'je, provide evidence of the human populations there during the Mousterian. The rock shelter of Kiik-Koba, southern Crimea (Bonch-Osmolovskii, 1940) has yielded bones of the hand (*ibid.,* 1941), leg and foot (*ibid.,* 1954) of a variety of 'Neanderthal' man. This was a burial in a fossa in the shelter floor, associated with a Mousterian industry predominantly of side-scrapers and some small hand-axes; it dates most certainly from an initial phase of the Last Glacial stage. The hand and foot show well-marked Neanderthal affinities and seem to bear a fundamental resemblance to the earlier Krapina people and to those people, roughly contemporaneous, from the Levalloiso-Mousterian of et-Tabūn.

Most recently the rock shelter of Starosel'je, farther south in the Crimea and nearer the Black Sea, has yielded skeletal remains of an infant (Formosov *et al.* 1954; also Ullrich, 1955; Vallois, 1956). It was found in association with a Mousterian industry not unlike that of Kiik-Koba, composed predominantly of side-scrapers with some small hand-axes and faint traces of an incipient blade technique. It, too, dates from an early phase of the Last Glacial stage. The post-cranial skeleton is so poorly preserved as to be largely useless for study, but the

TABLE 1

Distribution and relative dating of the skeletal remains of 'Neanderthal Man' and the earliest Cro Magnon men

AGE	Western and Southern Europe	Central Europe	Eastern Europe	Southwestern Asia	Southern Central Asia
Interstadial	Combe-Capelle	Lautsch			
Last Glacial I	Classic Neanderthals	Subalyuk Šipka	Starosel'je Kiik-Koba	Ksâr Akil Shanidar Skhūl (B), Qafzeh (L) Tabūn (C) ↑ Zuttiyeh	?
Last Interglacial	Fontéchevade (II) Saccopastore Montmaurin	Krapina ↓ Ehringsdorf	Ganovcé	↓ Tabūn (EA)	Teshik-Tash ?

skull (Ullrich, 1958) can be quite well reconstructed. The individual suffered perhaps from hydrocephaly, but nonetheless in a number of important features of the facial skeleton, as well as of the cranial vault, it resembled an early form of anatomically modern man. The cranial morphology calls to mind the pattern of growth of the slightly older child Sk. I from Mount Carmel. The Starosel'je specimen bears no basic resemblance to a child of similar age, for example that from Pech de l'Azé (Patte, 1958), of the classic Neanderthal people of western

Europe (and the only specimen known certainly to have been associated with a Mousterian industry of Acheulean tradition).

Another specimen is the child's skeleton, buried ritualistically, in the Teshik-Tash shelter (Uzbekistan), in southern Central Asia. The industry associated with the burial was not unlike that at the Crimean sites, with side-scrapers and some chopping-tools as well as indications of an incipient blade technique (Movius, 1953). The Teshik-Tash child *may* have been older than the skeletal remains from the Crimean sites, and dated possibly to the latter part of the Last Interglacial. The morphology of this specimen has now been thoroughly described (in Okladnikov *et al.,* 1949). It bears a rather close resemblance to some other Neanderthals of eastern Europe dating from the early Last Glacial, in particular the child from Subalyuk cave (Bartucz *et al.,* 1938). Its morphology differed markedly, as Weidenreich (1945) noted, from that of classic Neanderthal children, for example that of La Quina 18 (fig. 1).

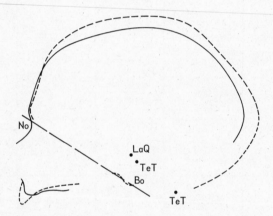

Fig. 1.

These skeletal remains from southern Russia and from central Asia enhance the significance of the fossil men of the Levalloiso-Mousterian of Palestine. They confirm the existence of a distinct human variety, a variety of 'Neanderthal' man loosely speaking, throughout the general area of western Asia during the earlier part of the Upper Pleistocene. The repeated occurrence of such a human variety, first made evident by the cranial fragment from ez-Zuttiyeh in Galilee, in widely separated regions of this area raises again the problem of interpretation brought about by the amazing discoveries in the caves of Mt. Carmel.

The writer finds it difficult to account for *each* of these situations on the basis of hybridization between distinctive prehistoric human races. However, Weckler (1954) has recently suggested that the Teshik-Tash child may be "the record of one of the earliest fusions between Neanderthal and *Homo sapiens,* physically and culturally." For that writer the et-Tabūn remains would "probably represent a group from central Asia that became interred before they had intermixed exten-

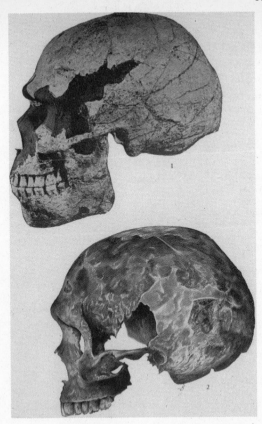

Fig. 2. Mousterian man in Palestine: Lateral views of (1) Skhūl 5 (after Snow, 1953) and (2) Qafzeh 6 (after Boule and Vallois, 1952). Both skulls were found in association with a Mousterian industry of Levallois facies in Palestine.

sively with the local *Homo sapiens* population." It is difficult to see any evidence which would lend support to this interpretation. In the fossil record there are no traces of any *Homo sapiens* population in this area before the middle of the Last Pluvial stage. These occur first in the Antelian, a stage of the Upper Paleolithic (Howell, *in litt.*). In fact, from the scant evidence available, the population of southwestern Asia during the Third Interpluvial (Interglacial) apparently resembled closely the people of the Levalloiso-Mousterian of et-Tabūn. Moreover there is no trace in the area of a 'Neanderthal' people (who are classic Neanderthal people in Weckler's sense of the term) to form the other ingredient of such a racial mixture. The classic Neanderthal people have never been found outside a circumscribed area of western and southern Europe where they lived during the early part of the Last Glacial. There is no substantial evidence to support, and there is some important evidence which disproves, that writer's thesis of "an easterly centered Neanderthal population and a *Homo sapiens* population oriented to the west and south" of this area which he regards as the "zone of contact" and hybridization.

During the Last Interglacial there were certain basic morphological similarities which linked early Neanderthal peoples throughout the European continent.[1] Climates were warmer than the present and there were no major natural barriers to prevent interbreeding between contiguous populations. A single variable racial group[2] seems to have been everywhere present in Europe.

The onset of the Last Glacial served effectively to disrupt this continuity of race. The early Neanderthals of the western and southern margins of the continent were segregated, in terms of gene interchange, from those of central and eastern Europe. Isolating mechanisms included the extensive glaciation of the

[1] Only a few sites of the Last Interglacial have yielded human skeletal remains. The best-dated and best preserved early Neanderthals are those from Ehringsdorf, Thuringia (Germany), Saccopastore (Italy) and Krapina (Croatia, Yugoslavia). The mandible from Montmaurin (Haute-Garonne, France) is perhaps of this age or possibly even the late Middle Pleistocene. The fragmentary cranial fragments from Fontéchevade (Charente, France) are generally presumed to be of Last Interglacial age because of their association with a warm fauna; however, there is no evidence to controvert a late Middle Pleistocene age and the fauna alone will not definitely settle the matter.

[2] The cranial fragments from the cave of Fontéchevade are regarded as of 'Pre-sapiens' rather than of early Neanderthal type by Vallois (1949, 1954) and some other workers. If this is in fact the case it would indicate that two distinctive forms of man occupied the western European region during the Last Interglacial. In order for these forms to remain distinct, and such has been implied in the designation 'pre-sapiens,' there must not have been genetic interchange as a result of interbreeding or else their differences would disappear as a result of hybridization. If these were population (demes) of the same species with a common origin but an isolated development, presumably there would be fusion into a single variable population due to their coming together. Otherwise they would have been distinctive sympatric species, sharing dissimilar ways of life characterized by differences in behavior or habit so that interbreeding did not normally take place. It is difficult to see any evidence which would favor this latter conclusion. If this were a case of a distinctive geographic area in which a particular species arose through isolation from other groups such an explanation would appear more likely. However, the area was occupied extensively by Neanderthal peoples throughout the earlier Upper Pleistocene. Similarly, if the Neanderthals were indigenous to the area, such a 'pre-sapiens' group must have had its origins elsewhere and expanded into western Europe subsequently. Where was this area and where is the fossil and other evidence necessary to support such an hypothesis?

The human skeletal remains from Fontéchevade are themselves inconclusive in the opinion of the writer. The writer is grateful to Prof. H. V. Vallois for permission to examine these specimens, a distorted and incomplete skull cap (No. 2) and a small fragment of frontal bone (No. 1), in 1953 and 1954. The calotte alone does not prove a 'sapiens' morphology since it falls readily, in all its main features, within the range of variation of the early Neanderthals. The real issue rests on the bit of frontal bone, comprising the glabellar region and frontal sinus, and which reveals no trace of a well developed supra-orbital torus. It appears to have been a mature (or at least adolescent) individual although clearly not the same individual represented by the skull cap. Application of the fluorine technique for relative age assessment has suggested that both specimens are of broadly the same age as the fauna from the Tayacian (pre-Mousterian) cultural horizon, situated below a calcified and stalagmitic horizon (Oakley and Hoskins, with Henri-Martin, 1951). However, at the time such tests were carried out, the technique was not yet sufficiently refined to differentiate absolutely between the Last Interglacial and early Last Glacial time ranges. The nitrogen analysis did not fully rule out a possible difference in age. The frontal fragment (No. 1) differs markedly from the skull cap (No. 2) both in general thickness of vault bone as well as in its degree of mineralization and state of preservation. This might well reflect a difference in geologic age (or merely the action of fire which had affected the skull cap). In view of the importance of the Fontéchevade discovery further tests, using more recently developed and refined techniques, would be particularly worthwhile in order to clarify these questions. At present, however, it would appear judicious to withhold judgement on this particular fragment (No. 1), and to resist basing a broad and far-reaching theory of human evolution on it alone.

Alpine ranges and their forelands, and the rigorous climate of the central European periglacial corridor south of the Scandinavian ice sheet. This is not to deny that some penetration of the country adjacent to the northern Alpine forelands took place. Mousterian habitation sites have been found sporadically in this region, and in areas to the north along the Rhine River, usually in hilly country and sheltered, probably at that time, wooded valleys. However, in terms of gene distribution this penetration was apparently ineffective. For all intents and purposes western and southern Europe were fairly circumscribed breeding areas. The classic Neanderthal people of the Last Glacial, now well documented by remains of a number of adult as well as juvenile individuals,[3] were the result of this isolation. They represented a distinctive local race which has been clearly delineated on morphological, temporal and geographic evidence. They were a local evolutionary development and became a stabilized variety during the initial Last Glacial due to this enforced genetic isolation, perhaps in response to the rigors of a subarctic climate (Howell, 1951, 1952).

Central and eastern Europe were not regions of isolation during the early Last Glacial stage. There was local glaciation in the Balkan and Carpathian mountains; but, tundra, which was widespread in the periglacial northern lowlands of Poland and western Russia, was restricted farther southward to the highland zones above the tree line. Most of the plains and low country were steppe lands, supporting a rich grazing fauna, while hilly regions and enclosed valleys were wooded. There were no major natural obstacles to prevent population shifts as bands moved from territory to territory nor to hinder free genetic interchange over this area, the regions bordering the Black Sea and southwestern Asia.

Southeastern Europe was broadly inhabited during the first part of the Last Glacial judging from the number of prehistoric sites already brought to light there. However, human skeletal remains are still relatively uncommon.[4] Those which are available reveal the presence of Neanderthal peoples morphologically not unlike those of the preceding interglacial stage. There was broad racial continuity at least as far east as the Crimea (Kiik-Koba) and southward into the Levant (et-Tabūn, Mount Carmel).

In the most easterly regions, however, there are clear indications of 'sapiensization.' The people from es-Skhūl and Djebel Qafzeh were well advanced toward

---

[3] Classic Neanderthal skeletal remains are restricted in geographic distribution to westernmost Germany, Belgium, France, Spain and Italy. The sites are as follows: (1) *Germany*: Neanderthal; (2) *Belgium*: Bay-Bonnet, Engis, La Naulette, Spy; (3) *Channel Islands*: St. Brelade (Jersey); (4) *France*: (a) Ariège: Malarnaud; (b) Charente: La Chaise, La Quina, Petit-Puy-moyen; (c) Corrèze: La Chapelle-aux-Saints; (d) Côte d'Or: Genay; (e) Dordogne: Combe-Grenal, La Ferrassie, Le Moustier, Pech de l'Azé; (f) Lot-et-Garonne: Monsempron; (g) Yonne: Arcy-sur-Cure (Hyena and Wolf caves); (5) *Spain*: Bañolas, Cova Negra, Gibraltar (Forbes Quarry, Devil's Tower), Piñar; (6) *Italy*: Monte Circeo, Santa Croce di Bisceglie.

[4] Only two sites in central-eastern Europe have yielded remains of peoples of the early Last Glacial. These are Šipka Cave in northern Moravia (Czechoslovakia) (Schaaffhausen, 1882; Virchow, 1892) and Subalyuk Cave in the Bükk Mountains of Hungary (Bartucz *et al.*, 1938; Szabo, 1935). Mottl (1938) has concluded that the Subalyuk skeletal remains dated from the latter part of the Last Interglacial, but both the faunal and the stratigraphic evidence (and the associated (Late) Mousterian industry) testify to the steppe condition of the initial part of the Last Glacial.

anatomically modern man, more so than populations of southeastern Europe at the time (or the Levant at a slightly earlier time). Was this the result of a movement into the region of an incipiently modern human people from regions to the east or south? Or was this the result of evolutionary transformation in the Levant proper? The morphology of the child from Teshik Tash, if it is really of late Last Interglacial age, would lend support to the view that the major transformation was occurring farther eastwards, more or less as McCown and Keith (1939) suggested, and that there was expansion subsequently of such peoples into the hilly uplands of the eastern Mediterranean littoral. The Starosel'je (Crimea) child would thus testify to the first penetration of such peoples into the eastern margins of the European continent. There is still too little evidence available from western Asia to answer either question in the affirmative with any degree of assurance.

It is difficult to escape the conclusion, although there is still inadequate evidence to fix exactly the region and time, that the southwest Asian area, and including southern Russia, was a primary one in the evolutionary transformation of protosapiens peoples, who had some general early Neanderthal affinities, into anatomically modern man of the European Cro Magnon variety. This conclusion can be drawn from the human skeletal material from the Levalloiso-Mousterian of Palestine and it is reenforced by more recent discoveries elsewhere in adjacent regions. The evidence is strongly in favor of looking to the east, away from Europe, for the ancestors of the earliest European Upper Paleolithic peoples since an appropriate base for such an evolutionary development is only evident there.

LITERATURE CITED

Ashley-Montagu, M. F. 1940: Review of: McCown, T. D. and A. Keith, 1939: The Stone Age of Mount Carmel. Vol. 2. The fossil human remains from the Levalloiso-Mousterian. Am. Anthrop., 42 : 518–522.

——— 1951: An introduction to physical anthropology. Second edition. 555 pages. Springfield, Ill.: C. C. Thomas.

Bartucz, L., J. Dancza, F. Hollendonner, O. Kadič, M. Mottl, U. Pataki, E. Palosi, J. Szabo, A. Vendl, 1938: A cserepfalui Mussolini-Barlang (Subalyuk). Geologica hungarica, series Palaeontologica, fasc. 14 : 1–320.

Bonch-Osmolovskii, G. A. 1940–41, 1954; Grot Kiil-Koba. Paleolit Kryma. Vyp. 1, 2, 3. Moscow-Leningrad: Akademiia Nauk SSSR Komissiia po izucheniia chetvertichnoyo perioda. 225 pages, 171 pages, 398 pages.

Bordes, F. 1956: Le Paléolithique inférieur et moyen de Jabrud (Syrie) et la question du Pré-Aurignacien. L'Anthropologie, 59 : 486–507.

Boule, M. and H. V. Vallois 1952: Les hommes fossiles. 4e ed. 583 pages. Paris: Masson et Cie.

Braidwood, R. J. 1943: Note on the age of the Galilee and Mt. Carmel skeletal material. Am. Anthrop., 45 : 642–643.

Coon, C. 1951: Cave excavations in Iran. University of Pennsylvania, Philadelphia.

Dobzhansky, T. 1944: On species and races of living and fossil man. Am. J. Phys. Anthrop., n.s. 2 : 251–265.

Formosov, A. A., M. M. Gerasimov and Ia. Ia. Roginskii, 1954: Novaia nahodka musterskogo cheloveka V SSSR. Sovetskaia Ethnografia, No. 1 (1954): 11–39.

Garrod, D. A. E. and D. M. A. Bate 1937: The stone age of Mount Carmel. Vol. 1. Excavations at the Wady el-Mughara. Oxford: Clarendon Press. 240 pages.

Gorjanovič-Kramberger, K. 1906: Der diluviale Mensch von Krapina in Kroatien. Ein Beitrag zur Paläoanthropologie. Wiesbaden: C. W. Kreidel's Verlag. 277 pages.

Hooton, E. A. 1946: Up from the Ape. Revised edition. New York: Macmillan Co., 788 pages.

Howell, F. C. 1951: The place of Neanderthal man in human evolution. Am. J. Phys. Anthrop., n.s. 9 : 379–416.

———— 1952: Pleistocene glacial ecology and the evolution of 'classic Neandertal' man. Southwestern J. Anthrop., 8 : 377–410.

———— 1956: Early man and Upper Pleistocene stratigraphy in the Levant. (in press)

Keith, A. 1927: A report on the Galilee skull, p. 53–106, in F. Turville-Petre: Researches in prehistoric Galilee, 1925–1926. London: British School of Archeology in Jerusalem. 103 pages.

———— 1931: New discoveries relating to the antiquity of man. 512 pages. London: Williams and Norgate, Ltd.

———— 1948: A new theory of human evolution. London: Watts and Co. 451 pages.

Keith, A. and T. D. McCown 1937: Mount Carmel man. His bearing on the ancestry of modern races. p. 41–52, in Early Man, ed. by G. G. MacCurdy. Philadelphia: E. B. Lippincott. 362 pages.

Köppel, R. 1935: Das Alter der neuentdeckten Schädel von Nazareth. Biblica, 16 : 58–73.

Le Gros Clark, W. E. 1955: The fossil evidence for human evolution. An introduction to paleoanthropology. The University of Chicago Press, Chicago.

McCown, T. D. 1933: Fossil men of the Mugharet es-Skhūl. Bull. Am. School Prehist. Res., 9 : 9–16.

———— 1934: The oldest complete skeletons of man. ibid., 10 : 12–19.

———— 1950: The genus Palaeoanthropus and the problem of superspecific differentiation among the Hominidae. Cold Spring Harbor Symposia on Quantitative Biology, 15 (Origin and Evolution of Man) : 87–94.

McCown, T. D. and A. Keith, 1939: The stone age of Mount Carmel. Vol. 2. The fossil human remains from the Levalloiso-Mousterian. Oxford: The Clarendon Press. 390 pages.

Movius, H. L., Jr. 1953: The Mousterian cave of Teshik-Tash, southeastern Uzbekistan, Central Asia. Bull. Am. School Prehist. Res., 17 : 11–71.

Neuville, R. 1951: Le Paléolithique et le Mésolithique du Désert de Judée. Archives de l'Institut de Paléontologie humaine, 25 : 1–270.

Oakley, K. P. and C. R. Hoskins, 1951: Application du test de la fluorine aux cranes de Fontéchevade (Charente), avec Remarques sur la Stratigraphie de Fontéchevade, par G. Henri-Martin. L'Anthropologie, 55 : 239–247.

Okladnikov, A. P., V. J. Gromova, P. V. Suslova, D. G. Rokhlin, N. A. Sinelnikov and M. A. Gremiatskii, 1949: Teshik-Tash: Paleoliticheskii Chelovek. Moscow: Trudy Nauchno-Issledovatelskogo Instituta Antropologii. 182 pages.

Patte, E. 1958: L'Enfant du Pech de l'Azé: Hundert Jahre Neanderthaler, G. H. R. von Koenigswald, ed., Utrecht, pp. 270–276.

Rust, A. 1950: Die Höhlenfunde von Jabrud (Syrien). 154 pages, 110 plates. Neumünster: Karl Wachholtz Verlag.

Schaaffhausen, H. 1882: Über den menschlichen Kiefer aus der Shipka-Höhle bei Stramberg in Mähren. Zeits. P. Ethnologie, 40 : 279–309.

Sergi, S. 1944: Craniometria e craniografia del primo paleoantropo di Saccopastore. Richerche di Morfologia, 20 : 1–59.

———— 1944: Il cranio del secondo paleantropo di Saccopastore, in A. C. Blanc and S. Sergi, L'uomo di Saccopastore. Paleontographia italica, 52 : 25–164.

Snow, C. E. 1953: The ancient Palestinian: Skhūl V reconstruction. Bull. Am. School Prehist. Res., 17 : 5–10.

Solecki, R. 1954: Shanidar cave, a Paleolithic site in northern Iraq. Smithsonian Inst., Ann. Rep. (4206) : 389–425.

Szabo, J. 1935: L'homme moustérien de la Grotte Mussolini (Hongrie). Bull. et Mém. Soc. d'Anthrop. de Paris, 1935 : 23–30.

Turville-Petre, F. 1927: Researches in prehistoric Galilee 1925–1926. 119 pages. London: British School of Archaeology in Jerusalem.

Ullrich, H. 1955: Palaolithische Menschenreste aus der Sowjet Union. Zeitschr. f. Morphol. u. Anthrop., 47 : 91–98, 99–112.

——— 1958: Neanderthalerfunder aus der lowjetunion: Hundert Jahre Neanderthaler, G. H. R. von Koenigswald, ed., Utrecht, pp. 72–106.

Vallois, H. V. 1949: The Fontéchevade fossil man. Am. J. Phys. Anthrop., n.s. 7 : 339–362.

——— 1954: Neandertals and Praesapiens. J. Roy. Anthrop. Inst., 84 : 111–130.

——— 1956: Un nouvelle homme moustérien en Crimée: La squelette d'enfant de Starosel'je. L'Anthropologie, 59 : 555–560.

Vaufrey, R. 1939a.: Paléolithique et Mésolithique palestiniens. L'Anthropologie, 49 : 612–616.

——— 1939b.: Paléolithique et Mésolithique palestiniens. Révue scientifique, 77 : 390–406.

——— 1944: De prehistorica palestiniana. Les culturas del Paleolitico y mesolitico. Actas y mem. soc. esp. anthrop., etnog. y prehist., 19 : 85–110.

Virchow, R. 1892: Der Kiefer aus der Šipkahohle und der Kiefer von La Naulette. Zeits. f. Ethnologie, 14 : 277–310.

Vlcek, E. 1953: Nález neadertálskcho cloveka na Slovensku (Find of a Neandertal man in Slovakia). Slovenská Archeologia: Časopis Slovenskej Akadémie Vled, 1 : 1–132. Bratislava.

Weckler, J. E. 1954: The relationships between Neanderthal man and Homo sapiens. Am. Anthrop., 56 : 1003–1025.

Weidenreich, F. 1928: Die Morphologie des Schädels p. 43–138, in F. Wiegers, F. Weidenreich, E. Schuster. Der Schädelfund von Weimar-Ehringsdorf. Jena: Gustav Fischer.

——— 1945: The Paleolithic child from the Teshik-Tash cave in southern Uzbekistan (Central Asia). Am. J. Phys. Anthrop., n.s. 3 : 151–163.

Zeuner, F. E. 1938: Die Gliederung des Pleistozäns und des Paläolithikums in Palestina. Geol. Rundschau, 29 : 514–517.

——— 1940: The age of Neanderthal man, with notes on the Cotte de St. Brelade, Jersey, C. I. Occasional Papers, Inst. of Archaeol., Univ. of London, 3 : 1–20.

——— 1945. The Pleistocene period. Its climate, chronology and faunal successions. 322 pages. London: The Ray Society.

——— 1952: Dating the Past. An introduction to geochronology. Third edition, revised and enlarged. 495 pages. London: Methuen & Co.

Man's Power as a Predator: A Controversial Issue

U NLIKE OUR CLOSEST COUSINS THE APES, WE HUMAN BEINGS have depended upon hunting for a considerable part of our food supply for many hundreds of thousands of years. Chimpanzees in the wild appear delighted to add a bit of meat to their diet when they get the chance. They have been observed to hunt, in groups, for such prey as monkeys and other small creatures. But they are not really well-equipped, anatomically, to be predators; and the proportion of meat in their diet is very small indeed. Our ancestors, not much better equipped anatomically, long ago devised various cutting and piercing tools which enabled them to hunt more efficiently. Many anthropologists, of whom I am one, are convinced that this was one of the major factors leading to the differentiation between humans and apes. We really exploited an aspect of the environment which they neglected, and we became very powerful by doing so. Our ancestors learned how to hunt and kill very large animals a long time ago. There is no controversy about this.

There is controversy, however, about the results of human efficiency at hunting. Quite a few species of large animals whch had been hunted by humans became extinct within a relatively brief time toward the end of the last glaciation. What role, if any, did man play in the extinction of these creatures? We know that in recent times our species has exterminated quite a few animal species: the routine example is the dodo, a large, flightless, and apparently succulent species of pigeon which lived on the island of Mauritius in the Indian Ocean. But of course during recent centuries human hunters have had firearms, whereas during the Paleolithic the human arsenal was much more meager. Competent scholars have disagreed, sometimes quite violently, on the answer to the question: "Was man responsible for the extinction of the Pleistocene megafauna?" The following article by Professor A. J. Jelinek is about the most judicious review of this question which has come to my attention.

10. Arthur J. Jelinek

Man's Role in the Extinction of Pleistocene Faunas

Abstract. The extinction of the Pleistocene megafauna appears to have been due to a variety of causes. The lack of replacement of most forms suggests that unusual patterns of selection were responsible for the large-scale disappearance of these animals. In the periglacial areas of the Old World the lack of plant resources stimulated the development of a human technology oriented almost exclusively to animal resources. It appears likely that toward the end of the glaciation many elements of the megafauna in this area may have disappeared as a result of hunting practices in increasingly constricted habitats. In Africa, however, less severe climatic restrictions and abundant sources of vegetal foods for human populations may have aided the survival of the megafauna. A totally different situation may have prevailed in the New World, where the megafauna had evolved independent of human contact. Here the intrusion of man, as a new and formidable predator, into a natural community unprepared for this stress may have been basic to the extinction of many genera of the Pleistocene megafauna. A major obstacle, however, to attributing a key role to man in the extinction of the New World megafauna is the lack of direct evidence of human association with many of the extinct genera.

> We may infer from these facts, what havoc the introduction of a new beast of prey must cause in a country, before the instincts of the indigenous inhabitants have become adapted to the stranger's craft or power [Darwin, *Voyage of the Beagle,* 1845, p. 386].

The particular nature of the large-scale extinction of the Pleistocene Nearctic megafauna continues to present several puzzling aspects. The problem, in brief, is this: Why, after surviving a succession of four or more major glacial advances, do most elements of the large mammalian faunas of the Northern Hemisphere disappear during the retreat of the last glaciation? In the New World alone this extinction encompasses at least twenty-nine genera (Hibbard, 1958; Hibbard et al., 1965) including probiscideans, edentates, ungulates, and carnivores. In contrast, small mammals (in continental populations) are conspicuous by their apparent continuity, with only a few species known from the late Pleistocene that did not survive into the Holocene.

A further puzzling factor accompanying this extinction is the lack of ecological replacement of most forms (Martin, 1958, p. 402), indicating that biological competition was probably not the reason for their disappearance. Recent pollen evidence from western America (Kapp, 1965) seems to indicate that in at least some areas occupied by the extinct fauna the conditions following the retreat of an earlier glaciation (Illinoian) were probably more arid and as warm or warmer than at present. Thus conditions of temperature and aridity do not appear likely as direct causes of extinction.

The few areas of the world in which this late-Pleistocene extinction is not present include most of Africa, especially sub-Saharan Africa, and portions of southern Asia. In fact, in discussions of a possible human cause of the extinction, Africa is frequently cited as negative evidence: the long cultural record of peoples known to hunt large animals, coexistent with the abundant megafauna, seems to indicate that human effects on the fauna should have been seen there, if anywhere. The lack of such effects is taken as evidence that the presence of humans where extinction occurred is not sufficient cause to postulate their major role in the extinction. I believe that this argument for the elimination of man as a factor can be shown to be invalid on cultural and paleobotanical grounds, and that for these reasons Africa is not comparable to the areas of the Northern Hemisphere in which extinction occurred. The relatively even topography of much of Africa meant that, whereas broad areas of vegetational zones shifted with varying temperature and precipitation, the dramatic climatic pressures on the megafauna found in the Northern Hemisphere probably did not exist there, and the faunal elements followed these shifts more or less undisturbed. The relatively lush flora, especially of the pluvial periods and throughout the sequence, as compared to Europe and northern Asia, provided an important food source for African hominids in the course of their cultural development. The continuing importance of these food sources into the historic period is confirmed by ethnological accounts of food-collecting groups. In contrast, Europe during the Würm glaciation provided few resources other than meat for man north of the Mediterranean. As a result, with the appearance of *Homo sapiens* in Europe, perhaps 40,000 years ago, we see the development of a series of cultures (the Upper Paleolithic) overwhelmingly oriented to a carnivorous subsistence pattern. The technological complexity of these cultures for hunting and processing animals had no equal at that time, and in many ways it compares favorably with the native technology of the modern Eskimo, the only surviving culture with a carnivorous orientation as extreme as the Eurasian Upper Paleolithic.

The efficiency of these hunters is attested by such sites as Solutré in east-central France, where a late-Perigordian level is estimated to contain the remains of over 100,000 horses (MacCurdy, 1933, p. 173). The restricted orientation of subsistence activities is evinced by a concentration on animal representation in the art forms of these cultures to the exclusion of virtually all other naturalistic motifs (with the exception of women). The effectiveness of this cultural adjustment is attested by the relatively dense population of Europe by the time of the terminal Upper Paleolithic Magdalenian Culture (Sonneville-Bordes, 1963, p. 354), a density unparalleled in any earlier period. Certainly in Europe the role of man in the depletion of the Pleistocene fauna as it followed the retreating ice merits serious consideration.

This same adaptation to an Upper Paleolithic way of life spread across northern Asia and made it possible for *Homo sapiens* to cross the tundra of the Bering land bridge into the New World (Jelinek, 1965). On the basis of currently acceptable dated cultural evidence, this entry may have taken place as late as 15,000–12,000 B.C. (see also Haynes, 1967).

The first men to enter the New World were most certainly hunters, because no likely food sources but game existed for most of the year in the tundra areas they traversed. It seems most likely that they were of the same Upper Paleolithic cultural tradition as the very proficient and highly meat-oriented cultures of the rest of northern Eurasia. They were entering a continent where, in contrast to virtually all of the Old World north of Australia, the large herbivorous fauna *had evolved removed from human contact*. Is it not reasonable to expect, then, that the initial presence of man among the New World faunas caused no more fear among these animals than the initial presence of man among the Antarctic fauna? Is it not also probable that throughout man's initial expansion over the New World, the fauna was exceedingly vulnerable to human attack? To go one step farther, does this difference in cultural history explain the survival of species of horses, elephants, large pigs, and large camels in the Old World, groups totally lost in the New?

Charles Darwin, who was very much interested in extinction as an inevitable concomitant of evolution, was deeply impressed by the evidence of the extinction of the large fauna of the New World. In his journal of *The Voyage of the Beagle* he gives striking accounts of the tameness of the animals which the expedition found in isolated areas such as the Falklands and the Galápagos. He describes a fox that could be coaxed into range of a knife held in the hand, or birds that could be killed with a hat or walking stick. These same animals were skilled in avoiding their natural predators, but showed only curiosity at the presence of man. It is of interest to note that a species of goose was very easily captured in the Falklands, where man was absent, but was as elusive in Tierra del Fuego as the wild goose of England (Darwin, 1845, p. 383–86). How long does it take, through natural selection, for an animal species to acquire the ability to flee or seek concealment at the sight or scent of man?

Given this unique relationship with native resources and his carnivorous cultural heritage, as well as a total lack of demographic or serious climate barriers (with a dependence on the ubiquitous large animals), it is not strange to find man at the southern tip of South America well before 8000 B.C. (Rubin and Berthold, 1961, p. 96), four to seven thousand years after his entry via the Bering Strait. All these factors, in conjunction with known data on the spread of success-fully introduced mammalian species through an available habitat (such as

European *Equus* in the New World and *Lepus* in Australia), even if differences in generational span and locomotive patterns are considered, suggest that if the date of 8760 B.C. ± 300 from Fells Cave on the Strait of Magellan really represents the earliest arrival of man at the tip of South America, his entry into Alaska may well have been closer to 12,000 than 15,000 B.C.

The nature of the hunting implements of the earliest well-defined New World cultures seems also to favor the hypothesis of a vulnerable fauna. Most character- istic of these horizons are stone points which show marked grinding of the sharp lateral edges adjacent to the base. Grinding would prevent the edges of the point from cutting the lashing that bound it to a shaft if the point was subjected to repeated lateral stress. The most likely circumstance in which such stress could occur would be in a point on a thrusting spear or lance whose shaft remained in the hand of the hunter after it penetrated the animal—a technique that would be most effective against a relatively easy quarry and of little use against a skittish and fearful prey. The problem of the extinction of the larger elements of this fauna, however, cannot be explained, except perhaps in part, by this initial spread of man through the New World.

Man's entry coincides with a period of climatic stress accompanying the retreat of the glacial ice. By about 10,000 B.C. the cooler flora of the glacial period was noticeably on the wane in most of North America south of Canada, being re- placed by plant communities similar to the present potential vegetation. In several areas of arid western America we have evidence of large Pleistocene animals surviving into this period and existing on a diet of vegetation essentially similar to that in the area at present (Martin et al., 1961). This fact has been offered as evidence that the conditions of natural habitat in the West at 8000 to 10,000 B.C. represent a favorable environmental setting for such forms as *Nothrotherium*† (Martin et al., 1961), when in fact they may represent the barely tolerable condi- tions under which a few survivors were able to continue to exist as remnants of an originally larger population. A similar claim can be made for mammoth and other large forms surviving as relict populations in the vicinity of the few remain- ing sources of water and relatively lush vegetation. The introduction of man into such an assemblage of animals not yet adapted to his presence might well have resulted in the extermination of local populations of animals.

It should also be stressed that it is difficult to anticipate the way the presence of humans might have interfered with the normal life cycle of animals whose evolu- tion had proceeded independently of such contact. The basic necessity for water, and man's presence at water sources, for instance, might well have created con- siderable difficulties for western faunas. While these animals had certainly been adjusted to the activities of carnivores, man's patterns of activity were quite different. The use of fire could have had drastic effects, especially in grassland areas. The narrative of Cabeza de Vaca, the first account of the southern and southwestern Indians, relates that peoples of what is now southwest Texas were in the habit of burning favorable areas of range, not to drive the game, but to

† Extinct genus.

deprive the animals of forage and force them into areas where they could be hunted more successfully (Covey, 1961, p. 81). Use of fire in this manner contrasts sharply with the effects of natural random firing of the range encountered by the game prior to the arrival of man; it is of interest to speculate how early such a practice might have been followed by New World hunters, and in what areas. This kind of burning could have had a significant effect on the populations of large herbivores in these areas.

Such explanations are not so useful in accounting for extinction in eastern North America in this period. The wide range of many eastern forms, such as mastodon, mammoth, and the peccary *Mylohyus*†, as well as the relatively abundant vegetation and water in this area, seems to preclude any climatic explanation for their disappearance. It is probable that within the great breadth of the natural habitat of these forms there occurred some zone in which the effects of Slaughter's proposed heat sterility and cold infanticide would not have been effective (Slaughter, 1966, 1967).

Throughout the New World one major puzzle exists with regard to linking man with the extinction. This is the absence of direct evidence of human activity associated with the remains of extinct animals. In fact, we have kill sites with implements in association with partially articulated skeletons for only one of the many genera that disappeared in western North America and Mexico—*Mammuthus*†. Several extinct species of bison are known in the same context; however, here the genus was successful in survival. Several extinct genera are linked to human activity on somewhat less secure grounds. These include *Equus, Nothrotherium, Paramylodon, Camelops, Tetrameryx,* and *Breameryx,* of which teeth or isolated bones have been reported from deposits containing cultural materials. Inasmuch as this type of vertebrate material has been shown to be derived from an earlier context in at least one instance (Jelinek and Fitting, 1963, p. 534) and exists in some abundance in earlier deposits near other postulated contexts of association, I feel that a demonstration of man's utilization of these forms is still to be made.

In this connection it may be helpful to consider the problems of preservation. Through much of western North America, deposits of the approximate age of the extinction are widely scattered and are frequently confined to a restricted set of environmental origins. The nature of the geologic record in most areas precludes the possibility of preservation of sediments and fossils from all but the lowest topographic levels of any particular age. Thus most of the events of this period are lost, and those recorded are only a very small selection, in deposits containing fossils that were fortuitously covered shortly after deposition and have recently been exposed by erosion or excavation. One area favorable for the preservation of relatively large numbers of animals is the northeastern United States, where an abundance of bogs in glaciated terrain serves as a repository for the remains of numerous mastodons and lesser numbers of mammoths, musk-oxen, and other forms. Although over 160 finds of *Mammut*† have been reported from Michigan alone (Skeels, 1962), not one specimen from Michigan or any other area of the eastern United States has yet been demonstrated in clear association with human artifacts or evidence of human alteration. The contemporaneity of man and these animals seems assured, however (Griffin, 1965, p. 657), and the most likely explanation for the lack of association of artifacts would seem to be that in this area man deliberately ignored the megafauna in favor of smaller, less dangerous, and perhaps more palatable animals. The only identifiable bone fragment from a site approximating this age in the East is from southern Michigan and assigned to *Rangifer arcticus,* the barren-ground caribou (Cleland, 1965). While the extinction of the larger forms in the east is puzzling, the extinction of *Mylohyus*†, a woodland peccary of smaller size than the surviving Cervidae, is even more so. Its ubiquitous distribution and probably omnivorous diet would also seem to have favored survival. It is possible that its habitat and diet coincided too closely with that of man.

In summary, while recent evidence indicates that climate was undoubtedly an important element in the extinction of the Nearctic Pleistocene megafauna, such factors as the survival of these genera under generally comparable conditions in earlier periods suggests that climate alone cannot be responsible. There is still no conclusive evidence that seasonal temperature fluctuations and annual temperature averages following the last glaciation were unlike those of earlier interglacials, and it is apparent that not all accessible habitats were made untenable by the factors that Slaughter suggests. The different times of extinction of the same species in different areas (Jelinek, 1957, p. 232) can be cited against any possible invoked catastrophe. Barring as yet undiscovered evidence of general pathologies, except in the case of the Old World *Ursus arctos spelaeus* (Kurtén, 1958), *Homo sapiens* remains as a new element in the environment, with a formidable potential for disruption, whether directly as an extremely efficient and rapidly expanding predator group, against whom no evolved defense systems were available, or indirectly as the source of profound changes in ecology already under the process of adjustment as a result of considerable climatic stress.

REFERENCES

Benninghoff, W. S., and Hibbard, C. W., 1961, Fossil pollen associated with a late-glacial woodland musk ox in Michigan: *Michigan Acad. Sci. Pap.,* v. *46,* p. 155–59

Cleland, C. E., 1965, Barren ground caribou (*Rangifer arcticus*) from an early man site in Southeastern Michigan: *Amer. Antiq.,* v. *30,* p. 350–51

Covey, C., *Editor,* 1961, *Cabeza de Vaca's adventures in the unknown interior of America:* New York, Collier, 152 p.

Darwin, Charles, 1845, *The Voyage of the Beagle:* London, Everyman ed., 1906, 496 p.

Griffin, J. B., 1965, Late Quaternary prehistory in the northeastern woodland p. 655–67, *in* Wright, H. E., Jr., and Frey, D. G., *Editors, The Quaternary of the United States*: Princeton Univ. Press, 922 p.

Haynes, C. V., Jr., 1967, Carbon-14 dates and Early Man in the New World: Pleistocene Extinctions, Vol. 6 of the Proceedings of the VII Congress of the International Association for Quaternary Research, P. S. Martin and H. E. Wright, eds., Yale Univ. Press, New Haven, pp. 267–286

Hibbard, C. W., 1958, Summary of North American Pleistocene mammalian local faunas: *Michigan Acad. Sci. Pap.*, v. *43*, p. 3–32

Hibbard, C. W., Ray, C. E., Savage, D. E., Taylor D. W., and Guilday, J. E., 1965, Quaternary mammals of North America, p. 509–25, *in* Wright, H. E., Jr., and Frey, D. G., *Editors, The Quaternary of the United States:* Princeton Univ. Press, 922 p.

Jelinek, A. J., 1957, Pleistocene faunas and early man: *Michigan Acad. Sci. Pap.*, v. *42*, p. 225–37

——— 1965, The Upper Paleolithic revolution and the peopling of the New World: *Michigan Archaeologist*, v. *11*, p. 85–88

Jelinek, A. J., and Fitting, J. E., 1963, Some studies of natural radioactivity in archaeological and paleontological materials: *Michigan Acad. Sci. Pap.*, v. *48*, p. 531–40

Kapp, R. O., 1965, Illinoian and Sangamon vegetation in southwestern Kansas and adjacent Oklahoma: *Univ. Michigan Mus. Paleont. Contrib.*, v. *19*, p. 167–225

Kurtén, B., 1958, Life and death of the Pleistocene cave bear: *Acta Zool. Fennica*, v. *95*, p. 1–59

MacCurdy, G. G., 1933, *Human origins*, v. *1*: New York, Appleton–Century, 440 p.

Martin, P. S., 1958, Pleistocene ecology and biogeography of North America, p. 375–420, *in* Hubbs, C. L., *Editor, Zoogeography:* Amer. Assoc. Adv. Sci. Publ. *51*, 510 p.

Martin, P. S., Sabels, B. E., and Shutler, D., Jr., 1961, Rampart cave coprolite and ecology of the Shasta ground sloth: *Amer. Jour. Sci.*, v. *259*, p. 102–27

Rubin, M., and Berthold, S., 1961, U.S. Geological Survey radiocarbon dates VI: *Radiocarbon*, v. *3*, p. 86–98

Semken, H. A., Miller, B. B., and Stevens, J. B., 1964, Late Wisconsin woodland musk oxen in association with pollen and invertebrates from Michigan: *Jour. Paleont.*, v. *38*, p. 823–35

Skeels, M. A., 1962, The mastodons and mammoths of Michigan: *Michigan Acad. Sci Papers*, v. *47*, p. 101–33

Slaughter, B. H., 1966, An ecological interpretation of the Brown Sand Wedge local fauna, Black-water Draw, New Mexico, and a hypothesis concerning late Pleistocene extinction, *in* Wendorf, F., and Hester, J. J., Assemblers, *Paleoecology of the Llano Estacado*, vol. 2: Santa Fe, Fort Burgwin Res. Center

——— 1967, Animal ranges as a clue to late-Pleistocene extinction: Pleistocene Extinctions, Vol. 6 of the Proceedings of the VII Congress of the International Association for Quaternary Research, P. S. Martin and H. E. Wright, eds., Yale Univ. Press, New Haven, pp. 267–286

Sonneville-Bordes, D., 1963, Upper Paleolithic cultures in western Europe: *Science*, v. *142*, p. 347–55

Adaptation to Climatic Differences

E VEN DURING THE PALEOLITHIC, AS WE HAVE SEEN, THERE was considerable variation in anatomical traits within the human species. Among living peoples it is clear that the same thing is true. Anyone can see that Chinese, Swedes, and Nigerians are quite dissimilar in appearance. Are these differences more than skin-deep? How have they come about? These are reasonable questions to ask, and it would be most helpful to learn the answers. During the earlier part of the present century, most anthropologists seemed content to accept such local differences in physique and appearance as being due to "race" but this explained nothing. Calling geographical varieties "races"—or calling them anything else—does not tell us why or how they became different from each other.

More recently, however, our increasing knowledge of genetics and our growing awareness of adaptive evolutionary processes have enabled us to think about human biology more clearly. Many of the earlier naturalists, even before Darwin, had attributed differences in physique and proportions, both in our own species and in others, to the influence of climate. During the 1920s it was suggested, on the basis of data collected from all parts of the world, that narrow nostrils have been selected for in frigid areas, and broad nostrils in torrid regions. By the 1950s, studies based on the idea that human variations are a consequence of adaptation to local conditions began to become popular. This following article, "Basal Metabolism, Race and Climate" by Professor D. F. Roberts, is a statistical survey of world-wide variations in an important aspect of human physiology.

11. D. F. Roberts

Basal Metabolism, Race and Climate

INTRODUCTION

The following study forms part of an extensive investigation into the physical characters of man in the light of environmental influence, a systematic attempt to evaluate, by the appraisal of data in terms of Place, the ecological significance of those characters about which information has been accumulated by students of physical anthropology. The present communication deals with basal metabolic rate.

The method comprises two complementary stages. The data are first examined cartographically, in order to allow the easier selection of those environmental features which appear to be influential, and subsequently more refined statistical methods are applied. To obtain dependable results, as in other comparative methods, all data which are not strictly comparable must be excluded.

Basal metabolism may, for present purposes, be defined as the minimal level of heat production of the body when it is at rest (not asleep), is not engaged in heavy digestive processes (*i.e.,* is in a post-absorptive condition), and is not undergoing marked mental activity or emotional stress. It is conventionally measured under temperature conditions of 20° C. It represents the total energy utilized in maintaining those body states and processes (*e.g.* body temperature, glandular activity, respiration, circulation, peristalsis, muscle tone) necessary to animal life.

It has been shown that heat production, like other biological characters, varies both in a given individual and from one individual to another. Both forms of variability can be represented by a Gaussian curve (Berkson and Boothby, 1938). Although the heat production of the human body may be measured directly, such direct calorimetry requires elaborate apparatus: the simpler indirect methods of calculation, from the respiratory exchange of gases, are more suitable for field work since the necessary apparatus is compact and portable. By the latter methods the amount of heat produced is computed usually from the amount of oxygen absorbed, rarely from the amount of carbon dioxide eliminated, sometimes from both.

The problem then may be stated thus: Do racial differences exist in basal heat production, and if so, to what extent may they be attributed to differences in climatic environment?

All available literature dealing with basal metabolic rate was examined. Data were thus collected relating to over two hundred human groups of varying race, sex, age, habits, etc., living in diverse parts of the world and under diverse climatic conditions.

DIFFICULTIES

Initially, a number of attendant difficulties have to be recognized and allowance made for them. They may be discussed under the following four headings:

1. *Presentation of material.* The material is presented in a variety of forms, which often prevents direct comparison. Frequently the figures are published in an unreduced condition, in which case it was necessary to calculate statistical constants. In the majority of cases where averages are given, measures of dispersion are not, so that it is not at present feasible to compare variabilities. Results are quoted in two ways in the literature:

(*a*) The actual figures may be given, in terms of O_2 consumed per minute, of heat production (Calories) per unit time, or of heat production per unit body surface area (or per unit weight or per unit stature) per unit time.

(*b*) The results may be referred to a standard and expressed as a percentage deviation from it. The standards in general use relate to Europeans dwelling either in western Europe or in the U.S.A., of known sex and age; the norms in common use include the Aub-Dubois (1917) and its modified form, the Harris-Benedict (1919), the Dreyer (1920), the Krogh (1925), and that of Boothby, Berkson and Dunn (1936), otherwise the Mayo Clinic. Since these standards are related to different physical characteristics or different mathematical coefficients for a given characteristic, they are not comparable save in a general way. Such is the precision of some investigators that occasionally the standard used is not specified, the result being given as a percentage of "normal" or "European." The values relating to any particular sample may be expressed in all, several, or any one of these terms, according to the inclination of the investigator.

This difficulty has been met by elimination of the less appropriate expressions and subdivision of the remainder into groups, each containing comparable data, which were then examined independently. It is interesting to note the emphasis on deviation from standards in the publication of results relating to different races. It would appear preferable and more logical in racial matters to use the actual figures, since this avoids the probably inaccurate premise that the variation of basal metabolic rate with age is similar in all races; the results of Genna (1938), shown in Fig. 1, seem to support this criticism. In the use of surface area

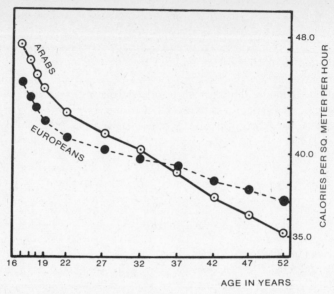

Fig.1.   Racial differences in changes in basal metabolic rate with age (after Genna, 1938).

it must be remembered that what is measured is not heat production in relation to actual surface, but heat production in relation to an estimate of surface by means of a mathematical function of height and weight (*e.g.* the Dubois formula); therefore, in racial matters, caution is necessary since it has yet to be shown that the relation of height and weight to surface area is constant for the different physiques observed among races.

2. *Apparatus used.* Another preliminary consideration is the extent to which the results are comparable as regards the apparatus used. Little work has been done on the comparison of absolute values obtained by different types of apparatus, their variability, and the frequency and magnitude of error. No fewer than 20 different named varieties of apparatus were used to determine the values dealt with here, and few investigators, especially in the earlier days, took the precaution of calibrating their apparatus or simply checking their results by alternative methods.

Comparative studies have, however, occasionally been made. Almeida (1924) compared his results obtained with the Tissot apparatus with those found with the Zuntz-Geppert type, and claimed that the latter caused exaggeration in some cases by as much as 17 per cent. Hindmarsh (1927) reviewed the three types of apparatus, closed circuit, open circuit (gravimetric) and open circuit (volumetric), and found that error tended to be greater in the closed circuit type (small leaks are magnified five times, since it is the volume of O_2, and not of total air, that is measured); while the third type of apparatus, *e.g.* the Douglas bag/ Haldane gas analysis, was the most accurate and gave the least variable results. Radsma (1931) gave figures determined with the Knipping and Douglas/

Haldane apparatus, the former appearing to be slightly but not significantly higher. Finally MacGregor and Loh (1940), after calibrating their spirometer, found that results obtained by the Benedict spirometer agreed with those of the Douglas/Haldane apparatus.

In short, in the subsequent analysis, the possibility of error due to apparatus must be borne in mind, since it is not feasible to eliminate it.

3. *Technique used.* That techniques are not always comparable is obvious from the fact that different workers obtain different results for the same population. Technical points to consider are whether check tests are performed by alternative means, how many times the determination is repeated to ensure the minimum level, which of such determinations are included in the final calculation, and whether conditions are definitely basal (*e.g.* the length of time since the last meal and its protein content). An extremely important though frequently unrecorded factor is the ambient temperature during the experiment.

4. *Nature of the sample.* When a particular worker using a constant technique obtains different results from samples drawn from a single population, the nature of the sample is clearly the deciding factor. It is remarkable that few investigators of heat production values have succeeded in obtaining samples which would be considered of adequate size for anthropometric purposes. The smaller the sample, the less reliable is its mean as an estimate of the mean of the population sampled; the results of many of the investigations, therefore, may not be relied upon. Incomparability on grounds of sex and age has been overcome by examining separately the results for each sex, and restricting consideration to adults aged between 20 and 50, since variation in basal metabolic rate between these ages is slight. While functional abnormality cannot be completely excluded as a possible source of variation, error on this account may be neglected if the investigator has visually examined the subjects and noted their temperatures, pulse rates, etc. It is more difficult to eliminate error due to their emotional condition, especially among primitive peoples examined by an unfamiliar observer. Few reports include details of the daily habits of the groups examined, though the position is rather better as regards the nature of their diets. Finally, many observers fail to state the area of provenance of the subjects or, more unforgivable from the anthropological point of view, describe but loosely their racial affinities; for example, the number of references to "Orientals" or "Indians" is astounding. Physiologists about to embark upon investigation of non-European peoples would be well advised to consult anthropological authorities as to their terms of reference.

GENERAL RESULTS

It has been usual, in comparative racial studies of basal metabolic rate, to tabulate deviations from "normal" standards and to suggest that variations in such figures represent possible racial differences. To indicate a line of approach to the present problem, all available deviations (154) for adults were translated into seven categories varying from "very high" to "very low," since it is only by the use of such general terminology that results expressed in relation to the various norms in current use may be equated. These categories represented 6 per cent. intervals on the Harris-Benedict scale, "medium" indicating −3 to +3, "high" +9 to +15, "very low" less than −15, and the other gradations similarly. Into this scale, results expressed in other standards were fitted by general considerations; the inter-standard correction factors of Jenkins (1931) could not be used, as slight coincidence was found between them and the differences actually observed when a particular result was referred to more than one standard. The data thus classified were then mapped, different symbols representing basal metabolic rate levels. The results (83) for indigenous groups are shown in Fig. 2, and those (71) for non-

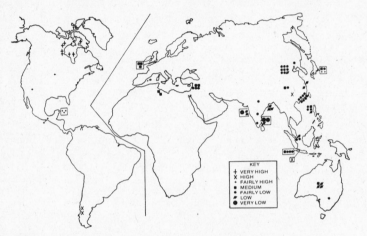

Fig. 2.   Distribution of basal metabolism in indigenous populations.

indigenous groups in Fig. 3. On account of the difficulties in comparison already outlined, it is possible to draw only limited general conclusions from these maps.

"Very high" basal metabolic rates are seen to occur only in arctic regions, and "high" levels only in the temperate regions of central Chile, Kweichow, and the mountainous areas of central Java. "Fairly high" levels do not occur within the tropics except in American Indian samples; these are, however, the lowest values recorded among New World indigenous peoples. Although for Europeans "medium" basal metabolic rates are demonstrated at all latitudes from that of temperate London to equatorial Batavia, in tropical regions lower levels predominate (in two cases "very low"). "Very low" levels do not occur outside the tropics save in the case of a single small European group at New Orleans (due in this instance to the use of minimum, instead of mean, basal readings). In India, European samples give results higher than those of local native inhabitants; in America, American indigenous peoples give higher results than do Europeans. The general level for Mongoloid peoples appears to be "medium" to "low," except where altitude interferes.

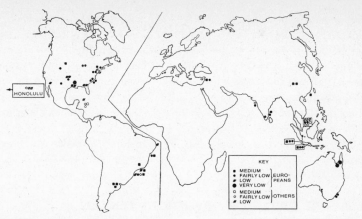

Fig. 3. Distribution of basal metabolism in non-indigenous populations.

From these very general preliminary maps, it was suggested that basal meta-bolic rate appeared to vary with altitude and latitude, and a certain amount of racial influence could also be postulated. Environmental temperature is also largely influenced by altitude and latitude, and further investigation into its relationship with basal metabolic rate, it seemed, might well be profitable. The maps make it abundantly clear that investigations into basal metabolic rate have so far been made only in a limited number of areas and on a small number of races, many of which are represented by samples of urban populations. Africa is an unexplored field, so is most of South America and Asia. Therefore any conclu-sions drawn from available data can only be tentative.

The material was then subdivided into more comparable groups. To ascertain that the suggested temperature relationship was not due to the method of con-struction of the maps, the first sub-group of data was considered. This related to adult male samples examined in the regions to which their parent populations are indigenous, conditions being stated explicitly as basal for each; their heat pro-duction could be expressed in terms of total Calories per 24 hours. This, the absolute value most frequently reported or obtainable from other figures given, was sometimes of necessity calculated from mean and not individual records; in these calculations differences in diet were taken into account by including such information as was provided on the respiratory quotient.

The means of these 37 comparable samples again suggested a relationship with mean annual temperature.[1] For example, in the New World, Chippewa Indians and Eskimos in the neighbourhood of Hudson Bay, with a mean annual temperature of less than 20° F., have a daily basal Calorie production of over

[1] Mean annual temperature is obtained in several ways, either from diurnal means, or from monthly means derived from them; diurnal means are calculated from the maximum and mini-mum temperatures, from regular readings at fixed hours, or from a combination of both, *e.g.*,

$$\frac{max. + min.}{2}, \quad \frac{9h + 21h}{2}, \quad \frac{7 + 13 + 21}{3}, \quad \frac{7 + 18 + max. + min.}{4}$$

all of which yield similar results.

1,800; Mapuche Indians in central Chile with a mean annual temperature of 53° F. have a Calorie production of 1,700 to 1,800; Maya Quiche Indians at high altitudes in Guatemala, where the mean annual temperature is 55° F., have a Calorie production of 1,600 to 1,700, while members of the same race occupied as planters on the lower hill slopes where the mean annual temperature is 76° have a Calorie production of 1,500 to 1,600; Maya Indians in Yucatan with a mean annual temperature of 80° F. have a Calorie production in the neighbourhood of 1,500.

The evaluation of this relationship by statistical methods was therefore undertaken.[2]

ANALYSIS OF DATA FOR INDIGENOUS GROUPS

Total Calorie Production and Mean Annual Temperature

1. *Results*. Temperature figures were obtained for each experimental locality, in some cases from the records of a local meteorological station, in others by interpolation from those of the nearest stations, after allowing for influences of altitude, latitude and other geographical factors.

Initially the degree of association, and its reliability, between the two variables was examined by calculating the correlation coefficient *r*, which for the 37 male

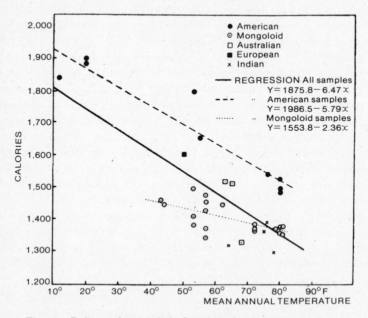

Fig. 4. Relationship of daily basal total calorie production to mean annual temperature: male indigenous populations.

[2] Statistical methods used throughout this study may be referred to in Snedecor (1946).

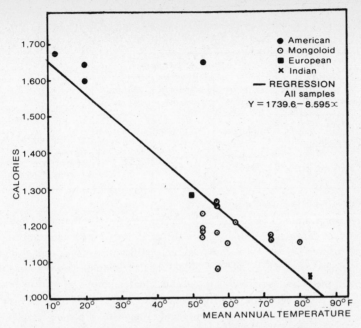

Fig. 5. Relationship of daily basal total calorie production to mean annual temperature: female indigenous populations.

samples proved to be −0.736, significant at 0.1 per cent. The relationship appearing linear, the regression line of Calories on temperature was fitted by the method of least squares (Fig. 4), with the regression coefficient b at a value of −6.47. A confirmatory result (Fig. 5) was obtained from the 21 similar samples relating to females, with $r = −0.845$, $b = −8.595$, significant at 0.1 per cent. Thus the indigenous groups exhibit a marked inverse relationship between their daily basal Calorie production and the mean annual temperature of the area in which they live.

These samples were drawn from a number of races representing several of the great varieties of *Homo sapiens*. It was necessary to enquire whether any variation in basal metabolism could be associated with or explained by the fact that a particular sample was drawn from a particular variety of man—in fact to separate variation on this account from the total, in order to arrive at a more accurate estimate of the temperature relationship. The indigenous samples were assigned, on the basis of affinities of morphology and ABO blood groups, to groups termed for present purposes Mongoloid, American (American Indian and Eskimo), European and Australian (aboriginal); and, for lack of more explicit description, all samples investigated in the Indian subcontinent were called Indian.

Analysis of covariance produced a number of interesting suggestions. Comparison of adjusted means, *i.e.*, after allowance had been made for the relationship with temperature (Table 1), indicated a high probability (at 0.1 per cent.) that differences in level of daily basal Calorie production among varieties were not due to chance. Varieties also appeared to vary in their responses to given temperature

TABLE 1. *Covariance analysis.   Test of significance of adjusted group means.*

Source of variation	Errors of Estimate			
	Sum of squares	Degrees of freedom	Mean square	
Total	406048	35		
Within groups	97625	31	3149	F = 24·48 significant at 0·1 per cent.
Among groups	308423	4	77106	

differences, since among the regression coefficients occurred differences significant at 0.1 per cent. Further, within varieties the relationship with temperature was again very marked ($r = -0.828$, $b = -4.642$, significant at 0.1 per cent.); indeed, by eliminating the variability due to the inclusion of samples drawn from different varieties, the relationship with mean annual temperature was seen to become more marked. It is regrettable that so few samples are available for each of the varieties; only the Mongoloid with twenty and American with nine samples may be regarded as at all adequate for curve fitting, the statistics obtained being shown in Table 2. There are differences significant at 0.1 per cent. between the regression

TABLE 2. *Relationship in Mongoloid and American groups of total basal Calorie production per diem and mean annual temperature*

Group	No. of samples	r	b	Significant at
Mongoloid	20	− 0·668	− 2·36	1 per cent.
American	9	− 0·953	− 5·79	0·1 per cent.

coefficients and between the adjusted means of these two varieties. It is interesting to note that the Miao of Kweichow, whose high positive deviation, contrasting with the low negative deviations of other Mongoloids, provoked some ingenious theorizing,[3] fall into their expected relationship with other Mongoloid results when total Calorie production and temperature are considered.

Data relating to females are too few to allow a satisfactory similar investigation of intravarietal regression. The occurrence of differences significant at 0.1 per cent. among adjusted means of varieties, however, seems to support the conclusion

---

[3] Kilborn and Benedict (1937) suggested that similar features of Miao and Maya political histories were accompanied by physiological parallels.

that there are differences in basal metabolic level among varieties not accountable by temperature influence.

2. *Discussion*. Although the statistical results are encouraging, the paucity of strictly comparable, adequately controlled samples induces caution in their interpretation. For the moment it must suffice to suggest that levels of mean basal total heat production, for a given mean environmental temperature, differ for different varieties of man, decreasing in the order American, European, Mongoloid, with the Indian series at the same level as the last; that within each variety there is a marked inverse relationship between mean basal total heat production and mean annual temperature of the area which the group inhabits, sufficient to account for many of the differences in basal metabolism that have been taken to be racial or intravarietal; and that between at least two of these varieties there is a difference in response to a given temperature difference.

The question now arises whether the correlation between basal metabolic rate and mean temperature is false, whether the heat production results do not depend rather on actual temperature conditions under which the experiments were done, which would themselves be related to mean annual temperature. Unfortunately comparatively few reports include the ambient temperature of the experiment, and of those, several state the outside temperature and add that the subjects were well blanketed and comfortable. It is, therefore, not feasible to examine the immediate environmental temperatures of the present samples. The following considerations, however, all point in one direction:

(*a*) The fact that the subjects were well blanketed where necessary reduces the possible range of immediate environmental temperature.

(*b*) Gagge, Winslow and Herrington (1938) showed experimentally no change in heat production of given individuals over a temperature range 60° F. to 103° F., though a tendency to increase was observed at lower temperatures in the clothed (not blanketed) subject. Of the samples at present considered, basal metabolism of ten Mongoloid groups, within the mean annual temperature range 62° F. to 81° F., gave a correlation coefficient with mean annual temperature $r = -0.805$, significant at 1 per cent., and the corresponding figure for five American Indian groups, within the range 55° F. to 80° F., was $r = -0.966$, also significant at 1 per cent.

(*c*) No seasonal fluctuations in basal metabolism were found by Tilt and Walters (1935), Benedict, Kung and Wilson (1937), or MacGregor and Loh (1940), while Gustafson and Benedict (1928) found in 20 individuals lower results in the cool season, and Necheles (1928) a lower result in a single individual in the warm season.

In the samples now considered, therefore, it may not be unreasonable to infer that the immediate environmental temperature of the determinations is of less importance in the correlations here found than the average temperatures to which the subjects are accustomed.

Differences of apparatus and of individual technique do not appear to have greatly influenced the regression lines as drawn. Crile and Quiring (1939) used a

Jones apparatus to obtain Eskimo, Chippewa, and both groups of Maya Quiche results; the curve obtained from these results is in slope and position very similar to that obtained for the other American populations by other workers using different kinds of apparatus. No single type of apparatus has been exclusively used in investigating any one variety.

The effect of diet on basal metabolic rate is a question which is not yet satisfactorily settled. Assuming that conditions are truly basal, *i.e.,* post-absorptive, the general opinion would seem to be that the everyday diet has little effect. For example, Benedict and Roth, confirmed by Harris and Benedict (1919), found no significant difference between the metabolism of vegetarians and non-vegetarians; Beard (1927) and Brooks (1929) both found constant dietary habits as regards protein among American college students in different parts of the U.S.A. although their basal metabolic rates varied; Wang and Hawks *et al.* (1930) found that feeding females on experimental diets over test periods produced no marked difference in basal metabolism; Hetler, Killinger and Plant (1932) found no significant relationship between basal metabolic rate and protein intake, nor did Radsma and Streef (1932) and Oliveiro (1937). With this consensus of views the present results would seem to be in accord. Although Eskimo and Chippewa samples, living under similar temperature conditions, have similar basal metabolic rates, there is a difference in the proportionate amounts of animal protein consumed. Both the Mapuche diet and that of the Central American Indians are poor in protein, but their Calorie production differs considerably. The slope of the American regression is scarcely altered if the high protein groups are omitted. As regards the Mongoloid regression, the Miao diet is largely cereal: the Chinese both of north and south, and the Japanese, use only small amounts of meat and animal products. Since the consumption of animal protein, very low by European standards, of all the present Mongoloid groups may be regarded as comparable, the slope of the curve in this instance obviously cannot be attributed to different amounts of animal protein in the diet.

Calorie Production per Unit Weight in Relation to Mean Annual Temperature

To what extent are these differences in heat production due to differences in body size? When weight was taken into account and correlation made between mean annual temperature and heat production expressed per unit weight, the male samples suggested a more scattered distribution about a more horizontal line (Fig. 6); nevertheless, for the 29 samples, the resulting statistics were $r = -0.430$ significant at 2 per cent., $b = -0.054$. This correlation coefficient compared with that found for total basal Calorie production ($r = -0.736$), indicates a clear decrease in the degree of relationship between the two variables. Comparison of the regression coefficients, after the necessary allowance has been made for the change of unit, shows a marked flattening of slope of the regression line. In subsequent covariance analysis, comparison of adjusted means indicated that in Calorie production per unit weight there are differences significant at 5 per cent. among

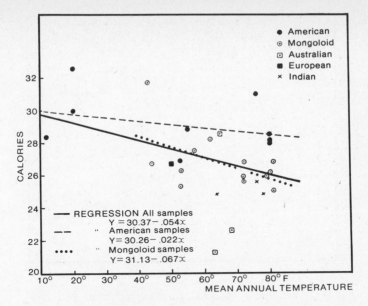

Fig. 6. Relationship of basal calorie production per kilogram body weight per diem to mean annual temperature:
male indigenous populations.

varieties which are not attributable to temperature influence. Within varieties,
however, the relationship between temperature and Calorie production per unit
weight, if the low significance level is admissible, is but slight ($r = -0.329$ significant at 10 per cent., $b = -0.033$), and among the regression coefficients of the
varieties there is no difference which can be regarded as significant. Statistics for
the two adequate intravarietal relationships are shown in Table 3.

When the female samples were considered (Fig. 7), the values found were $r = -0.644$ and $b = -0.083$, significant at 1 per cent. Analysis of covariance of the few
female data tended to confirm the slightness of the relationship within varieties
between heat production per unit weight and mean annual temperature ($r =$

TABLE 3. *Relationship of production of Calories per kilogram
per diem with mean annual temperature in Mongoloid and
American groups*

Group	No. of samples	r	b	Significant at
Mongoloid ..	13	-0.544	-0.067	10 per cent.
American ..	9	-0.356	-0.022	Not.

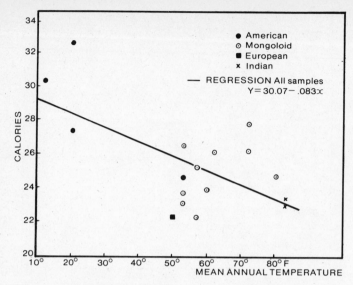

Fig. 7. Relationship of basal calorie production per kilogram body weight per diem to mean annual temperature: female indigenous populations.

—0.248, $b = $ —0.046, not significant), and indicated no significant differences among varieties. The flattening of the slope of the regression is again marked.

After consideration of the weight factor, then, it is suggested that intrinsic differences in basal metabolism exist among the varieties of man, irrespective of the influence of weight and temperature. The approach of the regression of heat production per unit weight towards a horizontal condition, both within varieties and when all samples are considered, may be interpreted as indicating that weight in indigenous populations has in some way become adjusted to environmental mean temperature conditions. This adjustment in turn would account for many of the differences in heat production observed among races. In other words the pattern, previously found, relating total basal Calorie production to mean annual temperature is seemingly attributable to the following factors: (*a*) the samples are drawn from different varieties of man, differing in their responses to temperature differences and in levels of response, but within the varieties the total Calorie output is closely related to temperature; (*b*) this relationship is achieved in part by an apparent adjustment of weight to environmental temperature, and in part by variation in output of Calories per unit weight.

Multiple Correlations

At this point it seemed imperative, on account of the number of relationships involved, to clarify the position by examining the inter-relationships of heat production, weight, stature and temperature, and to determine the relative effects of the last three factors. Analysis by multiple correlation of those 30 samples of male indigenous groups for which weight and stature were given produced the following total correlation coefficients:

TABLE 4.   *Total correlation coefficients of Calorie production, temperature, stature and weight*

—	Mean temperature	Stature	Weight
Correlation of total Calorie production with	− 0·773	− 0·173	+ 0·693
Correlation of weight with	− 0·573	+ 0·320	
Correlation of stature with	− 0·065		

The correlations of Calorie production with mean annual temperature and weight were significant at 1 per cent., of weight with mean annual temperature at 5 per cent. From these figures the following "prediction" formula was calculated:

$$Y = 2872.5 - 4.29T - 13.23S + 19.22W$$

where Y is daily basal Calorie production, T is mean annual temperature in degrees Fahrenheit, S is stature in centimetres, and W is weight in kilograms. Thus a negative difference of 50 Calories in mean daily basal heat production would be expected in association with any of the following: a positive difference of 11.7° F., or of 3.8 cm. stature, or a negative difference of 2.6 kg. weight.

Since, for example, there was a marked correlation between weight and mean annual temperature and between heat production and weight, it was of interest to know whether the high correlation between heat production and temperature was due rather to weight than to temperature. To determine the individual effects of the various factors, *partial* correlation coefficients were calculated, the following being significant at 1 per cent.:

TABLE 5.   *Partial correlation coefficients of daily basal Calorie production with temperature, stature and weight*

—	Mean temperature	Stature	Weight
Partial correlation of Calorie production with	− 0·679	− 0·631	+ 0·687

These may be interpreted as indicating marked independent linear relationships of heat production with each of the three factors; that, for example, the relationship with climate remains after the influence of physique has been eliminated. They show that for independent estimation of heat production, mean environmental temperature, formerly neglected in predicting "normal" values, is as useful as weight, while stature is slightly though not significantly less so. Comparison of the standard partial regression coefficients of Calorie production on each of the three factors illustrates this perhaps more clearly:

TABLE 6. *Standard partial regression coefficients of Calorie production on temperature, stature and weight*

—	Mean temperature	Stature	Weight
Standard partial regression coefficient of Calorie production on	− 0·493	− 0·375	+ 0·530

The degree of association of heat production and these factors in combination is interesting: the multiple correlation coefficient between Calorie production, weight and mean annual temperature was found to be 0.831, and when stature was included the value rose to 0.902, 30 samples being used in each case. It was therefore not surprising that the observed results showed fairly close agreement with those predicted for each sample from the formula. The Mongoloid series showed a predominance of values lower than predicted, the American series a predominance of higher values, suggesting that differences between these two varieties previously demonstrated in this study remain when stature is taken into account.

To the multiple correlation calculations was finally added the further climatic factor, relative humidity. This showed no significant correlation with basal metabolic rate, and no significant rise in the multiple correlation coefficient occurred. The evidence thus appears as yet inadequate to evaluate any humidity effect, on account either of the small number of samples, or of the difficulty of obtaining sufficiently accurate relative humidity values.

Calorie Production per Unit Surface Area and Mean Annual Temperature

In dealing with Calorie production per unit surface area, the same statistical procedure was used as in the examination of heat production per unit weight. Consideration of male samples gave, for the relationship between environmental temperature and production of Calories per square metre, values of $r = -0.644$, $b = -0.156$, significant at 0.1 per cent. (Fig. 8). After elimination of the variation

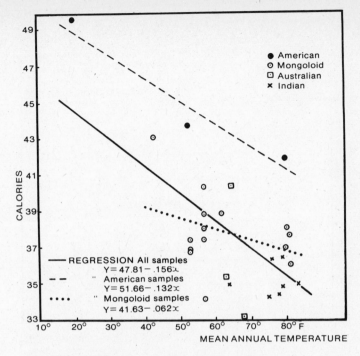

Fig. 8. Relationship of basal calorie production per square metre body surface per hour to mean annual temperature: male indigenous populations.

due to varieties, these values were reduced to $r = -0.528$, $b = -0.090$, significant at 1 per cent. Differences among varieties in the levels of heat production per unit surface area were significant at 0.1 per cent., but there were no significant differences among the regression coefficients. The few female results are shown in Fig. 9.

Climate and Body Shape

An interesting implication is now apparent, concerning the relationship between climate and body shape. The more nearly spherical a shape, the smaller the surface area in relation to its volume. The volume of the human body is not satisfactorily predictable, but for present purposes it may be considered proportionate to weight. It has been shown above that, for indigenous peoples, the output of heat per unit surface area decreases with increasing environmental temperature, while heat production per unit weight decreases less rapidly; further, it has been shown that, after elimination of variability due to the inclusion of samples drawn from different varieties of man, heat production per unit surface area still decreases markedly with increased temperature, while heat production per unit weight scarcely changes. Therefore, with increased temperature, surface area per unit weight must increase and weight per unit surface area must de-

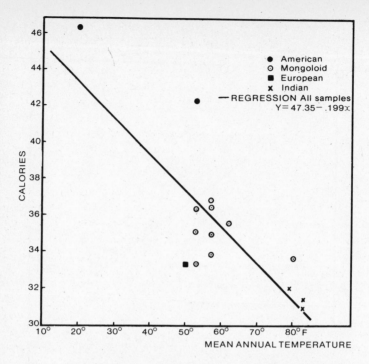

Fig. 9. Relationship of basal calorie production per square metre body surface per hour to mean annual temperature: female indigenous populations.

crease. In other words the human body tends towards linearity with increased temperature and, conversely, tends to become more spherical with decreased temperature. But surface area is related to stature and weight, so that either stature per unit weight tends to increase with increased temperature, or the relationship of surface area to stature and weight must vary among races adapted to different habitats, or a combination of both variations occurs.

The objection may be raised here that this inference depends on the assumption that Dubois' surface area formula is constant for all races, an assumption which has yet to be proved. However, a similar inference may be drawn directly from the multiple correlation calculations, where it was found that there was a significant relationship between weight and mean annual temperature, but none between stature and mean annual temperature. The argument runs thus: Dubois' formula, $A = W^{0.425} \times H^{0.725} \times C$, where A represents surface area, W weight, H stature, and C a constant, was based on Europeans of various sizes. It is not impossible that this relationship should vary from race to race, but it is probable that such variation would be relatively small (since differences in human body form are relatively small) and would be restricted to slight variations in the powers of W and H and in the value of C. So that, for any race the formula may be more generally written $A = W^p \times H^q \times K$, where p and q have positive values in the region of 0.425 and 0.725 respectively and K is a constant. Now, since stature does not apparently vary with mean temperature, for a given stature at any temperature A will be proportional to $W^p \times K$. However, a significant inverse linear relationship has been found between weight and temperature, so that, for a given stature, weight may be estimated thus: $W = a - bT$, where T represents mean temperature, and a and b are constants. Then

$$\frac{A}{W} = \frac{W^p K}{W} = \frac{K}{W^{1-p}} = \frac{K}{(a-bT)^{1-p}}$$

that is to say, that as temperature increases, the ratio of surface area to weight (A/W) increases also.

The results of this study are interesting in that they provide a mechanism by which variations in the morphology of the body in response to environmental demands may be understood. The hypothesis may be briefly stated as follows: in order to facilitate the balance of body heat exchange, less heat is produced, under those conditions in which heat loss is more difficult, by reduction of the amount of body tissue; under these conditions also, the ratio of surface area to weight (*i.e.,* the ratio of potential heat loss to potential heat production) is increased. Thus the functional mechanism underlying the application to zoological groups of Bergmann's rule (that within a polytypic warm-blooded species, the body size of a subspecies usually increases with decreasing mean temperature of its habitat) and Allen's rule (that in warm-blooded species, the relative size of exposed portions of the body decreases with decrease of mean temperature[4]) is also applicable to man.

NON-INDIGENOUS GROUPS

The position having been defined with regard to indigenous racial groups, it was obviously of interest to examine non-indigenous peoples, that is those groups who have inhabited a particular area for too brief a time to allow selective influences to function. Such groups include those who, having migrated to a particular area since adulthood (termed here "immigrants"), demonstrate effects of acclimatization over short periods, and those settlers born and brought up in a given area (termed here "local-born") who show effects both of acclimatization and of climatic influence during their growth period. To the latter group may be assigned for present purposes the white population of America. The only racial group at all adequately studied in varying environments is European, though the number of samples available is unfortunately small.

Of immigrant European males there were available only six samples (Fig. 10), on whose total basal Calorie production increased temperature would appear to have little if any depressing effect. There were only three samples of immigrant European females available. The series of local-born males was of little value since of the seven samples three were apparently invalidated by incomparability of

4 *See* Huxley, 1942, pp. 211, 213.

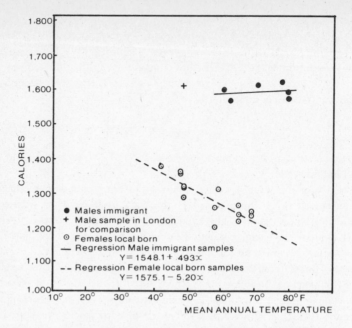

Fig. 10. Relationship of daily basal calorie production to mean annual temperature: European groups (not native).

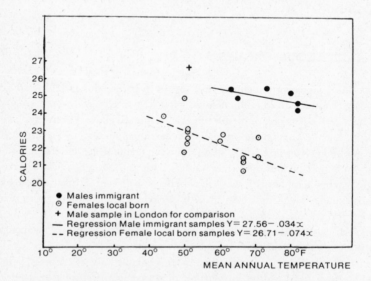

Fig. 11. Relationship of daily basal calorie production per kilogram body weight to mean annual temperature: European groups (not native).

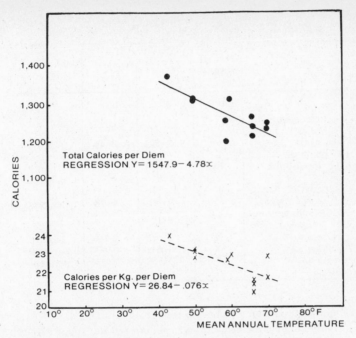

Fig. 12. Relationship of basal heat production to mean annual temperature: American college women.

technique. The position was rather better in the case of local-born females, since there were fourteen samples. Among these were eleven series (Fig. 12) relating to American college women in various parts of the U.S.A., possibly the most comparable series of samples in the literature, since age, diet, activities, etc., may be regarded as practically equivalent in each group, the only major varying factor (apart from ancestry) thus being climate. The statistics of the local-born female group ($r = -0.821$, $b = -5.20$, significant at 0.1 per cent.) indicated a marked inverse relationship between total Calorie production and environmental temperature. Perhaps then, although the evidence is as yet tenuous, a difference may be suggested in the total basal Calorie production of local-born and immigrant groups, the former showing a distinct relationship to temperature (resembling that found in native peoples), which is apparently absent, or at least much less marked, among the immigrant groups.

When production of Calories per unit weight was considered (Fig. 11) immigrant males again showed no significant relationship with temperature, though there was a suspicion of depressed results in warmer regions. There was however a marked inverse relationship among local-born females ($r = -0.641$, significant at 2 per cent.); also the slope of the regression line of Calories per unit weight in the local-born female samples showed a slight flattening relative to that of total Calorie production (after allowing for change of unit) similar to that observed among indigenous groups, suggesting again a certain amount of adjustment of

TABLE 7. *Statistics of the relationship for European groups between heat production and environmental temperature*

Group	No. of samples	r	b	Significant at
Total Calories per diem				
1. Males, immigrant	6	+ 0·193	+ 0·49	Not.
2. Females, all local-born	14	− 0·821	− 5·20	0·1 per cent.
3. Females, American college	11	− 0·805	− 4·78	1 per cent.
Calories per kilogram per diem				
1. As above	6	− 0·579	− 0·034	Not.
2. As above	14	− 0·641	− 0·074	2 per cent.
3. As above	11	− 0·781	− 0·076	1 per cent.

weight to temperature. The relationship between production of Calories per unit weight and mean annual temperature in local-born females appears to differ from that obtaining in samples of indigenous peoples.

The evidence then of this brief examination of the basal metabolism of non-indigenous groups would seem to suggest that the response of local-born samples to environmental temperature is intermediate between that of immigrant groups and that of native races, in that their total Calorie production approaches the condition of adjustment observed in indigenous groups and their weight shows a tendency towards similar adjustment; the relationship between production of heat per unit weight and temperature may perhaps indicate that the latter adjustment is not complete. It is not however possible, from evidence at present available, to say whether identity of response of local-born and native groups occurs, *i.e.,* whether or not adaptation involves genetic factors in addition to those of long-period acclimatization and climatic influence on the growing organism.

CONCLUSIONS

This investigation of basal metabolism by a combination of geographical and statistical methods has thus yielded a number of encouraging results and interesting inferences. The interim nature of the findings must however be stressed, on account of the difficulties innate in the material and also of its paucity. It is not claimed that the study is comprehensive or final, but only that treatment as objective as possible has been applied to all the material that could be obtained by searching the literature available in libraries. Indeed, the first conclusion to be drawn is that the amount of attention given to the basal metabolism of non-European peoples is minute and in great need of amplification.

The most striking feature emerging from the study is the importance of the relationship of basal metabolism of indigenous groups to mean environmental temperature, an association hitherto neglected in the establishment of so-called "normal" values and contrary to the axiom that the total basal heat production of the body is determined by its surface area. The temperature relationship is clear when total basal heat production and heat production per unit surface area are considered, somewhat less so though still significant when heat production is expressed per unit weight; it remains of major importance after allowance has been made for the influences of weight and stature. The three factors, temperature, weight and stature, together account for the greater part of the total variability in mean basal metabolism.

As to the existence of racial differences in basal metabolism, distinction has first to be drawn between differences between races belonging to the same variety of man, and differences between varieties. In the latter case, there appear to be intrinsic intervarietal differences in levels of heat production which cannot be accounted for by the influence of temperature, weight or stature, singly or in combination. On the other hand, intravarietal variations seem to be due essentially to differences in temperature of the localities inhabited; the necessary adjustment of heat production, it is inferred, being achieved with the assistance of adjustment in weight. Thus a solution is proposed to the problem stated at the outset.

Perhaps of more importance for the study of the morphology of the human body than this suggestion of adjustment of weight *per se* to environmental temperature, the inference is drawn from the relationships outlined that the ratio of surface area to weight, representing a measure of linearity of body form, is also to a certain extent adjusted to environmental conditions, the ratio tending to increase with increased temperature. The present study thus indicates a mechanism by which variations in the morphology of the body in response to environmental demands may be understood.

Acknowledgments

I wish to acknowledge my appreciation of the courtesy and co-operation, with which my enquiries have been met, of the staffs of the several libraries used for this and other studies, and especially my indebtedness to those of the library of the Royal Anthropological Institute, London, and the Radcliffe Science Library, Oxford; and finally to record my gratitude to my friend Dr. J. S. Weiner for his extremely helpful criticism of the work and the text.

Postscript

Since the foregoing was written, a report has appeared of an intensive statistical inquiry (Quenouille, Boyne, Fisher and Leitch, 1951) by a team of workers who have analysed individual results rather than group means. In their examination of records of nearly 9,000 subjects, racial differences as a feature of investigation *per se* have been relegated to a subordinate role, the emphasis being on the establishment of fresh basal metabolism standards. Their approach has been essentially statistical, aberrant results being discarded on grounds of mathematical probability rather than from consideration of technical factors.

However, their results show a very satisfying accordance with those outlined here: for example, our 30 comparable male indigenous groups show a regression coefficient of daily basal Calorie production upon temperature ($^{\circ}$ F) of -4.3, their corresponding regression coefficient for males -4.6. Differences appear between their regression coefficients for stature and weight and ours, as might be expected, since they consider the extra factor of surface area. The chief difference between the two sets of results is that theirs identifies, as in the following table, a relative

Regression coefficients of Calorie production upon relative humidity

U.S.A. and north European		Mixed	
Male	Female	Male	Female
-3.11	$+4.24$	-1.52	$+10.20$

humidity effect, varying considerably in intensity, however, among the groups, which in the present study did not reach a significant level. Bearing in mind the difference in approach in the two papers, it appears that the conclusions outlined in the present study are confirmed to a remarkable degree.

REFERENCES

The following list refers only to those papers quoted in the text; no attempt is made to list the large number of works from which data were collected, many of which are to be found in the extensive bibliographies given in Wilson (1945) and Dubois (1936).

Almeida, A. O. de 1924 *J. Physiol. et Path. Gen.*, **22**, 12.
Aub, J. C., and Dubois, E. F. 1917 *Arch. Intern. Med.*, **19**, 823.
Beard, H. H. 1927 *Am. J. Physiol.*, **82**, 577.
Benedict, F. G., Kung, L. C., and Wilson, G. D. 1937 *Chin. J. Physiol.*, **12**, 67.
Berkson, J., and Boothby, W. 1938 *Am. J. Physiol.*, **121**, 669.
Boothby, W., Berkson, J., and Dunn, H. 1936 *Am. J. Physiol.*, **116**, 468.
Brooks, F. P. 1929 *Am. J. Physiol.*, **89**, 403.
Crile, G. W., and Quiring, D. P. 1939 *J. Nutrition*, **18**, 361.
Dreyer, G. 1920 *Lancet* **2**, 289.
Dubois E. F. 1936 *Basal Metabolism in Health and Disease* (3rd ed.). Philadelphia.
Gagge, A. P., Winslow, C.-E. and Herrington, L. P. 1938 *Am. J. Physiol.*, **124**, 30.

Genna, G. 1938 *Zeit. f. Rassenkunde,* **7,** 209.

Gustafson, F. L., and Benedict, F. G. 1928 *Am. J. Physiol.,* **86,** 43.

Harris, J. A., and Benedict, F. G. 1919 *Carnegie Inst. Washington, Publ.* 279.

Hetler, R. A., Killinger, M., and Plant, M. 1932 *J. Nutrition,* **5,** 69.

Hindmarsh, E. M. 1927 *Aust. J. Exp. Biol.,* **4,** 225.

Huxley, J. 1942 *Evolution, the Modern Synthesis.* London.

Jenkins, R. L. 1931 *J. Nutrition,* **4,** 305.

Kilborn, L. G., and Benedict, F. G. 1937 *Chin. J. Physiol.,* **11,** 127.

Krogh, A. 1925 *Tables of Normal Metabolic Rates.* Copenhagen.

MacGregor, R. G. S., and Loh, G. L. 1940 *J. Malaya Branch, Brit. Med. Assoc.,* **4,** 217.

Necheles, H. 1928 *Chin. J. Physiol., Rept. Series, No.* **1,** 80.

Oliveiro, C. J. 1937 *J. Malaya Branch, Brit. Med. Assoc.,* **1,** 125.

Quenouille, M. H., Boyne, A. W. *et al.* 1951 *Commonwealth Bureau of Animal Nutrition, Tech. Comm. No.* 17.

Radsma, W. 1931 *Arch. Neerl. de Physiol.,* **16,** 91.

Radsma, W., and Streef, G. M. 1932 *Arch. Neerl. de Physiol.,* **17,** 97.

Snedecor, G. W. 1946 *Statistical Methods* (4th ed.). Iowa.

Tilt, J., and Walters, C. F. 1935 *J. Nutrition,* **9,** 109.

Wang, C. C., Hawks, J. E. *et al.* 1930 *J. Nutrition,* **3,** 79.

Wilson, E. A. 1945 *Am. J. Phys. Anth.,* New Series, **3,** 1.

Adaptation to Sunlight: Another Controversial Issue

ONE OF THE MOST OBVIOUS WAYS IN WHICH PEOPLE DIFFER from each other is in skin color. Since we lack a hairy coat, our skins are exposed to the elements and visible to each other's eyes, except where we cover them with garments. So, even in ancient times, Greeks, Egyptians, and others noted that fairness was typical of some of their neighbors, whereas others were much darker. They noted, too, that fair skins become tan when exposed to sunlight, and also that the darkest people lived in the tropics. Greek scientists assumed, therefore, that it is useful to be dark if you live where the sunlight is strong. European naturalists during the eighteenth and nineteenth centuries tended to agree: Linnaeus, in his taxonomy, classified *Homo sapiens* into races on the basis of pigmentation.

Darwin, however, was dubious about climatic adaptation in our species, tending to favor sexual selection as an explanation of racial differences. Other scientists have been skeptical too, pointing out—with respect to skin color—that a dark body absorbs heat more efficiently than a light one. This is quite correct, but the fact remains that Scandinavians are not black, nor Ethiopians blond. Consequently, anthropologists and other scientists interested in human biology have continued to explore the issue, seeking for a reasonable explanation and collecting more data. Fortunately we now have appropriate field equipment for recording skin color by measuring the percentage of light reflected at various wavelengths. Indeed, I have been engaged in such research myself in a number of countries. Other scientists have devoted themselves to the biochemistry involved in the development of skin pigmentation. Only by learning the function of skin pigmentation can we hope to discover its adaptive significance. The following paper by Professor W. Farnsworth Loomis, "Skin-Pigment Regulation of Vitamin-D Biosynthesis in Man," is a very clear exposition of this problem.

12. W. Farnsworth Loomis

Skin-Pigment Regulation of Vitamin-D Biosynthesis in Man

Variation in Solar Ultraviolet at Different Latitudes May Have Caused Racial Differentiation in Man

Vitamin D mediates the absorption of calcium from the intestine and the deposition of inorganic minerals in growing bone; this "sunshine vitamin" is produced in the skin, where solar rays from the far-ultraviolet region of the spectrum (wavelength, 290 to 320 millimicrons) convert the provitamin 7-dehydrocholesterol into natural vitamin D (*1*) (Fig. 1).

Unlike other vitamins, this essential calcification factor is not present in significant amounts in the normal diet; it occurs in the liver oils of bony fishes and, in very small amounts, in a few foodstuffs in the summer (see Table 1). Almost none is present in foodstuffs in winter.

Chemical elucidation of the nature of vitamin D has made it possible to eradicate rickets from the modern world through artificial fortification of milk and other foods with this essential factor. Before this century, however, mankind resembled the living plant in being dependent on sunshine for his health and well-being, a regulated amount of vitamin D synthesis being essential if he were to avoid the twin dangers of rickets on the one hand and an excess of vitamin D on the other.

Unlike the water-soluble vitamins, too much vitamin D causes disease just as too little does, for the calcification process must be regulated and controlled much as metabolism is regulated by the thyroid hormone. The term *vitamin D* is, in fact, almost a misnomer, for this factor resembles the hormones more closely than it resembles the dietary vitamins in that it is not normally ingested but is synthesized in the body by one organ—the skin—and then distributed by the blood stream for action elsewhere in the body. As in the case of hormones, moreover, the rate of synthesis of vitamin D must be regulated within definite limits if both failure of calcification and pathological calcifications are to be avoided.

Synthesis of too little vitamin D results in the bowlegs, knock-knees, and twisted spines (scoliosis) associated with rickets in infants whose bones are growing rapidly. Similar defects in ossification appear in older children and women deprived of this vitamin; puberty, pregnancy, and lactation predispose the individual toward osteomalacia, which is essentially adult rickets. In osteomalacia

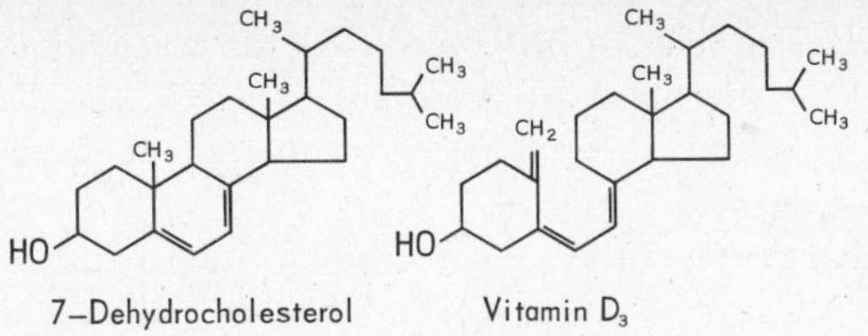

Fig. 1. Chemical structures of 7-dehydrocholesterol and vitamin D_3.

7-Dehydrocholesterol   Vitamin D_3

the bones become soft and pliable, a condition which often leads to pelvic deformities that create serious hazards during childbirth. Such deformities were common, for example, among the women of India who followed the custom of purdah, which demands that they live secluded withindoors and away from the calcifying power of the sun's rays (2). Cod-liver oil or other source of vitamin D is a specific for rickets and osteomalacia, the usual recommended daily dosage being 10 micrograms of 400 international units (1 I.U.=0.025 microgram of vitamin D).

Ingestion of vitamin D in amounts above about 100,000 I.U. (2.5 milligrams) per day produces the condition known as hypervitaminosis D, in which the blood levels of both calcium and phosphorus are markedly elevated and multiple calcifications of the soft tissues of the body appear. Ultimate death usually follows renal disease secondary to the appearance of kidney stones (3). Although this condition has been described only in patients given overdoses of vitamin D by mouth, similarly toxic results would probably follow the natural synthesis of equal doses of vitamin D by unpigmented skin exposed to excessive solar radiation. The

TABLE 1

Vitamin-D content of two fish-liver oils and of the only foodstuffs known to contain vitamin D

Fish-liver oil or foodstuff	Vitamin-D content (I.U./gram)
Halibut-liver oil	2000–4000
Cod-liver oil	60–300
Milk	0.1
Butter	0.0–4.0
Cream	0.5
Egg yolk	1.5–5.0
Calf liver	0.0
Olive oil	0.0

From K. H. Coward, *The Biological Standardization of the Vitamins* (Wood, Baltimore, 1938), p. 223.

body appears to have no power to regulate the amount of vitamin D absorbed from food and no power to selectively destroy toxic doses once they have been absorbed. These facts suggest that the physiological means of regulating the concentration of vitamin D in the body is through control of the rate of photo-chemical synthesis of vitamin D in the skin.

It is the thesis of this article that the rate of vitamin-D synthesis in the stratum granulosum of the skin is regulated by the twin processes of pigmentation and keratinization of the overlying stratum corneum, which allow only regulated amounts of solar ultraviolet radiation to penetrate the outer layer of skin and reach the region where vitamin D is synthesized. According to this view, different types of skin—white (depigmented and dekeratinized), yellow (mainly kera-tinized), and black (mainly pigmented)—are adaptations of the stratum corneum which maximize ultraviolet penetration in northern latitudes and minimize it in southern latitudes, so that the rate of vitamin-D synthesis is maintained within physiological limits (0.01 to 2.5 milligrams of vitamin D per day) throughout man's worldwide habitat.

Figure 2 provides evidence in support of this view, for it is apparent that there is a marked correlation between skin pigmentation and equatorial latitudes. In addition, the reversible summer pigmentation and keratinization activated by ultraviolet radiation and known as suntan represents a means of maintaining physiologically constant rates of vitamin-D synthesis despite the great seasonal variation in solar ultraviolet radiation in the northern latitudes.

Ultraviolet Transmission and Vitamin-D Synthesis

In 1958 Beckemeier (4) reported that 1 square centimeter of white human skin synthesized up to 18 I.U. of vitamin D in 3 hours. Using this figure, we calculate that an antirachitic preventive dose of 400 I.U. per day can be synthesized by daily exposure of an area of skin approximately equal to that of the nearly transparent pink cheeks of European infants (about 20 square centimeters). Perhaps this explains why mothers in northern climates customarily put their infants out of doors for "some fresh air and sunshine" even in the middle of winter.

From this high rate of synthesis by only a small area of thin unpigmented skin, one can calculate the daily amount of vitamin D that would be synthesized at the equator by the skin of adults who exposed almost all their 1½ square meters (22,500 square centimeters) of body surface during the whole of a tropical day. Such a calculation shows that the skin of such individuals would synthesize up to 800,000 I.U. of vitamin D in a 6-hour period if the stratum corneum contained no pigment capable of filtering out the intense solar ultraviolet radiation.

Direct evidence that pigmented skin is an effective ultraviolet filter was pro-vided by Macht, Anderson, and Bell (5), who used a spectrographic method to show that excised specimens of whole skin from Negroes prevented the trans-mission of ultraviolet radiation of wavelengths below 436 millimicrons, while excised specimens of white skin allowed radiation from both the 405- and the 365-millimicron bands of the mercury spectrum to pass through.

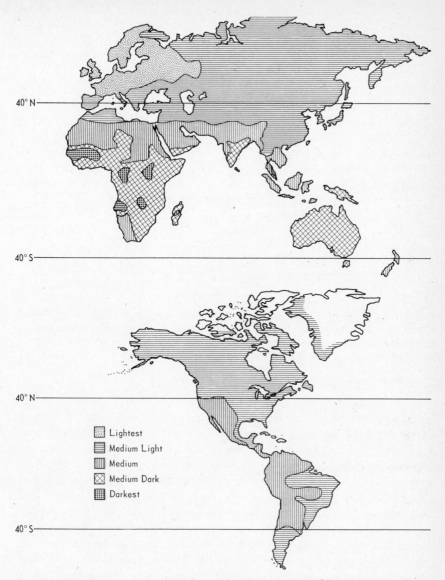

Fig. 2. Distribution of human skin color before 1492. [Adapted from Brace and Montague, *Man's Evolution* (Macmillan, New York, 1965), p. 272]

These early studies with whole skin were refined by Thomson (6), who used isolated stratum corneum obtained by blistering the skin with cantharides. He found that the average percentage of solar radiation of 300- to 400-millimicron wavelength transmitted by the stratum corneum of 22 Europeans was 64 percent, while the average for 29 Africans was only 18 percent. There was no overlapping

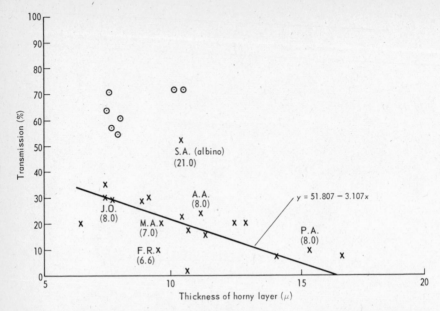

Fig. 3. Variation of transmission of solar ultraviolet light (3000 to 4000 angstroms) through the stratum corneum, plotted against thickness of this layer. ⊙, Europeans; ✕, Africans. The numbers in parentheses after initials are percentages for reflectance of blue light on the forearm. [From M. L. Thomson (6)]

of values for the two groups (Fig. 3), but there was considerable variation within each group, the values for the Europeans varying from 53 to as high as 72 percent and those for the Africans (who were mainly Ibos but also included men from most of the Nigerian tribes) varying from 36 to as low as 3 percent.

In his careful studies, Thomson measured skin thickness as well as pigmentation and found that the former was a minor variable. Studies on the degree of blackness of the various African specimens were made by skin-reflectance measurements. These showed that the darker the skin is, the lower is the percentage of ultraviolet radiation transmitted. One specimen from an albino African showed transmission of 53 percent—a value within the range for the European group. Thomson concluded from these studies that skin pigmentation was mainly responsible for protecting the African from excessive solar ultraviolet radiation, the thickness of the horny layer in Africans playing only a minor role. Thomson did not mention the fact that skin pigmentation and thickening of the horny layer in Africans would protect against excessive vitamin-D synthesis as well as sunburn.

Thomson's results indicate that African stratum corneum filters out solar ultraviolet radiation equivalent to between 50 and 95 percent of that which reaches the vitamin-D synthesizing region of the skin of Europeans. This explains "the fact, agreed to by all, that of all races the Negro is most susceptible to rickets" (7). It is clear from Thomson's figures that exposure of the face of Negro infants to winter sunlight in Scandinavia would result in synthesis of too little vitamin D to meet the infant's body requirements.

It was Hess who first proved that sunlight could cure rickets (8). Seeking experimental proof of a relationship between skin pigmentation and rickets, he took six white and six black rats and placed them on a rachitogenic diet containing low amounts of phosphorus. Exposing both groups to a critical amount of ultraviolet light, he found that all the white rats remained healthy while all the black rats developed rickets. He concluded (9), "It is manifest that the protective rays were rendered inert by the integumentary pigment."

To return now to Thomson's results and consider their bearing on hypervitaminosis, they explain why deeply pigmented Africans living near the equator and exposing almost all their body surface to the ultraviolet of the tropical sun do not suffer from kidney stones and other evidences of hypervitaminosis. Under conditions where untanned Europeans would synthesize up to 800,000 I.U. per day, deeply pigmented Africans would synthesize 5 to 10 percent as much; thus their daily production would fall within the acceptable range.

In this connection it is significant that Reinertson and Wheatley (10) found that the 7-dehydrocholesterol content of human skin does not vary significantly between Negroes and Whites. Skin from the back, abdomen, and thigh of adults of both races averaged 3.8 percent (standard deviation, 0.8 percent), the lowest result in their series being obtained in a specimen of the epidermis of the sole, an area that receives no radiation at all, while the highest result among adults was from a Negro. The highest content of all was found in a specimen from a 2-week-old infant that showed 8.8 percent of the provitamin, a fact that correlates well with the especially high need for vitamin D during the first 2 years of life.

In their paper and ensuing discussion, the above workers emphasize that 7-dehydrocholesterol is found almost entirely beneath the stratum corneum, thus establishing the fact that in man it is not present in the secretions of the sebaceous glands as it is in birds and some northern fur-covered animals which, respectively, obtain their vitamin D by preening or by licking their fur after the provitamin has been converted into the vitamin on the surface of the body. It would appear that vitamin D is made in man solely by the irradiation of the provitamin in the layers underneath the stratum corneum, a mechanism that would allow efficient regulation of the biosynthesis of this essential factor by varying the degree of ultraviolet penetration through differing amounts of pigmentation in the overlying stratum corneum.

Origin of White Skin

Having originated in the tropics where too much sunlight rather than too little was the danger, the first hominids had no difficulty in obtaining sufficient amounts of vitamin D until they extended their range north of the Mediterranean

Sea and latitude 40°N (Fig. 2), where the winter sun is less than 20 degrees above the horizon (*11*) and most of the needed ultraviolet is removed from the sun's rays by the powerful filtering action of the atmosphere through which the slanting rays have to pass. Before the present century, for example, there was a very high incidence of rickets among infants in London and Glasgow, because in these latitudes the midday sun is less than 35 degrees from the horizon for 5 and 6 months, respectively, of the year; in Jamaica and other southern localities, on the other hand, the sun's midday altitude is never less than 50 degrees and rickets is almost unknown (*2*). The farther north one goes, the more severe becomes this effect of latitude on the availability of winter ultraviolet radiation, an effect compounded by cloudy winter skies.

Having evolved in the tropics, early hominids were probably deeply pigmented and covered with fur, as are most other tropical primates. The first adaptation one might expect therefore to lowered availability of ultraviolet light as they moved north of the Mediterranean would be a reduction of fur, for Cruikshank and Kodicek have shown (*12*) that shaved rats synthesize four times more vitamin D than normal rats do.

As early hominids moved farther and farther north, their more deeply pigmented infants must have been especially likely to develop the grossly bent legs and twisted spines characteristic of rickets, deformities which would cripple their ability to hunt game when they were adults. In this connection, Carleton Coon has written (*13*), "Up to the present century, if black skinned people were incorporated into any population living either north or south of the fortieth degree of latitude, their descendants would eventually have been selected for skin color on the basis of this vitamin factor alone." Howells agrees (*14*): "This variety of outer color has all the earmarks of an adaptation, of a trait responding to the force of sunlight by natural selection." The skin, he continues, "admits limited amounts of ultraviolet, which is needed to form vitamin D, but presumably diminishes or diffuses dangerous doses by a screen of pigment granules."

Even in 1934 Murray clearly recognized the implications of these facts (*15*): "As primordial man proceeded northwards into less sunlit regions, a disease, rickets, accomplished the extinction of the darker, more pigmented elements of the population as parents and preserved the whiter, less pigmented to reproduce their kind and by progressive selection through prehistoric times, developed and established the white race in far northern Europe as it appears in historic times; its most extreme blond types inhabiting the interior of the northern-most Scandinavian peninsula."

It is a curious fact that Murray's thesis is almost unknown to the general public, including physiologists, biochemists, and physicians, and that it is not generally accepted by anthropologists, with the exception of Coon and Howells, quoted above, even though it fits the facts of Fig. 2. Both in Europe and China, skin pigmentation becomes lighter as one goes north, and it is lighter in young children; in almost all races the skin is lighter in the newborn infant (*16*) and gradually darkens as the individual matures, a change that parallels the declining need for vitamin D.

When Did European Hominids Begin To Turn White?

On the basis of the conclusion that white skin is an adaptation to northern latitudes because of the lowered availability of winter ultraviolet radiation, it appears probable that the early hominids inhabiting western Europe had lost much of their body hair and skin pigmentation even half a million years ago. Anthropological evidence indicates that early hominids such as the Heidelberg, Swanscomb, Steinheim, Fontechevade, and Neanderthal men lived north of the Mediterranean Sea—particularly during warm interglacial periods (*17*). It is important to recognize that the effect of latitude on the availability of ultraviolet light in winter is not related to climate but operates steadily and at all times, through glacial and interglacial periods alike.

Hand axes and other early stone tools have been found throughout the tropics of the Old World and also in Europe as far north as the 50th degree of latitude (Fig. 4). The presence of such stone tools as far north as England and France

Fig. 4. Distribution of early stone tools throughout the tropics of the Old World and in Europe as far north as 50° N. [From Brace and Montague, *Man's Evolution* (Macmillan, New York, 1965), p. 231]

shows that some early hominids must already have adapted to the lowered level of ultraviolet radiation and consequent danger of rickets by partial loss of body hair and skin pigmentation, for without such adaptation they would have probably been unable to survive this far north.

England is at the same latitude as the Aleutian Islands, and no stone tools such as those found in southern England and France have ever been found in other areas at this latitude—for example, Mongolia and Manchuria. The unique combination of temperate climate and low levels of winter ultraviolet radiation in England and France is due to the powerful warming effect of the Gulf Stream on this particular northern area, which is unique in the world in this respect, for the Japan current in the Pacific is not as powerful as the Gulf Stream and warms only the Aleutian Islands, where no hominids existed until very recently.

Occupation of northern Europe and even Scandinavia up to the Arctic Circle seems to have taken place during the Upper Paleolithic, when presumably partially depigmented men already adapted to latitude 50°N lost nearly all their ability to synthesize melanin and so produced the blond-haired, blue-eyed, fair-skinned peoples who inhabit the interior of the northernmost part of the Scandinavian peninsula.

It has been held that the abundant appearance of stone scrapers in the Upper Paleolithic indicates that this far-northern extension of man's habitat followed his use of animal skins for clothing, a change that would select powerfully for infants with nearly transparent skin on their cheeks, who were thus still able to synthesize a minimum antirachitic dose of vitamin D even when fully clothed during the Scandinavian winter. Certainly the pink-to-red cheeks of northern European children are uniquely transparent; their color is due to the high visibility of the blood that circulates in the subepidermal region.

The one exception to the correlation between latitude and skin color in the Old World is the Eskimo; his skin is medium dark and yet he remains completely free of rickets (*18*) during the long dark arctic winters. Murray noted long ago that the Eskimo's diet of fish oil and meat contains several times the minimum preventive dose of vitamin D, concluding (*15*), "Because of his diet of antirachitic fats, it has been unnecessary for the Eskimo to evolve a white skin in the sunless frigid zone. He has not needed to have his skin bleached by centuries of evolution to admit more antirachitic sunlight. He probably has the same pigmented skin with which he arrived in the far north ages ago." Similar considerations would apply in the case of any coastal peoples of Europe and Asia, who would have been able to expand northward without depigmentation as long as they obtained sufficient vitamin D from a diet of fish; only when they ventured into the interior would antirachitic selection for blond types, as in Scandinavia, presumably have taken place.

Yellow, Brown, and Black Adaptation

Human skin has two adaptive mechanisms for resisting the penetration of solar ultraviolet: melanin-granule production in the Malpighian layer and keratohyaline-granule production in the stratum granulosum. Melanin granules are black, whereas the keratohyaline granules produce keratin (from which nails, claws, horns, and hoofs are formed), which has a yellowish tinge. Particles of both types migrate toward the horny external layer, where they impart a black (melanin), yellow (keratin), or brown (melanin and keratin) tinge to the skin.

Thomson has shown (*6*) that, in Negroes, melanization of the stratum corneum plays the major role in filtering out excessive ultraviolet radiation, keratinization of the horny layer playing only a minor part. Mongoloids on the other hand have yellowish skin, since their stratum corneum is packed with disks of keratin (*13*) that allow them to live within 20 degrees of the equator even though their skin contains only small amounts of melanin (Fig. 2). On the equator itself, however, even Mongoloid-derived peoples acquire pigmentation—

for example, the previously medium-light-skinned Mongoloids who entered the Americas over the Bering Straits at latitude 66°N as recently as 20,000 to 10,000 years ago (Fig. 2).

Even white-skinned peoples have to protect themselves against excessive doses of solar ultraviolet radiation in summer, for, as Blum has pointed out (*19*), on 21 June the solar ultraviolet is as intense in Newfoundland as it is at the equator, since at that time the two regions are at the same distance from the Tropic of Cancer (at 23°27′N). (At the equator, the solar ultraviolet is never less than on this date, while in Newfoundland it is never more.) In other words, adaptation to the variable intensities of solar ultraviolet in the north requires not only winter depigmentation but also the evolution of a reversible mechanism of summer repigmentation to keep the rate of vitamin-D synthesis constant throughout the year. It is significant that both the keratinization and melanization components of suntan are initiated by the same wavelengths which synthesize vitamin D, for it would be difficult to design a more perfect defense against excessive doses of vitamin D than this reversible response to ultraviolet light of these particular wavelengths—a pigmentation response that is further protected by the painful alarm bell of sunburn, which guarantees extreme caution against overexposure to solar ultraviolet in untanned individuals suddenly encountering a tropical sun.

Defenses against production of too much vitamin D therefore range from (i) reversible suntanning, as in Europeans, through (ii) constitutive keratinization, as in the Mongoloids of Asia and the Americas, to (iii) constitutive melanization, as in African and other truly equatorial peoples. The physiological superiority of melanization as a means of protection against ultraviolet was demonstrated by the ability, historically documented, of imported Nigerian slaves to outwork the recently adapted American Indians in the sun-drenched cane fields and plantations of the Caribbean and related tropical areas.

Additional evidence for the view that melanization of the stratum corneum is primarily a defense against the oversynthesis of vitamin D from solar ultraviolet is provided by the fact that the palms and soles of Negroes are as white as those of Europeans; *only* the palms and soles possess a thickly keratinized stratum lucidum (Fig. 5) under the external stratum corneum, which renders melanization of the latter unnecessary. The same reasoning explains the failure of the palms and soles of whites to sunburn during the summer.

Coon has written (*13*), "We cannot yet demonstrate why natural selection favors the prevalence of very dark skins among otherwise unrelated populations living in the wet tropics, but the answer may not be far away." Since overdoses of vitamin D administered orally are known to result in prompt and serious consequences, such as calcifications in the aorta and other soft tissues of the body, kidney stones, secondary renal disease, and death, it would appear that oversynthesis of vitamin D is sufficiently detrimental in young and old to favor the gradual selection for deeply pigmented skin near the equator, as seen, for example, in the repigmentation that has taken place among the equatorial American Indians during the last 10,000 years (Fig. 2).

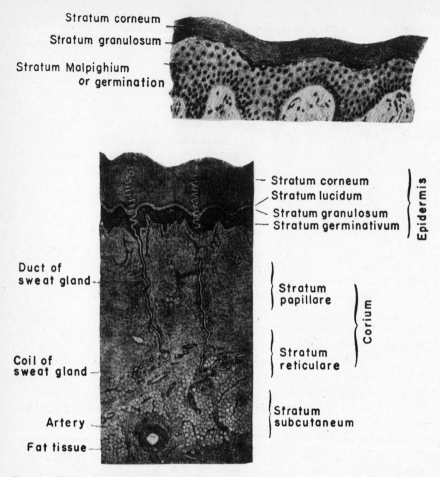

Fig. 5.   Vertical section from (top) the shoulder and (bottom) the sole of the foot of a Caucasian adult. [From J. L. Bremer, *A Textbook of Histology* (Blakiston, Philadelphia, 1936)]

Secondary Results of Pigmentation and Depigmentation

It is known that black skin absorbs more heat than white skin; the studies of Weiner and his associates (20) show that black Yoruba skin reflects only 24 percent of incident light whereas untanned European skin reflects as much as 64 percent. Of themselves, these facts would lead one to expect that reflective white skin would be found near the equator while heat-absorbing black skin would be found in cold northern climate.

Since the exact opposite is true around the world, it seems clear that man has adapted his epidermis in response to varying levels of ultraviolet radiation despite the price he has had to pay in being badly adapted from the standpoint of heat absorbance and reflectance of visible and near-infrared wavelengths. Similar considerations naturally apply to summer pigmentation due to suntan; ultraviolet regulation rather than heat regulation explains why Caucasians are white in the winter but pigmented in the summer.

In addition to being badly adapted for maximum heat absorbance, white-skinned northern peoples are known to be particularly susceptible to skin cancer (21) and such skin diseases as psoriasis and acne. Therefore, only some powerful other advantage, such as relative freedom from rickets, would explain the world-wide correlation between high latitudes and white skin, for without some such factor it would seem that black or yellow skin would be the superior integument.

From this and other evidence, such as the fact that lion cubs and the young of other tropical animals develop rickets in northern zoos unless given cod-liver oil (2), it appears probable that depigmentation occurred north of latitude 40°N (a line marked by the Mediterranean Sea, the Great Wall of China, and the Mason-Dixon line) as an adaptation that allowed an increased penetration of winter ultraviolet radiation and consequent freedom from rickets. Certainly no other essential function of solar ultraviolet is known for man besides the synthesis of vitamin D.

Summary

The known correlation between the color of human skin and latitude (Fig. 2) is explainable in terms of two opposing positive adaptations to solar ultraviolet radiation, weak in northern latitudes in winter yet powerful the year around near the equator. In northern latitudes there is selection for white skins that allow maximum photoactivation of 7-dehydrocholesterol into vitamin D at low intensities of ultraviolet radiation. In southern latitudes, on the other hand, there is selection for black skins able to prevent up to 95 percent of the incident ultraviolet from reaching the deeper layers of the skin where vitamin D is synthesized. Selection against the twin dangers of rickets on the one hand and toxic doses of vitamin D on the other would thus explain the worldwide correlation observed between skin pigmentation and nearness to the equator.

Since intermediate degrees of pigmentation occur at intermediate latitudes, as well as seasonal fluctuation in pigmentation (through reversible suntanning), it appears that different skin colors in man are adaptations of the stratum corneum which regulate the transmission of solar ultraviolet to the underlying stratum granulosum, so that vitamin-D photosynthesis is maintained within physiological limits throughout the year at all latitudes.

REFERENCES AND NOTES

1. A. White, P. Handler, S. L. Smith, *Principles of Biochemistry* (McGraw-Hill, New York, ed. 3, 1964), p. 981.
2. C. H. Best and N. B. Taylor, *The Physiological Basis of Medical Practice* (Williams and Wilkins, Baltimore, ed. 3, 1943), pp. 1102, 1105.

3. F. Bicknell and F. Prescott, *The Vitamins in Medicine* (Grune and Stratton, New York, ed. 3, 1953), p. 578.
4. H. Beckemeier, *Acta Biol. Med. Ger.* **1**, 756 (1958); ——— and G. Pfennigsdorf, *J. Physiol. Chem.* **214**, 120 (1959).
5. D. I. Macht, W. T. Anderson, F. K. Bell, *J. Amer. Med. Assoc.* **90**, 161 (1928); W. T. Anderson and D. I. Macht, *Amer. J. Physiol.* **86**, 320 (1928).
6. M. L. Thomson, *J. Physiol. London* **127**, 236 (1955).
7. A. F. Hess and L. J. Unger, *J. Amer. Med. Assoc.* **69**, 1583 (1917).
8. ———, *ibid.* **78**, 1177 (1922).
9. A. F. Hess, *ibid.*, p. 1177.
10. R. P. Reinertson and V. R. Wheatley, *J. Invest. Dermatol.* **32**, 49 (1959).
11. F. Daniels, Jr., in *Handbook of Physiology,* D. B. Dill, E. F. Adolph, C. G. Wilber, Eds. (American Physiological Society, Washington, D.C., 1964), pp. 969–88.
12. E. M. Cruikshank and E. Kodicek, *Proc. Nutr. Soc. Engl. Scot.* **14**, viii (1955).
13. C. Coon, *The Living Races of Man* (Knopf, New York, 1965), pp. 232, 234.
14. W. W. Howells, *Mankind in the Making* (Doubleday, New York, 1959), p. 270.
15. F. G. Murray, *Amer. Anthropol.* **36**, 438 (1934).
16. E. A. Hooton, *Up from the Ape* (Macmillan, New York, 1946), p. 466.
17. It is possible that the most northern or "classic" Neanderthal died out some 35,000 years ago in western Europe because of rickets which became severe when the arctic weather of the last glaciation made it necessary for him to dress his infants warmly in animal skins during the winter months, a change that would drastically reduce the area of their skin exposed to solar ultraviolet.
18. W. A. Thomas, *J. Amer. Med. Assoc.* **88**, 1559 (1927).
19. H. F. Blum, *Quart. Rev. Biol.* **36**, 50 (1961).
20. J. S. Weiner, G. A. Harrison, R. Singer, R. Harris, W. Jopp, *Human Biol.* **36**, 294 (1964).
21. H. F. Blum, in *Radiation Biology,* A. Hollaender, Ed. (McGraw-Hill, New York, 1955), vol. 2, pp. 487, 509, 529.
22. The work discussed here was partially supported by grant E-443 of the American Cancer Society to Brandeis University, Waltham, Massachusetts. This article is Graduate Department of Biochemistry Publication No. 505.

Cold Adaptation: Testing an Hypothesis in the Laboratory

I N 1950 A STIMULATING BOOK CALLED *Races: A Study of the Problems of Race Formation in Man*, by C. S. Coon, S. M. Garn, and J. B. Birdsell, was published. This rather brief work was full of interesting suggestions proposed by the authors to explain how populations living in different parts of the world came to evolve different physical characteristics. Among the most popular of these hypotheses is that of the "cold-engineered mongoloid face," which was based upon the assumption that the ancestors of modern East Asians and American Indians had been subjected to frigid environments for hundreds of generations during the Paleolithic period. Hunting would have been required throughout the winter, as among recent Eskimos, and even the best tailored garments, which would keep the body warm, would not have given as much protection to the face. In accordance with Allen's rule, facial flatness—which includes slight browridges, flat, narrow noses, and massive malars—should have been selected for under these conditions.

Fortunately this explanation is a testable hypothesis. Volunteers of various racial backgrounds can be subjected, in a laboratory, to conditions simulating those encountered by an Arctic hunter, and their physiological reactions recorded and compared. This is precisely what Professor A. T. Steegmann has done. One article in which he reported some of his results forms a part of a Symposium on Human Adaptation which took place at an Annual Meeting of the American Association of Physical Anthropologists held at Mexico City in 1969. These results are well worth reading.

13. A. T. Steegmann, Jr.

Cold Adaptation and the Human Face

Abstract. A framework is suggested within which the evolutionary biology of the human head and face can be explored; it includes several channels of natural and behavioral selection as well as modes of "plasticity" change.

One aspect of the model is then examined by means of physiological and anthropometric experimentation. A cold room study of 33 Japanese and 25 whites, all born and raised in the tropics, was conducted at Hawaii's Pacific Biomedical Research Center. Thermal response during 70 minutes of exposure (face and hand) to moving 0° C air was electrically recorded. Assuming skin and body temperature is partially dependent upon morphology, detailed anthropometric measurements were taken and employed in thermal-morphological correlation analysis.

Though results are not yet thoroughly analyzed, it appears that head surface temperatures relate to sub-cutaneous fat thickness, but not clearly to other form factors; the oriental face, supposedly a product of selection by cold, seems to respond little differently than any other.

The human hand and foot are often featured in studies of cold adaptation; not only are they known sites for what surely has long been selective cold injury, but must also function adequately under the daily demands upon the cold-adapted hunter or herder. Consequently, these appendages are assumed to reflect both genetic and ontogenetic response to survival at low temperature. Furthermore they can be conveniently tested experimentally.

It is likely that none of the above statements apply to the face, though the face suffers great cold exposure. Man's head simply does not experience cold injury equivalent to that of the extremities and indeed shows little at all (Steegmann, '67). Functionally, the head and face must support the cranial sensory system, but under extreme conditions will not be put to demands such as those made upon the hand. In short, the head and face cannot be placed in an evolutionary model together with the other extremities.

The northern Asian face has been widely assumed in recent years to have arisen as some sort of adaptive response to an arctic or sub-arctic environment (Garn, '65), yet this conflicts with the content of the preceding paragraph. Since not all responses are adaptive, and since selection in cold areas may result from factors other than cold, and especially because there is more to evolution than natural selection alone, it seems appropriate at this point to review some research goals, approaches, and problems of a cranio-facial biology of cold. A second section will consist of preliminary findings derived from an experimental test of specific hypotheses.

RESEARCH OBJECTIVES

The research topics may be classed into two broad categories (morphological and physiological) each of which demands a manifold approach.

Selection and Morphology of the "Arctic" or "Classic" Mongoloid Face

The peculiar cranio-facial morphology which typifies human populations of north and north central Asia and arctic North America is distinctive and must ultimately be placed in evolutionary context; that is, we can start by assuming it is a complex of dependent variables and must try to decipher those conditions and histories upon which it "depends."

As with most analyses of selection in man, the direct evidences of frostbite selection are lost in the past and are otherwise approached only by utilization of contemporary population data. I previously noted (Steegmann, '67) that all evidences point to facial frostbite as constituting a selective force of negligible strength. Of course, any force exerted on a population over a long period will leave its product, but inquiry into alternative or additional selective channels is needed.

Cold may operate selectively on man in many ways other than by freezing peripheral tissue, though I must admit I am hard pressed to understand how it could act differentially on the face. One group of possibilities here may be classed as *injuries to deep or sensory structures* of the head. The suggestion that European (neanderthal) facial structure was a modification to protect the internal carotids (and therefore the brain) from cold belongs in this category (Coon, '62, page 533); how this would have developed (*i.e.,* "selection" evidences from modern medical data) is not quoted nor is any convincing discussion offered as to why the same problem was handled in a morphologically "opposite" way by arctic mongoloids (Coon, '65, pp. 249–251).

Various studies have implicated the nose in another possibly cold-related role; nose size and shape (or more properly, that of the internal nasal chamber) is clearly related to vapor pressure and therefore secondarily to cold. In addition, a direct function of the narrowing of nasal passages at low temperature may be that of air warming; by implication the structures protected are the deep respiratory passages and a number of discussions are available (Proetz, '53; Veghte, '64;

Coon, '65; Wolpoff, '68). However, I have serious reservations as to whether this relationship is a product of cold selection alone. Nose shape follows clinal gradients in non-cold as well as in cold areas (Newman, '53). Also, the work of Veghte ('64) implies that the nose may exhibit a high, low variability warming capacity. Investigation of the mechanism of any such selection is yet to be done and is sorely needed. Low nasal width heritability estimates (Vandenberg, '62) and nose ecosensitivity under certain circumstances (Hulse, '64; Shapiro, '39) are relevant, and Post's work ('66) shows nasal septum form may be balanced by selection and suggests a particularly appropriate guide for further efforts.

On a less specific level, the original "cold-engineered mongoloid face" hypothesis (Coon, Garn and Birdsell, '50) held that several features such as facial fat, nose form, sinus and malar size are products of selection by low temperature; if that selection were not frostbite as was held in 1950, then it was at least some manner of cold selection resulting in protection of the eyes and face (Garn, '65, page 63). In other words, we still do not understand how cold selection could have molded facial morphology and this is still a pivotal research problem.

Natural selection by disease is generally one of our best understood selections and should be applied to the biology of arctic facial form. I have discussed elsewhere (Steegmann, '67) the possible interaction between facial frostbite and infection and would only like to add here a speculation concerning deeper facial structures, the sinuses. Certainly, if selective pressures should change sinus shape (especially of the maxillary and paranasal sinuses) then we would come a long way by that discovery. The circum-orbital, circum-nasal face stays much warmer than anticipated in cold (Edwards and Burton, '60; Steegmann, '65) and the same should be even more the case for deeper structures. Consequently, I would suggest that direct effects of cold on the sinuses are selectively negligible, and that infection would be a much more plausible source of sinus shape or size change. How this would have worked is the limiting problem for now. Though I observed remarkably few reports of sinusitis or sinus-related complications while gathering data on frostbite injury in the arctic, a separate survey should be taken; also death by frostbite might leave no trace on the skeleton but the same may not be true of severe sinus conditions (Wells, '64, pp. 80–81, 143). We need skeletal "selection" studies as additional means of clarifying selection for facial shape. On logical grounds alone, however, I would predict that such selection would operate more upon the capacity of sinuses to drain than upon their shape (to the extent that size and shape are unrelated).

Let me now turn from discussions of natural selection and facial form to problems of social and sexual selection in this context. The only reason this may appear to be straying from the point is that we currently know so little about it (Clark and Spuhler, '59; Damon and Thomas, '67; Schreider, '67). Man is a resourceful and adaptable animal with extensive skills for avoiding at least some types of mortality selection. There may well be differential fertility associated with effects of cold adaptation, but even more likely, sexual selection based upon differences in facial traits. Bielicki and Welon ('66) have also presented data suggesting that some aspects of head form may be involved in balancing selection (sexual or natural). There is so much yet to learn about the entire problem that I will present here only a plea that it be investigated. What part of the body should be more involved than the face? We cannot afford at this point to research origins of distinctive facial form in reference to "cold selection" alone.

In the same way, it is appropriate to speculate that at least part of the variation contributing to northern mongoloid facial morphology may once have been and could now be "cold-associated" but not "cold-selected"; that is, the head and slow-to-mature face may grow differently in cold than elsewhere. Additionally, final phenotype might be effected by secular trends in face form (Laughlin, '63, pp. 11–12) whether these be of dietary, heterotic, or other origin. There may be, as well, allometric relationships between head and body form such that changes (by whatever means) in the body involve the head indirectly. We harbor the hope that various International Biological Program (IBP) projects will further illustrate differential growth (Eskimo/other), and we expect work will continue with animal experiments of which a discussion may be found in Steegmann and Platner ('68). Evolutionally interpretation of "plasticity" is complicated by the situation stated in the following quote:

> It is an important attribute of the environment that usually it selects what it itself in part determines, though the selecting component, of course, need not necessarily be the same as the determining one. (Harrison, '60, p. 3)

Finally, I think (pending the outcome of these several lines of research) that we could arrive at a position in which north Asian face morphology simply had not been explained as a product of either selection or plasticity. If so, alternative possibilities should be considered:

(a) It actually is such a product, but we have been unable to decode its evolutionary biology on available data.

(b) It has undergone little or no recent major selective modification and is rather a product of "chance," "founder effect," or accident. Aspects of this interpretation would agree with that of Oschinsky ('62), Hartle ('62) and others, in many details. It would also call for further detailed anatomical analysis with a historical emphasis.

Another possibility would be that the arctic face *is* arctic adapted, but not primarily by means of its gross morphology. Thus, the explanation of morphology would be left to one of the preceding causes.

Physiology of the Head in Cold and Its Role in Thermoregulation

Our extremities normally react to local or whole-body cooling by vasoconstriction; heat is thereby conserved and core temperature preservation takes biological precedence over peripheral tissue warming. The effect may be modified by cyclical release of vasoconstriction and active vasodilation for peripheral rewarming; but localized cold injury to the extremities can occur.

The head is not an extremity in reference to its superficial circulation; cold does not induce reflex vasoconstriction though vasodilation occurs (Cooper, '62; Fox and Wyatt, '62). Consequently, the head not only keeps itself "warm" at low temperatures but also radiates great quantities of heat away from the body (Froese and Burton, '57). By implication, these physiological observations suggest that the head may function in environmental adaptive changes involving heat loss, but less so in heat conservation. This of course assumes that, though circulation is not the only means of getting warmth to the head's surface, it is the major and most rapid channel.

What then could be the physiological role of this unique anatomical area in cold adaptation? (A) Local circulatory changes could evolve to protect the tissue on those areas of the head, nose, and ears most exposed to local effects of cold. Indicators of adaptation would be lowered sensitivity to cold injury or the maintenance of high skin temperatures during cooling. This has never been carefully studied in the field. (B) By means of increases in arteriovenous anastomoses, vasodilation pattern shifts, increased head surfaces, or combinations of these, the head could be made to function as a somewhat more efficient heat radiator. Whether variation in these traits, sufficient to make any physiological difference, is available or extant in our species remains to be seen. (C) Since cephalic circulation characteristics are probably related to vascularization of the brain and special senses (rather than to cold protection), it is doubtful that the reverse of "B" would evolve or has evolved (*i.e.*, a head and face surface which could conserve heat).

Therefore, it would appear that arctic man carries a legacy which promotes heat loss. This, in turn, would mean that such a physiological role may either be strictly incidental to other functions of cephalic and bodily physiology, or has evolved to help one lose heat. I will first elaborate upon the latter view which I do not accept. The nature of life in the arctic winter may require of man periods of heavy exertion at sub-zero temperatures. Excessive perspiration, depending on the circumstances, can lead to cold injury and/or general hypothermia, this suggests that mechanisms aiding in dissipation of surplus heat are essential. Morphological, physiological, and behavioral solutions come to mind, but a large radiating head, particularly if uncovered, does drain off a great deal of heat. It should be noted that Eskimos are relatively large of head and face. However, I feel that with limited ranges of variation in human head size and temperature, and because arctic man is so adroit at clothing design (and notably, its ventilation), it is currently impossible to accept a "heat-loss" hypothesis for head evolution in a natural selective context. Of course, the head may certainly aid in heat dissipation, should it be large and highly vascular for other reasons, but I don't think it would undergo such a specific cold-related evolution *per se*.

Lastly, I would like to add this strictly speculative possibility. The hypothalamus of the brain is not only the seat of central thermoregulation, but is anatomically central to the precise areas under discussion. Thermoregulatory reception by the hypothalamus is at least partly dependent upon direct effects of blood temperature on its tissues (Fusco, Hardy and Hammel, '61). In extreme cold, respiratory cooling of the tissue and vessels anterior and inferior to the hypothalamus might interfere with normal thermoregulation. Results of brain cooling experiments upon monkeys suggest that aortic blood moves to the brain at sufficient speed and volume that there is negligible heat loss on the way (Hayward and Baker, '68; Baker, personal communication). The head apparently participates in blood cooling, as do the other extremities, by contributing relatively cool venous blood to the total blood volume. However, the ambient temperatures (28–32° C) employed in Hayward's and Baker's experiments were cool only relative to core blood temperatures. Had there been a higher contrast between internal carotid blood and respiratory passage temperatures, heat exchange might have been greater. These relationships are assessable in man (Benzinger and Taylor, '63) and must be clarified eventually in reference to race and adaptation.

A summary of the objectives of this research may now be stated. (A) One general goal is an understanding of the adaptive role of the human head in cold (and indeed in all environmental extremes). We would like to determine anatomical involvement in any such adaptation whether it is "racial" (polytypic) in this species or not. Naturally, the head cannot be analytically separated from the body (despite its physiological singularity) and it will be seen that no attempt is made to do so in the research outlined in this paper. If there exists a polytypic (and truly "genetic") physiological cold adaptation of the head, with anatomy playing a secondary (and perhaps biologically "dependent") role if any, it will be most difficult to interpret selectively.

(B) A second, pressing, and more traditionally anthropological problem has to do with clarifying the history and distribution of the "arctic mongoloid face." Its origins may or may not involve biological adaptation to the arctic. Though this singular facial morphology may have arisen in the late Pleistocene, in fact, we have little more than impressions (in time or space) of arctic "facial flatness" from osteological work (Woo and Mourant, '34; Hartle, '62; Oschinsky, '64), and only

TABLE I

Microevolutionary forces acting upon the northern mongoloid face and head

---

A. Selection (leading to genetic change)
 1. Frostbite
 2. Cold injury of the brain
 3. Damage by cold or dryness to the pulmonary system
 4. Disease or cold injury of the sinuses
 5. Sexual selection and differential fertility
 6. Cold disturbance of the para-hypothalamic anatomy[1]

B. Non-selective modification
 1. Differential growth (ontogenetic "plasticity") in cold
 2. Effects of diet, heterosis, etc. on growth
 3. Historical chance, "drift," or "founder" effect

---

[1] Those areas influencing the temperature of the hypothalamus.

limited comparative quantified data upon the living (Levin, '63). Difficulty in quantifying facial shape in contemporary populations is partly responsible for the deficiency, but it need not stop work on relationships between selection and physiology or shape. Approaches to those ends have been discussed above and are summarized in table 1.

AN INVESTIGATION OF RACE, MORPHOLOGY, AND COLD RESPONSE: PRELIMINARY REPORT AND TENTATIVE CONCLUSIONS

Ideas are traditionally easier to propose than to test, and those within environmental human biology are no exception. While the research described here will examine only a modest aspect of the problem outlined previously, it is designed to approach some of the primary questions. (a) Is there any relationship between various aspects of human face size or shape and face temperatures in the cold? Morphology is determined by wholly or partially independent skeletal factors (Landauer, '62) and other factors including subcutaneous tissue, and nasal cartilage; these must be separated, if possible, for correlation to temperature variation. (b) What are the involvements of body traits (weight, sitting height, etc.) with face and head temperature? (c) Do head size and head temperature influence loss of core body heat? (d) Are there racial differences in cranio-facial temperature control and expression which are not attributable to accessible morphological differences? This might include such phenomena as the "hunting" response (Steegmann, '65) (see footnote 1, p. 190).

A research design including some of the following elements was deemed absolutely essential in order to reach firm conclusions: (a) It is assumed that the patterns of surface cooling at pre-cold injury levels, seen in the laboratory, are homologous to patterns of actual cold injury. Supporting data are offered elsewhere (Steegmann, '65; '67). (b) Morphological "models" of a highly quantified nature must be examined for their relationships to assumedly "dependent" thermal variables (for instance, does nose temperature depend upon nose protrusion?). Thus the approach was inherently intra-populational and correlational, rather than comparative. By analyzing thermal and physical variation *within* a population, many obvious sources of error could be avoided. (c) However, not all human populations could be assumed to follow morphological-thermal standards derived from a single group; indeed, man may exhibit genetically based polytypic physiological patterns. Consequently, the concept outlined in "b" should be applied to at least two separate racial population samples. This would also expand the study to a comparative one, both as to raw data, and as to correlation-regression standards. (d) Finally, the standardization of environmental conditions for such tests (*i.e.*, exposing all subjects to nearly identical conditions) is both mandatory in "model-testing" and nearly impossible to attain under arctic winter field conditions. Such is especially critical for most facial temperature testing.

With these problems to manage, I decided to run the primary experiments under laboratory conditions.

Experimental Setting and Design

A chronic and unresolved problem in the anthropological study of human cold response is based in our inability to separate the contribution of differing acclimatization levels from that of "genetics" or "race." It becomes a problem of importance in between-group comparisons, and is certainly one even within populations. For this study, a second and quite practical problem was the location of adequate samples of subjects of equivalent age, socio-economic status, and cultural pattern, and yet of two unmixed racial groups. Both problems, and many others, were solved by locating the project in Hawaii. Not only were the populations found, but so was a good professional setting, the Pacific Biomedical Research Center. In theory, then, cold responses were produced in subjects with no cold experience, and at least part of any "racial" differences would be due to genetic differences or to differences in morphology.

Sample. The sample ultimately collected consisted of college-age men born and raised in the tropics; 33 were of unmixed Japanese ancestry and 25 of "Northwestern European" descent. A segment of the entire sample was repeat-tested.

Morphological assessment. Before each experiment, the subjects were interviewed and measured for 20 anthropometric and 18 cephalometric traits, including complete sagittal and transverse profiles of the face. A number of derived measurements and indices were also calculated.

Physiological assessment. After taking blood pressure and the vital signs, thermocouples were applied to the forehead, malar, cheek, chin, nose tip, chest, finger and core (rectal). Subjects were tested for room temperature responses, then warmly clothed and introduced into the 0° C environmental room; there they were seated upright in aluminum-webbing lawn-chairs against one wall. Air was blown over the face by a 12" fan at an average speed of 10 f.p.s.; although it gusted from 7 to 12 f.p.s., the flow was reasonably constant, and was the same for all subjects. Temperatures and air speeds were recorded by a Honeywell *ElectroniK 16* and a Gelman-Wallac anemometer, respectively. Cooling lasted for seventy minutes in every case.

Analysis. During the end of this period (64–70 minutes) most face temperatures were stable and averages for the last six minutes were used as "final" temperatures. These were then tested for relationship to over a hundred physical and physiological variables, both singly ("forehead temperature") and combined ("total head temperature"); simple and multiple correlations as well as regressions were computed.

Preliminary results. While the simple correlation analysis is complete, its conclusions may be substantially modified by results of regression or multiple-partial correlation tests now in progress. Nevertheless, a few trends have already appeared.

A. *Face temperature–morphology relationships.* Viewed as a strictly morphological model, the nose offers the best test of a temperature–morphology relationship. It varies appreciably in relative and absolute size (especially protrusiveness), is somewhat independent of other factors in face shape such as subcutaneous fat and malar size, and like the chin, is rather "peripheral" anatomically. It is of particular interest to this study that nose temperature showed no relationship in either sample to any of the more than ten measurements and indices of nose size and shape. Nose temperature was positively correlated to overall head size in the Japanese sample and probably behaved the same way in the "Europeans." In addition, the white sample showed a positive pulse rate to nose temperature correlation and others to be considered elsewhere.

The malar region is morphologically more complex and even more important to the anthropological discussion. Malar temperature increased as face width and other measures of malar size decreased. When the effects of facial skinfolds are held constant, this low correlation may remain, or may be negated. If it is sustained, the more protrusive or larger malar is actually more exposed to cold and does get colder. The "white" malar is better protected from cold than the Japanese malar.

B. *Face temperature–adipose tissue relationships.* Temperatures of the cheek surface (and probably those in other areas since subcutaneous tissue thickness is hard to measure on the head) are inversely related to both skinfold thickness and actual cheek thickness.

C. *Relationships between face temperature and bodily characteristics.* Remarkably few interrelations were found between the cranio-facial temperatures and bodily characteristics. The odd exception (such as a forehead–sitting height positive correlation) will be considered later. Likewise, there appears at the present state of analysis to be little association of core heat or its loss with overall head and face temperature.

D. *Racial differences.* A number of non-agreements appeared between results on the two samples. Furthermore, the rather dramatic differences in "hunting response"[1] frequency at facial sites, in which Japanese were more reactive than whites (Steegmann, '65), may be reversed here; likewise, the higher Japanese facial temperatures seen before were not duplicated in this sample. Curiously, the only really striking racial difference had to do with finger temperature. Thermal analysis of finger cooling is complicated and I have not yet attempted it on this sample. But, we observed during the experiments that the Japanese seemed to have less finger pain and obviously maintained higher finger temperatures. The uniqueness of extremity cooling both biologically and analytically suggests further comment would be premature; it should only be noted that any racial difference in extremity cooling was not mirrored in the face.

---

[1] "Hunting" waves (also known as Lewis waves) are cold-induced cycles of alternating vasodilitation and vasoconstriction in peripheral tissue. One function is to balance the necessity to conserve core heat against the advantage of tissue rewarming.

CONCLUSIONS[2]

A. Cranio-facial form appears to have little to do with surface temperatures, and I conclude that the "frostbite" selection of Coon, Garn and Birdsell ('50) is not sustained. If anything, the thin and hawklike visage of the European is better protected from cold than that of the Asiatic. Adipose tissue padding (as gauged by skinfold thickness) may protect deeper structures but permits surface temperatures to fall. Actual facial temperatures were overall slightly lower on the mean for the Japanese sample as compared to the "European" one and may be associated with less "hunting."

B. There may be a racial dimorphism in finger temperature, the oriental sample maintaining the higher temperature in cold.

ACKNOWLEDGMENTS

My gratitude goes to the National Science Foundation for support under grant GS-1569. Field research was greatly facilitated through numerous courtesies by Dr. T. A. Rogers (Pacific Biomedical Research Center, University of Hawaii), his staff, and many other people in Hawaii whom it is a pleasure to thank here. Particularly, to my Research Assistant in Hawaii, Mr. Sidney Kent, I owe sincerest thanks.

LITERATURE CITED

Benzinger, T. H., and G. W. Taylor 1963 Cranial measurement of internal temperature in man. In: Temperature: Its Measurement and Control in Biology and Medicine. J. D. Hardy, ed. *3:* 111–120.

Bielicki, T., and A. Welon 1966 The operation of natural selection on head form in an Eastern European population. In: Yearbook of Physical Anthropology 1964. S. T. Genoves, ed. *12:* 137–145. From Homo, *15:* 22–30, 1964.

Clark, P. J., and J. N. Spuhler 1959 Differential fertility in relation to body dimensions. Hum. Biol., *31:* 121–137.

Coon, C. S. 1962 The Origin of Races. Knopf, New York.

——— 1965 The Living Races of Man. Knopf, New York.

Coon, C. S., S. M. Garn and J. B. Birdsell 1950 Races: A Study of the Problems of Race Formation in Man. Charles C Thomas, Springfield.

Cooper, K. E. 1962 The peripheral circulation. Ann. Rev. Physiol., *24:* 139–168.

Damon, A. J., and R. B. Thomas 1967 Fertility and physique—height, weight, and ponderal index. Hum. Biol., *139:* 5–13.

Edwards, M., and A. C. Burton 1960 Temperature distribution over the human head, especially in the cold. J. App. Physiol., *15:* 209–211.

Fox, R. H., and H. T. Wyatt 1962 Cold induced vasodilatation in various areas of the body surface of man. J. Physiol., *162:* 289–297.

[2] A detailed report of experimental findings is now in preparation.

Froese, G., and A. C. Burton 1957 Heat losses from the human head. J. App. Physiol., *10:* 235–241.

Fusco, M. M., J. D. Hardy and H. T. Hammel 1961 Interaction of central and peripheral factors in physiological temperature regulation. Am. J. Physiol., *200:* 572–580.

Garn, S. M. 1965 Human Races, second ed., Thomas, Springfield.

Harrison, G. A. 1960 Environmental modification of mammalian morphology. Man, *60, 2:* 3–5.

Hartle, J. A. 1962 A Study of Certain Features of the Mongoloid Face. Columbia University Dissertation, University Microfilms, Ann Arbor.

Hayward, J. N., and M. A. Baker 1968 Role of cerebral arterial blood in the regulation of brain temperature in the monkey. Am. J. Physiol., *215:* 389–403.

Hulse, F. S. 1964 Exogamy and heterosis, Yearbook of Physical Anthropology. G. W. Lasker, ed. *9:* 241–257. Translated from Exogamie et Heterosis. Arch. Suisse d'Anthrop. Gen., *22:* 103–125, 1957.

Landauer, C. A. 1962 A factor analysis of the facial skeleton. Hum. Biol., *34:* 239–253.

Laughlin, W. S. 1963 Eskimos and Aleuts: their origins and evolution. Science, *142:* 1–13.

Levin, M. G. 1963 Ethnic Origins of the People. of Northeastern Asia. University of Toronto Press, Toronto.

Newman, M. T. 1953 The application of ecological rules to the racial anthropology of the aboriginal New World. Am. Anthrop., *55:* 311–327.

Oschinsky, L. 1962 Facial flatness and cheekbone morphology in arctic mongoloids. Anthropologica, *4:* 349–377.

——— 1964 The Most Ancient Eskimos. The Canadian Research Centre for Anthropology, Ottawa.

Post, R. W. 1966 Deformed nasal septa and relaxed selection. Eugen. Quart., *13:* 101–112.

Proetz, A. W. 1953 Essays on the Applied Physiology of the Nose, Annals, St. Louis.

Schreider, E. 1967 Possible selective mechanisms of social differentiation in biological traits. Hum. Biol., *39:* 14–20.

Shapiro, H. L. 1939 Migration and Environment, Oxford, New York.

Steegmann, A. T. Jr. 1965 A study of relationships between facial cold response and some variables of facial morphology. Am. J. Phys. Anthrop., *23:* 355–362.

——— 1967 Frostbite of the human face as a selective force. Hum. Biol., *39:* 131–144.

Steegmann, A. T. Jr., and W. S. Platner 1968 Experimental cold modification of cranio-facial morphology. Am. J. Phys. Anthrop., *28:* 17–30.

Veghte, J. H. 1964 Respiratory and microlimate temperatures within the parka hood in extreme cold. Aerospace Medical Research Laboratory–TDR–64–79.

Wells, C. 1964 Bones, Bodies, and Disease. Praeger, New York.

Wolpoff, M. H. 1968 Climatic influence on the skeletal nasal aperture. Am. J. Phys. Anthrop., *29:* 405–423.

Woo, T. L. and G. M. Mourant 1934 A biometric study of the flatness of the facial skeleton in man. Biometrika, *26:* 196–250.

Ancestry and Adaptation: An Asian Example

By the end of the paleolithic, if not before, it is clear that tribal migration from one area to another was not at all uncommon. In the modern world, as we all know, millions of people are found living in regions far from those inhabited by their ancestors. Most Americans are of European or African origin. Blonds live in the tropics, and Blacks in the Arctic. At present, technology shelters us from many environmental stresses, but many migrations took place long before this was so. Both historical and archaeological evidence demonstrate that some tribes moved from one climatic zone to another hundreds of generations ago: from the lowlands to the mountains, from the plains to the jungles, as well as north or south.

If, indeed, our biological characteristics are adaptive to environmental conditions, it might be expected that some evolutionary changes might have taken place among such peoples. Although natural selection is rarely a rapid process, under certain circumstances it may be speeded up. A disease which is almost universal among the inhabitants of any area may kill many more individuals having one genetic trait than it would those who possess another. The distribution of sickle cell in the malarial region of Africa is commonly explained on this basis. There may well be many examples of this process which have not yet come to the attention of scientists. In all cases, the result should be that tribes of quite varied racial origins would come to resemble one another more and more. Dr. J. C. Sharma presents interesting evidence of such a process in the next selection, "Convergent Evolution in the Tribes of Bastar."

14. J. C. Sharma

Convergent Evolution in the Tribes of Bastar

Abstract. An investigation of the ABO blood groups, the sickle cell trait, and the ability to taste phenylthiocarbamide among four endogamous tribal groups of Bastar in Central India is reported. These tribes, the Raj Gonds, the Murias, the Bhatras and the Halbas are shown to resemble one another in the genetic traits investigated to a remarkable degree, despite genetic and social isolation from each other. It is suggested that similarities between the tribes is due to their having shared a common geographical environment for hundreds of generations.

It is now increasingly realized that genetic resemblance in human populations is not always indicative of a common descent and conversely, that populations of a common descent may show genetic diversity. This realization seems to take into account a greater role of environment as a modifying factor on the genetic constitution of populations through natural and social selection. Obviously, while natural selection can bring about great genetic diversity in a population spread out over different environments, it can also at the same time smooth out genetic differences in populations of diverse origins which live in the same environmental conditions for a long enough period (say many hundreds of generations).

In a vast territory like India, for instance, where human populations live in all possible geographical environments from arctic to tropic, in deserts and forests, on plains and at high altitudes, geography could form the biggest single factor responsible for the genetic diversity of the people. Since there is also found a strong correlation between geography and diseases, and since some diseases are associated with certain genotypes, geography as a selective agent may operate on populations independently, though indirectly. This effect of natural selection on the genetic constitution would be more pronounced in tribal populations which have been living in the same environment comparatively longer and away from modern civilization and thus more free of such "anti-selective" forces as medical care, public sanitation, and knowledge of hygiene.

There is also now a considerable body of evidence to show that most of the biochemical factors are highly selective in nature. Certain genotypes of the sickle cell trait, thalassemia and glucose-6-phosphate dehydrogenase (G-6-PD) deficiency are said to confer a measure of resistance against malaria, which is a disease of humid tropical climates all over the world. This would, therefore, provide such genotypes a greater chance of survival against malaria. Similarly a close relationship is found between various blood types and diseases (Aird et al., '53, '54; Clarke et al., '55, '56; Anand, '64 inter alia) showing that even blood group alleles may be of some selective value.

Thus, judgments concerning genetic relationships among populations on the basis of allele frequencies in such traits should be viewed in the light of their environment and the standing of the populations in such an environment. Howells' ('66) conclusions based on the population of Bougainville, that differences in living populations reflect the pre-existing differences of their ancestral stocks are not perhaps universally true. At least they need not hold good for those physical and genetical traits which confer greater or lesser selective value for one reason or the other.

The present paper reports the frequency of three genetical traits, namely the ABO blood groups, the sickle cell trait, and the ability to taste phenylthiocarbamide among four endogamous tribal groups living in the same environment for hundreds (or possibly a thousand) generations. An analysis of the findings requires us to ask whether a part of the great homogeneity discernible among the tribal groups with regard to these genetical traits could be due to environmental factors through natural selection. Direct evidence to support such a conclusion is rather difficult to furnish. In the absence of effective gene flow through interbreeding among the tribal groups, hybridization as a factor responsible for this homogeneity is ruled out, unless, of course, the effect of sporadic gene exchange through extra-marital or illegitimate relationship among the members of the different tribal groups (because of their close proximity to each other) is also accounted for, which in itself is a difficult task indeed.

There is considerable historical, linguistic and cultural evidence supported by physical data to suggest that the Indian tribal populations have three basic elements, namely, Negrito, proto-Australoid and palae-Mediterranean, mixed in various proportions in different tribes. Of these the Negrito, which is said to be the oldest racial strain, is represented by the tribal population of Andaman and Nicobar in a comparatively less hybridized form. Mixed with proto-Australoid, it is represented by the Kadars and Paniyans of South India. In the tribal population of central India the most predominant racial strains are the proto-Australoid and the palae-Mediterranean though the Negrito element in the substratum of the population cannot be completely ruled out. There is also an unmistakably Mongoloid element in the tribal population of central India which is more marked in the hill populations than in those of the plains. This perhaps has entered through the eastern coastal regions (Hutton, '41).

The Bastar district, which forms a part of the central India Plateau region, is inhabited by numerous jungle tribes such as the Raj Gonds, Muria, Halba, Bhatra and others. These tribal populations, though each is endogamous, have undergone a lot of linguistic and cultural interchange because they live close together. It is on

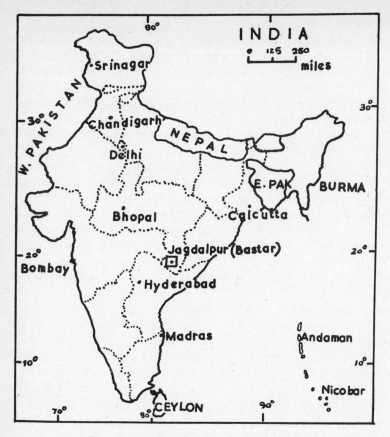

Fig. 1.　Showing the area of investigation.

these four tribal groups that the present study is based. Despite considerable diversity in the ancestral origin (based on historical, linguistic and cultural data, Grigson, '38, and physical data by Guha, as quoted by Elwin, '47) of these tribal groups and despite an apparent genetic isolation of each group the population shows a remarkable degree of homogeneity in the genetical traits under investigation. This gives rise to a logical speculation that perhaps we have here a case of convergent evolution due to common selective forces.

MATERIALS AND METHODS

The data for the present investigation were collected in September–October 1966 from the Bastar village (10 miles north of Jagdalpur) and other adjoining villages and the Tribal Training Centre in the Bastar village which draws tribal students from all over Bastar district. Blood samples of 54 Raj Gonds, 35 Murias, 25

Bhatras and 26 Halbas were subjected to ABO grouping and investigations for the sickle cell trait. ABO testing was done by the open slide method, while the sickle cell trait was examined under a microscope after allowing a drop of blood to mix with a drop of freshly prepared 2% solution of sodium metabisulphite on a glass slide under a coverslip.

The testing ability of 64 Raj Gonds, 41 Murias, 25 Bhatras, and 26 Halbas and their thresholds were studied by serial dilutions of phenylthiocarbamide. The solution number 2 (650 mg P.T.C./liter of water) was half as concentrated as solution number 1 (1300 mg P.T.C./liter of water), solution number 3 was half as concentrated as solution number 2, and so on till solution number 14. Individuals who failed to taste any of the solutions were classified as group O. The respondent was given solution number 14 (lowest concentration) first to taste, and if he failed to taste it, then solution number 13 and so on. The solution at which he or she first perceived any taste was recorded as his or her threshold (T.S.N.). Only in doubtful cases was the sorting technique of Harris and Kalmus ('49) employed.

Both males and females have been included and treated together under each group.

OBSERVATIONS AND DISCUSSION

ABO System

The distribution of ABO blood groups among the various tribal groups has been presented in table I. The table illustrates that B blood has the highest frequency in all the populations, closely followed by blood group O. The X^2 test has failed

TABLE 1

The frequency distribution of ABO blood type in Raj Gond, Muria, Bhatra and Halba

Tribal groups	Total no.	A		B		O		AB		X^2
		no.	%	no.	%	no.	%	no.	%	
Raj Gond	54	11	20.4	21	38.9	17	31.5	5	9.3	0.008
Muria	35	5	14.3	15	42.9	14	40.0	1	2.9	0.040
Bhatra	25	3	12.0	11	44.0	10	40.0	1	4.0	0.036
Halba	26	6	23.0	10	38.4	8	30.8	2	7.6	0.086

$X^2 = 4.37$, d.f. $= 9$, $0.90 > p > 0.80$.

Tribal groups	Allele frequency		
	p	q	r
Raj Gond	0.16	0.28	0.56
Muria	0.09	0.26	0.63
Bhatra	0.08	0.28	0.63
Halba	0.17	0.27	0.56

to show any statistically significant difference among Raj Gonds, Murias, Bhatras, and Halbas in regard to ABO blood group distribution.

A high frequency of the allele B is quite uniformly common in practically all the castes and populations in India except in some of the tribal groups or more isolated jungle communities, in whom A or O preponderates. The South Indian tribal groups (Pulayans, Kaders, etc.) who are said to be of proto-Australoid descent also have a higher frequency of O and A and a low frequency of blood group B. In the present tribal groups the high frequency of B may, however, be partly accounted for by the Mongoloid strain from the eastern coastal regions. Majumdar ('58) has found a high percentage of B blood among those social groups, castes and tribes in India who are exposed to unhealthy and inhospitable regions or are habitual victims of malaria. If this is so then the alleles for B and for the sickle cell trait must have developed some selective mechanism among groups living in such an inhospitable and malarious area as Bastar.

Sickle Cell Trait

Results of the test for the sickle cell trait among the four tribal groups are recorded in table 2. All the populations exhibit a fairly high frequency of the trait and the X^2 test suggests that the populations are quite homogeneous.

TABLE 2

Distribution of the Sickle cell trait among the four tribal groups

Tribal groups	Total no.	No. of persons affected	Frequency of sickle cell trait
Raj Gond	54	15	0.278
Muria	35	10	0.286
Bhatra	25	7	0.280
Halba	26	6	0.231

$X^2 = 0.53$, d.f. $= 3$, $0.95 > p > 0.90$.

It is interesting to note that in spite of close inbreeding practiced by each of these populations, they all show a remarkably high frequency of the sickling trait. It would seem that the heterozygote (Hb^AHb^S) must have a greater survival value than either of the homozygotes (Hb^SHb^S or Hb^AHb^A). It is now well established that heterozygotes (Hb^AHb^S) suffer less from malaria than homozygotes (Hb^AHb^A) (Barnicot, '64) thereby increasing the chances of heterozygotes surviving more frequently than homozygotes. Hence this balanced polymorphism in the case of the sickle cell trait seems to be responsible for maintaining a high allele frequency in the present tribal groups. Besides, it may well be possible that the homozygous condition (Hb^SHb^S) did not always produce lethal effect. In the present investigation, six out of 38 sicklers who showed severe sickling phenomena (the sickling of the blood cells was quicker and the cells were badly reduced when incubated with sodium metabisulphite solution) than the rest, may well have been those homozygous sicklers (Hb^SHb^S) who have survived anaemia. This, however, requires further investigation.

Tasting Ability

The results of the test of ability to taste phenylthiocarbamide and the taste threshold of individuals among Raj Gonds, Murias, Bhatras and Halbas are presented in tables 3 and 4. The histograms in figure 2 show a good deal of

TABLE 3

Distribution of P.T.C. taste threshold among the four tribal groups

Tribal groups	T.S.N.															Mean T.S.N.
	0	1	2	3	4	5	6	7	8	9	10	11	12	13	14	
Raj Gond	32	—	11	5	6	—	2	2	1	1	1	1	2	—	—	4.6
Muria	14	—	2	3	4	4	—	1	3	3	4	2	1	—	—	6.7
Bhatra	7	—	3	5	4	3	—	—	—	1	1	—	1	—	—	4.6
Halba	10	—	2	5	—	3	—	1	1	2	1	1	—	—	—	5.5

TABLE 4

Frequency of tasters and nontasters among the four tribal groups

Tribal groups	Total no.	Tasters		Nontasters		Allele frequency	
						T	t
		no.	%	no.	%		
Raj Gond	64	32	50.0	32	50.0	0.293	0.707
Muria	41	27	65.8	14	34.1	0.416	0.587
Bhatra	25	18	72.0	7	28.0	0.471	0.529
Halba	26	16	62.5	10	37.4	0.388	0.612

$X^2 = 4.736$, d.f. $= 3, 0.20 > p > 0.10$.

consistency in the taste threshold distribution in the four populations. The percentage frequency and the allele frequencies of tasters and nontasters have been calculated after noting that the antimode is at solution number 1, in all the populations under study. Of the four populations Raj Gonds are found to possess the maximum frequency (50.0%) of nontasters, while Bhatras are found to possess the minimum frequency (28.0%). The difference between the two is statistically significant at the 2% probability level ($X^2 = 4.32$ for 1d.f.). However, when the four populations are treated together they fail to show any statistically significant difference as is shown in table 4.

Natural selection is alleged to exert a strong selective influence on the alleles for tasting ability also, since there exists a correlation between adenomatous goitre and a high frequency of the nontaster allele (Harris, Kalmus and Trotter, '49), an association of toxic diffuse goitre and the taster allele (Kitchin et al., '59) and an associaton of higher incidence of the nontaster allele with cretinism (Fraser, '61). In some regions of India (Himachal Pradesh for instance), the iodine content of

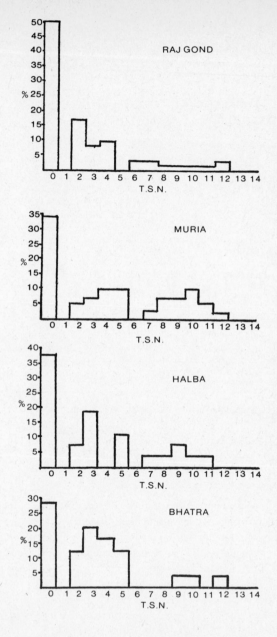

Fig. 2. Taste threshold distribution among the four tribal groups.

the soil and water is so low that it has affected the bulk of the population and has caused thyroid deficiency diseases. Thus, selection of the taster allele in such a region must have been in operation during the past. However, recent attempts on the part of the government to introduce iodized common salt, would certainly affect the selective power of such genotypes and change the allele frequencies at the taster locus among such populations in the future.

CONCLUSIONS

In conclusion it may be remarked that these four intrabreeding tribal groups of the Bastar district, who lived in the same environment for hundreds of generations, although of diverse racial origin, show a considerable degree of mutual similarity of such genetical traits as ABO blood groups, the sickle cell trait and the ability to taste phenylthiocarbamide. Table 5 shows the extent to which these

TABLE 5

Values of X^2 for each pair of groups with regard to the three genetical traits

Pair of groups	ABO	Sickle cell	P.T.C.
Raj Gond × Muria	2.29	0.03	2.59
Bhatra × Muria	0.18	0.00	0.27
Muria × Halba	1.73	0.34	0.15
Raj Gond × Bhatra	1.77	0.00	4.32 [1]
Bhatra × Halba	1.14	0.21	0.54
Raj Gond × Halba	1.48	0.28	1.25
d.f.	3	1	1

[1] Except Raj Gonds and Bhatras who differ significantly from each other $(0.05 > p > 0.02)$ in regard to the P.T.C. tasting ability only, none of the other tribal groups differ with each other in regard to any of the genetical traits.

populations differ at the loci under consideration. Since such biochemical traits as these are said to possess a great selective value, the homogeneity among these tribal groups may be in part due to environmental reasons, and offer an example of convergent evolution due to common selective forces.

Acknowledgments

Thankful acknowledgments are due to the authorities of the Tribal Training Centre at Bastar whose help enabled the author to stay in the region and collect the data. Thanks are also due to Miss Gurbir Dhillon and Mr. D. P. Bhatnagar who helped the author while collecting the data.

LITERATURE CITED

Aird, I., H. H. Bental and J. A. Roberts   1953   A relationship between cancer of the stomach and the ABO blood groups. Brit. Med. J., *1:* 799.

Aird, I., J. A. Mehigan and J. A. Roberts   1954   The blood group in relation to peptic ulceration and carcinoma of colon, rectum, breast and bronchus. Brit. Med. J., *2:* 315.

Anand, S.   1964   The relationship of ABO, MN and Rhesus blood groups to Asthma. Ind. J. Chest Dis., *4:* 74–79.

Barnicot, N. A. 1964 Biochemical Variation in Modern Populations. Human Biology, Oxford University Press, London.

Clarke, C. A., W. K. Cowan, J. W. Edwards, A. W. Howell Evans, R. B. McConnel, J. C. Woordraw and P. M. Sheppard 1955 The relationship of ABO blood groups to duodenal and gastric ulceration. Brit. Med. J., 2: 643.

Clarke, C. A., J. W. Edwards, D. R. W. Haddock, A. W. Howell Evans, R. B. McConnel and P. M. Sheppard 1956 The ABO blood groups and Secretor character in duodenal ulcer. Brit. Med. J., 2: 725–731.

Das, S. R., and L. Ghosh 1954 A genetic survey among the Paniyans, a South Indian aboriginal tribe. ABO, MN blood groups, Secretor factor and taste ability. Bull. Dept. Anthrop., Govt. India, 3(1).

Elwin, V. 1947 The Muria and their Ghotul. Oxford University Press, London.

Fraser, G. R. 1961 Cretinism and taste sensitivity to phenylthiocarbamide. Lancet, 1: 964–965.

Guha, B. S. 1951 The Indian Aborigines and their Administration. Delhi.

Grigson, W. V. 1938 The Maria Gonds of Bastar. Oxford University Press, London.

Harris, H., and H. Kalmus 1949 The measurement of taste sensitivity to phenylthiocarbamide (P.T.C.). Ann:Eugen. Lond., 15: 24–31.

Harris, H., H. Kalmus and W. R. Trotter 1949 Taste sensitivity to phenylthiourea in goitre and diabetes. Lancet, 11: 1038.

Howells, W. W. 1966 Population distances: Biological, Linguistic, Geographical and Environmental. Curr. Anth., 7: 531–535.

Hutton, H. H. 1941 Primitive tribes, Modern Indian and the West. Census of India, 1: 3.

Kitchin, F. D., A. W. Howell Evans, C. A. Clarke, R. B. McConnel and P. M. Sheppard 1959 P.T.C. taste response and thyroid diseases. Brit. Med. J., 1: 1069–1074.

Majumdar, D. N. 1958 Races and Cultures of India. Asia Press, New Delhi.

Negi, R. S. 1964 The incidence of sickle cell trait in Bastar, III. Man, 64: 171–174.

Ancestry and Plasticity: An African Example

ANTHROPOLOGY DEVELOPED IN EUROPE DURING THE NINE-teenth century. Despite the increased social mobility which accompanied the industrial revolution, the intellectual climate of the time was still strongly influenced by the hereditary principle upon which society was founded. The science of genetics was in its infancy, and everyone took it for granted that all human biological characteristics were inherited without change, although of course natural selection could "improve the breed." Early in the twentieth century, however, the American anthropologist Franz Boas (himself an immigrant from Europe) made a careful study comparing the physical traits of immigrant parents to those of their American-born offspring. He found that the two generations differed in many respects; an improved environment apparently leads to more rapid growth and greater size in adulthood.

Many European anthropologists were quite incredulous, but his work has been fully confirmed by later research among other migrants, their children, and their kinfolk in the old country. It is now clear that the human body responds to environmental stress to a far greater extent than scientists had supposed. When the conditions of life improve, people grow more: we do not inherit precise dimensions. In some parts of the world, both nutrition and child health have improved during the past two centuries, and a secular trend toward greater stature has occurred. This has been notable in Europe and Japan as they have become more and more industrialized. The next essay, by Professor Jean Hiernaux, "Heredity and Environment: Their Influence on Human Morphology," tells us what has happened in nonindustrialized Equatorial Africa.

15. Jean Hiernaux

Heredity and Environment:
Their Influence on Human Morphology

A Comparison of Two Independent Lines of Study*

Two broad categories of methods have been used for studying the relative influence of heredity and environment on anthropometric variability:

1. The comparison of intrapair differences in mono- and dizygotic twins. Provided the average between-twin difference of environment is similar for the monozygotic and the dizygotic twins, the ratio of the mean intrapair variances of DZ and MZ twins provides a test of a heredity component of the variability of the concerned character. Since its formulation by Dahlberg ('26), this F-ratio has often been termed a "heredity estimate." Vanderberg ('62) recently compared six anthropometric studies on twins by its means. As Osborne and De George ('59) emphasize, a low, eventually unsignificant value of the F-ratio may however result from a small genetic variability, or large environmental influences, as well as from a low degree of genetic control.

The method comparing MZ and DZ twins opposes two levels of genetical difference between individuals: nul between MZ twins, fraternal between DZ twins. Similarly, the fraternal level of hereditary difference may be opposed to that of the mean hereditary difference in the population. This was done by Howells ('49) by comparing the differences between brothers to the differences between random pairs of males taken in the population to which the brothers belong. The potential efficiency of such a study is lower than that of the twin studies: as an average, the members of the random pairs will tend to differ from brothers in their conditions of living much more than DZ from MZ twins.

2. The comparison of the phenotypes resulting from different environments acting on the same genotypes. The phenotypical differences may be assigned to the action of environment.

This category of methods can be applied at the individual or at the population level.

a. At the individual level, one method consists of studying several individuals

* Partly supported by a grant of the Fonds National de la Recherche Scientifique (Belgium). Elaborated for the most part during a stay of the author at the Department of Anthropology of Harvard University as a visiting professor.

submitted to environmental changes. The change may be experimental, as in the work of Keys, Brozek, Henschel, Mickelsen and Taylor ('50) on the biology of human starvation, or natural as in the observations of Ivanovsky ('23) on the modifications of the population of Russia during a three year period of famine. The last type of study is based on the physical modifications of individuals, even if the results are expressed under the form of shifting arithmetic means.

Another way to study the action of different environments on the same genotype is to compare MZ twins reared in dissimilar conditions, and to oppose them to MZ twins reared together (see for example Newman, Freeman and Holzinger, '37).

b. At the population level, the comparison will bear on genetically similar populations living in different environments.

The first purpose of the present paper is to compare the results of a study opposing MZ and DZ twins for several anthropometric variables, thus isolating the part played by Heredity, with those of a study of the second category, isolating the part played by Environment on the same variables. It must be stressed at first that no strict antithetic correspondence may be theoretically expected between the two lines of evidence: the differences of environment acting in the second study could be such as to have little influence on some characters of low heritability, or inversely to have a strong influence on the environmentally-determined part of a feature showing a high heritability.

Studies Selected for Comparison

The selected twin study was that of Osborne and De George ('59). It was chosen because it deals with adults, as the selected study of the second category. The authors took care to minimize the environmental differentiating influences by collecting their subjects within a single socio-economic stratum of a community living in a more or less homogeneous geographical environment. Only the data on male twins will be considered here, for avoiding eventual sex differences in heritability to disturb the comparison with the data of the populational study, which deals with males only.

The work concerning the influence of environment was selected in the group of studies based on the comparison of genetically similar populations living in different ecological conditions. For the present purpose, they have an advantage over the data on physique variation under adverse conditions: the ecological differences play since birth and even, through the mother, since conception, and not, as in Ivanovsky's and Keys' studies, on already built-up organisms; they therefore allow a better estimate of the result on adult morphology of factors having acted during the entire growing period. Such studies also imply a more systematic action of more easily identified environmental variables than in the case of the twins reared apart vs. twins reared together approach. They require however a great care in establishing that the two compared groups are really similar in heredity. Especially, if one group represents the offspring of migrants from the other group, the possibility of selective migration and of random genetic drift (in the sense of a random difference between small samples and the large population from which they are drawn) must be carefully investigated. If several generations have elapsed since the parting of the two groups, the possibility of selection having differentiated the two gene pools must also be faced, as well as that of mixture with different contiguous populations. Finally, attention must be paid to the mating system within both groups: migration often results in a breaking up of the isolates, which can influence some metric variables through heterosis, as Hulse ('58) demonstrated in Man.

The study here considered is that of Hiernaux ('54) in which two subgroups of Hutu, the agriculturalist cast of Rwanda, are compared. The subgrouping conformed to a purely geographical criterion: birth place and residence both higher or lower than 1900 m above sea level. Culturally and historically, both subgroups belong to the same entity. Geographically, the higher group does not inhabit a single circumscribed area, but several areas of higher altitude scattered through the country. The higher zones have been occupied recently and gradually, the forest front receding higher and higher as the Hutu, exclusive savannah dwellers, cut it down for tilling new fields, a necessity owing to their progressing population density and to the pressure exerted on them by relatively recent newcomers, the pastoralist Tutsi, who imposed themselves as the dominant class, and required large grazing-lands for their cattle. This gradual expansion of the cultivated land at the expense of the forest is still going on. These conditions minimize the possibility of a difference between the gene pool of the two subgroups by selection or drift: no barrier to mating divides them; they keep their cultural and social unity; there has been no real migration, but just an expansion over several large fronts. There is no evidence of different rates of gene flow from the two other ethnic groups of Rwanda: Tutsi and Twa: the features that are the most sensitive to such influences, like nasal index, do not show any significant difference between the two Hutu altitudinal subgroups. It is therefore sound to assign to environment most if not all the difference found between the latter.

In what does the environment of the two subgroups differ? Both live at a fairly high altitude: as an average, 2057 m and 1778 m, the difference being 279 m. This difference in altitude, on which the subdivision was based, seems too moderate for considering the difference in atmospheric oxygen concentration an important mesological factor. We lack data on mean temperature, but the difference can be estimated to 2.3°C from meteorological data collected in Rwanda at different altitudes. This is not negligble, but it does not seem to be of a magnitude that could matter much in the development of the individuals. At least, such mesological factors seem to be of minor importance in comparison with two other ones: nutrition and malaria.

In the higher zone, the soil is more fertile: it has been recently reclaimed from the forest, while that of the lower zone has been impoverished by erosion and intense cultivation. Owing to altitude and proximity of the forest, the rainfall is higher and the dry season reduced in the higher zone. There is no doubt that food production is considerably greater in the higher altitude group, with a smaller risk of periods of scarcity.

A food survey was conducted in Rwanda in '54 and '55 by several members of the Institute for Scientific Research in Central Africa (I.R.S.A.C.). Only its preliminary, purely qualitative stage has been published yet (Close, '55). The quantitative survey consisted of two parts: an extensive one, based on collecting one-day-per-family data on a large sample, and an intensive one, in which everything eaten during several days by each member of a restricted number of families was weighed. I extract from the latter stage's results the ones concerning the adult diet of the two Hutu subgroups (the full results will be published later by Hiernaux and Maquet). The values (table 1) have been computed by Close from the '54 F.A.O. tables.

TABLE 1

Mean daily intake of adult males and females in the two Hutu subgroups

Group	Sex	Number of subjects	Total number of days	Calories	Proteins	Carbo-hydrates	Lipids
					g	g	g
Higher altitude Hutu	♂	14	55	2648	109	542	13.2
	♀	9	35	2258	90	466	12.0
Lower altitude Hutu	♂	17	70	2357	75	499	12.0
	♀	23	96	1800	57	378	11.0

For both sexes, the dietary difference between the samples is important; only the fat intake is similar in the two groups. The higher altitude Hutu have a much higher caloric intake, due to more proteins and more carbohydrates. An analysis of the staple foods shows that most of them are common to the two groups: plantains, sweet potatoes, corn, sorghum, legumes (mainly peas in the higher regions, only beans in the lower ones). Both groups consume relatively important amounts of home-made beer (from bananas or sorghum). In both groups, the proteins are almost entirely of vegetable origin, at least in the adult's diet: milk, though favored, is nowhere available in large quantities and usually reserved for children; meat is everywhere a rare food (its consumption was recorded in one household only during the survey). Fat and fat-soluble vitamins are deficient in both diets. The contrast between the food intake of the higher and lower altitudinal Hutu groups is not a matter of a well-balanced against a deficient diet: both show qualitatively similar deficiencies, but the higher altitude group benefits of a higher caloric intake, from higher vegetable protein and carbohydrate intakes.

Another important factor differentiating the environment of the two Hutu subgroups is the severity of malaria. Malaria is now present nearly everywhere in Rwanda, but its frequency is much lower at high altitude. Some quantitative information on this point is available from the Health Department of Rwanda: in

'51 (the year during which the Hutu were measured), the percentage of cases of malaria in the total number of patients (all patients in treatment at the beginning of the period excluded) for a period of four months (two in the rainy season, two in the dry one) was the following: 8.7 for three dispensaries in the high part of the district of Byumba (at 2,200, 2,275 and 2,275 m altitude) against 21.7 for three dispensaries in the lower part of the same district (at 1,300, 1,450 and 1,596 m altitude). The report states that probably an important proportion of the malarial cases in residents of the high altitude zone were contracted while traveling in the lower areas. If this is the case, the difference in malarial morbidity between the two zones is more marked for the children (more sedentary than adults) than the one suggested by the preceding percentages on the whole population. Some doubt could be cast on the strict validity of such data, since full confidence in the diagnosis of malaria may not be possible owing to the conditions in which it was usually made. The possible bias would consist in attributing to malaria attacks of fever of other origin, thus giving to high values of the frequency of malaria and a less marked difference than the real one. A recent study by Meyers, Lips and Caubergh ('62) on the distribution of malarial infestation in Rwanda shows a stronger contrast between the higher and lower altitude zones. Over 2,000 m, they state, malaria is not transmitted; the rare cases observed in this zone were contracted when visiting lower regions. The population of the high altitude North-South stretch (i.e. the habitat of our high Hutu subgroup) shows a plasmodic index of 1%, contrasting with an index of 10 to 40% on the central plateau (from 1,500 to 1,800 m) where the majority of our lower altitude Hutu live, and sometimes reaching 80% in the eastern savannah (1,250–1,500 m) which has also contributed to our lower altitude sample. The high altitude Hutu group is undoubtedly greatly favored from the viewpoint of malaria. This advantage can, at least partly, be considered as nutritional (including both quantitative and qualitative aspects) in nature.

As a summary, the main ecological factors differentiating the response of the two Hutu subgroups to environment seem to be nutrition and malaria, which may perhaps be grouped as nutrition in a broad sense, if malaria is considered as an additional source of nutrient expenditure.

In view of the large difference in malarial incidence between the two Hutu subgroups, their similar sickle-cell trait frequency (4.92% in 142 higher altitude adult Hutu against 5.36% in 261 lower altitude adult Hutu) indirectly confirms their belonging to the same ethnic group. Intertribal correlation between altitude and sickle cell trait frequency in the Rwanda–Burundi–Kivu area, to which the Hutu belong, amounts to $r = 0.73$ as computed by Livingstone, Gershowitz, Neel, Zuelzer and Solomon ('60) from the data published by Hiernaux ('56). They interpret this correlation by the strong selective advantage of the sicklemic heterozygote in a malarious environment, and by the attenuation of malaria with altitude. If this is the right explanation, a similar sickle cell gene frequency between two subgroups having a common origin but largely differing by their malarial infestation means a very recent separation or a large intermingling, both factors indicated by the ethnological data.

Results and Discussion

The comparison between Osborne and De George's twin study and Hiernaux' Hutu study is based on the following anthropometric characters, for which the technique of measuring is identical in both studies: stature, total arm length, upper arm length, forearm length, biacromial breadth, chest breadth, chest depth, bi-iliac breadth, upper arm circumference, thigh circumference, calf circumference, weight, head length, total face height, upper face height, nose height, nose breadth, bigonial breadth, mouth width, interocular width, biocular width, and head height. Total leg length was added, though differently measured by Hiernaux (height of the spina iliaca) and by Osborne and De George (stature minus sitting height), because of the importance of this character and the similitude of the information provided by both techniques. Head breadth was dropped, because the F-ratio of variances computed by Osborne and De George between their male twin series for this character differs greatly from any corresponding value found in five similar studies listed by Vandenberg ('62), while the agreement between the six studies is fairly high for the other measurements (moreover, the very large difference in F-ratio between Osborne and De George's male and female twins makes the more likely that their exceptionally high value for head breadth in males—nearly four times the second highest value of F-ratios—is aberrant). The head breadth factor was partly re-introduced by including the cephalic index in the list.

The comparison will start from the viewpoint of the statistical significance of the results of both studies: the significance of the F-ratios of the DZ and MZ within pair variances (from data on 10 and 24 or 25 pairs respectively), and the significance of the differences between the two Hutu subgroups (from data on 70 higher altitude—and 184 lower altitude Hutu) for the same measurements (table 2).

Table 2 shows a strong tendency toward a balanced opposition between the two columns of significances. Disregarding the degree of significance, among the ten measures for which the F-ratio is significant, only five show a significant difference between the Hutu subgroups; among the 19 measures significantly differentiating the Hutu, only five show a significant F-ratio. A better environment resulted in a significantly higher mean in all but one (head height) characters whose variability has no detectable hereditary component in Osborne and De George's series. Moreover, all five characters for which both heritability and sensitivity to environment are demonstrated at the level of .05 show the probability of one factor below .01, that of the other above .01. There is a strong tendency for heritability and ecosensitivity being mutually exclusive.

This tendency can be quantitatively expressed by comparing the values instead of their significance. The correlation between the F-ratio of DZ and MZ within pair variances and the distance between the two Hutu subgroups has been computed. The distance used is the value $(\bar{x}_1 - \bar{x}_2)/\Sigma$ in which $\bar{x}_1$ and $\bar{x}_2$ are the two arithmetic means, and Σ the estimated standard deviation of the pooled Hutu population (this value is a true measure of divergence, independent of the size of

TABLE 2

Significance of the F-ratios of the DZ and MZ within pair variances in Osborne and De George's male series and significance of the difference between the two Hutu subgroups.

Two stars indicate P-values below 0.01, one star P-values below 0.05, no star P-values above 0.05. Characters are listed by decreasing F-ratios.

Character	Significance of the F-ratio of DZ and MZ variances	Significance of the difference between Hutu sub-samples
Cephalic index	**	
Total arm length	**	*
Stature	**	
Total leg length	**	
Nose height	**	*
Upper face height	**	
Bigonial breadth	**	*
Forearm length	*	**
Upper arm length	*	
Biocular width		**
Biacromial breadth	*	**
Chest breadth		**
Mouth width		**
Chest depth		**
Total face height		*
Interocular width		*
Max. calf girth		**
Bi-iliac breadth		**
Nose breadth		**
Upper arm girth		**
Weight		**
Bizygomatic breadth		*
Thigh girth		**
Head height		
Head length		**

the samples). Table 3 gives the values of the two variables. Figure 1 shows the corresponding scatter. The computed value of the coefficient of correlation r is —.471. This value is significantly different from zero (P < .01).

A more favorable environment (with respect to diet and malaria) tends to increase all physical measurements in a proportion inverse to their heritability.

TABLE 3

*F-ratios of the DZ and MZ within pair variances
in Osborne and De George's male series and distances between the two Hutu subgroups. Characters are listed by decreasing F-ratios.*

Character	F-ratio of DZ and MZ variances	Distance between the two Hutu subgroups
Cephalic index	9.90	0.064
Total arm length	4.97	0.316
Stature	4.73	0.198
Total leg length	4.41	0.240
Nose height	4.03	0.273
Upper face height	3.49	0.145
Bigonial breadth	3.17	0.435
Forearm length	2.89	0.356
Upper arm length	2.68	0.219
Biocular width	2.39	0.387
Biacromial breadth	2.29	0.538
Chest breadth	2.17	0.623
Mouth width	1.86	0.451
Chest depth	1.83	1.419
Total face height	1.81	0.204
Interocular width	1.76	0.292
Max. calf girth	1.58	0.814
Bi-iliac breadth	1.50	0.509
Nose breadth	1.39	0.365
Upper arm girth	1.36	0.915
Weight	1.05	0.968
Bizygomatic breadth	0.99	0.356
Thigh girth	0.91	0.930
Head height	0.73	0.241
Head length	0.44	0.458

This might seem evident; it is not however. An ecological factor could act
strongly on the relatively small ecosensitive part of a feature with a high heritability; the specific environmental factors that vary between the two Hutu subgroups could have little differentiating influence on features with a low heritability.

Figure 1 deserves several remarks. Cephalic index shows the highest heritability
and no ecosensitivity. A better nutrition has increased both head length and
breadth, but without affecting head shape. A similar situation exists for the face:

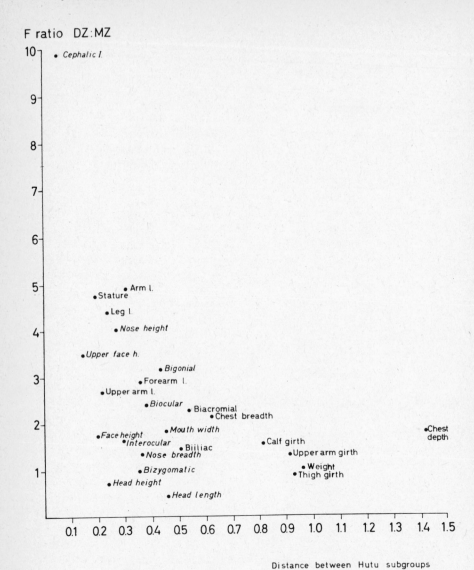

Fig. 1. Scatter diagram. Horizontal: distance $(x_1-x_2)/\Sigma$ between Hiernaux' two Hutu subgroups. Vertical: Osborne and DeGeorge's MZ : DZ F-ratio. Head measurements in italics.

significant differences appear in face height and breadth between the two Hutu subgroups, but their facial index is nearly identical (see appendix for means and standard deviations of the Hutu subgroups). For the nose again, they show a non-significant difference for the nasal index, while they differ significantly for both nose height and breadth. This gives an advantage to these indices over absolute measurements when comparing populations living at different health and nutrition levels.

Stature and leg length show a high heritability and no significant ecosensitivity. This agrees with the conclusions of Schreider ('62) on the low influence of environment on adult stature. Arm length, though showing a high heritability, reveals an ecosensitivity significant at the .05 level; the longer arm of the higher altitude Hutu is due merely to an elongation of its distal segment. A similar influence of the environment on the segmental proportions of the arm has been found by Prevosti ('49) in the school children of Barcelona, Spain: throughout the studied growth period, the higher socio-economic class shows a higher radio-humeral index than the lower class.

The distance between the two Hutu groups is moderate for all head and face measurements, though significant for most features; much higher distances are obtained for some postcranial measurements. If we consider cephalic and post-cranial measurements separately, they show different trend lines on figure 1. The coefficient of correlation between heritability and ecosensitivity, computed for head and face measurements equals $-.650$; that for postcranial measurements equals $-.729$. Both are considerably higher than the overall coefficient of correlation ($-.471$). The trend line is more oblique for the postcranial measurements: for a similar fall of heritability, the between-Hutu-distance increases more for the postcranial measurements. Stature, leg length, length of the arm and of its segments are near to the trend line of cranial measurements. Biacromial and bi-iliac breadths are slightly more influenced by environment, relatively to heritability, than the previous measurements, and chest breadth still more. A much higher distance between ecogroups appears for limb circumferences and weight. The main differentiating factor in this respect seems to be the importance played by bone in the feature: stature and longitudinal measures of the limbs are mostly bony measurements, as are most cephalic and facial characters. Limb circumferences and weight have a large non-bone component, while biacromial and bi-iliac diameters have a much lower soft tissue component, though more important than for stature, limb lengths and most head and face measurements. Chest breadth includes superficial soft tissues and the thoracic organs. As do the soft tissues, bony structures show an ecosensitivity inversely correlated with heritability, but the action of an environmental difference is more marked on the soft tissues than on bone (at least, the kind of difference playing between the Hutu groups; it is conceivable that differences of other nature could act more on bones).

The situation of chest depth on the scatter is exceptional: the highest distance between the Hutu subgroups is obtained for this character, despite the fact that superficial soft tissues are of little importance in this dimension. Here the altitude (and corresponding cold) factor, which we have considered of relatively little importance, could play as an additive factor. Citing the observations of Monge, Newman ('61) mentions the tremendous size of the chest of Indians who lived for many generations at high altitude, some of them being even barrel-chested. Though the altitude differential between the Hutu group is moderate (279 m), it is possible that this factor marked its impact on the one feature especially sensitive to it.

For limb circumferences, soft tissues mean merely muscle and fat. Our data do not allow to answer directly to the question: how much of the higher weight and limb circumferences observed in the better-nourished and less malarious Hutu group consists in more fat and how much in more muscle? Limb teleroentgeno-graphs and skinfolds would have provided the right data for a direct answer; we unfortunately did not have the necessary equipment. We can however approach the question indirectly. The difference between the Hutu subgroups is more marked for flexed arm with contracted biceps than for extended arm (22.7 against 17.4 mm); this indicates a more developed musculature in the higher Hutu group. Hand dynamometry confirms it; the mean for the right hand grip is 42.40 kg in the higher group, 38.04 kg in the lower group; the difference is highly significant and the computed distance is .543, a very large one indeed. We may be sure that muscle plays a part in the difference in limb girths (hence in weight). The data do not allow to estimate the part played by fat or by bone circumference.

The main postcranial differences between the Hutu subgroups may be summarized in this way: they are similar in stature but the group favored by the environment is heavier and has a stronger musculature, a wider and deeper thorax, wider shoulders and hips. One can but be struck by the fact that all the mentioned features are important in somatotyping. Whatever the method of typing used, the higher altitude Hutu, though genetically similar to the lower altitude ones, would show a higher mean rating in endomorphy and meso-morphy, and a lower one in ectomorphy. Lasker ('47) has already demonstrated the influence of nutrition on somatotype: the 34 volunteers subjected to a famine diet for 24 weeks in the Minnesota starvation experiment showed a mean decrease of 49% in endomorphy and of 43% in mesomorphy, and an increase of 77% in ectomorphy when somatotyping was based on measurements from standardized photographs, and slightly less marked changes when the photographs were rated by reference to observational standards.

Though the Minnesota experiment and the Hutu study both indicate a similar trend for the impact of nutrition on somatotype, they largely differ in the extent and timing of the nutrition differential. In the Minnesota experiment, adults were submitted to an intense dietary restriction (such as to induce a weight loss of 19 to 28%) during a limited period (six months). The Hutu subgroups have been submitted to a milder ecological difference, resulting in a mean adult weight 10.8% lower in the handicapped group, but bearing on the entire growth period. (Our unpublished food survey shows a consistent difference in diet through all ages. Lactation has not been estimated, but a better nourished mother may be expected to have a better lactation, and even to supply her offspring better with nutrients in utero. Malaria, on the other hand, differentiates the two environments since birth.) Comparing the distance between the two Hutu subgroups with the distance between pre- and post-starvation volunteers will reveal the influence of timing on the action of nutritional differences. Table 4 gives these values for a few characters; the standard deviation used for computing the distance for

TABLE 4

Distance between Hutu subgroups and between pre- and post-starvation Minnesota volunteers (see text)

Character	Distance between Hutu subgroups	Distance between pre- and post-starvation Minnesota volunteers
Stature	0.198	0.055
Biacromial breadth	0.538	0.506
Bi-iliac breadth	0.509	0.037
Chest breadth	0.623	0.601
Chest depth	1.419	0.304
Upper arm girth	0.915	3.916
Thigh girth	0.930	3.210
Calf girth	0.814	2.754

Minnesota volunteers is that of the pre-starvation series (means and standard deviations from Keys et al., '50).

The two sets of differences show a very different pattern: while the difference between the two stages of Minnesota volunteers is more than three times greater for limb girths than between the Hutu groups, it is a little less for biacromial and chest breadths, and much less for chest depth and bi-iliac breadth. Partial starvation in adulthood affects the measurements in which the bony parts are important much less than the ones in which fat and muscle are important; one may even wonder if bone dimensions are affected at all. On the contrary, differences in nutrition since birth that lead to much smaller differences in weight and limb girths produce larger differences in measurements of laterality. This confirms the evidence drawn from figure 1: the skeletal frame is involved in the difference between the Hutu subgroups; a better nutrition since birth leads to a laterally more developed skeleton. A body-build typology based on bone traits measured by x-ray techniques or other osteometric methods, as suggested by Lasker ('47) from the Minnesota experiment evidence, would still estimate morphophenotypes and not morphogenotypes (this was besides suspected by Lasker who writes: "However, one should still need to take into account environmental factors which might affect the shapes of bones during the developmental period"). Adult somatotype, or more generally adult morphology, is determined by three categories of factors: the genotype, environmental influences during growth, and environmental influences on the built-up organism (the process of aging is not considered here). Bone sensitivity to environment is much higher during and through growth than after it.

The preceding comments imply that the Hutu data allow a more fundamental approach to the problem of the influence of nutrition on constitution than data of the Minnesota experiment type. We have already noted that the most ecosensitive characters in the Hutu study are all important in somatotyping. Could this relation be quantified? For this we need an evaluation of the importance played by the individual characters in the process of somatotyping. Such an evaluation is provided by the factor analysis made by Howells ('52) on the measurements of 15 individuals, five of which are extremely dominant in endomorphy, five in ecto-morphy and five in mesomorphy when rated by Sheldon's method. Three factors have been extracted. Factor I accounts for the major fraction of the total variance. Endomorphy and ectomorphy appear to be the two halves of the scale of scores of individuals for this factor: the five extreme endomorphs are ranged around one pole of F_1, while the five extreme ectomorphs are tightly clustered around the opposite pole. Lasker ('52) remarked the relation between the starvation-induced changes in the Minnesota volunteers and the scores of the measurements on this F_1 factor; the correspondence is however far from perfect, especially in the case of bony characters like chest depth and bi-iliac diameter: both measurements show high scores in factor I but little change in the Minnesota starvation experiment. Is the relation tighter when we compare Howells' scores with the distance between the Hutu subgroups? To answer this question, let us put Howells' scores of measurements on F_A I factor (F_A represents an orthogonal rotation of the factor that is "approximately the best solution attainable") and the between-Hutu distances for the 23 common measurements on a scatter diagram (fig. 2).

The two variables are strongly associated. The computed value of the coefficient of correlation is $r = 0.828$. The bony measurements do not show any systematic deviation from the trend line. In particular, chest depth and bi-iliac width conform to the trend. Chest depth deviates from the trendline towards a larger ecosensitivity, a tendency already observed on the heritability/ecosensitivity scatter diagram (and suggesting that a supplementary ecological factor—altitude supposedly—acts on this feature). The correlation between Howells' scores and the changes in Minnesota subjects has not been computed, but the values of the variables suggest that it is much lower. It must finally be noted that head and face measurements follow the same trend as postcranial ones.

Ecosensitivity of a feature, as revealed by the Hutu study in which diet and malaria could print their impact on morphology since birth, is highly correlated with the score of the feature on factor I, which is essentially an endomorphy-ectomorphy scale. This shows how much nutrition (in a broad sense) during the growing period can affect the adult's somatotype. Acting on the same genotype, a better nutrition will produce a more endomorphic and less ectomorphic individual. Will all the genotypes be equally sensitive to nutrition? We must remember here that the scale of ecosensitivity is inversely correlated with the scale of heritability. An individual whose genotype favors high values of the variables located near the negative pole of factor I will tend to display these high values in any condition, because they are little affected by the environment and mainly determined by heredity. He will undoubtedly be wider and heavier if reared in

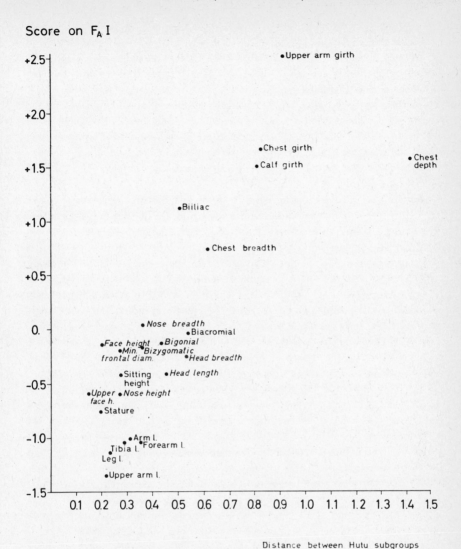

Fig. 2. Scatter diagram. Horizontal: distance $(x_1-x_2)/\Sigma$ between Hiernaux' two Hutu subgroups. Vertical: Howells' scores on F_A I.

better health and diet conditions, and this will shift his somatotype on the ecto-morphic-endomorphic scale towards the endomorphic pole, but this shift will be much more moderate than the one shown, in the same conditions, by an individual whose genotype favors low values of the negative pole variables. This one will have a much wider range of possible somatotypes in response to environment: in adverse conditions, he will be predominantly ectomorphic; in good conditions, predominantly endomorphic. High genetic ectomorphy protects against acquired endomorphy. Low genetic ectomorphy allows a wide range of somatotypes, from ectomorphy to endomorphy, depending on environmental factors. At the reduced level of adult ecosensitivity, this probably explains why, in the Minnesota experiment on initially well-fed individuals from a population enjoying high health standards, the ectomorphic subjects changed less than the endomorphic ones (Lasker, '47).

As a corollary to the preceding remarks, the location of an individual along the factor I scale is no criterion of his nutritional state: it depends on his genotype as well as on his past and present nutrition. If we look for metrical criteria of the nutritional state, we should use the features that exhibit both the largest ecosensitivity and the lowest heritability: limb circumferences for example, in the range of features here considered.

The fact that genotype controls the range of possible changes in morphology makes it imaginable that selection could exert a pressure on that range. Genotype here concerns many multifactorial characters, hence a large number of loci. Does it mean that, for narrowing the range of morphological ecosensitivity, selection should act at many loci? Not necessarily. The polygenic systems controlling different measurements might have one or more loci in common. By the cross-twin analysis, Osborne and DeGeorge ('59) showed evidences of genetically influenced covariation of two measurements. A genetic communality could partly be behind the correlations between measurements, and behind the factors extracted by factor analysis from the panel of correlations. A simple theoretical model working on the degree of heritability, and hence indirectly on Howells' factor I, can be built in a way to control the degree of genetic ectomorphy, hence the range of morphological ecosensitivity. It consists of two assumptions: a. a locus is common to all polygenic systems controlling body dimensions correlated with factor I; it has two alleles: one responsible for higher values, the other for lower values of the variables; b. this locus interacts with the other ones in each system as a multipler by a factor higher than one for the first allele, lower than one for the second one. In this model, any increase in the frequency of the first gene in a population would increase the mean of the measurements in which heredity plays a part, proportionally to the heritability of the feature (this model was presented for the sake of simplicity: of course, a model with more than two alleles and more than one common locus would meet the requirements as well). An increased frequency of the first allele would change the mean morphology of the population: the characters having a high heritability would increase more than those having a low heritability; in particular, linear dimensions like stature and leg length would increase more than lateral ones like biacromial and bi-iliac diameters, and still more than weight and limb circumferences. The relation between the scale of heritability and the scores of the metric variables on factor I implies, beyond the evidence provided by the above description, that ectomorphy would increase and endomorphy decrease in the population.

It is not suggested that the mechanism here described operates on a factor evidenced by a factor analysis of metrical features, such as the factor reflecting the antagonism between the linear and lateral tendencies discovered by Schreider ('56) in all samples on which he made a factor analysis (but accounting for only a small fraction of the total variance). Howells' analysis aims only to discover the factors subjacent to somatotyping, and his sample is built for that purpose, far from a representative sample of a population. Our suggested model operates on the scale of heritability, and the relation between Howells' factor I and this scale causes it to operate also along the scale of scores on this factor.

The existence of such an "auxogene" (mono- or multifactorial) acting on several measurements and directly controlling the situation of the morphogenotype on the ectomorphy-endomorphy continuum would be substantiated if we could find an evolutionary sequence along such a line. Patent cases of morphological evolution by selection have rarely been completely elucidated in Man: the necessary data on several successive generations of a population on which no other evolutionary force is acting are rarely available. An indirect approach to the checking of our model would consist in finding two populations that differ in a way consistent with the model, though living in the same environmental conditions. The check could consist in opposing the mean endomorphy or the mean ectomorphy in the two populations. Still better, it could consist in opposing the means of indices whose components have different degrees of heritability: in our model in which the frequency of the "auxogene" would increase, stature would increase more than bi-iliac, biacromial and thoracic diameters, arm length more than upper arm girth, leg length more than thigh girth, and so on.

In Rwanda, two populations show mean morphologies that seem contrasted in a way similar to the contrast between ectomorphy and endomorphy, although no somatotypological research has been made on them: the Tutsi are tall and narrow with low limb circumferences; the Hutu are shorter and heavier, they have larger limb perimeters and wider shoulders, hips and thorax in relation to stature (means are reproduced in appendix from Hiernaux, '52, '54 and '56). As explained before, the Hutu are the agriculturalist caste of the country, while the Tutsi are relatively recent newcomers; their former homeland is not known with certitude. These invaders were transient pastoralists and imposed themselves as the aristocratic class.[1] Any phenotypical difference between Hutu and Tutsi is to be interpreted in terms of heredity and environment. Since the difference seems to be partly of a more endormorphic vs. more ectomorphic type, data on their nutrition and health are of paramount importance.

Our Tutsi sample of 177 adult males came from the same regions as our lower altitude Hutu. They will be compared with the latter, both in their conditions of living and in their physique. Tutsi, currently settled, and Hutu live on the same hills; they are subjected to the same malarial infestation. The already cited food survey was made on the Tutsi as well as the Hutu. The following values have been computed from the data on adult Tutsi: for eight males totalizing 33 days of survey, the mean caloric intake is 2,422; the mean intakes are 90 g for proteins, 466 g for carbohydrates, and 23.6 g for lipids. The corresponding values for 11 females totalizing 43 days of survey are 2,392 calories, proteins 86 g, carbohydrates 488 g and lipids 16.7 g. If we compare these values with the means for the lower

---

[1] The sociological data refer to the situation that existed at the time of the survey: 1950–1952.

altitude Hutu (table 1), we see that the Tutsi sample has a higher caloric intake than the Hutu one in both sexes; the difference concerns mainly the "noble" nutrients: protein and fat. This is essentially due to more milk in the Tutsi diet. Data on children have not yet been statistically elaborated, but the difference appears to be of the same nature as among adults: the pastoralist Tutsi can give more milk to their children, and their lord-to-serf relationship with the Hutu provides their households with an at least equal amount of starchy foods. The food survey confirms the sociological data. Without discussing the significance of the differences in diet observed in such small samples, one may safely state that the Tutsi diet is at least as good as that of the surrounding Hutu, and probably richer in proteins and fat of animal origin. We are thus on safe ground for interpreting the leanness of the Tutsi in terms of heredity, and for applying the above described check to the hypothesis that the morphological difference between Tutsi and Hutu is consistent with the model of higher and lower frequencies of an "auxogene" indirectly acting on the ectomorphy-endomorphy factor. Table 5

TABLE 5

Tutsi and Hutu means of indices whose terms have one, a high heritability, the other a low heritability

Index	177 Tutsi	184 Hutu
Bi-iliac/stature	15.0	15.1
Biacromial/stature	20.8	21.6
Chest breadth/stature	14.6	15.6
Arm girth/arm length	30.7	34.3
Thigh girth/leg length	45.6	50.7

lists the mean values of the indices selected above for having one term high, the other term low in heritability.

This panel of values is entirely consistent with the hypothesis: all indices are higher in the Hutu. Moreover, the contrast between Tutsi and Hutu is most marked for indices in which the contrast of heritability of their terms is maximum: those involving limb perimeters. We have seen that diet, had it any differentiating influence, would act in the opposite direction. The striking leanness and linearity of the Tutsi, as compared to the Hutu, is genetical, not nutritional. This has an important corollary: the use of the various weight-to-stature indices, or of the limb perimeters related to stature, or even of the absolute limb perimeters as criteria of the nutritional status may be misleading. Such indices are valid only for following the evolution of the nutritional status of a population in the absence of selection, or for comparing the nutritional status of populations that are similar in their genetic location along the ectomorphy-endomorphy continuum.

All indices listed in table 5 are based on postcranial measurements. The analysis can be extended to the face. Compared to nose height, nose breadth shows a much lower F-ratio in the twin study, a higher ecosensitivity in the Hutu study and a higher score on $F_A I$. In our model, an increase in the frequency of the "auxo-gene" would thus lower the nasal index. The Tutsi actually have a much lower nasal index than the Hutu. A similar relation appears between the bizygomatic diameter and total face height: the former has a much lower F-ratio, a larger ecosensitivity and a higher score on $F_A I$. The model would show an increasing facial index. The facial index of the Tutsi is actually much higher than the Hutu's.

For facial proportions as well as for general body proportions, the nature of the morphological difference between Tutsi and Hutu is thus consistent with the hypothesis: in the same environment, with a diet at least not worse, the Tutsi systematically differ from the Hutu in the direction predicted by a model of higher genetic ectomorphy through an increased frequency of a general auxogene. It is not suggested here that all the difference between Tutsi and Hutu is due to such a mechanism; the Tutsi are evidently no Hutu transformed by selection. But what the data suggest is that part of the difference is due to an evolution of the ancestors of the Tutsi toward extreme genetic ectomorphy.

What selective forces could favor such an evolution? From experimental and actuarial data, Baker ('58) constructed a model or "ideal" man for tolerance of desert heat. Its morphological characteristics are a large surface area per unit weight and low subcutaneous fat. The Tutsi conform to this model: their rela-tively long legs and short trunk, their narrow thorax and shoulders, and their low relative weight give them a large surface area per unit weight. Their skinfolds have not been measured, but observation on the field and on photographs and the evidence from limb perimeters allow us to assert that their subcutaneous fat-layer is thin. Hot desertic conditions, or conditions approaching this extreme climate, like those of the dry and hot steppes of the Sahel and of some parts of East Africa (especially Somaliland), or of the similar steppes that covered part of the Sahara during the neolithic period, could characterize the environment in which the Tutsi developed their current morphology.

From the published data, Hiernaux ('52) noted that the population anthro-pologically the nearest to the Tutsi is the Somali (excepting the Hima of Uganda, who are the neighbors of the Tutsi and akin to them). The Somali live in hot desertic conditions. The Peuls or Fulani of West Africa, savannah or steppe dwellers, also have morphological affinities with the Tutsi. The selective mecha-nism here proposed as a partial explanation of the Tutsi's morphology might have worked on the ancestors of several other populations, and those ancestral popula-tions might have been geographically and genetically nearer to each other than their current descendants (unless a phenomenon of convergence took place). This matter will not be discussed further here. Diversity in time and space of selective pressures, hybridization, drift and mutations makes the search for phylogenetic affinities between populations a very difficult task. Originally, the purpose of this paper was only to study the relative influence of Heredity and Environment on human morphology; the findings lead us to face the possibility of a still uncon-sidered modality of evolution; this possibility is supported by the evidence from Rwanda. Generalization is, at least, premature.

Summary

Heritability of anthropometric variables, as estimated from data on twins, is compared with their sensitivity to differences in nutrition and health, especially when these differences operated since birth. A negative correlation is found, stronger when computed for postcranial and head measurements separately; bone measurements and those including a large non-bone component follow different trends.

The influence of nutrition on somatotype is discussed. Heritability of metrical characters, their ecosensitivity and their score on the main factor extracted from the factorial analysis of extreme somatotypes are compared. The ranking of the features is similar on the three scales. A different sensitivity to nutrition of the genetical endomorphs and ectomorphs is deduced.

A simple genetical model producing high genetic ectomorphy is elaborated. The differences between Rwanda's Hutu and Tutsi are consistent with this evolu-tionary model. The selective forces favoring high genetic ectomorphy in Africa seem to be related to hot and dry climatic conditions.

Acknowledgments

Gratitude is expressed to all members of the Department of Anthropology of Harvard University; discussion with them was highly stimulating in the prepara-tion of this paper. I am especially indebted in this respect to Dr. William Howells and Dr. Edward Hunt. Mr. Frank Saul was very helpful in the collection of references.

LITERATURE CITED

Baker, P. T. 1958 A theoretical model for desert heat tolerance. Headquarters Quartermaster Research and Eingeering Command, U.S. Army, *Technical Report EP-96*, Natick, Mass.

Close, J. 1955 Enquête alimentaire au Ruanda-Urundi. Acad. Roy. Sci. Colon., Cl. Sci. Nat. et Méd., n.s., 2, fas. 4, Bruxelles.

Dahlberg, G. 1926 Twin births and twins from a hereditary point of view. Stockholm Tidens Tryckeri.

F.A.O. 1954 Tables de composition des aliments (minéraux et vitamines) pour l'usage inter-national. F.A.O., Rome.

Hiernaux, J. 1952 Influence de la nutrition sur la morphologie des Bahutu du Ruanda. Actes du IXe Congrès International des Sciences Anthropologiques et Ethnologiques (Vienne 1952), *1*: 157–162.

———— 1954 Les caractères physiques des populations du Ruanda et de l'Urundi. Mém. Inst. Roy. Sci. Nat. Belgique, 2e sér., 52.

——— 1956   Analyse de la variation des caractères physiques humains en une région de l'Afrique centrale: Ruanda-Urundi et Kivu. Ann. Mus. Roy. Congo Belge, Sci. de l'Homme, Anthrop. 3, Tervuren.

Howells, W. W.   1949   Body measurements in the light of familial influences. Am. J. Phys. Anthrop., n.s., 7: 101–108.

——— 1952   A factorial study of constitutional type. Am. J. Phys. Anthrop., n.s., 10: 91–118.

Hulse, F. S.   1958   Exogamie et hétérosis. Arch. Suisses d'Anthrop. gén., 22: 103–125.

Ivanovsky, A.   1923   Physical modifications of the population of Russia under famine. Am. J. Phys. Anthrop., 6: 331–353.

Keys, A., J. Brozek, A. Henschel, O. Mickelsen and H. L. Taylor   1950   The biology of human starvation. University of Minnesota Press, Minneapolis.

Lasker, G. W.   1947   The effects of partial starvation on somatotype. An analysis of material from the Minnesota starvation experiment. Am. J. Phys. Anthrop., n.s., 5: 323–342.

——— 1952   Note on the nutritional factor in Howells' study of constitutional type. Am. J. Phys. Anthrop., n.s., 10: 375–379.

Livingstone, F. B., H. Gershowitz, J. V. Neel, W. W. Zuelzer and M. D. Solomon   1960   The distribution of several blood group genes in Liberia, the Ivory Coast and Upper Volta. Am. J. Phys. Anthrop., n.s., 18: 161–178.

Meyers, H., M. Lips and H. Caubergh   1962   L'état actuel du problème du paludisme d'altitude au Ruanda-Urundi. Ann. Soc. Belge Méd. Trop., 42: 771–782.

Newman, H. H., F. N. Freeman and K. Holzinger   1937   Twins: a study of heredity and environment. University of Chicago Press, Chicago.

Newman, M. T.   1961   Biological adaptation of Man to his environment: heat, cold, altitude, and nutrition. Ann. N.Y. Acad. Sci., 91: 617–633.

Osborne, R. H., and F. V. DeGeorge   1959   Genetic basis of morphological variation. Harvard University Press, Cambridge, Mass.

Prevosti, A.   1949   Estudio del crecimiento en escolares barceloneses. Trabalhos del Instituto "Bernardino de Sahagun" de Antropologia y Etnologia, Barcelona.

Schreider, E.   1956   Morphologie et physiologie. Bull. Inst. National Orientation Professionelle, 12: 301–312.

——— 1962   Les modifications actuelles de l'Homo Sapiens. Actes VIe Congr. Intern. Sci. Anthrop. et Ethnol. (Paris 1960), 1: 691–693.

Vandenberg, S. G.   1962   How "stable" are heritability estimates? A comparison of heritability estimates from six anthropometric studies. Am. J. Phys. Anthrop., n.s., 20: 331–338.

APPENDIX

Means and standard deviations for higher-altitude Hutu, lower-altitude Hutu and Tutsi of Rwanda

Character	70 Higher-altitude Hutu		184 Lower-altitude Hutu		177 Tutsi	
	x̄	s	x̄	s	x̄	s
Weight (kg)	64.50	6.77	57.51	6.36[1]	57.42	6.81[2]
Stature (cm)	168.40	6.22	167.08	6.79	176.52	7.29
Total leg length (cm) (from iliospinale ant)	98.12	4.43	96.93	4.99	104.29	5.65
Total arm length (cm)	76.98	3.36	75.85	3.59	78.50	3.83
Upper arm length (cm)	31.82	1.73	31.42	1.88	32.98	2.05
Forearm length (cm)	27.79	1.27	27.31	1.35	28.07	1.50
Biacromial breadth (cm)	37.31	2.04	36.18	2.06	36.79	1.99
Bi-iliac breadth (cm)	25.94	1.35	25.23	1.38	26.49	1.22
Chest breadth (cm)	27.04	1.39	26.16	1.39	25.72	1.23
Chest depth (cm)	20.98	1.47	19.17	1.14	18.67	1.18
Chest girth (cm)	92.27	4.33	88.46	4.17	86.55	3.54
Upper arm girth (cm) (in relaxation)	27.72	1.82	25.99	1.83	24.09	1.85
Upper arm girth (cm) (biceps contracted)	31.03	1.83	28.79	1.94	26.76	2.13
Thigh girth (cm)	52.51	3.03	49.11	3.05	47.55	3.09
Calf girth (cm)	35.69	2.49	33.57	2.41	32.56	2.15
Right hand grip (kg)	42.40	7.78	38.04	7.71	35.98	7.86
Head length (mm)	198.32	7.07	195.06	6.96	197.32	6.10
Head breadth (mm)	149.45	4.43	146.66	5.32	146.97	5.07
Frontal min. breadth (mm)	110.38	4.04	109.10	4.57	106.15	4.25
Bizygomatic breadth (mm)	140.90	4.77	138.99	5.63	134.45	4.98
Bigonial breadth (mm)	104.60	5.41	102.10	5.72	97.87	4.81
Total face height (mm)	121.47	6.04	120.19	6.48	124.58	6.88
Upper face height (mm) (nasion-prosthion)	72.92	4.59	71.93	4.62	74.96	4.85
Nose height (mm)	53.10	3.67	52.12	3.53	55.80	3.54
Nose breadth (mm)	43.94	3.03	42.82	3.01	38.71	3.05
Biocular width (mm)	100.25	3.73	98.54	4.55	95.96	3.82
Interocular width (mm)	34.72	2.63	33.85	3.06	32.58	2.65
Head height (mm)	121.38	4.30	120.32	4.33	121.18	4.17
Cephalic index	75.40	2.75	75.21	3.11	74.45	2.65
Nasal index	83.15	7.03	82.29	7.57	69.42	7.03
Facial index	86.30	4.37	86.53	4.98	92.82	5.36

[1] 179 subjects.
[2] 172 subjects.

Ancestry and Tradition

As the previous article makes perfectly clear, some human biological characteristics, such as anatomical dimensions, are more or less influenced by environmental conditions, whereas others, such as hemoglobin types, are not. Neither are the blood groups, eye color, hairy ears, and a wide variety of items; these are called "genetic markers." Their frequencies in a breeding population may be altered by natural selection, but in each individual's constitution they are fixed. Consequently they are used as the best indications of kinship in cases of disputed paternity and are often used as indications of genetic kinship between peoples who now live in different regions. Under some circumstances, this is perfectly reasonable.

In dealing with the genetics of laboratory animals and plants, it is customary to assume random mating among them, unless there is evidence to the contrary. In dealing with the genetics of human populations, on the other hand, it is vital to remember that random mating never exists. Different peoples have different customs about mating, of course, just as they do about diet, the disposal of the dead, and so on. But in all aspects of human activity, custom rules. And this cannot help but skew the flow of genes from one generation to the next, and consequently the distribution of gene frequencies in a population. Some societies insist that all known kinfolk be avoided as mates: this obviously promotes gene flow. Others are highly endogamous, feeling that all "outsiders" must be avoided as mates: this promotes genetic isolation. A genetic isolate might be expected to retain its ancestral characteristics for quite a long while. Dr. Batsheva Bonné, in the next article "Are There Hebrews Left?" writes about such an isolate.

16. Batsheva Bonné

Are There Hebrews Left?

Abstract. The Samaritan sect in the Middle East traces its ancestry over a period of more than 2,000 years from the Biblical Samaritans. The Samaritans are the guardians of a unique and very ancient religious literature which together with other historical accounts makes their claim of such a length of existence probable.

Comparison of blood group frequencies as well as other genetic markers (such as PTC sensitivity, color blindness and G6PD deficiency) indicate that the Samaritans are unlike any of the existing surrounding groups whom they might be expected to resemble. From comparison of anthropometric data the Samaritans appear to exhibit their own "typical" features which do not resemble those of any other Jewish or non-Jewish community in the Middle East. These differences support the contention that the Samaritans' separation and isolation from the communities is not a recent event. The possibility that the Samaritans today can be regarded as modern representatives of the ancient Hebrews and the living offspring of a particular branch of the Israelite kingdom is discussed.

One generally associates the name Samaritan with the famous parable of "The Good Samaritan" (John IV) and several other references in the New Testament. The Samaritan people, however, as a distinctive national group made their appearance in history earlier than the first century.[1]

While there seem to be abundant references to the Samaritans in Biblical

---

[1] The name "Samaritan" is derived from the Greek word "Samareitai" which is a transliteration of the Hebrew in the Old Testament:

Omri "bought the hill Samaria of Shemer for two talents of silver and he built on the hill and called the name of the city which he built after the name of Shemer the owner of the hill, Samaria" (Kings, I, 16:24).

The name of the town therefore was Shomeron and that of the inhabitants shomeronim or shomerim. The application of the name varied from time to time. At first it probably referred only to the town of Samaria; then it was used for the whole of the northern province. Later it was restricted to those who sided with the Samaritans in their dispute with the Jews and worshipped at Mt. Gerizim and not at Jerusalem.

sources and in later writings, it is not an easy task to draw a clear and uniform picture of their history, especially during the earlier periods. Historians claim that their history has been written "by their adversaries and consists mainly of stray allusions in the Biblical and Rabbinic literature coloured by the bias of the writers" (Gaster, '25). Their own ancient literature has been destroyed with the exception of a few fragments. It, too, was probably biased. Only since the middle of the last century have historical records of the Samaritans become known, which made possible the piecing together of the whole history from the various sources.

The beginning of the Samaritans are viewed by Jews and Samaritans from two opposite standpoints. According to Biblical sources, the Samaritans are the descendants of the settlers that were transplanted into Palestine in 722 B.C., by the Assyrian King Sargon (Kings, II, 17:5). The settlers included people from Babylon, Hamath, Kuth (or Kutah) after which the Samaritans were called "Kuthim" in Jewish sources.

Other transplantations were made successively by the Assyrian Kings between 680–670 B.C. Those who were left behind and were not led into captivity interbred with the transplanted foreign elements. Jerusalem, the center of the Southern kingdom, fell in 586 B.C. and the Judahites were led into Babylon. Fifty years later they were allowed to return to Jerusalem and to rebuild their temple; the Judahites regarded the Samaritans now as people of doubtful purity who corrupted their worship with that of heathen Gods and turned down their offer to help.

The Samaritans, on the other hand, deny vehemently their foreign origin and regard themselves as pure Israelites. They explain the schism between them and the Jews in terms of religious, not political differences tracing it to their dispute about the chosen place of worship.

They claim that the holiness of Mt. Gerizim, the one and true sanctuary was declared by Moses himself and therefore Joshua built the temple on the summit of the mountain.

According to the Samaritans their history begins with the settlement of the tribes in the Holy Land. They claim to be the descendants of the tribes of Ephraim and Manasseh who populated the central region known as Samaria. The choice of Jerusalem as the religious and political center by David and Solomon is deeply resented by the Samaritans who saw in it a definite break with God's decrees. Gaster ('25) maintains that until the proposals to rebuild the temple were made there had been considerable friendship and intermarriage between the Samaritans and the Jews.

It is only during the attempts of Ezra (around 200 B.C.) to purify the Jewish nation when a complete social break between Jews and Samaritans took place.

From that time the history of the Samaritans is a long succession of misfortunes interrupted by only brief periods of peace.

During the earlier part of the Roman regime (up to 70 A.D.) the emperors applied severe laws to both Jews and Samaritans. The ancient city of Schechem was destroyed and replaced about 1.5 miles to the west by the new city Flavia Neapolis, which has become modern Nablus.[2]

For most of the remainder of the Roman period Samaria had practically no peace. In the fourth century, Baba Rabba, the eldest son of the high priest instituted a great religious revival and reformation of the Samaritan State. Soon, however, came Byzantine Christian rule, which for 250 years cruelly oppressed both the Jews and the Samaritans. There were frequent revolts by the latter, which in turn prompted further oppression and persecutions. In 474 A.D. the emperor Zeno expelled the Samaritans from Mt. Gerizim and built a church on the mountain in honor of the Virgin Mary.

Ben Zevi ('56) feels that the great revolts against the Byzantines from the fourth to the fifth centuries A.D. show that the Samaritans constituted, even in those times, a strong nation whose population numbered at least 100,000 individuals, or even families. But such revolts mark also the end of the nation. The losses suffered, the enormous number of prisoners, the forced deportations and most of all the extensive conversions following the persistent persecutions, resulted in a great reduction in their numbers. There is, however, a record of the existence of still large Samaritan settlements in the seventh century too; for example, in Caesarea and its neighborhood there were 80,000 Samaritans (Jaqut, in Montgomery, '07) or according to Baladhur (Vilmar, 1865) some 30,000.

From the Islamic period onwards (634–970 A.D.) the Samaritans begin to appear as a small and fragmentary sect only. There were still thousands of Samaritan peasants during the reign of Harun el Rashid in the neighborhood of Ramleh Lydda, Yavneh and Arsuf (Vilmar, 1865 and Ben Zevi, '56).

For subsequent periods information regarding the history of the Samaritans is rather meager. We get some glimpses of the community from sources such as Arabic historians and geographers. Christian chronicles for the age of the Crusades almost ignore the Palestinian sect. The references found in medieval Judaism and in the writings of several Hebrew scholars and tourists to the Holy Land make it clear, however, that the sect, small as it was, never disappeared completely.

The following landmarks will summarize some of the major events in the Samaritans' story after the eleventh century:

1099 A.D. Samaritan chieftains from the mountains came to the Christian conquerors of Jerusalem, bringing presents and inviting the Crusaders to take possession of their territory, an offer which was immediately accepted (Montgomery, '07).

1137 A.D. The governor of Damascus murdered all the citizens of Nablus, took 500 Samaritans captive and transported them to Damascus. These served as an important component in the development of the Samaritan community there. Part

---

[2] The *New York Times* of October 28, 1964 reports: "Under the recently discovered ruins of a Roman temple in Jordan, archeologists have uncovered the remains of another temple which may turn out to be the ancient sanctuary of the Samaritans. The twin finds were made in a mount known as Tel-el-Ras on Mount Gerizim . . ."

of the captives were redeemed by a generous Samaritan citizen from Acre and went to live in Gaza (Montgomery, '07).

1163 A.D. The Jewish traveller Benjamin of Tudela visited Palestine, and writes about the Samaritans:

> Thence it is two parasangs to Nablous, which is Shechem on Mount Ephraim, where there are no Jews; the place is situated in the valley between Mount Gerizim and Mount Ebal, and contains about 1,000 Cuthim, who observe the written law of Moses alone and are called Samaritans. They have priests (of the seed of Aaron) and they call them Aaronim, who do not intermarry with Cuthim but wed only among themselves. These priests offer sacrifices and bring burnt-offerings in their place of assembly on Mount Gerizim, as is written in their law "And thou shalt set the blessing on Mount Gerizim." They say that this is the proper site of the Temple. On Passover and the other festivals they offer up burnt-offering on the altar which they have built on Mount Gerizim . . . They say that they are descended from the tribe of Ephraim. . . .

(From the Itinerary of Benjamin of Tudela) Adler, '04

1187-1516 A.D. The Mameluk period: The Samaritans formed part of the general Jewish community at whose head was a Jewish exilarch who resided in Egypt. Samaritans in Palestine, Syria and Egypt were under his jurisdiction.

1488 A.D. Rabbi Obadiah of Bertinura describes the Samaritans in Egypt as employed in financial business and as agents for the government, so that the community was a rich one. He travelled with many Samaritans from Egypt to Mt. Gerizim. He indicates the existence of 500 Samaritan families; about 150 in Cairo, and the rest in Damascus, Gaza Shechem and some other Palestinian localities.

1516 A.D. Ottoman Conquest and empire: Ottoman registers in the archives in Istanbul report the existence of some 25 Samaritan households in Gaza, 34 in Shechem. Their occupation was trade and manual work. Most of them were poor with only a few rich individuals.

1538 A.D. A large number of Samaritans returned from Damascus to Shechem, among them the high priest. (The "diaspora communities" especially that at Damascus, fostered the mother community, which otherwise would have perished. Many members of the high priest's family often lived in Damascus.) From this time on, until 1625, the community in Damascus decreased in number; this was a period of persecutions, and conversions by Damascus rulers.

1616 A.D. Shechem became the center of the Samaritan community.

1624 A.D. The priestly house claiming descent in the male line from Aaron died out and the high priests have henceforth been drawn from men tracing descent from Uzziel, son of Kohath, son of Levi.

1648–1687 A.D. A period of oppression and confiscation of lands; there were many conversions to Islam.

1708 A.D. The Samaritan community in Egypt became extinct.

1785–1820 A.D. The sect was restrained from its worship on the holy mountain.

1841 A.D. A conspiracy was formed to murder all the Samaritans. Nablus Arabs persecuted severely the Samaritans who did not want to accept the Moslem religion, under the pretense that the Samaritans do not possess any religion and do not believe in any one of the following: Moses, New Testament, Psalms, Prophets and Koran. The Samaritans were saved by the chief Rabbi of Jerusalem who gave them a "certificate" stating that "the Samaritan people is a branch of the Children of Israel, who acknowledged the truth of Torah" (Rogers, 1865) thus proving that they were "people of the book" and so entitled like Christians and Jews to protection.

1854 A.D. The Samaritans came under the protection of the British rule. "Through the friendly notice of European governments, especially that of England and its consuls in Jerusalem, the Samaritans have been preserved from the violent annihilation that threatened them. But the wealth they possessed was gone and they have become a community of alm-seekers forced to sell their sacred manuscripts for subsistence" (Montgomery, '07).

1855 A.D. Mills visited the Samaritan community in Nablus and found 40 families (150 individuals) all living together Ghetto-like on the south-western side of the city (Mills, 1864).

1927 A.D. A serious earthquake caused destruction of several sections of the city of Nablus, including the Samaritans' buildings. The Samaritans moved from their street to about four miles outside of the city where they live today.

1965 A.D. A total of 381 Samaritans regard themselves as the descendants of the original Samaritans described previously. They are divided into two groups that live under different political allegiances, and are therefore separated socially and geographically except for seven days a year during their Passover. There are 225 Samaritans residing in Nablus, Jordan and 156 in Cholon (near Tel-Aviv), Israel. (For demographic and anthropological studies on the community, see Bonné, '63 and '65.)

Previous Studies

It would be wrong to conclude from a brief historical account of the Samaritans that except for mention of them by various visitors or tourists to the Holy Land in recent centuries the Samaritans have not themselves been studied as a group.

An increasing interest in the Samaritans grew among European scholars since the time of Scaliger (1583) and a correspondence was opened with them. Two letters, one from a Samaritan of Gaza, the other from Egypt, were the beginning of an extensive correspondence between the Samaritans and several Europeans, which for nearly 250 years served as a major source of information concerning their condition (Silvestre de Sacy, 1823).

Later, travellers such as E. Robinson ('57), Petermann (1865) and M. E. Rogers (1867) devoted several pages of description to the Samaritan community in their publications about their tours to Palestine and the Orient. A very full account is found in Mills (1864). Most of these reports deal primarily with the small size of the group and problems of marriage and in more detail with their religious rites and customs.

In the beginning of the present century, several more anthropological studies of the Samaritans were published. These can be divided in two categories: cultural and physical.

The first centers around cultural and religious affinities between Samaritans and Judaism, or between the Samaritans and surrounding religions and cultures. These affinities were traced along lines of archaeological remains and linguistic data as well as social customs and traditions (Gaster, '25; Ben Zevi, '35).

At the turn of the century, another aspect of the Samaritan sect aroused the interest of European scholars, who organized special scientific expeditions to study the group. This aspect was the second anthropological category, the physical or biological, which grew out of interest in the problems of race and environment. In particular it developed from the desire to define physical types and assign them to geographical areas of the world. In addition, the whole issue of Jewish features at that period added impetus to above movement. The Samaritans, who claimed descent from the early Biblical tribes in Palestine, and who never left their place of residence, were considered to be an excellent group for the study of the pure physical type of the ancient Hebrews.

Among the people who did work from this viewpoint on the Samaritans as well as on some other ethnic groups in the neighborhood for comparisons were: H. M. Huxley ('05), S. Weissenberg ('05), Fishberg ('11) and Von H. Spizdbaum ('26). These reports were based primarily on anthropometric measurements on samples of various sizes of the Samaritan population and gave physionomic characteristics in detail.

Probably the most thorough investigation of the Samaritans was carried out by the Italian expedition to Palestine under the direction of Professor G. E. Genna ('38). The primary motivation for the study was that the Samaritans, a community then reduced to but a few representatives, seemed to be destined, according to the opinion of many anthropologists, for rapid extinction. Along with other studies of "primitive and decadent people" this Italian committee for the study of populations wished to report on the Samaritans' characteristics as long as it was still possible.

While no degenerative symptoms could be found, the hope of finding which had in fact prompted the study, the authors predicted that the Samaritans in 1933 were at a turning point of their history. "It has been a most unusual and lucky chance that we could study them thoroughly at this moment which is the beginning of the gradual fusion with the Hebrew race" (Genna, '38). That they were not the last to investigate the Samaritans is obvious from the existence of more recent studies (Bonné, '63, '65).

Samaritans, Hebrews and Others

The Samaritans' own claim of being the descendants of the early Israelite tribes residing in Northern Palestine, as well as their present geographical location and the continuous evidence throughout the ages that they have existed there, often led early investigators to examine such speculations (see Huxley, '06; Spizdbaum, '27; and Genna, '38).

Although it is true that Jewish people throughout the world regard themselves as ultimate though not perhaps direct offspring of the old Hebrew Nation, there does not exist any other well-defined community in the same area (present-day Israel and Jordan) which can claim a comparable length of existence with as complete a set of records as the Samaritans.

Not having today a group of people whom we can label as Ancient Hebrews and not possessing anthropological and genetic data for the old Israelite kingdom, makes the task in establishing the Samaritans' relationship to such an early population difficult.

There are, however, several Jewish communities in various Middle Eastern countries who have lived in a somewhat similar form of isolation for extended periods in history and probably in similar economical and social ways of living. Moreover, some of these communities also claim to go back to an early stage in Biblical history and claim descent from Hebrew people who were exiled from Palestine during Biblical times. Among these are the Iraqi Jews who are considered to be the descendants of the Jews deported from Palestine to ancient Babylonia after the destruction of the first temple in 586 B.C. (Gottheil, '02; Safanow, '40). Others are the Jews from Kurdistan, a mountainous area divided today between Iraq, Persia and Turkey, who consider themselves to have lived in Kurdistan from ancient times being the descendants of the ten lost tribes (see Lipman, '04; Brutzkus, '34).

For a short historical account of Jewish dispersal migration waves, see Ronen ('63).

At the end of the eighteenth century, Jews began to gather back to Israel in successively larger waves of immigrations. Early immigrants were mostly Ashkenazim, but a substantial number of Sephardim and Jews from Iraq, Kurdistan, Persia, Yemen, Turkey, Syria, and North Africa also entered Israel.

This variety of human populations settling in the State of Israel gave stimulus to anthropological projects and investigations (see Goldschmidt, '63). There exists much information on the blood groups of the various Jewish communities (Gurevitch, '53, '55, '56; Margolis, '57, '60a, b and others).

Other investigations in more recent years have accumulated data on additional genetic traits, such as the incidence of color-blindness, taste sensitivity, haptoglobin and Gc types, etc. (Kalmus, '61; Sheba, '62a; Goldschmidt, '62; Ramot, '62; Cleve, '62). It thus becomes possible to use this information for comparing the different Jewish populations with the Samaritans.[3]

[3] It should be mentioned that the criteria for selection of these communities was first in terms of their historical and geographical relevance to the Samaritans, and secondarily, in terms of availability of data. It is rather obvious that none of the groups chosen can in fact be regarded as an ideal comparable "control group" like those used in a laboratory experiment. Each population differs in the background setting, i.e. the population among whom they have lived, as well as in their geographical and climatic environments, all of which must have had an influence upon the biological history of these groups.

TABLE 1

Gene frequencies of the common blood-group systems in Samaritans and in ten Jewish communities[1]

Community	O	A	B	M	N	CDe	cDE	cDe	cde	Rare chromo-somes
Yemen	72.4	18.5	9.1	75.6	24.4	56.1	7.9	6.4	28.2	1.4
Cochin	73.1	10.1	16.8	60.6	40.0	41.5	5.0	6.2	44.4	2.9
Baghdad	49.3	30.1	20.6	60.5	39.5	53.5	15.8	4.1	19.8	6.8
Kurdistan	51.2	32.0	16.8	52.9	47.1	53.0	17.9	5.2	15.0	8.9
Persia	55.0	26.5	18.5	59.2	40.8	60.5	10.9	6.0	22.7	0.0
Morocco	62.2	23.1	14.7	55.9	44.1	53.4	6.3	9.4	30.8	0.1
Tunisia	62.9	21.2	15.9	55.5	44.5	56.1	6.6	8.5	28.4	0.4
Tripolitania	62.4	21.2	16.4	50.5	49.5	43.0	7.8	9.5	36.4	3.3
Sephardim	54.4	32.1	13.5	50.0	50.0	46.8	8.6	11.0	26.4	7.2
Ashkenazim	61.6	26.2	12.2	53.5	46.5	51.5	12.1	5.2	30.4	0.8
Samaritans	82.2	11.5	6.3	39.8	60.2	42.8	8.7	5.6	42.9	0.0

[1] From Nelken, D. ('63).

Table 1 presents the frequencies of the three common blood-group systems in various Jewish communities. The data indicates that Jewish communities differ widely from each other and from the Samaritans in almost all of the gene frequencies presented. While Yemenites and Samaritans may be similar in their ABO frequencies, the MN system differs immensely, and this is the situation with other communities as well. From the blood-group picture it seems impossible to define a standard Jewish group, or characteristic Jewish frequencies.

The same phenomenon of diverse frequencies in the various communities is also apparent from table 2.

The differences among Jewish populations has been recognized for some time by various investigators and led to a series of discussions in the literature as to whether or not the Jews form a distinct race (see Mourant, '54; Shapiro, '60). It is generally agreed that the Jews are not a homogeneous population and that the various communities differ from each other too significantly to be grouped together as a single race.

Several studies have also dealt with the related issue of Jewish intermarriage and mixture with their neighboring populations among whom they have lived in various parts of the world. Comparisons of the blood types of Jews in different countries have demonstrated that each Jewish population tends to resemble its local non-Jewish neighbors sometimes to a very close degree (Mourant, '54). The question then arises: is this tendency a result of the effect of intermarriage between Jews and non-Jews, or perhaps due to the operation of natural selection working on both Jews and non-Jews in a common environment?

Most investigators, perhaps, tend to accept the hypothesis that Jews have through intermarriage approximated the frequencies characteristic of the countries

TABLE 2

Comparison of genetic markers in different Oriental communities

Community	Color blindness (Kalmus, '61) %	Non-tasters (Sheba, '62a) %	G6PD (Sheba, '62b) %	Rh negative (Goldschmidt, '63) %	Hp[1] gene (Ramot, '62 and Goldschmidt, '62) %	Gc[1] gene (Cleve, '62) %	Increas. Hb A_2 (Ramot, '64) %	Lipoprotein (C. de. B+) (Blumberg, '63) %
Ashkenazim	8.0	20.7	0.4	9.0	30.2	66.2	2	—
Sephardim	5.5	21.7	1.6	7.0	37.5	—	—	—
North Africa	6.2	15.0	0.8	11.0	28.2	72.0	1.4	—
Kurdistan	5.7	13.0	58.2	4.0	30.8	81.0	6.4	70.6
Iraq	3.9	16.0	24.8	6.0	27.3	75.9	—	—
Persia	5.7	—	15.1	5.0	29.2	75.5	2.2	70.3
Yemen	4.7	18.0	5.3	10.0	25.0	80.6	(b[2])	—
Arabs	—	19.0	4.4	11.0	26.5	74.0	(b[2])	71.8
Samaritans	27.7	8.0	0.0	19.0	39.6	79.6	13.5	61.6

[1] Except Arabs and the Samaritans, all communities are Jewish.
[2] According to Ramot ('64) the frequencies of increased Hb A_2 in these communities is low (less than 2%).

where they have long been established. My personal view is that Jews on the whole have intermingled less than is usually assumed, and that the similarity found (and many have to be further studied and confirmed) are largely the result of the exposure of Jews and non-Jews to the same influences. This issue, though interesting and even somewhat related to the comparisons between the Samaritans and other Jewish communities, lies however, outside the scope of the present presentation.

The aim of this comparative section is limited to establishing whether the Samaritans are like other Jewish communities, and if so, like which ones. Also, to seeing if one may evaluate from such comparison the extent to which the modern Samaritans represent a population descendant from the old Hebrew Kingdom.

Table 3 gives a quantitative evaluation of the differences found between the Samaritans and the other Jewish populations for the genetic characteristics studied.

The statistical significance of most of the differences is indeed very high. This is less true in the Haptoglobin groups, and the differences in the Gc types between Samaritans and other communities are not statistically significant. It is too early to say whether this is due to very small numbers in samples typed for these factors, or rather to the operation of selective forces, acting in the same direction.

From the above tables there does not seem to be any one Jewish community which closely resembles the Samaritans in more than one genetic characteristic.

Comparison of the common blood group systems of Samaritans and *non-Jewish populations* in the Middle East, yields a similar picture. While there are no data with respect to markers as those presented in table 2 in countries like Syria, Lebanon, Jordan, Iraq, Yemen, and Egypt, the χ^2 figures for the ABO, MN and Rh groups are in the same range as those given in table 3, with a probability level of 1×10^{-7} or higher.

An obvious conclusion from the data is that the Samaritans are presently different from every population, Jewish and non-Jewish among whom they have been living, or with whom they may have shared an ancestral gene pool. Whatever forces account for the differences encountered (i.e. drift, selection, etc.) they do support the contention that the Samaritans' separation and isolation from other communities is not a recent event. Their insistence on and claim for endogamous relationships gain credibility from their gene frequency picture. Even if some mixture has occurred, I think it has been slight, and has had almost no visible effect on their distribution.

The probability of mixture with other non-Mediterranean populations is also diminished by absence of genes which, because of their distribution, are often called "African genes," or "mongoloid genes." All Samaritans tested in Israel were negative for the Diego, Gm(x) and Gm(c) alleles.

In Jordan, 82 Samaritans were tested in addition for V, Js and the Henshaw alleles, which when present may indicate African ancestry. All were negative.

While it is by no means evident that polygenic traits are less exposed to quick effects of selection than monogenic traits (Boyd and Li, '63) it is often believed

TABLE 3

Values of χ^2 for intergroup differences between Samaritans and other Jewish communities for seven genetic systems

Community	ABO χ^2	ABO p	MN χ^2	MN p	Rh χ^2	Rh p	PTC χ^2	PTC p	CB χ^2	CB p	Hp χ^2	Hp p	Gc[3] χ^2	Gc[3] p
Ashkenazim	39.0	1×10^{-7}	17.4	2×10^{-4}	2.91[1]	0.08	10.7	1.2×10^{-3}	30.4	1×10^{-7}	9.5	1×10^{-2}	9.9	1.5×10^{-3}
Sephardim	60.2	1×10^{-7}	12.3	2.5×10^{-3}	3.03[1]	0.08	—	—	28.1	1.3×10^{-7}	0.7	0.29	—	—
North Africa[2]	40.2	1×10^{-7}	19.7	4×10^{-5}	35.8	3×10^{-6}	3.9	5×10^{-2}	36.3	1×10^{-7}	5.9	5×10^{-2}	4.1	0.05
Kurdistan	65.8	1×10^{-7}	59.8	1×10^{-7}	181.3	1×10^{-7}	2.3	0.135	37.0	1×10^{-7}	1.4	0.21	0.2	0.40
Iraq	46.8	1×10^{-7}	31.6	2×10^{-7}	39.9	1×10^{-7}	5.0	5×10^{-2}	80.9	1×10^{-7}	6.3	5×10^{-2}	1.0	0.27
Persia	50.2	1×10^{-7}	27.5	1.5×10^{-6}	53.1	1×10^{-7}	5.0	5×10^{-2}	32.1	1×10^{-7}	4.0	0.0	2.6	0.10
Yemen	10.8	1.8×10^{-3}	118.5	1×10^{-7}	19.1	4×10^{-3}	6.7	1×10^{-2}	45.1	1×10^{-7}	5.5	1.7×10^{-2}	2.4	0.10
Cochin	17.5	1×10^{-3}	31.5	2×10^{-7}	6.3	0.25	27.9	3×10^{-7}	—	—	—	—	—	—

[1] Differences only between Rh(+) and Rh(−).

[2] The North African community includes Morocco, Tunisia and Tripolitanian Jews. Each of these communities separately also differs significantly from the Samaritans.

[3] The numbers in the Gc phenotype 2–2 were very small (less than 5), yet no significant differences were observed.

TABLE 4

Comparative series of anthropometric measurements in Samaritans and in selected Jewish populations (males only)

Population	Stature cm	Head length cm	Head width	Cephalic index	Face height	Nose height	Nose width	Nose index
Mzab[1]	166.10	195.50	140.70	72.00	123.40	55.80	37.60	68.10
Sephardim[2]	165.90	189.10	147.60	78.00	121.40	58.20	35.60	61.50
Syria[3]	165.80	183.00	148.00	80.90	126.00	56.00	33.00	58.90
Iraqi[4]	164.50	181.05	148.20	82.05	123.70	54.98	33.89	62.78
Morocco[1]	164.90	188.20	141.70	75.00	125.20	58.00	34.00	64.70
East-Europeans[5]	171.70	193.00	157.10	81.40	120.30	57.70	35.90	62.30
Samaritans[6]	170.93	184.69	149.31	79.86	124.52	57.45	35.89	63.12

[1] (Briggs, '58). [3] (Weissenberg, '11). [5] (Saller, '33).
[2] (Wagenseil, '25). [4] (Field, '52). [6] (Bonné, '65).

that differences in blood group frequencies, for example, result from more recent racial divergence than do differences in morphological traits. In table 4 some of the more recent studies of anthropometric measurements in various contemporary Jewish populations together with the Samaritans' data have been assembled.

Once again, two facts appear in the comparison:

1. Lack of identity and considerable variation between the populations.

2. The Samaritans have their own "typical features" not resembling those of any other group.

A similar situation is demonstrated when comparing Samaritans to non-Jewish Middle Eastern populations:

It has been argued that the blood groups offer a more precise and objective method for comparison than anthropometric measurements. The anthropometric differences observed in various studies may reflect only differences in techniques rather than "real" differences in the measurements.

The criticism, however, cannot be applied to the work of Huxley (table 5) since both Samaritans and other populations were examined by him. This is also true for the studies of Weissenberg and Spizdbaum ('09 and '26). Both scholars examined a group of Fellachim and Sephardic Jews, in addition to the Samaritans, in Palestine in those years, and reported wide variations in measurements between each group. The difference of the Samaritans from the others was striking.

From all above comparisons, it seems reasonable to accept the conclusion that the Samaritans reveal a gene-frequency picture unique to themselves.

A question which remains to be answered is whether the particular Samaritan type, as disclosed by the study, portrays that of the ancient Israelites. The assumption that the Samaritans are perhaps a group of people who were converted to

TABLE 5

Comparison between Samaritan males and other Near Eastern groups[1]

	Samaritans	Bedawins	Akeydat	Maualy	Moslems	Turkomans	Maronites	Nusairiyeh	Druse
Number	38	115	120	176	258	19	31	25	46
Stature	172.26	166.86	168.50	170.12	168.00	169.74	167.61	169.68	167.55
Head length	188.28	189.09	191.35	190.42	189.48	191.04	179.13	176.16	178.89
Head breadth	146.17	144.46	146.14	147.06	147.28	143.89	151.96	152.56	151.72
Head height	140.22	134.50	122.76	125.36	136.26	136.54	139.10	138.84	138.90
Min. frontal diam.	103.54	103.42	117.64	118.50	104.86	104.62	105.46	105.86	106.94
Bizygomatic diam.	132.15	135.30	134.58	135.91	137.25	137.70	137.00	139.00	140.70
Total face height	123.95	119.70	123.32	124.04	120.65	120.40	118.95	124.00	120.35
Upper face height	78.95	74.05	71.82	73.00	74.60	75.25	73.95	76.00	73.65
Nose height	55.38	52.70	54.66	55.42	52.98	54.14	51.58	54.94	53.06
Nose breadth	36.74	36.41	36.28	36.82	36.71	35.78	36.74	35.84	36.77

[1] From Seltzer ('40).

their faith like the Falasha, or some other Jewish communities (i.e. in Mexico) can hardly be supported from historical and literary records. Assuming then, that the Samaritans and all other Jewish populations once comprised one nation, and ignoring, for the sake of speculation, the possibility that neither the Samaritans nor any other living population today typifies exactly the ancient Hebrews, there remain two possible alternatives:

(a) All other Jewish communities, as result of migration, mixture, drift and selection, changed their biological attributes in the course of history, while the Samaritans have retained theirs.

(b) During the years the Samaritans developed their own particular character-istics, and thus diverged from all other Jewish communities.

Most probably, both of these processes have occurred and it is not necessary to believe that present-day Samaritans' gene frequencies were exactly those of the Biblical Hebrews living in Palestine some 2,000 years ago. Yet, because all other Jewish communities reflect such heterogeneity and because their geographical locations have indeed changed, it seems that present-day Samaritans can be regarded as Modern representatives of the ancient Hebrews, perhaps more than any other living Jewish community.

In other words, the distribution of traits among them today is perhaps that which might have been found in a biblical tribe had they remained living con-tinuously in Palestine. Whether present gene frequencies are related or unrelated to those of many generations—a fact we cannot know—the Samaritans represent a descendant population from the old Hebrew kingdom; not of the total Israelite kingdom but of a small branch of it, as indeed they claim.

In itself, the usefulness of concluding that the Samaritans are the living repre-sentatives of ancient Hebrews, is doubtful. It is perhaps most meaningful to them themselves who have claimed to be the only true and faithful adherents of the original Hebrew faith.[4]

LITERATURE CITED

Adler, M. N.   1904   The itinerary of Benjamin of Tudela. Jewish Quart. Review, *17:* 123–131.
Ben Zevi, I.   1935   Sefer Hashomronim (in Hebrew). Shtibel, Tel-Aviv.
———   1956   Eretz Yisrael veyeshuvah biyemei hashilton haotomani (in Hebrew). Bialik, Tel-Aviv.
Blumberg, B. S.   1963   Polymorphisms of the human serum. In: The genetics of migrant and isolate populations. Edited by E. Goldschmidt. Williams and Wilkins Co., New York.

[4] The following incident points this out: when the Samaritans were told about G6PD deficiency which was investigated among them, and that the defect was sex-linked, namely transmitted from mothers to sons, the head of the community had his own explanation for the absence of the deficiency existing in both Ashkenazi Jews and in Samaritans. According to their beliefs, the Ashkenazi are the sons of Benjamin and the Samaritans the sons of Ephraim, both sons of the same mother, Rachel. That both Ashkenazi Jews and Samaritans do not show the defect indicates to him that Rachel did not possess the gene and could not transmit it to her sons, as other mothers did.

Bonné, B. 1963 The Samaritans: a demographic study. Hum. Biol., *35:* 61–89.

———— 1965 A genetic view of the Samaritan isolate. Unpublished dissertation, Boston University School of Medicine.

Boyd, W. C., and C. C. Li 1963 Rates of selective action on unifactorial and multifactorial traits. Am. J. Phys. Anthrop., *13:* 447–454.

Briggs, L. C. 1958 The living races of the Sahara desert. Papers. Peabody Museum, Harvard University, *28:* no. 2.

Brutzkus, J. 1934 Kurdistan. Encyclopedia Judaica, *10:* 514–519. Verlag Eschkol, Berlin.

Cleve, H., B. Ramot and A. G. Bearn 1962 Distribution of the serum group specific components in Israel. Nature, *195:* 86–87.

Field, H. 1952 The anthropology of Iraq. Papers of the Peabody Museum, Harvard University, *46:* no. 2–3, 3–217.

Fishberg, M. 1911 The Jews: a study of race and environment. Charles Scribners and Sons, New York.

Gaster, M. 1925 The Samaritans. Their history, doctrines and literature. Oxford University Press, London.

Genna, G. E. 1938 I Samaritani. Spedizioni scientifiche del comitato Italiano per la studio dei problemi della populazione, Roma.

Goldschmidt, E., P. Bayani-Sioson, H. E. Sutton, K. Fried, A. Sandor and N. Bloch 1962 Haptoglobin frequencies in Jewish communities. Amer. J. Hum. Genet., *26:* 39–46.

———— 1963 The genetics of migrant and isolate populations. (Edit.) The Williams and Wilkins Co., New York.

Gottheil, R. 1902 Bagdad, In: The Jewish Encyclopedia. Vol. 2, Funk and Wagnalls, New York and London.

Gurevitch, J., and E. Margolis 1955 Blood groups in Jews from Iraq. Ann. Hum. Genet., *19:* 257–259.

Gurevitch, J., E. Hasson and E. Margolis 1956 Blood groups in Persian Jews. Ann. Eugen., *21:* 135–138.

Gurevitch, J., E. Hermoni and E. Margolis 1953 Blood groups in Kurdistani Jews. Ann. Eugen., *18:* 94–95.

Huxley, H. M. 1905 Zur anthropologie der Samaritaner. Z. Demograph. Statistik. Juden., *2:* 137–139.

Kalmus, H., A. Amir, O. Levine, E. Barak and E. Goldschmidt 1961 The frequency of inherited defects of colour vision in some Israeli populations. Ann. Hum. Genet., *25:* 51–55.

Lipman, J. G. 1904 Kurdistan, In: The Jewish Encyclopedia. Funk and Wagnalls, New York and London.

Margolis, E., and D. Hermoni 1960a Blood groups in Sephardic Jews. Am. J. Phys. Anthrop., *18:* 197–199.

———— 1960b Blood groups in Ashkenazi Jews. Am. J. Phys. Anthrop., *18:* 201–203.

Margolis, E., J. Gurevitch and E. Hasson 1957 Blood groups in Jews from Morocco and Tunisia. Ann. Hum. Genet., *22:* 65–68.

Mills, J. 1864 Three months' residence at Nablus and an account of the modern Samaritans. J. Murray, London.

Montgomery, J. A. 1907 The Samaritans: the earliest Jewish sect. The John C. Winston Co., Philadelphia.

Mourant, A. E. 1954 The distribution of the human blood groups, Blackwell Scientific Publications, Oxford.

Petermann, Von H. 1865 Reisen im Orient, Von Veit and Co., Leipzig.

Ramot, B., P. Duvdevani-Zikert and G. Kende 1962 Haptoglobin and transferrin types in Israel. Ann. Hum. Genet., *25:* 267–271.

Ramot, B., A. Abrahamov, S. Prier and D. Gafni 1964 The incidence and the types of thalassameia trait carriers in Israel. Brit. J. Haemat., *10:* 155–158.

Robinson, E. D. D. 1841 Biblical researchers in Palestine, Mount Sinai and Arabia Petraea. Vol. III, Crocker and Brewster, Boston.

Rogers, M. E. 1865 Domestic life in Palestine, Jennings and Pye, Cincinnati.

Ronen, A. 1963 Immigrant waves into Israel, In: The genetics of migrant and isolate populations, Edited by E. Goldschmidt, Williams and Wilkins, New York.

Sacy, Silvestre de 1829 Notices et extraits de divers manuscripts Arabes correspondence de Samaritain de Naplouse, Imprimerie Royale, Paris.

Safanow, A. 1940 Babylonia, In: The Universal Jewish Encyclopedia, Universal Jewish Encyclopedia, Inc., New York.

Saller, K. 1933 Beitrag zur anthropologie der Ostjuden. Morphol. Anthrop., *32:* 125–131.

Seltzer, C. C. 1940 The Samaritans of the Near East, In: Contributions to the racial anthropology of the Near East, Papers of the Peabody Museum, Harvard University, Cambridge.

Shapiro, H. L. 1963 The Jewish People: a biological history. Unesco series, George Thone, Liege, Belgium.

Sheba, Ch., I. Ashkenazi and A. Szeinberg 1962a Taste sensitivity to Phenylthiorea among the Jewish population groups in Israel. Amer. J. Hum. Genet., *14:* 44–51.

Sheba, Ch., A. Szeinberg, B. Ramot, A. Adam and I. Ashkenazi 1962b Epidemiologic surveys of deleterious genes in different population groups in Israel. Amer. J. Public Health, *52:* 1101–1106.

Spizdbaum, Von H. 1926 Samaritaner. Mitteil. Anthrop. Gesel. In: Wien., *56:* 134–158.

Vilmar, E. 1865 Abullfathi annales Samaritani, Gothae.

Wagenseil, F. 1925 Beitrage zur physische anthropologie der Spaniolischen Juden und zur Judischen rassenfrage. A. Morphol. Anthrop., *23:* 33–150.

Weissenberg, J. 1911 Die Syrischen Juden anthropologisch betrachtet. Z. Ethnol., *43:* 80–90.

Weissenberg, S. 1909 Die autochthone bevolkerung Palastinas in anthropologischen beziehung. Z. Demograph. Statistik, Juden., *5:* 129–139.

Evolution in Isolation

SOME ETHNIC GROUPS CLING FAST TO THEIR HOMELANDS, DE-spite generations of misfortune. They retain their identity and traditions by avoiding ties, either cultural or genetic, with their neighbors. This is very difficult, as the case of the Samaritans demonstrates. But the natural environment surrounding them remains the same, as a rule, for a very long time, so they are not subjected to sudden, stressful changes in that aspect of their life. Other ethnic groups or (more often) subsections of ethnic groups migrate to new homes, where conditions are likely to be very different indeed. Unaccustomed foods, diseases, and climates, as well as new neighbors with odd customs, are likely to affect those who have gone to live in a strange place. Often, as the generations pass, migrant groups merge into the general population surrounding them: this is why the United States has been called a melting pot.

In some cases, however, a migrant group may occupy an area which is naturally isolated, such as an island. This gives it a better chance to retain its identity, since it lacks neighbors with whom to merge. During the last few centuries a number of groups like this have become estab-lished: this has been one incidental result of the expansion of Europeans throughout so much of the world. Some, like the people of Pitcairn Island in the Pacific, the Seychelles in the Indian Ocean, and Tristan da Cunha in the Atlantic, are of mixed genetic origin, and also very remote. In the West Indies, one small island was settled by families from France three centuries ago. In "Saint-Barthélemy: Physical Anthropology of an Isolate," Professor J. Benoist writes lucidly about this interesting popula-tion, which has lived for many generations in a climate so different from that of Western Europe.

17. J. Benoist

Saint-Barthélemy:
Physical Anthropology of an Isolate*

Human populations have different ways of being influenced by the various forces that work upon, and sooner or later transform, their hereditary patrimony. A certain evolutionary factor becomes privileged depending upon the population's demographic situation, its social structure, and its geographic environment; being thus highlighted, it brings more clearly to light the nature and modalities of its incidences than it would in the observation of a group where it is less forceful. Thus, the study of human evolution can greatly profit by the analysis of populations where one of these mechanisms is especially predominant.

Admitting that these models can translate real situations, it is easier to portray them than to verify their accord with these situations. In the latter cases, the relatively simple relations which the models translate are perturbed by interferences with other relations which mask them in a web that is difficult to disentangle. That is why the analysis of particular cases, of populations where one of the extreme characteristics (mixture, isolation, strong selection) is especially predominant, seems to be fruitful.

In a first study on this theme, we have examined a mixed population, and have tried to analyze its own dynamics, and the factors contributing to it (Benoist, '63). But race-mixture is only one of the aspects of the transformation of human groups. If it plays a fundamental role in the formation of new hereditary configurations, it seems to be able to do so only because other causes of evolution have given it sufficiently differentiated material. In fact, race-crossing is essentially the erosion of the differences. In the present paper we shall try to examine a mechanism that brings out these differences: isolation and its evolutionary consequences.

The research took place in a small island in the Caribbean.[1] We realized very

* This study was made possible by grants from National Research Council of Canada and the Canada Arts Council.
1 For the warm welcome they have given me I particularly wish to thank Mr. and Mrs. Jean Morice, Dr. Hourtiguet and the families of Saint-Barthélemy where I have been so kindly received.

soon that a simple classical study of its population's biological or morphological characteristics would give us only taxonomic data, and that the understanding of the actual mechanisms required a deeper knowledge of the social modalities that regulate the relations between persons. We have to place ourselves at their own level in order to know the meaning and the validity of the documents we have been able to acquire. Thus, this study contains two main parts: the first gives the main conclusions which are arrived at by the analysis of the historians and the geographers, and of the ethnological study that has been carried out parallel to the physical anthropology one, the second gives the results of the physical anthropology study.

The conclusions will rely as much as it is possible upon both of these data. Indeed, we cannot insist enough upon the importance, for the physical anthropologist as well as the ethnologist, of the confrontation of the data gathered on the same population. Many have expressed this wish, but unfortunately the number of researches done with this aim in mind are still rare. Nevertheless we can mention those of Neel et al. ('49), of Kluckholn and Griffith ('50), of Glass et al. ('52), of Oliver and Howells ('57), of Salzano ('61).

It appears from these studies that the main area in which social structures interfere with the biological facts is at the level where the hereditary patrimony is manipulated by the marriage system existing in the society. It is upon this point also that we shall concentrate our attention, but without engaging in the analysis of the cultural anthropologist who tackles the causalities of the system of which we shall use but the description.

GEOGRAPHICAL AND HISTORICAL REVIEW

The island of Saint-Barthélemy, situated at 200 kilometers to the north of Guadeloupe, belongs to the archipelago that ends the Lesser Antilles to the north. Its surface is less than 25 km², as of 1961, its population numbered 2216 inhabitants (of which 324 lived in the village of Gustavia and 1892 in the rural areas), and it differs greatly from Guadeloupe to which it is administratively attached.

To the differences in dimension and climate are added particularities concerning the conditions of its settlement, its history, and its social and economic characteristics.

Although it is situated in the heart of "Plantation America," Saint-Barthélemy does not share its social and economic characteristics. The following salient features of this system have never been able to take hold: the growth of a great servile labor-force, a racially defined social stratification, the concentration of land into large units of cultivation held by a white aristocracy, the transformation of family structures and the formation of the matrifocal system.

Only a very small number of Blacks have come to the island. They have never formed the majority, and after a period of prosperity in the early nineteenth

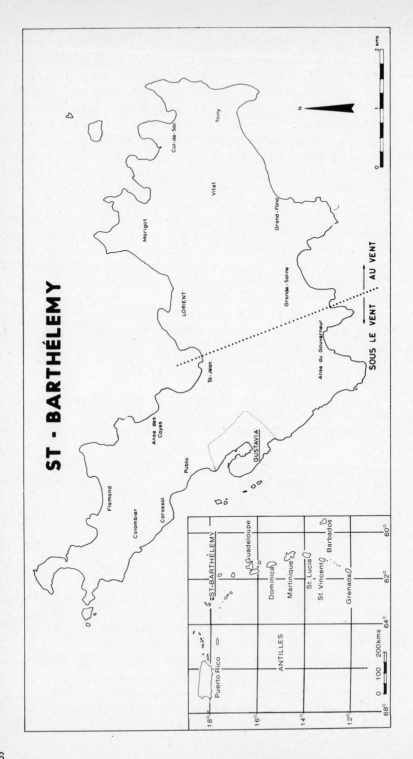

ST - BARTHÉLEMY

Tony

Cul-de-Sac

Vitet

Grand-Fond

Marigot

LORIENT

Grande-Saline

St-Jean

Anse du Gouverneur

Anse des Coyas

Flamand

Colombier

Corossol

Public

GUSTAVIA

SOUS LE VENT   AU VENT

N

0   1   2 kms

ANTILLES

Puerto Rico

ST-BARTHÉLEMY

Guadeloupe

Dominica

Martinique

St. Lucia

St. Vincent

Barbados

Grenada

18°

16°

14°

12°

68°   64°   62°   60°

0   100   200kms

century, most of them have left. Particularly significant is the fact that now they are not at all located in the rural areas, and it would seem that they have never owned any great amount of land on the island.

These facts seem to have respected the cultural and genetic continuity of the white population on the island. Lasserre ('61, pp. 845–883) mentions that a text written in 1772 points out that the Whites of Saint-Barthélemy are the descendants of about 30 men sent in 1659 to colonize the island, and that in 1664 they amounted to about 100 persons. Relying upon other documents from the seventeenth and eighteenth centuries, he proves the continuity of this population during this period. Since then, the parochial registers as well as the study of patronyms permit us also to infer that to this day it would seem that no major contribution has been added to the initial group.

The published documents do not give precisions as to the exact geographical origin of the first settlers, nor of those who later joined them. Local tradition affirms a Norman origin, which many ethnographical elements would confirm, but there are no studies that would allow us to limit the area more precisely, or to judge the extent to which other regions of western France have contributed.

SAINT-BARTHÉLEMY: THE LIMITS AND STRUCTURE OF AN ISOLATE

Social rules delimit the area within which chance plays a role. They leave a more or less wide margin according to the strictness of their prohibitive and of their prescriptive rules. This conditions the number of potential mates and the number of real unions, for each individual. Every human group has its own characteristics in this field, and their influence upon evolution encourages us to analyze them.

In the case of Saint-Barthélemy we must specify on one hand the relation between the island's white population seen as a unit and those populations with whom there are geographical, cultural and economic ties, and on the other hand the internal organization of this population as to the factors that act upon the transmission of the hereditary patrimony.

By "isolate" we mean the unit of "population" in the genetic sense of the word. We do not then restrict its sense to those individuals who are of age to be married, as has been proposed. But this distinction does not, in our case, have the importance it has in quantitative demographic studies.

The Isolate

The insular position is not the essential factor of isolation: there is much coming and going between islands. Genetic isolation is due to socio-cultural factors that find geographical support in the exiguity of the island. Saint-Barthélemy is the only territory of the archipelago that is inhabited by Whites, where French is spoken and the official religion is Catholic. These three have comprised an efficient shield against all immigration ever since the group owned almost all the land in the island, that is to say since several centuries.

There is frequent contact with the Blacks from neighboring islands, but this does not stimulate any important immigration. A small number of them have settled down in the town of Gustavia. They keep their English language and their Anglican religion, and they are culturally much more integrated with the neighboring islands than with Saint-Barthélemy. Moreover strong racial prejudice keeps these Blacks from settling in the rural areas. The town of Gustavia is also the most important port of the island, and economic traffic runs through it. But, contrary to what happens in larger islands, this port is not a place of ethnic mixing. The exiguity of the town (324 inhabitants) does not make it a stop-over place for sailors, and facilitates the strong control that the white families and many Blacks practice in this matter.

Thus, genetic isolation is extreme. In 1954, of 2,075 persons living in the island, 2,039 were born there; of the 36 who were born elsewhere 16 were mainland French (officials and their families), some were Blacks from Martinique and Guadeloupe, and the rest were Blacks coming from English and Dutch neighboring islands. All strangers, except one hotelkeeper from France and his wife from Martinique lived in Gustavia, and mingled with rural Saint-Barts only occasionally. Among these there was no immigrant who had settled after marrying a resident. The survey of the couples of the three major districts, and also the survey of the marriages registered in the island, show a very high rate of endogamy (table 1). If we keep in mind the fact that the descendants of the

TABLE 1

Endogamy of the Whites of Saint-Barthélemy

Origin of the partner	1862–1914	1914–1961
White St.-Barthélemy	296	421
Colored St.-Barthélemy	1	7
White France	0	1

marriages between Whites and Colored leave the white community, and that the only stranger having married a girl from Saint-Barthélemy has gone back to France, we come to the conclusion, based on 617 marriages, that *since at least one century ago, the endogamy of Saint-Barthélemy reaches the exceptional rate of 100%*. This rate is without equivalence in the Caribbean, even in the other white groups isolated in a colored mass (the Békés of Martinique, the Blancs Matignons of Guadeloupe).

One reserve can nevertheless be made over a longer period of time, as certain slightly mixed individuals have been able to cross the color line, particularly in Gustavia where certain families whose position in the white group is contended now live. The same is true for certain rural families in the districts of Flamand, Anse des Cayes and Lorient. The population's insufficient knowledge of their genealogy makes the reintegration of a few mixed individuals possible after several generations, if their physical features do not give away their origins. However, this phenomenon is quantitatively very limited.

Structure of the Isolate

The structure of the isolate mirrors all the genetic exchanges determined by forces other than those of chance, and that separate the group under study from the theoretical schema of panmixia. In order to analyze it, we have at our disposal some documents relative to the Catholic marriages registered in the parish of the island. As all the Whites of Saint-Barthélemy are Catholics and hold church marriages, these documents permit us to carry out an exhaustive study. First, we shall examine their validity regarding our problem, and then see how they permit us to specify the structure of the white population of Saint-Barthélemy.

The family. The rules of kinship, and sexual behavior in general influence the genetic structure of populations. By the examination of marriages we can obtain precise answers for the needs of the study of this structure, but first we have to assure the validity of the information obtained.

Numerous studies have shown us the fluidity of the Caribbean family structures. The instability of homes, the high rate of illegitimacy, the fact that the same person has children by several others, and residential mobility determine an intense genetic stirring within the population of the area. Without ever achieving panmixia, it comes close to it within broad territorial limits. Geographical and social barriers are overcome by informal and often fecund relationships that assure the flow of genes exterior to the community and their rapid diffusion. Marriage registers reflect these facts very imperfectly and cannot be of direct use for the study of these populations.

Is this the case in Saint-Barthélemy? The conclusions of the ethnological study would prove the opposite. This study will be published elsewhere but it shows that extramarital sexual relations are quite exceptional for the women, and that those of the men all take place outside of the island.

In Saint-Barthélemy the home is composed of only a couple and their children, and the nuclear family constituted after a religious marriage is very stable (4 divorces for 426 marriages from 1927 to 1961). Social control of the women's sex life is very strict, and cases of concubinage and of illegitimate births are exceptional. All these social facts support the opinion that the official documents regarding marriages clearly reflect the real exchanges, and that one could not suspect a secret canal of genetic exchange perturbing the current.

The Social Units: Districts and Parishes

The whole island is one commune, directed from Gustavia, but it is divided into two parishes each of which groups several rural "districts." These districts form the basic agglomerations. The parish of Gustavia includes the town of Gustavia with its church, as well as the rural districts called "Sous le Vent" which are serviced by another church (the church of Colombier). The other parish, named Lorient, includes all the districts called "Au Vent" centered upon only one church. Moreover Gustavia also has an Anglican temple where the Blacks go.

Thus besides the administrative unit of the island there are three religious units: Anglican, the parish of Lorient, and the parish of Gustavia (including Gustavia and the rural districts).

As the religious structure conditions most of the collective activity of the island, the latter takes place in each parish: the schools are generally parochial and the children attend the schools of their parish. Mass is attended in one's own parish, and one is a member of the associations (religious groups, handicraft societies) of one's own parish. Political activity, the circles one is associated with, and economic activity, are also clearly defined by the parish. Most daily activity, especially that of the women takes place in one's own neighborhood, moving is done within the parish or to the town of Gustavia, and contact between the rural districts of different parishes remain scarce. The question could be raised whether these facts have an influence upon marriages, if these social units are or are not endogamous, and if they do or do not correspond to units of population.

Parishes. Table 2 shows that parishes are highly endogamous. The socio-cultural sections that divide the island into two halves (the Blacks of Gustavia being considered apart) can be found in the marriages.

TABLE 2

Place of birth of the partners, and endogamy of the parishes

	Same parish	Colored	Other parish	Total
Lorient				
1862–1914	141 (97.9%)	0	3	144
1914–1961	195 (94.6%)	5	6	206
Gustavia				
1862–1914	142 (92.8%)	1	10	153
1914–1961	199 (87.2%)	7	22	228

Districts ("quartiers"). A survey of the origins of the partners of the couples actually living in several districts of the island (table 3) and a study of the origins of the partners from the marriage registers (table 4) show that the districts are endogamous, but at a lesser rate than the parishes. It would seem that the genetic flow from one district to another is sufficiently important and constant that we can consider the real unit of population as the parish, and not the district. Movement is irregular from one parish to another. Because of general virilocal residence, women go to the parishes of their husbands. The movement of women from "Au Vent" regions to the "Sous le Vent" ones occurs more often than the reverse. This partially compensates the definitive emigration of a good number of men from the "Au Vent" districts.

Thus the isolate of Saint-Barthélemy is divided: in fact *two highly endogamous*

TABLE 3

Endogamy of three rural districts

District	No. of couples (1962)	Both partners of the same district	Both partners of the same parish	Total population
Corossol	42	31 (73%)	40 (95%)	158
Anse des Cayes	20	15 (75%)	16 (80%)	115
Lorient	33	18 (57%)	33 (100%)	151

TABLE 4

Origin of marriage partners

District	Same district	Other districts of the parish	Other parish
Corossol			
1862–1914	17	9	0
1914–1961	22	14	2
Anse des Cayes			
1914–1961	16	10	6
Lorient			
1914–1961	25	16	0

isolates exist in Saint-Barthélemy; they correspond geographically to the two halves of "Au Vent" and "Sous le Vent" and sociologically to the two parishes. Therefore the case of Saint-Barthélemy offers the possibility of comparing two isolates of the same origin, living in the same environmental conditions. This situation is particularly favorable: Glass et al. ('52) point out that "genetic drift and selection are not alternative explanations but are factors which may often act in conjunction, as Sewall Wright has constantly maintained," and that "what appears to be needed for a clearer solution of this problem is the analysis of a genetic isolate of known size, age and origin and which in particular shares an environment indistinguishable from that of the major population with which it is to be compared." But two types of criticism could be made concerning this method: (1) One never knows exactly what was the original population, and if it has not undergone some transformation; (2) one can never be sure that differences, even only such as religious ones, would not be enough to disturb a selective balance.

In Saint-Barthélemy we will indeed be able to refer to the original population, but above all we will be able to compare two isolates of the same origin, and also to try to distinguish between differences that could only be due to drift, and those changes which they both underwent simultaneously but independently and which could be due to selection.

Consanguinity. The intensity of endogamy inevitably determines a high rate of consanguinity. The relation between the dimension of an isolate and its consanguinity are indeed theoretically sufficiently strict that the knowledge of one permits the estimation of the other (Dahlberg, '42). Nevertheless this is not our problem. Besides the fact that one must be prudent in estimating isolates by this method (Sutter and Goux, '61) in the case of Saint Barthélemy, we have the possibility of directly observing the isolates. But the knowledge of the frequency of consanguineous marriages will allow us to complete the interpretation of biological data. The analysis of the dispensations granted by the Catholic church for the marriages between first cousins and second cousins gave us the following table. This table seems to be complete, for all white marriages in Saint-Barthélemy are religious ones and are registered by the parish priest.

TABLE 5

Consanguinity and its evolution

	No. of marriages	First cousins		Second cousins		Total	
		N	%	N	%	N	%
Parish of Lorient							
1862–1914	144	23	15.9	37	25.8	60	41.7
1914–1961	206	17	8.2	44	21.3	61	29.5
Parish of Gustavia							
1862–1914	153	13	8.5	13	8.5	26	17.1
1914–1961	228	17	7.4	25	10.9	42	18.3

Table 5 shows us that: the proportion of marriages between first cousins and second cousins is different from what we would find in random mating, particularly in the parish of Gustavia. This could be interpreted as an increase of marriages between first cousins due to economic pressure, but in the case of Saint-Barthélemy it seems to be a basically ecological phenomenon, and it corresponds to the distance between the dwellings of the future partners: The general tendency is that sons establish their homes close to their father's and this increases the chance of marriage between first cousins.

The consanguinity of the parish of Lorient is clearly the highest, although it is the largest parish. We have seen that it is also the most endogamous one, and these two facts are in all likelihood related.

The total rate of consanguinity is very high, and is not comparable to that of western nations. In France the rate of consanguineous marriages is 1.76% (Sutter and Tabah, '48), and approximately the same rate was found in different European countries. In the larger communities of Brazil, Freire-Maia ('57) found some rates close to those of Saint-Barthélemy. In groups of smaller dimension Salzano ('61) found that 14% of the marriages were between first or second cousins (Neel et al., '49).

Emigration. The general census of the population in 1954 gives a demographic structure which characterizes populations where men emigrate while women stay on.

This emigration is mainly directed toward Saint-Thomas (Virgin Islands), but some also go to Curaçao, New York and France. Nevertheless 80% of the emigrants go to Saint-Thomas. There are several types of emigration: the permanent emigration of a married man and his family; the temporary emigration of young men who later return to Saint-Barthélemy to settle down; semi-permanent emigration—men live in Saint-Thomas but return to Saint-Barthélemy to marry and to settle their family, and then go back to Saint-Thomas, returning home only a few weeks every year.

Of 88 men born on the island between 1903 and 1939 and who were living abroad in 1962, 66 or 75% of them were in Saint-Thomas and 15 were in different cities of the U.S.A. particularly in New York.

In Saint-Thomas this has resulted in the formation of a population closely related to Saint-Barthélemy, and there also it seems to have formed an isolate within the colored population, representing thus an off-shoot of the isolate of Saint-Barthélemy, and formed of its excess of population.

It would be interesting to estimate to what degree and in what sense it is selective, for its consequences not only upon the population of Saint-Barthélemy but also upon the formation of that of Saint-Thomas. It would also be interesting to undertake its comparative study, because here also we can foresee the appearance of certain phenomena of drift. In fact, this emigration is not equally distributed throughout the whole of the island, but seems mainly from the parish of Lorient. Moreover, in the island of Saint-Thomas the Saint-Barts originating from the two parishes do not settle in the same areas, and the dichotomy of their island is perpetuated in this new environment. Here we have a favorable situation for a more ambitious study of the dynamics of populations.

STUDY OF ANTHROPOLOGICAL CHARACTERS

Methods

The anthropometric measures have been taken according to Martin's classical techniques, and the determination of blood groups according to Beth-Vincent's technique.

The anthropometric sample is made up of 103 adult men between the ages of 21 and 50, and chosen at random in their homes or at their working places. We were mainly preoccupied by trying to secure a geographically representative sample, but we must mention that the "Au Vent" area is slightly less represented than the "Sous le Vent" area. Gustavia men are included in the Sous le Vent group. The places of birth and residence of all subjects were verified, and the usual precautions were taken in order not to perturb the sample by an overrepresentation of certain families or by the inclusion of closely related persons. But the high rate of consanguinity of the group permits us to consider that many of the persons measured are related, a fact that is impossible to avoid in such populations.

In the sample of blood groups we have tried to be as inclusive and exhaustive as possible when it was found that the frequency of B was quite particular. We have examined several times the serum of the subjects known to be of group B. Finally the study included 734 Whites from all of the island, the distribution of which is given below, and 52 Colored persons, that is 35.47% of the whole population. This percentage necessarily implies results in data of several members of the same family. However, this is justified by the kind of problem involved. Furthermore, it may be stated that less than 5% of homes were not sampled.

Anthropometric Characteristics

Table 7 sets forth measurements and indices obtained.

General results. Features and indices of the populations of Saint-Barthélemy fit with the data of the inhabitants of western France, as reported by Giot et al. ('57). It must be emphasized, however, that stature is tall, nasal index is higher, although still leptorrhinean, and that the face is narrow.

Stature seems to have increased during the last 50 years in both populations, while remaining shorter in the "Sous le Vent" side. Table 6 shows its trend from

TABLE 6
Evolution of the stature

Years	"Au vent"		"Sous le vent"		Total	
	n	M	n	M	n	M
1928–1945	63	168.8	76	167.7	139	168.2
1946–1958	39	170.9	30	169.9	69	170.5

an analysis of draft records which include annual measurements of men of 20 years of age. Before drawing conclusions it is well to remember the caution with which such data must be treated.

But the most important point emerges from an examination of variability: *despite a very rigid endogamy, variability from one individual to another remains of the same order of magnitude of that of much larger and less consanguineous populations.* This is apparent not only for the total population but also for each of the two sub-populations.

Comparison between the two populations. Both "Au Vent" and "Sous le Vent" halves of the island had been compared after the individuals measured had been regrouped according to their birth places and present domiciles, both of which were located in the same parish.

Certain differences in the means (table 7) are significant at the 5% level of significance: the stature, the cephalic index, the nasal index and the cephalo-facial index.

We shall not consider the differences found in the absolute values of most of

TABLE 7

	"Au vent"				"Sous le vent"				Total			
	n	M	σ	V	n	M	σ	V	n	M	σ	V
1. Body measurements (cm)												
Stature	42	172.4	5.5	3.2	61	169.6	7.2	4.3	103	170.7	6.9	4.0
Sitting height	32	88.8	2.9	3.3	32	88.6	3.9	4.4	64	88.6	3.5	3.9
Biacromial breadth	42	38.7	2.2	5.7	54	38.3	2.4	6.3	96	38.4	2.3	6.1
2. Head measurements (mm)												
Head length	42	188.3	7.5	4.0	61	189.9	6.2	3.2	103	189.4	6.6	3.5
Head breadth	42	157.8	5.1	3.2	61	154.2	4.6	3.0	103	155.4	5.1	3.3
Minimum frontal breadth	42	106.2	4.8	4.5	61	104.6	3.7	3.5	103	105.1	4.1	3.9
Bigonial breadth	42	110.4	6.1	5.5	61	108.3	4.6	4.2	103	109.1	5.8	5.3
Bizygomatic breadth	42	140.4	6.2	4.4	61	138.8	4.9	3.5	103	139.3	5.4	3.9
Morphological face height	42	123.2	7.8	6.3	61	119.1	7.9	6.6	103	120.4	8.1	6.7
Physiognomic face height	42	182.7	11.1	6.0	60	178.5	11.1	6.2	102	180.7	11.2	6.1
Nose height	42	53.4	3.3	6.1	61	52.7	2.8	5.3	103	53.0	3.0	5.6
Nose breadth	42	38.2	3.4	8.9	61	35.7	4.8	13.4	103	36.7	4.4	11.9
Inter-canthic diameter	42	33.6	3.1	9.1	61	32.3	2.9	8.9	103	32.7	3.0	9.1
Extra-canthic diameter	42	88.6	4.6	5.1	61	88.2	3.8	4.4	103	88.3	4.1	4.6
Mouth breadth	42	49.9	4.0	8.0	61	50.8	4.0	7.8	103	50.4	4.0	7.9
Ear length	42	65.6	5.3	8.0	61	64.1	4.7	7.3	103	64.7	4.8	7.4
Ear breadth	42	34.0	2.8	8.2	61	33.4	2.7	8.1	103	33.6	2.7	8.0
Lips height	42	13.6	4.6	34.1	61	14.3	3.8	26.8	103	14.1	4.1	29.2
3. Indices												
Relative sitting height	32	51.4	1.3	2.6	32	51.9	1.4	2.7	64	51.7	1.4	2.7
Relative biacromial breadth	42	22.3	1.3	5.9	54	22.6	1.3	5.6	96	22.5	1.3	5.7
Cephalic index	42	83.7	3.0	3.6	61	81.2	3.0	3.7	103	82.0	3.2	3.9
Morphological face index	42	87.8	5.5	6.2	61	85.8	6.2	7.2	103	86.5	6.0	6.9
Physiognomic face index	42	76.8	4.6	5.9	60	77.6	4.9	6.3	102	77.2	4.8	6.2
Transverse fronto-parietal index	42	67.4	2.6	3.5	61	67.8	2.3	3.4	103	67.7	2.4	3.6
Fronto-zygomatic index	42	75.7	2.6	3.5	61	75.4	3.0	4.0	103	75.5	2.9	3.8
Cephalo-facial index	42	89.0	2.4	2.7	61	90.0	2.6	2.9	103	89.6	2.6	2.9
Gonio-zygomatic index	42	78.7	3.5	4.5	61	78.0	2.8	3.6	103	78.3	3.1	3.9
Nasal index	42	71.9	8.5	11.8	61	68.0	9.7	14.3	103	70.2	9.4	13.3
Ear index	42	52.2	5.3	10.1	61	52.1	4.9	9.5	103	52.1	5.0	9.5
Mouth index	42	27.2	9.3	34.1	61	28.3	7.8	27.4	103	28.0	8.3	29.5

the measurements, for they closely depend upon the stature. In any case the important fact seems to be that several metric characteristics are significantly different from one area to the other, from one isolate to the other.

Moreover, these differences are very clearly perceived by the population who can recognize the physical type of certain districts by the stature and the form of the face: the tall stature on the Windward side is an often mentioned fact.

Blood Groups

Our results concern only the ABO system, but they bring to light some very interesting facts (tables 8 to 11).

In the tables we have put down Gustavia and "Sous le Vent" separately in order to bring our results closer to the sociological reality. Indeed it seems that

TABLE 8
Blood groups. Phenotypes. Whites

	A	B	AB	O	Total
"Sous le Vent"	146	0	0	200	346
Gustavia	26	3	0	49	78
"Au Vent"	117	14	5	174	310
Total	289	17	5	423	734

TABLE 9
Blood groups. Frequency of phenotypes. Whites

	A	B	AB	O
"Sous le Vent"	42.20	0	0	57.80
Gustavia	33.33	3.85	0	62.82
"Au Vent"	37.74	4.52	1.61	56.13
Total	39.37	2.32	0.68	57.63

TABLE 10
Blood groups. Distribution of genes. Whites

	p	q	r
"Sous le Vent"	0.2397	0	0.7603
"Au Vent"	0.2210	0.0310	0.7480
Total	0.2256	0.0152	0.7592

TABLE 11
Blood groups. Phenotypes. Blacks

	A	B	AB	O	Total
Phenotypes	19	6	1	26	52
Frequencies	36.54	11.54	1.92	50.00	100

although it is partially integrated in this area, Gustavia forms a quite particular unit within it. On the other hand, in the examination of the blood groups of Gustavia we included individuals whom certain informants consider to be remotely mixed.

Tables 12 and 13 show that:

(1) *The two populations of Saint-Barthélemy are significantly different* (P 0.001) *from all French populations* chosen as a reference. These differences are so great that neither q nor r are within the limits of the maximal values found in 28 studies of the west of France. Because of the small sample, gene frequencies were not calculated for Gustavia and for the Blacks.

(2) *Blood group B has sharply decreased* over the whole of the island and has completely disappeared from the "Sous le Vent" side. Thus the two halves seem to be qualitatively different.

(3) Group A has clearly decreased, especially "Au Vent."

(4) The frequency r of I° has sharply increased.

The mass of these transformations result in a considerable alteration of the genic frequencies, so that the frequencies now existing in Saint-Barthélemy are quite different from those found in other groups of the white race.

TABLE 12

Comparison of the blood groups of Saint-Barthélemy and of several regions of France

Locality	Number	O	A	B	AB	p	q	r
St.-B. "Sous le Vent"	346	200	146	0	0	23.97	0	76.03
		(57.80)	(42.20)	0	0			
St.-B. "Au Vent"	310	174	117	14	5	22.56	1.52	75.92
		(56.13)	(37.74)	(4.52)	(1.61)			
Whole France (Vallois, '58)	34174	14593	16066	2473	1042	29.34	5.28	65.38
		(42.70)	(47.01)	(7.24)	(3.05)			
Calvados (Kherumian, '58)	8658	3931	3734	712	281	26.76	5.91	67.33

TABLE 13

Extreme values of p, q and r in the west of France (Mourant, '58, pp. 30–35)

	p	q	r
Min.	19.51	2.05	66.1
Max.	32.52	9.66	73.08

DISCUSSION

The results of the study show that:

(a) Saint-Barthélemy is populated by a highly endogamous human group, the group itself being divided into two very endogamous sub-groups.

(b) The serological characters of this population differ greatly from those of the original population. The two subgroups are themselves different one from the other in this respect.

(c) The metric characters partially differ from one area to the other.

There are two types of biological facts we have to try to explain: (1) the fluctuation of blood groups, characters possessing a simple and well-known genetic determinism; (2) the morphological differentiation of the two sub-populations affecting metric characters the determinisms of which are as yet insufficiently well known. Nevertheless these characters are to a great extent determined by heredity, especially, as is the case in this study, when one compares populations living in very similar conditions.

Theoretical Considerations

These differences can be traced to several classical causes that determine the changes in the genetic structure of a population: mutation, selection, random or oriented fluctuations.

(a) It is impossible to say anything about the possibility of a different rate of *mutation* in the two halves of the island, or even about the chance appearance of a mutation in only one of the halves. Moreover, the facts we have noted could not be justified by this type of explanation, as we are considering the disappearance of an allele in one population and its sharp decrease in another, and not the appearance of a new character.

(b) The *immigration* of Whites and Blacks in both groups is very limited. The exchanges themselves between the two groups are so rare that they are far from enough to erode their differences, so that this factor cannot play any major part. If the differences in the morphological characters could leave a doubt as to this fact, the serological results would immediately erase it.

Nevertheless we must theoretically consider the possibility of an original variant sample, or of a differential emigration. If these facts are called upon to explain the difference between the Saint-Barts and the French, it is difficult to see how they could have sufficed to later distinguish the two groups of Saint-Barts. The ancientness of the division of the island is nevertheless underlined by the unequal distribution of the patronyms. It is possible that this division had been outlined since the very first settlement, but we have to remember that for a very long time the population was very scant, and that several districts are of quite recent occupation, the distribution of patronyms should rather be interpreted as a drift, as a few ancient genealogical fragments testify.

(c) The *fluctuations* of frequencies of the alleles can be caused by chance (the Wright effect) or by selection.

It is difficult to think that the differences found in the two halves of this island could be due to a selective factor. Ecology, dimensions of the populations, standard of life and pathology are too much alike in both areas to have introduced the variations noted. But the demographic characteristics (isolation, endogamy, dimensions of the population) make possible great fluctuations due to genetic drift.

Nevertheless we must ask if the decrease of B, and, less clearly, that of A, in *both* sub-populations could not be traced to another cause, even if the differences of intensity of these reductions seem to be related to drift. Penrose ('59) pointed out that a gene can be quite rapidly eliminated if the selective balance by which polymorphism is maintained becomes perturbed. In the case of the ABO system it seems that the characteristic frequencies of the habitual polymorphism are maintained by a slight advantage to the heterozygotes OA and OB (Livingstone, '60; Brues, '63). On the other hand, due to the hemolytic disease, there is nevertheless a certain disadvantage of the heterozygotes: the balance thus realized is unstable, and any change in the genetic structure of the population will perturb it. An increase of the number of homozygotes will be shown in particular by an increase of the pressure against B; in order to maintain the polymorphism, that is to say that B should persist, there should be a greater selective advantage of the heterozygotes, which we have no reason to presume. The high rate of consanguinity of small endogamous populations transforms the ratio homozygotes-heterozygotes in favor of the homozygotes, and, if the balance of genic frequencies is related to the selective value of the genotypes, it is through this channel that the dimension of the population and selection will interfere.

Penrose ('59) studying only the incidences of the foeto-maternal incompatibility which is to the disadvantage of the heterozygotes concludes (p. 7): "A rare immunizing antigen, unbalanced by mutation of heterozygous advantage of some kind, would be very rapidly selected against, like an ordinary bad dominant trait, and would disappear in relatively few generations. Correspondingly, a very common antigen would tend to become universal. Perhaps there has been selection of this kind against antigen B, in favor of O, while A, nearer 50%, has held its own throughout the world."

Without drawing conclusions about the mechanisms, we must take into account the evidence of selective mechanisms in the determination of p, q and r in a certain population. Changes in the genotypic structure of this population will influence the balance of the alleles. The dimension of the population thus plays a fundamental role not only in regulating the extent of the fluctuations caused by chance, but also in favoring selection which is demonstrated by a change of balance. Thus we must avoid looking for too simple an explanation by simple drift, and, through the comparison with other isolates, see if the constant variations follow a general direction.

Comparative Data Concerning Blood Groups: Other Studies of Isolates

(a) The studies of isolates having not found changes in the genic frequencies of the ABO system, as compared to surrounding populations, are very rare. We can mention that of Van der Heide and Van Logjem ('52) on two Dutch villages.

(b) The majority of studies show a decrease of B as compared to larger groups belonging to the same racial stock. This is the case in the following works:

— the study of the Dunker (Glass et al., '52) B = 3.1% = 9 = 0253.

— the study of the Walzer (Kaufmann, '54) where these groups always show a smaller proportion of B subjects than the surrounding non-Walzer.

— the study of polar Eskimos by Heinebecker and Pauli (Laughlin, '50) B = 5.3% ♭ = 0.31 in Thule, and B = 2.40% 9 = .013 with other polar Eskimos. On the other hand we can relate these results with those found among the Basques, where B always remains low, and with the American Indians, where it is absent.

(c) Only one study (Dunn, '60) shows a relative and absolute increase of B: in the Jewish community of Rome B = 27%, this percentage being higher than that of the Italian population. But the author, while considering the possibility of genetic drifts, points out that in other Jewish communities, the phenotype B is more common than in the surrounding population, and that this may be due to the origins of the group.

(d) The group O is increased, in compensation, in all the populations mentioned above, except for the Dunker where the decrease of B is made in favor of A (A = 59.3%).

(e) Another study (Donegami, Dungal, Ikin and Mourant, '50) shows, in Iceland, a decrease of A in favor of O, B remaining stable.

This review shows that *changes in the frequency of the genes in the ABO system in small endogamous populations seem to have a general tendency toward an increase of O and a decrease of B*. This tendency is not a rule, but it occurs with a significant frequency. But this result can also be explained by genetic drift as well as by selection, for drift tends to make the less frequent genes disappear. Nevertheless, excepting for this possible disappearance, it should not lead so often to the regular decrease of B and to almost general increase of O. Observation as well as theory thus leads us to conclude as to a conjunction of a selection against B, and a great fluctuation due to chance around the transformations following this tendency. The global evolution of Saint-Barthélemy and the differential evolution of its two halves illustrate very well both of these factors. In fact it is only to drift that we can trace the differences between "Sous le Vent" and "Au Vent" but the reduction of B and the increase of O on both sides are perhaps due to another factor, and could be related to a certain selective pressure in this direction.

Anthropometric Characters

Variability. In spite of the homogeneity of the population and its high rate of endogamy, the variability is not diminished. The standard deviation and the coefficients of variability (table 7) are never low and are sometimes very high. We have not found, in this population, the morphological homogeneity that we had expected, and this is confirmed not only by the whole but also by each sub-group.

The variability can be related to several causes, and is connected to the dimension of the population only if it has a high rate of consanguinity. Kluckhohn and

Griffith ('50) have in particular underlined the influence of the type of kinship, opposing the very small variability of a population practicing marriage between first cousins (cross cousins, a study by Buxton on the Ashanti) to the larger variability of smaller populations, but where marriages take place between second cousins (Australians, study by Howells and Warner). We also know that the variability of mixed populations is most of the time of the same order as that of other populations.

On the other hand we must remember that variability is not necessarily reduced by consanguinity. In experimental animal populations the variability of consanguinial groups is often larger than that of the hybrids (Lerner, '54). This increase in the variability of environmental origin, in populations where homozygotes are more numerous has been related to the decrease, in a consanguinial population, of the homeostatic regulation that is made possible by the diversity of alleles (Robertson and Reeve, '52). We must also remember that for the polygenic characters, the extreme types correspond to the homozygotes. We can recall that an increase in number of homozygotes, will, in the absence of selection, flatten the distributional curve. It would be interesting to take up this question within human groups.

The results found in this domain in Saint-Barthélemy raise a few questions, and it would be useful to examine different types of isolates from this point of view, in order to be able to judge the relative importance and the respective influence of the forces which tend to increase and to diminish the variability within them.

Diversity of the two sub-populations. We must mention that the nasal index, especially because of the width of the nose, is relatively high, clearly higher than in other white populations. It reaches the values found by Thieme ('59) in Puerto-Rico. It is only a sign of mixture, or is it climatic adaptation? We dare not settle the problem.

The differences between the two sub-groups, no matter what their causes may be, show that morphological differences can be constituted within a relatively short period of time between two populations of small dimension, isolated one from the other and placed in identical ecological and social conditions.

It is easily proven that a character determined by several genes has less chances of fluctuating in its phenotypic expression than a character determined by only one gene (Boyd, '63). This seems to greatly reduce the possibility of drift for the anthropometric characters. But if this argument is true at a theoretical level of evolution, it does not take into consideration the fact that the nonrepresentative sample which presides over the constitution of each generation is not made gene by gene but character by character, and that drift can affect the mass of genes which determine the character. The high rate of homozygotes, that is, of the extreme phenotypic expression of polygenic traits, will tend this way and encourage drift. It then seems that we must consider that the differences between "Au Vent" and "Sous le Vent" are caused by genetic drift.

CONCLUSION AND SUMMARY

The island of Saint-Barthélemy (Guadeloupe) is populated by the descendants of a group of European immigrants who arrived three centuries ago. Genetically completely isolated for more than 100 years, this population itself is divided into two highly endogamous isolates. These isolates of Saint-Barthélemy have extended by emigration and have constituted in Saint-Thomas (Virgin Islands) another population, the comparative study of which should complete the present results and broaden their perspective.

The stability of marriages, and the absence of illegitimacy while distinguishing this group from other Caribbean populations, also maintain its isolation and permit its division.

As a result of these facts, certain anthropometric characters differ significantly from one isolate to the other, which fact can be explained only by drift, either in the population sample which was at the origin of each isolate, or generation by generation with the reproduction of these populations.

The frequencies of ABO differ greatly from those of the regions from which the original inhabitants of Saint-Barthélemy came. Group B is strongly reduced, group A is a little less reduced, while O is strongly increased. In one of the isolates the allele B is apparently absent. It is possible that drift explains the differences between these two isolates of the island (disappearance of B), but it seems that a certain selection must have operated in the transformation of the frequencies of the alleles; the majority of studies concerning isolates give results parallel to ours, and theory shows us that we must expect selection to act in this sense.

Ethnological analysis has shown the fundamental importance of the rules of social structure in the evolution of the biological phenomena thus brought to light, and the case of Saint-Barthélemy can contribute to the widening of our documentation on the biological incidence of the social organization of human groups.

LITERATURE CITED

Benoist, J. 1963 Les Martiniquais, anthropologie d'une population métissée. Bull. Mém. Soc. d'Anthrop. Paris IV–XI: 241–432.

Boyd, W. C. 1963 Four achievements of the genetical method in physical anthropology. American Anthropologist, 65: 243–252.

Brues, A. M. 1963 Stochastic tests of selection in the ABO blood group. Am. J. Phys. Anthrop., 21: 288–299.

Dahlberg, G. 1942 An analysis of the conception of race and a new method of distinguishing races. Human Biology, 14: 372–385.

Donegami, J. A., N. Dungal, E. W. Ikin and A. E. Mourant 1950 The blood groups of Icelanders. Annals of Eugenics, 15: 147–152.

Dunn, L. C. 1960 Heredity and Evolution in Human Populations. Harvard University Press, 156 pp.

Freire-Maia, N.   1957   Inbreeding in Brazil. Am. J. Human Genet., *9:* 284–298.

Giot, P. R., J. L'Helgouach and J. Briard   1957   Données anthropologiques sur les populations du Nord-Ouest de la France. Bull. Mem. Soc. d'Anthrop., Paris, *8-X:* 183–195.

Glass, B., M. S. Sacks, E. F. Jahn and C. Hess   1952   Genetic drift in a religious isolate: An analysis of the causes of variation in blood group and other gene frequencies in a small population. Am. Nat., 145–159.

I. N. S. E. E.   1956   Résultats statistiques du recensement général de la population des départements d'Outre-Mer effectué le 1 juillet 1954. Antilles françaises. Martinique et Guadeloupe, Paris, P. U. F. et Imprimerie nationale.

Kaufmann, H.   1954   Aspects nouveaux du problème des Walser suisses par l'étude des groupes sanguins. Arch. Suisse d'Anth. Gén., *XIX:* 58–65.

Kluckhohn, C., and C. Griffith   1950   Population genetics and social anthropology. Cold Springs Harbor Symposia Quant. Biol., *15:* 129–140.

Lasserre, Guy   1961   La Guadeloupe, 2 vol. 1135 pp., U. F. I., Bordeaux.

Laughlin, W. S.   1950   Blood groups, morphology, and population size of the Eskimos. Cold Springs Harbor Symposia on Quantitative Biology, *15:* 165–173.

Lerner, I. M.   1954   Genetic Homeostasis. Edinburgh: Oliver & Boyd, 134 pp.

Livingstone, F. B.   1960   Natural selection, disease, and ongoing human evolution, as illustrated by the ABO blood groups. In: The Processes of Ongoing Human Evolution. G. Lasker, ed. Wayne State University Press.

Mourant, A. E. et al.   1958   The ABO blood groups. Blackwell Scientific Publications, Oxford.

Neel, J. V., M. Kodani, R. Brewer and R. C. Anderson   1949   The incidence of consanguineous matings in Japan, with remarks on the estimation of comparative gene frequencies and the expected rate of appearance of induced recessive mutations. Am. J. Human Genet., *1:* 156–178.

Oliver, D. L., and W. W. Howells   1957   Microevolution: cultural elements in physical variation. American Anthropologist, *59:* 965–978.

Penrose, L. S.   1959   Natural selection in man: some basic problems. In: Natural Selection in Human Populations. D. F. Roberts and G. A. Harrison ed., Pergamon Press.

Robertson, F. W., and E. C. R. Reeve   1952   Heterozygoty, environmental variation and heterosis. Nature, *170:* 296.

Salzano, F. M.   1961   Studies on the Caingang Indians. I. Demography. Human Biology, *33:* 110–130.

Sutter, J., and J. M. Goux   1961   L'aspect démographique des problèmes de l'isolat. Population, *16:* 447–462.

Sutter, J., and L. Tabah   1948   Fréquence et répartition des mariages consanguins en France. Population, *3:* 607–630.

Thieme, Frederick P.   1959   The Puerto Rican Population. Study in Human Biology. Anthrop. pap. Museum of Anthropology, University of Michigan, Ann Arbor, 156 pp.

Van der Heide, H. M., and J. J. Van Loghem   1952   Répartition des groupes sanguins en Hollande. Rapports et comm. du IVe Congès int. de trans. sang. Exp. Scient. franc., 383–388.

Gene Flow and Social Selection in the United States

M ILLIONS OF MIGRANTS HAVE MOVED TO NEW COUNTRIES because they thought they might find life better than at home: more profitable, more free, or more comfortable. Other millions, during the last few centuries, have been moved most unwillingly to new homes— some being driven into exile by conquerors, and some being kidnapped into slavery and brought from Africa to America to serve European masters. Probably about one eighth of the ancestry of the inhabitants of America today is of African origin. In the southern parts of the United States the proportion is much greater, and in the tropics greater still. It was always possible for masters to impregnate their female slaves, which they often did, at the same time "protecting" their own wives, daughters, and sisters from male slaves. In consequence, almost all gene flow was from Europeans into the Black population.

But another consequence of slavery was the tragic reversal in esthetic standards among the slaves themselves. Physical traits characteristic of Europeans came to be much admired by most of them. Negro men tended to seek mates who looked less African, when they had any choice. Of course, they were unaware of, and therefore could not be interested in, such things as blood types or sicklemia, which have nothing to do with exterior appearance. The genetic consequences of miscegenation between Africans and Europeans, as influenced by this sort of sexual selection, are excellently described and analyzed by Professor W. S. Pollitzer in "The Negroes of Charleston (S.C.); A Study of Hemoglobin Types, Serology, and Morphology." Note especially the differences between the two diagrams in Figure 3.

18. W. S. Pollitzer

The Negroes of Charleston (S.C.); A Study of Hemoglobin Types, Serology, and Morphology*

Introduction

With the rise of the modern concept of races as populations differing in the frequencies of certain genes, questions of the comparative meaning of "morphological" and "genetical" methods of racial analysis have inevitably followed. Both the fundamental assumptions and the practicality of application have been subjects of debate. Sanghvi ('53) undertook a comparison of the two methods in the study of several castes of India and found considerable agreement in results. The present study of the Negroes of the Charleston area, comparing populations over a wider span of miles, seeks to answer the following problems: What is the biological position of the Charleston Negro compared with the Negro of West Africa, the Negro of the United States, and the Whites of the United States? How does the answer from conventional physical anthropology compare with that from gene frequency determinations? What evolutionary factors most likely account for the biological position of the populations? And what associations may exist within an individual between racially significant morphological and genetical traits? Abnormal hemoglobin frequencies, especially in view of the hypothesis of the relationship between sickle cell trait and falciparum malaria, may be considered a distinct study in itself.

The coast of lower South Carolina has long been known as the home of the Gullah Negro, the approximate territory being indicated in figure 1. Stoney ('30) and others have popularized the speech and personality of the colorful Negroes. After seven years of study the linguist Turner ('49) concluded that hundreds of words and much of the syntax of the Gullah dialect show evidence of its kinship to languages of West Africa. The survival of magic and other practices from West Africa among the coastal Negroes have also been noted. But no study of physical anthropology in the area has been published.

The sources of slaves imported to Charleston from 1733 through 1807, as

* Submitted in partial fulfillment of requirements for Ph.D. degree, Columbia University. Presented at annual meeting of Association of Physical Anthropology and American Society of Human Genetics, Ann Arbor, Michigan. April 12–14, 1957.

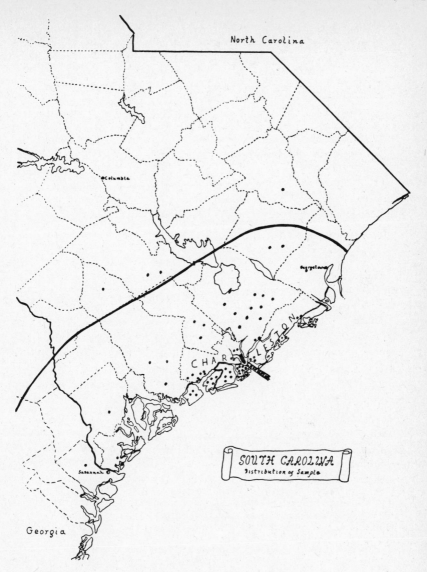

Fig. 1. Coastal Carolina, home of the Gullah Negroes.

compiled by Donnan ('35), are shown in table 1. Omitting the small numbers from the West Indies and such indefinite regions as "Guinea," the slave trade may be grouped into six regions with the percent contribution of each ás indicated in the table and in figure 2. The vast numbers from the Congo and Angola contrast strikingly with the few from the "Slave Coast" (Whydah). The word "Gullah" appears to be derived from "Angola."

According to Herskovits ('41), difficulty of travel and hostility between tribes

TABLE 1

Sources of slaves imported to Charleston 1733–1807

SOURCE	NUMBER	AREA TOTAL[1] IN PERCENT
Senegambia		19.7
Senegal	3015	
Gambia	9468	
Windward Coast		23.3
Rio Pongo and Los Island	440	
Sierra Leone	3906	
Grain (Rice) Coast	4157	
Windward Coast	6247	
Gold Coast	8508	13.4
Whydah-Bennin-Calabar		3.7
Whydah and Bennin	992	
Calabar	1345	
Congo	10705	16.9
Angola	14618	23.0
Others		——
Guinea	1046	
East Africa, Mozambique	473	
Africa	4376	
West Indies	2175	
Unknown	1406	
TOTAL	72877	100.0

[1] The percent column for the six areas is computed after subtracting "others" from the total.

made the "thousand-mile-coffle" unlikely and infrequent. The great majority of slaves probably came from within a few hundred miles of the coast. Slaves imported to the United States after the ban of 1808 were destined primarily for the newly opened lands of the Gulf States rather than coastal Carolina. Although the Gullah isolate has been dissolving in recent decades as rural homes lose members to the cities, Negro migration into the area has been negligible. It is thus highly probable that the Negroes of the Charleston area today are the descendants of those living two centuries ago in the African areas indicated above. On the rice and cotton plantations of coastal Carolina, Negroes from different regions were blended into large and relatively isolated communities, where they vastly outnumbered Whites. Phillips ('49) reasons that large plantations in which many Negroes in the fields were in little contact with the White owners is a significant factor in the development of the language and culture unique to the Gullahs. The possible influence of this situation upon human biology will be considered presently.

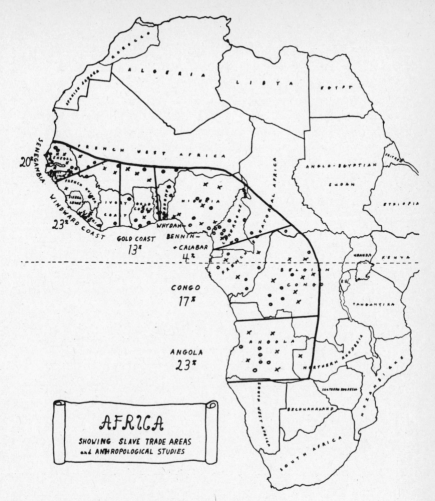

Fig. 2. West Africa, with six slave trade areas.

The Sample

Subjects were obtained through the "colored" clinics of the Medical College of South Carolina, in Charleston, chiefly obstetrics, medicine, and less frequently orthopedics; a few came from surgery and gynecology wards of the affiliated Roper Hospital. The sample consists of 479 women and only 57 men, with an age range from 14 to 79. For blood studies all age groups were included; for morphology, only those 18 and above. Among females the 18 to 30 age group constituted almost half of the total.

Of the 513 subjects reporting birthplace, one-third were born in the city of Charleston, over two-thirds within the county of Charleston, and almost 95% within the coastal tier of counties in South Carolina considered the land of the

Gullah Negro. (In figure 1 each dot represents the approximate location of the birthplace of five subjects.) Of the parents whose birthplace was known to the subject, 11% were natives of the city, 60% were natives of the county, and 85% were from the coastal strip. It thus appears highly likely that the vast majority of subjects studied are geographically representative of the Gullah Negro. Of the subjects who reported on the birthplace of their parents, 46% named the same place for father, mother, and self. On the average the distance between the birthplace of the father and that of the mother was 25 miles; and in 73% of the cases, the two parents were born within ten miles of each other. These figures suggest that the coastal Negro of recent decades neither forms small breeding isolates nor wanders afar in search of his mate.

Hemoglobin

The method of analysis followed the electrophoretic techniques of Larson and Ranney ('53), which differentiate among normal (AA), sickle cell (SS), and C (CC) hemoglobin, and any combinations of them (AS, AC, and SC). Results of the survey are presented in table 2. The high incidence of hemoglobin S is slightly

TABLE 2

Distribution of hemoglobin types in Charleston sample

HEMOGLOBIN	NUMBER	FREQUENCY
AA	393	.814
AS	73	.151
SS	2	.004
AC	14	.029
CC	1	.002
SC	0	.000
TOTAL	483	1.000

above the 13.6% sickling incidence which Switzer ('48, '50) found by wet smear studies of 4066 Negroes of the area. As shown in table 3 the Charleston gene frequencies are remarkably close to those of Africa. Wet smear determinations yield results similar to electrophoretic studies.

In view of Allison's ('54) hypothesis that falciparum malaria has an effect in maintaining the frequency of the sickle cell gene, it is noteworthy that the lower Carolina region has known malaria in endemic proportions since colonization in the late seventeenth century (Childs, '40). Although the disease is virtually non-existent today, as recently as 1937–44 McDaniel found among 58,658 Negro school children in 23 coastal counties, 2219 positive malarial smears, of which 1840 were

TABLE 3

Comparison of hemoglobin in four populations[1]

GENE	WEST AFRICA	CHARLESTON	U.S. NEGRO	WHITE
A	898	904	937	1,000
S	084	080	050	000
C	018	016	013	000
% Sickling	15.8	13.6	7.3	0.0
% Sickling calculated from gene frequencies	16.6	15.5	9.6	0.0

[1] Gene frequencies have been computed from electrophoretic studies and sickling percent from wet smear studies. Gene frequencies for Charleston are from the present study; all other figures are from the literature. A complete bibliography of the sources in this and subsequent tables is on file with Dissertation Office of Columbia University.

falciparum. Although the extent of falciparum infection in the distant past cannot be determined, the large number of known deaths from malaria in general plus the high incidence in school children cited above suggest that it has been of prime importance in the Carolina low country. As the abnormal hemoglobin genes may have been thus influenced by selection, they will not be averaged in with the serological genes in the determination of biological distance which is to follow.

One significant finding of the present study is the age distribution of subjects with abnormal hemoglobins, as revealed in table 4. Subjects under 30 have almost twice the frequency of abnormal hemoglobins of those over 30. If the heterozygous sickle cell hemoglobin confers a selective advantage it is difficult to explain this marked differential. Is it possible that the virtual disappearance of malaria in recent decades has destroyed the advantage of the heterozygote and even reduced it in viability to a level below that of the normals? Whatever factor is operative apparently effects both S and C hemoglobin.

TABLE 4

Association of hemoglobin and age in Charleston sample
(both sexes)

AGE	AA	AS	AC	TOTAL
14–29				
Number	181	42	9	232
Percent	78	18	4	100
30 and up				
Number	210	26	5	241
Percent	87	11	2	100
TOTAL NUMBER	391	68	14	473

Chi-square, 2 d.f. $= 6.81$

$p = .033$

Serology

Almost all subjects were typed for ABO group, subgroup, Ulex, M-N, Henshaw, Duffy, and the Rh factor. The Rh antisera routinely used were D, including D^u, C, E, c (if C was positive) and usually e (if E was positive). A smaller number were typed for Kell. Tests were made in small tubes with suitable controls, and read with a hand lens. Of the 515 blood samples 327 were typed at the Institute in New York; 188 were typed by the author in Charleston. Combined results are

TABLE 5

Distribution of blood types in Charleston sample

PHENOTYPE	NUMBER TESTED	NUMBER POS.	FREQUENCY[1]
ABO	514		
A_1		67	.1304
A_2		46	.0895
B		127	.2471
O		256	.4980
A,B		5	.0097
A_2B		13	.0253
M-N	515		
M		128	.2485
MN		268	.5204
N		119	.2311
Rh	515		
Dccee		291	.5650
DccEe		21	.0408
DccEE		6	.0116
DccE/		34	.0660
DCcee		73	.1417
DCcEe		3	.0058
DCcE/		6	.0116
DCCee		12	.0233
DCCEe		1	.0019
DCCE/		1	.0019
DC/ee		1	.0019
DC/E/		1	.0019
D^uccee		17	.0330
D^uccEe		1	.0019
D^uccE/		1	.0019
D^uCcee		4	.0078
D^uCCee		1	.0019
dccee		34	.0660
dccE/		1	.0019
dCcee		6	.0116
He	471	15	.0318
Fy^a	515	16	.0311
K	119	3	.0252

[1] Gene frequencies are presented in table 6.

shown in table 5. Of the 15 Henshaw positives two were associated with M, one with N, and 7 with MN. Gene frequencies were computed by Bernstein's formulas for ABO (Mourant, '54), Wiener's for Rh ('54), homozygotes plus half the heterozygotes for M-N, and unity minus the square root of the negatives for He, Fy^a, and K.

The gene frequencies of blood types of Africans, Charleston Negroes, American Negroes, and Whites are presented in table 6. In nearly all genes a gradation from

TABLE 6

Comparison of gene frequencies in four populations

	WEST AFRICA	CHARLESTON	U.S. NEGRO	WHITE
p	157	137	169	260
q	155	153	133	060
r	688	710	698	680
m	535	509	510	530
n	465	491	490	470
R_z	000	004	004	001
R_1	094	087	143	422
r'	040	022	027	009
R_2	056	069	102	143
r''	000	004	004	013
R_0	586	558	465	023
r	224	257	255	389
He	063	016	016	000
Fy^a	000	016	140	413
K	004	013	018	042

Africans to Whites through the Charleston and American Negroes is evident. To measure the biological distance between the populations the Chi-square method of Sanghvi ('53) was employed, based on:

$$x^2 = \frac{100 \sum_{i=1}^{n} \sum_{j=1}^{r} \dfrac{(p'_{ij} - q_{ij})^2}{q_{ij}} + \dfrac{(p_{ij} - q_{ij})^2}{q_{ij}}}{\text{Total number of degrees of freedom}}$$

where $n =$ number of discrete characters, each character having two to r classes; p_{ij} is the proportion of j-class of i-character for one population and p'_{ij} for another; and $q_{ij} = (p_{ij} + p'_{ij})/2$. In the distances presented in figure 3, compared with the American Negro, the Charleston Negro appears closer to Africa and farther removed from the White-African axis.

Morphology

Skin color was observed in the scapular region and recorded in terms of Gates' ('49) chart. Prognathism was recorded as none, slight, moderate, or marked, or half grades between, transformed for computation to a scale from o to 6. The following measurements were made according to the technique of Martin ('28), whose number follows in parentheses: nose length (21) and width (13), lip thickness (25), face length (18) and width (6), stature (1), and sitting height (23). Also made but not included in the analysis were hip and shoulder measurements (too inaccurate) and hair color and form (uniformly black or gray and usually artificially straightened). The results of the morphological study are compared with findings in the other three populations in table 7. The numbers

TABLE 7

Comparisons of morphology in four populations[1]

TRAIT	MALES				FEMALES			
	West Africa	Charleston	U.S. Negro	White	West Africa	Charleston	U.S. Negro	White
Skin color	2.2	3.0	5.0	9.0	2.2	2.8	5.0	9.0
Nose length	47	57	53	54	42	55	51	51
Nose width	44	46	41	35	39	42	39	32
Lip thickness	25	21	21	16	24	22	19	15
Face length	113	126	123	121	105	119	117	112
Face width	135	139	139	140	127	132	132	130
Prognathism	4.8	3.4	3.0	0.0	4.3	3.7	3.0	0.0
Standing height	1678	1675	1712	1738	1557	1593	1606	1623
Sitting height	836	856	872	911	768	822	830	863

[1] Skin color numbers refer to Gates' chart. Prognathism is on a scale from 0 = none to 6 = marked. All other measurements are in millimeters. Techniques are explained in the opening paragraph of the section on morphology.

for skin color in Charleston may be translated as fairly dark chocolate and those for prognathism as just less than moderate. Although some gradation from Africa to Whites is shown in most of the traits, precise measure of distance is complicated by variances and correlations between traits. The generalized distance, or D^2, of Mahalanobis ('49) has been used to allow for these factors. The procedure rests upon the formula: $D^2 = \Sigma\Sigma\ w^{ij}d_id_j$ where w^{ij} is the inverse of the matrix of covariance and d is the difference between two populations with respect to each continuous morphological trait employed. The method is accurate only where the traits are normally distributed, the standard deviations and correlations are similar in the populations compared, and the populations themselves live under similar environmental conditions. All traits except prognathism are normally distributed in the Charleston sample. As the standard deviations and correlations are but rarely given for the populations in the literature, those for the Charleston series have been used. The physical and cultural environment in Africa and America is obviously different. Thus, the present analysis is at best an approximation to the method of Mahalanobis. The figures suggest an unreasonable discrepancy between nose and face lengths in Charleston and in Africa. Many workers in Africa were apparently locating nasion too low (perhaps using sellion as the superior point of the measurements) and the author was locating it too high. These two dubious measurements have therefore been omitted from the analysis. Since the discriminant coefficient is given by: $l_i = \Sigma d_j w^{ij}$ for any trait, the difference in each trait between two populations was multiplied by the appropriate item in the inverse covariance matrix. The sum of products is the discriminant coefficient, an indication of the value of that trait in differentiating between the populations considered. The difference in each trait was next multiplied by its discriminant coefficient, and the sum of these products is the D^2. The square root of this value is the distance between two populations. The results of these computations, made for each sex for each of the 6 possible distances, are shown in figure 3. As the findings for males and for females were resonably

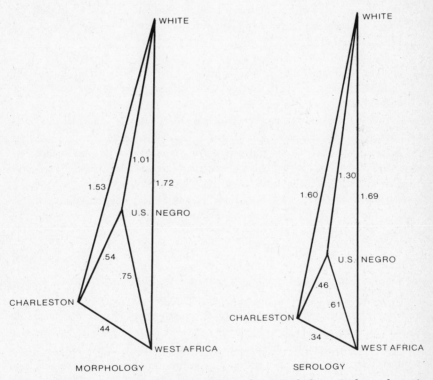

Fig. 3. Distance between four populations by morphology and serology in mean units.

similar, they were averaged. The Charleston Negro again appears closer to Africa than the average American Negro and further removed from the White-African axis.

A comparison may now be made between the "genetical" and "morphological" methods of distance ascertainment. The two sets of distances may be transformed into mean units; each of the 6 morphological distances is divided by the average of the 6, and the genetical distances are treated in a comparable manner. It is evident from the results shown that distances derived by both methods are essentially similar.

Associations Between Morphological and Genetical Traits

To compute a "morphological score" for an individual, the discriminant coefficient between Africans and Whites for each trait may be multiplied by the individual's value for each trait and the products summed. Females in the Charleston sample were arranged according to their morphological scores and the sample divided at the mean into moieties containing approximately equal numbers. The "more Negroid" fractions were then compared by Chi-square tests as to the frequency of certain genetical traits. Those selected as showing marked differences between Negroes and Whites were the abnormal hemoglobins AS and AC, Group B, Rho (Dccee) plus all variants (D^u), Henshaw, and Duffy. The results are presented at the top of table 8, which shows Chi-square and p values and degrees of freedom. The genetical trait showing the highest Chi-square value is B, followed closely by Fy^a; the hemoglobins, Rh and He are lower.

To test the association of genetical traits with each morphological trait, the female subjects were ranked by each particular morphological trait and divided at the mean into two moieties. The genetical data were counted and tested for significance, results of which are also shown in table 8. The only associations which are significant at the five percent level are the Fy^a blood factor with prognathism and skin color, and Group B with lip thickness. The small value of association of Rh_o (and D^u) with most Negroid morphological traits is noteworthy. The total for each morphological trait is in the column at the right, and the total for each genetical trait in the row at the bottom, both ranked by descending value. If the genes listed at the top of the table are indicative of negroidness, then the value of any morphological trait for racial differentiation may be read from the total column at the right. By such a test prognathism and lip thickness would be superior. If the morphological traits listed are valid indicators of negroidness, then the value of any given gene may be read from the bottom line. According to this procedure, Fy^a is the most important genetical trait for differentiation, followed by B and the abnormal hemoglobins, with Rh_o and Henshaw least important. This rating of genes by summation of their value with individual morphological traits yields a picture similar to, but not identical with, the results found through the discriminant function.

TABLE 8

Association of morphology and genetic traits by chi-square value
(adult females only)

TRAIT	Hb	Fy^a	B	Rh° + D^u	He	TOTAL
Deg. Freed.	2	1	1	1	1	6
By discriminant function[1]	0.7	2.7	3.0	0.3	0.2	6.9
Prognathism	3.4	3.9*	0.1	1.8	0	9.2
Lip thickness	1.5	3.7	3.8*	0	0	9.0
Nose width	5.4	0	1.4	0	0.2	7.0
Sitting height	4.6	1.1	0	1.0	0.3	7.0
Nose length	4.6	0 .	0.5	0.5	0	5.6
Face length	1.4	1.0	2.1	0	0.4	4.9
Skin color	0.1	3.8*	0.9	0	0	4.8
Standing height	0.8	0	0	2.1	0.2	3.1
Face width	1.2	0	0	0.2	0	1.4
Deg. Freed.	18	9	9	9	9	54
Total (9 traits)	23.0	13.5	8.8	5.6	1.1	52.0

* Significant at .05 level.

[1] The Discriminant Function is a composite measure of negroidness based on all of the nine traits listed. It is found by multiplying a coefficient (the value of any given morphological trait for Negro-White differentiation) by the individual's score for each trait, and summing the products.

Discussion

On the basis of morphological and serological findings the Charleston Negro has been compared with the West African Negro, the American Negro, and Whites to determine the degree of similarity among them. What biological meaning can be assigned to the distance thus computed? Although the aim of the calculations is the measurement of actual genetic kinship, both genetical and morphological methods fall short of this goal. In theory the blood type frequencies dependent upon single genes inherited in a known Mendelian manner, fully expressed, and not subject to environmental modification *within the individual,* should be perfect indicators of the degree of affinity. Such genes, especially those showing wide variations in frequency among the populations considered, appear to be ideal for the modern genetic concept of race. Yet the monogenetic nature of the blood type genes permits them to be readily affected by random fluctuations and sampling error. The same frequency of a gene may occur in diverse and obviously unrelated people, while groups as closely akin as two North American Indian tribes may show a striking difference. Only recently has a start been made in unravelling the possible role of selection in the blood types. Other major drawbacks to the genetical approach at the present time are the complexities of technique and the rather few "gene" traits known which occur in suitably high frequencies. Nevertheless, a large number of blood factors should yield a fairly accurate measure of biological relationship, especially where adequately supported by data from such other disciplines as history, archeology, or physical anthropology. The totalled Chi-square calculations based on serology may be considered a reasonable approximation to genetic kinship among the populations involved.

The morphological traits present a different kind of problem. In addition to the difficulty of precise measurement, no simple pattern of inheritance is known for these polygenic traits. Many if not all are subject to environmental modification *within the individual,* skin color, hair color, and hair form being especially malleable. Selection through many millennia probably plays the major role in the formation of most such racial traits; chance fluctuations should wield relatively little influence. Many morphological features, distinctive among the populations of the world with little or no overlap, have been used by anthropologists for over a century in racial classification. In the absence of known artificial deformation or time enough for appreciable natural selection, morphology should yield a reasonably accurate index of relationship. The generalized distance, allowing for intercorrelations and range of variation of the traits, should provide the best estimate.

Satisfactory agreement of the two methods is indicated by the present study.

The major evolutionary factor most likely responsible for the biological positions of the populations appears to be hybridization between West Africans and Whites. This phenomenon is indicated by the gradation in serological and morphological factors. Among the blood factors this effect is well illustrated by the ABO, Rh, Kell, Duffy, and Henshaw systems, in addition to the abnormal hemoglobins. Of the morphological traits, skin color, prognathism, lip thickness, stature, and sitting height present a similar picture. The implication of the data and the diagram is that, although both intermediate groups have undergone admixture with Whites, the Negroes of Charleston have received far less White genes than Negroes elsewhere in the country. That the average American Negro shows evidence of significant admixture is known from the studies of Herskovits ('30) in morphology and genealogy and those of Glass ('55) in genetics. Coon, Garn, and Birdsell ('50) even consider them distinct enough to be called a separate "race."

Why should the Gullah Negro have less genetic contribution from Whites than those Negroes elsewhere in the United States? The ratio of the races on the low-country plantations may provide one answer. Just as the social situation molded the language and culture characteristic of the Gullah Negro, it may have played a dominant role in shaping the physical man as well. Besides offering less opportunity for mixture, the social situation probably created a psychological factor opposing it. Wherever Negroes are in close association with a dominant White society in large numbers, White physical traits seem to be held at a premium. Those Negroes with indications of Caucasian admixture have greater opportunities for transmitting their genes. But in isolates composed overwhelmingly of distinctly Negroid individuals a sense of social cohesion develops which militates against those showing signs of admixture. Mate selection, operating on visible traits, might be strong enough to discourage miscegenation or to lead to the migration of hybrids away from the area. Although documentary proof is lacking, it is likely that such a mechanism has had significant influence among the Negroes long isolated in the coastal counties of lower South Carolina.

The Charleston Negroes are not only nearer to Africa biologically; they are also somewhat removed from the African-White axis relative to the general American Negro. This fact suggests that somewhat different parental stocks may have fused in the formation of the Negroes of Charleston and those elsewhere in the United States. The provenance of Negroes brought to America, other than to Charleston, is inadequately known. Areas to the south and east in Africa were apparently engaged in the slave trade, especially in the illegal operations following 1808. Even within West Africa the relative contribution of tribes to the Gullahs may have differed significantly from that to other Negroes of America. The White component which fused with the Negro may also have varied appreciably in different parts of America.

The question of Indian admixture with the American Negro has been raised by Herskovits ('30) and by Glass ('55). The former, basing his argument chiefly on genealogy, suggests a significant degree of Indian contribution to the amalgam. The latter, relying primarily upon the serological genes, concludes that the Indian flow has been virtually negligible. In frontier days many opportunities existed for miscegenation, and a few communities of today bear witness to such racial fusion. Some physical and verbal evidence for Indian admixture came to the author's attention during a survey of the sea-island area of Carolina and Georgia. Although Indian gene frequencies in general (as reported by Mourant, '54) are compatible with the theory that that race did contribute genes to the American Negro, too little information is available for a precise statement of the degree of Indian influence. Serological studies are almost entirely of tribes beyond the range of possible fusion with Negroes, and these exhibit wide variability.

As the difference in degree of admixture and in ancestral stocks may not be the sole explanation of the divergence of Charleston from other American Negroes, other evolutionary factors should be considered. Could natural selecton produce significant differences in the two hybrid populations? It is difficult to conceive of environmental agents, differing between coastal Carolina and the rest of the nation, potent enough to create detectable differences in a mere dozen generations. The relative isolation of the Gullah Negroes on large plantations through one or two centuries appears to offer an ideal situation for the operation of genetic drift. Until recent decades the vast majority of the native Negroes of the coastal strip probably spent their entire lives within a few miles of their birthplace. But any random fluctuations in gene frequencies thus produced should tend in varying directions within any small isolate. The 25-mile average distance between birthplace of the subject's parents in the present sample suggests that any deviations produced in the isolates of the past would be cancelled out in the formation of the larger gene pools of recent generations. It therefore appears likely that neither natural selection nor genetic drift has played an appreciable role in the biological position of the Charleston Negro.

The significant association between morphology and the blood factor genes is probably due to hybridity. If genes for a negroid physical trait and those for a negroid blood factor enter a mating together, they would tend to remain together, especially if they are on the same chromosome. If they are close together on the chromosome many generations might be required to achieve random association. Association between morphology and blood factors should thus yield some indication of the position of the genes on the chromosomes. However, the polygenes for morphological factors are unknown and of unequal value in differentiating the races; nearly all of the negroid serological genes and hemoglobin genes occur in only a minority of Negroes; and the statistical procedure used to measure the relationship is affected by chance, especially in small categories. Thus no reliable estimate of the chromosomal relationship between morphological and other genes can be made from the present data. Ideally racial analyses should include a large battery of both morphological and genetical traits. Such an approach not only permits each method to serve as a check on the other; it might also point the way toward a better understanding of the chromosomal or physiological association between traits.

Summary

Data have been presented on approximately 500 Gullah Negroes of the Charleston, South Carolina, vicinity. Comparisons have been made with natives of West Africa, average American Negroes, and Whites. Values for abnormal hemoglobin in the Charleston sample are close to African ones and may have been maintained at this high level through the action of falciparum malaria. The degree of similarity between Negroes of Charleston and other populations has been analyzed by two methods: Sanghvi's Chi-square of the gene frequencies for blood types and Mahalanobis' generalized distance for the morphological traits. Results of the methods are quite similar; both show that the Charleston Negro is distinct from, and closer to Africans than, the general American Negro. Hybridization to a lower degree appears to be the major cause of the biological position noted. Study of the association of genetical and morphological traits within the individuals tends to confirm hybridization and suggests traits useful in racial study.

Notes

Tables of data on hemoglobin, serology, and morphology collected from the literature on West Africans, American Negroes, and Whites are on file with the Dissertation Office of Columbia University. On the map of West Africa each circle or cross indicates the approximate location of one morphological and one serological study respectively. An effort was made to include all known studies on Negroes within the slave trade regions, omitting pygmies and those with obvious Caucasian admixture and a few studies of ancient vintage, doubtful techniques, small sample, and those giving no means. Sickling and blood type data are based on Mourant's ('54) and Boyd's ('39) compilations, but original sources have been checked wherever possible and additions made wherever necessary. All genetical data were reduced to gene frequencies. Bernstein's correction was applied to ABO frequencies which did not total between .999 and 1.001.

To obtain an average for any value in Africa, the available studies within each of the six regions were first weighed by sample size (which emphasizes the more accurate modern studies with large samples) and averaged. Then the 6 means for the trait were averaged according to the contribution of each region to the Charleston slave trade. Figures for American Negroes and Whites were averaged with equal weight for each study, with the exception of the serological studies in New York City which were first averaged by sample size to yield a single study.

Wide variations in hemoglobin values in Africa tend to cast doubts on the validity of the data from the literature, but close agreement of the African average by electrophoresis with that by wet smears of sickling lends substantiation to the figures. Except for ABO groups blood typing data are still too scarce in most of Africa to provide reliable estimates. Studies on American Whites and Negroes are purposely aimed at sampling primarily the South. As insufficient serological data, other than ABO, are available on Southern Whites, who are about 85% of English stock, English blood type frequencies have been substituted. The similarity of the two in ABO frequencies tends to justify the procedure. Skin color has been subjected to such a bewildering array of scoring techniques that any estimate for a large territory is unavoidably poor. An effort was made to translate verbal and numerical estimates to numbers of Gates' chart. Evaluation of prognathism is equally difficult. The scarcity of morphological data on African females is also regrettable.

In using Sanghvi's measure of genetical distance, a $2 \times r$ contingency table was set up for each different blood type system. As the "expected" value for each class is the average between the two "observed" values, the difference between observed and expected will be the same in any one class. Thus it is simpler to compute half of the Chi-square value. Since the number of genes compared is the same for all four populations, the number of degrees of freedom can be ignored. The square root of the sum of all the Chi-square values yields the distance between any two populations. ABO, MN, Rh, Fy^a, He, and K have been employed as separate systems; using within the Rh system 4 major genes (R^1, R^2, R^0, and r) and the sum of R^z, r', and r''. As sub-group data are scarce, often unreliable, and highly variable in the 4 populations, they have been omitted in the calculations.

In the diagrams of distance morphology is an accurate representation; serology has been slightly distorted in order to convert a three-dimensional figure to a flat surface.

Acknowledgments

This investigation was supported in part by Predoctoral Fellowship no. HF-6131, from the National Heart Institute, U.S. Public Health Service; and in part by fellowships from Columbia University. The author is grateful for this financial aid. He is also happy to express his appreciation to: Ortho Research Foundation, Raritan, N.J., and The New York City Board of Health, for sera; Mrs. F. Innella, First Army Area Medical Laboratory, and Miss N. Gibbel, Mt. Sinai Hospital, New York, for blood typing; Drs. L. C. Dunn, H. Levene, H. L. Shapiro, P. Levine, R. E. Rosenfield, and Helen Ranney, all at Columbia University, for their kind help and advice; Drs. M. H. Knisely, L. Hester, V. Moseley, J. R. Siegling, and W. McCord, and their staffs at the Medical College of South Carolina, as well as the nurses, students, and patients for making this research possible; Mr. J. Robbin, Watson Scientific Computing Laboratory, New York, for the mathematical analysis of the data; Dr. G. W. Hervey, American National Red Cross, Washington, D.C., Dr. G. E. McDaniel, State Board of Health, Columbia, S.C., Mr. S. G. Stoney, Charleston, S.C., and Dr. Marion Waller, University of Virginia Medical School, Richmond, Va., for their personal communications; and his wife, Peggy, for typing, preparing maps and diagrams, and tolerating him during two years of his labors.

LITERATURE CITED

ALLISON, A. C.   1954   The distribution of the sickle-cell trait in East Africa and elsewhere, and its apparent relationship to the incidence of subtertian malaria. Trans. Roy. Soc. Trop. Med. Hyg., 48: 312.

BOYD, W. C.   1939   Blood Groups. Tabulae Biologicae. The Hague, 17: 113.

CHILDS, ST. J. R.   1940   Malaria and the Colonization of the Carolina Low Country. 1526–1696. The Johns Hopkins Press, Baltimore.

COON, C. S., S. M. GARN AND J. B. BIRDSELL   1950   Race . . . a study of the problems of race formation in man. C. C. Thomas, Springfield, Ill.

DONNAN, E.   1935   Documents Illustrative of the History of the Slave Trade to America. Carnegie Inst. Publ. no. 409. vol. IV.

GATES, R. R.   1949   Pedigrees of Negro Families. Blakiston Co., Phila.

GLASS, B.   1955   On the unlikelihood of significant admixtures of genes from the North American Indians in the present composition of the Negroes of the United States. Amer. J. Human Genetics, 7: 368.

HERSKOVITS, M. J.   1930   The Anthropometry of the American Negro. Columbia Univ. Press, New York.

——   1941   The Myth of the Negro Past. Harper and Bros., New York.

LARSON, D. L., AND H. RANNEY   1953   Filter paper electrophoresis of human hemoglobin. J. Clin. Invest., XXXII, 11: 1070.

McDANIEL, G. E. (S. C. Board of Health) Personal communication.

MAHALANOBIS, P. C., MAJUMDAR AND C. R. RAO   1949   Anthropometric survey of the United Provinces, 1941: A statistical study. Sankhya, 9: 89.

MARTIN, R.   1928   Lehrbuch der Anthropologie. G. Fischer, Jenna.

MOURANT, A. T.   1954   The distribution of the Human Blood Groups. C. C. Thomas, Springfield, Ill.

PHILLIPS, U. B.   1949   Life and Labor in the Old South. Little, Brown, and Co., Boston.

SANGHVI, L. D.   1953   Comparison of genetical and morphological methods for a study of biological differences. Amer. J. Phys. Anthrop., 11: 385.

STONEY, S. G., AND G. M. SHELBY 1930 Black Genesis. A Chronicle. Macmillan Co., New York.

SWITZER, P. K., AND H. H. FOUCHÉ 1948 The Sickle-cell trait: incidence and influence in pregnant colored women. Amer. J. Med. Sci., *216:* 330.

SWITZER, P. K. 1950 The incidence of the sickle cell trait in Negroes from the sea-island area of South Carolina. Sthn. Med. J., *43:* 48.

TURNER, L. D. 1949 Africanisms in the Gullah Dialect. Univ. of Chicago Press, Chicago.

WIENER, A. S. 1954 An Rh-Hr Syllabus: the types and their applications. Grune & Stratton, New York.

Gene Flow and Social Selection in the Jungle

FOR THOUSANDS OF GENERATIONS OUR ANCESTORS ARE PRE-
sumed, with good reason, to have lived in very small groups which
were widely scattered. Such conditions, according to the calculations of
mathematical geneticists, are likely to have consequences which Darwin
would not have predicted. In very small groups which are really genetically isolated, chance is more important than adaptive selection in
determining the relative frequencies of contrasting alleles. This is
known as genetic drift, or the Sewell Wright effect. And, of course,
widely scattered small groups have few opportunities to exchange
genes.

Since most people now live in much larger groups, and in proximity to
thousands of potential mates, anthropologists and human geneticists
eagerly seek for genetic isolates to study. In this way, genetic theory,
they hope, may be confirmed by data—or if not confirmed, suitably
modified. Some religious groups have intentionally isolated themselves
from the world and become endogamous breeding populations; a
number have been studied. But there are also some groups living under
"primitive" conditions in remote places who are attractive targets for the
more adventurous human biologists; a few of these have been
studied too.

One aspect of genetic drift is known as the Founder Effect. If some
individuals or families leave an established population to found a new
group by themselves, it is highly unlikely that they will be a random
sample of the population that they left. This has been amply demonstrated by research among several different religious isolates in the
United States and Canada. At the same time, geneticists appear to assume that when two groups, previously separated, interbreed, random
samples from each are involved. Thus, it is further supposed that the
proportion of ancestry among the mixed group which is derived from

each of the two original groups can be calculated, provided that we know the allele frequencies of all three groups.

But it ain't necessarily so. The following study, by a team of geneticists and anthropologists of whom Professor Chagnon is the senior author, demonstrates how mating patterns, as regulated by social status, can produce quite different results. It is correctly titled "The Influence of Cultural Factors on the Demography and Pattern of Gene Flow from the Makiritare to the Yanomama Indians."

19. Napoleon A. Chagnon, James V. Neel, Lowell Weitkamp, Henry Gershowitz, and Manuel Ayres

The Influence of Cultural Factors on the Demography and Pattern of Gene Flow from the Makiritare to the Yanomama Indians*

Abstract. A single village of Yanomama Indians was found to have frequencies of Di^a of 0.06 and of Ap^a of 0.08, in contrast to 40 other villages were Di^a was absent and Ap^a quite rare. The source of these genes was identified as a village of Makiritare Indians, but the two allele frequencies were approximately the same or even higher in the Yanomama than in the Makiritare village. Demographic, social and cultural parameters affecting marriage and reproduction in the two tribes explain this. Genealogical relationships and informants' accounts collected in the field, when viewed against the traditional marriage practices, reproductive advantages of headmen, and differential treatment of captured women, indicate that the mating and reproduction parameters inherent in tribal social organization of this kind constitute an essential part of the explanation of the genetic findings. It is argued that mating systems of this sort are such that the probability of a new gene introduced by a captive surviving in the recipient population is a function of the sex of the initial carrier. The implications for tribalization and potentially radical changes in allele frequencies are briefly explored by considering aspects of settlement pattern and population fissioning known to characterize the tribes in

* This work has been supported in part by grant AT(11-1)-1552 of the U.S. Atomic Energy Commission. Paper presented in part at the Twelfth International Congress of Genetics and the Eighth International Congress of Anthropological and Ethnological Sciences, Tokyo, Japan, 1968.

287

question. Finally, it is shown that genetic sampling from a single location can and does result in unrepresentative allele frequencies when this single sample is taken to characterize the tribe as a whole.

The question of the extent to which the gene frequencies for a population, however defined, are the result of deterministic as opposed to random genetic forces is, of course, one of the central issues of population genetics. In the past, two kinds of random events have been commonly recognized, namely, the founder effect, the luck of the draw when a relatively small group which is to serve as an ancestral population separates from a much larger group, and genetic drift, *sensu strictu,* the random walk of gene frequencies in successive generations of a small population. Recently we have recognized, under the term "lineal effect," a third kind of event, random in the genetic but not in the social sense, and especially applicable to human populations (Neel, '67; Arends et al., '67). This effect is based on the observation that the social structure of tribal populations usually ensures that break-away groups contain many related persons, so that in such a group the number of independent genomes is well below the numerical count of individuals.

In the present communication we propose to begin to define a fourth type of event, more properly, a group of social phenomena, which although "random" in the genetic sense is, like the lineal effect, inherent in the social organization of many tribal populations. Specifically, we shall, on the basis of a concrete example, begin to explore the genetic consequences of the socially-conferred reproductive advantages of headmanship and the differential fertility of abducted women. At the same time, we shall present a very concrete illustration of how gene flow occurs between two tribal populations of American Indians. While it would obviously be unwise to generalize from a single anecdote such as this, the changes in gene frequencies with which the population geneticist deals are, in the final analysis, based on such grass-roots events as these; our formal treatments can be no better than our knowledge of the detailed events upon which our assumptions depend.

The Populations

The tribes on which this study of gene flow and socially-influenced gene frequency changes are based are the Makiritare and Yanomama of southern Venezuela and adjacent portions of Brazil (see fig. 1). The former is a Carib-speaking group of some 2,000 individuals whose population is distributed in numerous villages along the upper reaches of the navigable rivers that drain the border mountains between Venezuela and Brazil. They are a "canoe" people and have been known to take long river journeys to European settlements on which they have traditionally depended for steel tools, firearms, salt and glass beads. Their villages range in size from 50 to 150 inhabitants. Economically, the Makiritare rely principally on the slash-and-burn cultivation of bitter manioc, which they refine into manioc flour or cassava bread, especially the latter.

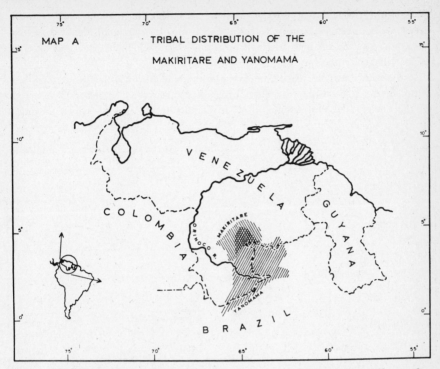

Fig. 1. Tribal Distribution of the Makiritare and Yanomama. The villages discussed in this communication are found at the southeastern corner of the area commonly held by the two tribes.

The Yanomama, by contrast, are a "foot" people, avoiding larger rivers for lack of a watercraft tradition. Their palisaded settlements are found deep in the tropical forest. Thus, where their territory overlaps with that of the Makiritare, villages of the two tribes tend to be in complementary distribution. Like the Makiritare, the Yanomama also are slash-and-burn cultivators, but the staple food in this case is now plantains, a post-Columbian introduction (Reynolds, '27; Zerries, '58; Simmonds, '59; Becher, '60; Chagnon, '66, '68b, in press). Both groups hunt, fish and collect wild foods to supplement their agriculture, but neither group can be called a "hunting and gathering" tribe. The number of Yanomama has been roughly estimated at 10,000 (Chagnon, '66, '68b), but our recent work in several large, uncontacted areas leads us to believe that the total population may be even larger (Chagnon, N.D.). The Yanomama are divided into some 125 villages that range in size from 40 to 250 inhabitants. They are more aggressive than the Makiritare and still retain their aboriginal warfare pattern (Chagnon, '66, '68a, b).

The two tribes live contiguously, sharing a common border (fig. 1). At a number of points the Yanomama, in the process of expanding away from their tribal center (Chagnon, '68a), have within the past several generations forced the Makiritare out of their old territory. On the other hand, recently, with some 20 years of peaceful relations between the two tribes, Makiritare villages have moved deep into Yanomama territory, to be near missions. In some areas the two groups have now established such amicable relations with each other that they live in mixed villages.

In the course of field work among the Yanomama and Makiritare in 1967, we sampled one Yanomama village in Brazil, Borabuk (2°45′N; 62°05′W, see fig. 2) that differed from the some 40 other Yanomama villages on which we now

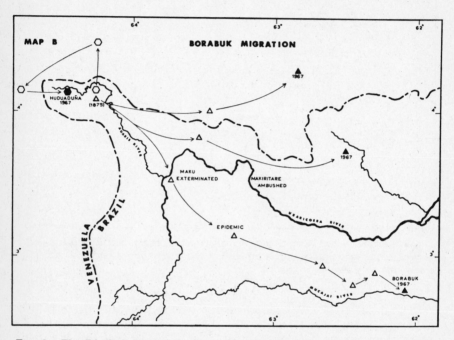

Fig. 2. The Borabuk Migration. The two villages discussed originated in the upper left-hand corner of the diagram, our informants' accounts of village history and migration going back to about 1875. Makiritare villages are indicated by hexagons and Yanomama villages by triangles. Present ('67) locations are indicated by shading. The locations of the epidemic and the conflict with the Makú are approximate, as are abandoned village sites.

have blood group frequency data, including the ten villages in which we have previously reported (Arends et al., '67). The village in question was characterized by modest frequencies of Diego a-positive and erythrocyte acid phosphate type A-positive individuals and, in one family, a rapidly-migrating serum albumin variant (Weitkamp and Chagnon, '68). The first and third genetic traits had not previously been encountered in the Yanomama and acid phosphatase type A in only four other villages, all in the northern portion of the tribal distribution, contiguous to the traditional distribution of the Makiritare. However, the Di^a and Ap^a genes do regularly occur in the Makiritare villages studied to date (Layrisse and Wilbert, '66; Gershowitz et al., in press; Weitkamp and Neel, in press). At the time of this study, the nearest Makiritare village, Huduaduña, was located on the Auaris River (4°10′N; 64°20′W) some 200 miles to the northwest of the village of Borabuk (fig. 2). The albumin trait was found in an abducted Makú woman and her progeny then living in Borabuk, being thus far unknown in either the Makiritare or the Yanomama tribe.

Our field work procedure and method, in addition to collecting biological specimens, involves the systematic interviewing of as many villagers as time permits for the purpose of establishing recent village histories, settlement pattern and genealogies. By this means we learned that the Borabuk and Huduaduña populations lived contiguously on the Auaris River for some time prior to turn of the century in a mixed village, and that some intermarriage took place between them. Informants in both the Makiritare and Yanomama villages independently corroborated this, and genealogical data explicitly show some of the intermarriages. Indeed, a sizeable fraction of the current population of the Yanomama group reckon descent from a deceased headman and his two brothers whose father was Makiritare and whose mother was Yanomama. (See discussion of genealogy, below.)

The laboratory analyses of the blood samples thus confirmed the village histories and pedigree information, but in a somewhat puzzling manner: the Yanomama village was characterized by approximately the same or even higher frequencies of Di^a and Ap^a than was found in the present population of Huduaduña, the Makiritare village from which the two alleles were most probably introduced. Specifically, among 91 individuals, 12 were Diego positive and 16 were, on electrophoresis, erythrocyte acid phosphatase type AB, a Di^a gene frequency of 0.06 and an Ap^a gene frequency of 0.08. Layrisse and Wilbert ('66) had previously established that in a pooled sample gathered from two Makiritare villages, the Di^a gene frequency was 0.17. In subsequent work, we (Gershowitz, Layrisse, Neel, Brewer, Chagnon and Ayres, in press) have encountered Di^a frequencies between 0.02 and 0.52 in seven Makiritare villages, and in addition (Weitkamp and Neel, in press), Ap^a frequencies from 0.00 to 0.13. In the Makiritare village of Huduaduña the Di^a gene frequency among 71 persons was 0.04 and the Ap^a gene frequency, 0.05. Thus the frequency of the Di^a and Ap^a genes was approximately the same or even higher in the Yanomama village of Borabuk than in the Makiritare village from which the genes were probably introduced.

The explanation of the situation appears to rely in large part in the sociocultural practices relating to reproduction in the Yanomama mating structure, particularly those having to do with the prerogatives of headmanship in the context of polygyny and in the differential treatment of female captives from non-Yanomama groups. Secondly, the demographic structure of the Yanomama population must be considered in interpreting the marriage practices and how these relate to the probability of retaining an introduced allele, a probability that, when the gene is introduced by a captive, varies with the sex of the introducer, as will be shown in the discussion of tribal marriage practices below.

Village Histories

Before turning to the discussion of the mating structure a brief resumé of the village histories will be in order to give some idea of the general cultural milieu within which the mating structure operates. Prior to 1900 both the Borabuk (Yanomama) and Huduaduña (Makiritare) populations maintained contiguous villages on the upper reaches of the Auaris River (fig. 2). The histories of the respective groups are not known prior to this point in time, so there is a possibility of earlier intertribal admixture in either or both groups previous to ca. 1875, the approximate date that the two groups are estimated (by inspection of genealogies and informant's accounts) to have lived contiguously.

The Makiritare have long had contact with the more remote colonies of European settlers and through these they acquired steel tools and glass beads. Even at the present time the village of Huduaduña obtains glass beads that originate in Guyana; these are traded westward in a network of several intermediate tribes, processed manioc and dugout canoes being exchanged for them. The fact that the Makiritare have established and maintained this relationship with European settlements has given them a trading hegemony over the Yanomama, who have remained isolated and thereby avoid direct contacts with outsiders. The Yanomama have traditionally relied on the Makiritare for steel tools, which according to Yanomama informants as far away from this point as the upper Orinoco (Chagnon, '66) eventually reached very remote Yanomama villages via a long, inter-village trading network. (Until the advent of missionary activity in this area, 1955–1960, the Yanomama relied exclusively on the Makiritare for their supply of steel tools.) It is for this reason that groups of Yanomama periodically take up temporary residence with the Makiritare: they work for them in order to obtain the necessary and extremely desirable steel tools that make their agricultural economy more efficient.

Although both the Yanomama and Makiritare have very low opinions of each other, the fact that the Makiritare have a monopoly on steel tools, which they jealously guard, has given them the advantage in the various social relationships that emerge in mixed villages. One way in which this advantage is expressed is that Makiritare men (in mixed villages) demand and usually obtain sexual access to Yanomama women. If intermarriage or semi-permanent co-residence does take place, it invariably involves a Makiritare man with a Yanomama woman. The issue of these unions are somewhat disadvantaged in both tribes from a matrimonial point of view, for the respective notions regarding marriage are such that half-Yanomama sons are not readily incorporated into either marriage system. Daughters of mixed marriages, on the other hand, are always marriageable although they do not enjoy the status of full tribal members in every case, particularly among the Makiritare. There are subtle sociological issues involved here, but these do not speak directly to the immediate problem and will be handled in other publications.

During the period of time when the members of Borabuk resided in close proximity to Huduaduña, men of the Makiritare group persistently had affairs with Yanomama women, much to the chagrin of the Yanomama men. In addition to this cause of friction, the Yanomama suspected the Makiritare of practicing harmful magic against them, and their general interrelationships were potentially strained, if not hostile. According to Borabuk informants, matters came to a climax when a Yanomama man was accused of stealing tobacco from the garden of a Makiritare, which eventually led to arguments and then to an inter-village fight in which a Yanomama man was badly injured with a knife. The Yanomama decided to separate from the Makiritare and moved down the Auaris River to its junction with the Uraricoera (Parima), probably just prior to 1900. (A dissident faction of the Yanomama group also separated and moved eastward, to Venezuela.)

The headman of the Yanomama group at this point in time was half-Makiritare, having been sired by a prominent shaman of the latter group but raised by his mother among her people. The dissident Yanomama group remained in this general area until about 1910 when a feud within the village over the possession of a woman caused a fission, and part of the group migrated to the east, entering into active hostilities with those who remained behind. The latter group moved further to the southeast and settled on a branch of the Mucajai River known as Koroknai-u (not shown on fig. 2).

Shortly after the split in the Yanomama village a serious epidemic of unknown etiology struck and killed a large number of men. We do not know why only men died in this particular epidemic, but similar situations are known to occur among the Yanomama elsewhere. Yanomama men frequently take long trips to visit or trade with distant groups and occasionally are exposed to disease long before it reaches their natal village. We have informants' accounts of such groups becoming seriously ill and their members dying in large numbers before they return home. Presumably this is what happened in this epidemic. It should be pointed out that the Yanomama have just one word to describe a situation in which many people become sick and die and our (Chagnon's) translation of the word is not meant to coincide precisely with our medical notions of epidemic. The Makiritare and the Makú (a tribe now extinct save for three or four survivors who reside among the Yanomama on the Mucajai and Uraricoera Rivers) were blamed for the epidemic. One important consequence of the epidemic was that the half-Makiritare Yanomama headman acquired as his wives several of the widows of men who perished, a prerogative he exercised largely because of his status.

Some time after the epidemic the Yanomama raided the Makú and abducted a woman from them during the skirmish; she still lives in Borabuk (Weitkamp and Chagnon, '68). A few years later the Makiritare of Huduaduña sent a party of workers down the Uraricoera to cut logs and make canoes to trade with the Brazilians in the town of Boa Vista, several days journey further downstream. The members of Borabuk took this opportunity to get their revenge on the Makiritare and visited the temporary camp on the Uraricoera. They were invited into the hut, and, discovering that they greatly outnumbered the Makiritare, at a signal from Iro, the instigator of the attack, set upon the men and killed many of

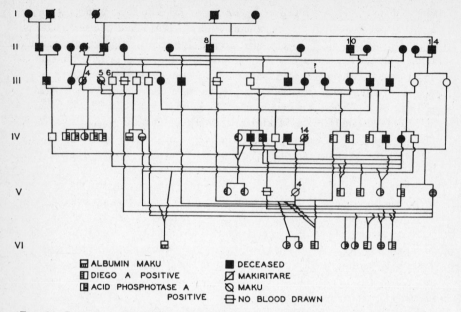

ALBUMIN MAKU   DECEASED
DIEGO A POSITIVE   MAKIRITARE
ACID PHOSPHOTASE A   MAKU
            POSITIVE   NO BLOOD DRAWN

Fig. 3. Partial genealogy of individuals carrying the Di^a, Ap^a and Albumin Makú genes. The genealogy shows only the putative family ties among affected individuals as given by informants. This particular Yanomama genealogy is somewhat distinct in the more-than-usual level of polyandry, polygyny and paternity uncertainty compared to genealogies collected in other villages. Note that some individuals have more than one possible father.

them with staves. Our informant for the raid details was a Makiritare woman who was captured at this time and who now lives among the Borabuk (individual III-4 of fig. 3). Two other women were captured with her, and likewise live with the Borabuk, incorporated as wives. This raid took place sometime around 1930.

Mating Structure and Status of Headmen

We have noted (Salzano, Neel and Maybury-Lewis, '67) that among the Xavante, a tribe of approximately the same cultural level, there is a significant difference in the reproductive performance of males and females. Whereas women are uniformly exposed to the risk of pregnancy and rarely fail to reproduce, men, on the other hand, are characterized by an appreciably higher variance in their reproductive performance. The basis for this difference is sociological in origin, since males in this type of society are "rewarded" for political and military astuteness and prowess by being in a much better position to acquire multiple wives. Consequently, some men will reproduce very little and others will make significantly large, often dramatic, contributions to the gene pool. Thus, in one Xavante village the headman's contribution to the present generation amounted to 23 surviving children. The same phenomenon is also observed in many Yanomama villages (Chagnon, unpublished). In one Yanomama village south of the Orinoco River the two headmen sired 28 children (25 of whom were alive at the time of the study), amounting to approximately one-fourth of the total village population.[1]

Mating Structure and Status of Abducted Women

Borabuk includes four non-Yanomama women, three abducted Makiritare and one Makú (see fig. 3, individuals III-4, III-5, IV-14 and V-4). With the exception of one of the Makiritare women (individual IV-14), abducted while she was well along in her reproductive lifespan, these women have substantially larger families than is characteristic for Yanomama women (they average 7.3 living children, as compared to 3.8 for Yanomama women of comparable age (Neel and Chagnon, '68)).

One cultural difference between the Yanomama and Makiritare is the practice of preferential female infanticide by the former, partially accounting for the remarkably low "achieved" fertility in this population (Neel and Chagnon, '68). We have no information on the Makú in this regard, since they were effectively extinct before their culture was recorded. The Makiritare, however, are not known to practice either male or female infanticide.

If after delivery the woman picks the newborn child up and carries it to the village, it is allowed to live. Given that the decision rests with females, abducted women from tribes *not* practicing infanticide are therefore predisposed to have larger families and, in this case, have in fact achieved this. More importantly, the attitude of abducted females toward killing their offspring, particularly female babies, can affect the probability of retaining an introduced gene: since women rarely fail to reproduce despite their tribal status, in this particular circumstance chances are greater that the gene will be maintained when introduced by a female carrier from the outside because such women are less prone to kill their offspring. The effect is compounded when female offspring are considered, since females, as we have noted several times above, almost invariably reproduce.

The Yanomama also practice coitus taboos during lactation (Chagnon, '66, '68b), a phenomenon that has some bearing on the size of completed family (Neel and Chagnon, '68). The length of time that the taboo is maintained depends on the receptivity of the female to sexual advances made by men. In the case of the abducted Makiritare and Makú females, neither tribe known to have this taboo (or if they did it would largely be inoperative because of the disadvantage of captive status), exposure to the risk of pregnancy is somewhat higher when compared to their Yanomama counterparts.

1 When the offspring of these men are counted, two-thirds of the village are lineal descendants of just two men. Although not germane to the reproductive performance of headmen, in the case mentioned here, the two men were married to each other's sisters or half-sisters, giving a rough notion of how consanguineous some villages are as a result of traditional marriage practices.

The Yanomama practice regarding abducted women is as follows: men who participated in the raiding party rape the captive before reaching home, and the men in the village are later given the same opportunity. For some considerable time these women are "seduced" by men in the village until one of them can claim her as a wife and thereby limit the access of his covillagers to her sexual favors. In the village of Borabuk, where there is an acute shortage of women as a result of female infanticide (male/female sex ratio: 1.45), the lower status of the abducted women and their consequent higher than usual opportunities to reproduce is reflected not only in their reproductive performance but in the fact that two of them had multiple, simultaneous husbands (polyandry), one of them having six "legal" husbands at the same time.[2]

In addition to the role of attitudes regarding coitus taboos, infanticide and polyandrous marriages, it can be shown that when a gene is introduced through a captive, the sex of the initial carrier also affects the probable retention of an introduced gene in another way. Genes introduced by male captives are less likely to be retained in the recipient population for two reasons. First, the status of the captive males (usually the immature sons of abducted women, since adult males are never taken captive) is uniformly lower than that of captured females, so low that the Yanomama are even known to kill young male captives once they have them back in their village (Chagnon, '68b). If the male is allowed to live and reaches adulthood, he must have exceptional personal attributes to compete effectively in a demographic situation where there are fewer marriageable women than competing men, especially in a social system where marriage is arranged by one's male kinfolk. These kinsmen, of course, are non-existent for a captive male unless the husband of his mother adopts him without undue qualification as his legitimate offspring. Given that he has only average capabilities, he will marry later than his peers and have difficulty maintaining possession of and exclusive sexual access to his wife. In many cases the young man, if he retains his natal language, returns to his mother's village even though he knows nobody there, largely because he hopes his kinsmen will provide him with a wife within the context of the tribal marriage practices. Without male kin to support him a young man is at a severe disadvantage in seeking a spouse. Both the Yanomama and the Makiritare have a prescriptive bilateral cross-cousin marriage system, the essence of which is that a male must marry a female who belongs to a single (social) category of women, two genealogical specifications of which are mother's brother's daughter and father's sister's daughter. (See Chagnon, '68b, for more complete details.) Since marriage in both societies is arranged by kinsmen of the ascending generation, a young man with only half of his kinsmen (and adopted ones at that) in his village will be severely restricted as to possible mates in a way

---

[2] One Makiritare woman was quite old at the time she was abducted and therefore somewhat undesirable (individual IV-14) and another (individual III-4) was a lineal descendant of the Makiritare man who sired the Borabuk headman. She was accorded somewhat special treatment in that her new husband (individual III-6), her known kinsman, managed to limit his peers sexual advances toward her.

that a female captive would not be. Secondly, he is at a different kind of disadvantage because males marry, in general, later than females. Of the two kinds of cross cousin he could legitimately marry, those on his mother's side live in enemy villages, leaving only his (adopted) patrilateral cross cousins as possible choices. Because females marry, on the average, some seven years earlier than men in this particular case, the man in question would have only his (adopted) father's sister's daughters (and their categorical equivalents) to choose from, most of whom would be married by the time he comes of age. This demographic situation, lower probability of marrying a father's sister's daughter, has been demonstrated for other populations (Hajnal, '63; Rose, '60) and characterizes the Yanomama as well (Chagnon, unpublished data). In brief, the probability of a gene introduced by a captive surviving in a population with these socio-cultural parameters appears to be in large measure a function of the sex of the initial carrier. Indeed, it would appear that an introduced gene by an abducted female carrier would stand a better chance of retention than a newly arisen mutant within the non-mixed population because of the social and cultural factors influencing the reproductive performance of captured women.

With respect to the population of Borabuk and the frequencies of Di^a and Ap^a, the headman of the group (i.e., the half-Makiritare founder, individual II-8) appears to have carried the Di^a gene and possibly Ap^a so their frequency in the population might be in some measure a result of his fecundity. This, in turn, was the result of his acquiring three additional wives during the epidemic, by whom he had a total of 13 children (of whom 12 are presently living). Although we do not have precise information regarding the politics of acquiring the widows of the epidemic, we do know that the same phenomenon occurs in Yanomama villages at the present time. Whenever there is a controversy regarding the disposition of a widow or a separated woman, the headman often takes her into his household as a wife in order to maintain village order. He may, if he wishes, give her to a bachelor in the village, preferably his younger brother, but often he simply keeps her as an additional wife.

Of the 12 living offspring, only two men (1 of them a headman) had the Di^a allele (only 10 were sampled). However, depending on how the genealogy is interpreted, and several interpretations are possible because of unsampled or dead individuals, as many as three-fourths of the village's present Di^a positive individuals may have gotten the allele from this man or his offspring. On the other hand, the headman's brother (individual II-10) may have carried the allele and passed it on to some of his descendants. Some individuals are presumed to have derived their Di^a positive alleles from Makiritare admixture prior to the separation of the two groups at a time beyond the genealogical recall of our oldest informants.

Regarding the Ap^a allele, it can be seen from the genealogy that over half of the individuals carrying the positive factor are either the abducted Makiritare women or their offspring. Finally, all of the individuals with abnormal albumin are descendants of the abducted Makú woman (individual III-5).

Discussion and Conclusions

The manner in which previously absent genes are introduced into populations and then increase in frequency is, of course, a basic phenomenon in population genetics. The present communication has been devoted to a small case history. As a result first of what appears to be a concatenation of unlikely sampling events ("drawing" individuals with the Di^a, Ap^a, and albumin Makú genes) and secondly of cultural practices which result in abducted women having larger than usual families, a Yanomama village now finds itself with two genes (Di^a and Ap^a) in higher frequency than in the Makiritare village which was the presumed source of the gene flow. In addition, raids on another tribe have introduced a third "new" gene to the group. Ethnographic studies provide a partial explanation for otherwise puzzling findings. The picture would be clearer if we could document all the introductions of these three "foreign" genes, but this would be too much to expect in such a population. It should be emphasized that the events we are discussing occurred prior to the intrusion into this region of outsiders, aside from a few expeditions that moved through, so that these events would seem to mirror the traditional pattern of gene flow. Although we cannot rigorously preclude the possibility that the Di^a and Ap^a genes were introduced into the Mucajai population of Borabuk prior to 1875, we believe that events since then could account for the entire situation. On that basis, these two genes have "moved" over 200 miles in three generations.

A question which can in part be answered by future studies, but to which there may never be a completely satisfactory answer, is the extent to which "microevents" such as here described may dominate "macro phenomena." If, were it not for the European intrusion, events such as those just described were destined to occur at multiple points along the Makiritare-Yanomama frontier, then indeed the gene frequencies in the mixed population might have reflected the degree of admixture more accurately. If, by contrast, the Borabuk population, now on the periphery of the tribal distribution, were to separate still further, multiplying disproportionately in the process, while the remainder of the tribe did not fare so well in its exchanges with the Makiritare, then this small event could play an important role in establishing certain allele frequencies in an emergent tribe. Elsewhere we (Neel and Salzano, '67) have pointed out how stochastic events might be of importance in enabling a polymorphism which is frequency dependent under schemes of normalizing selection (cf. Fraser et al., '67) to reach a point of stable equilibrium; these findings provide an actual illustration of the possibilities inherent in this breeding structure.

Matson et al. ('68) have recently reported on the allele frequencies of the "Uaica," "Xirixano," "Cacarapai" and "Paramiteri" Indians of northern Brazil. These are simply local names for parts of villages, distinct villages or groups of villages of the Yanomama. The "Xirixano" (Xirixana?), "Cacarapai" (Kasrapai?) and "Paramiteri" (Parimiteri?) specimens were in fact collected in 1963 at Mucajai station of the Unevangelized Fields Mission (Borabuk), then the most accessible of the Brazilian Yanomama villages. Failure to investigate carefully the genealogical and historical relationships among the several groups in the sample has led to an unfortunate lumping and separating of the samples. Thus, the "Paramiteri" (Parima-teri) individuals sampled at Mucajai were visitors to that village from the location of Matson's second sampling point (Waika station of the Unevangelized Fields Mission), and should have been included among them. However, the sample collected at Waika station (Matson's "Uaica"), according to local missionaries, included individuals from five distinct villages; three groups of people happened to be visiting there at the time, and the local population at Waika station is, from genealogical and informants' historical accounts, a composite of two distinct groups. Again the "Cacarapai" (Kasrapai?) individuals are, from our genealogical and ethnohistorical evidence, merely a small fraction of the Borabuk population living a few miles upstream from the latter. Finally, a few members of the Waika station population have recently (one generation ago) migrated there from Borabuk.

Matson et al. ('68) report, without comment, a Di^a positive allele frequency of 0.10 for the "Xirixano" and a 0.01 frequency for the same allele among the "Uaica." From the foregoing it is apparent how very unrepresentative these frequencies are of the Yanomama tribe as a whole, or of any definable demographic sub-unit of the tribe. That our own findings and theirs are puzzling and/or unrepresentative could only be determined by comparing them to allele frequencies found in other, related villages and viewing the results in the light of the specific mating structure, the village history, the genealogical relationships and actual village composition at the time of the study.

LITERATURE CITED

Arends, T., G. Brewer, N. Chagnon, M. L. Gallango, H. Gershowitz, M. Layrisse, J. V. Neel, D. Shreffler, R. Tashian and L. Weitkamp 1967 Intratribal genetic differentiation among the Yanomama Indians of southern Venezuela. Proc. Nat. Acad. Sci., Wash.; 57: 1252–1259.

Becher, H. 1960 Die Surára and Pakidái: Zwei Yanonámi-Stämme in Nordwest-brasilien. De Gruyter and Co., Hamburg.

Chagnon, N. A. 1966 Yąnomamö Warfare, Social Organization and Marriage Alliances. (Ph. D Thesis) University Microfilms, Ann Arbor.

———— 1968 Yąnomamö social organization and warfare. In: War: The Anthropology of Armed Conflict and Aggression. M. Fried, M. Harris and R. Murphy, eds. Natural History Press, Garden City, pp. 109–159.

———— 1968b Yąnomamö The Fierce People. Case Studies in Cultural Anthropology. Holt, Rinehart and Winston, New York.

———— The culture-ecology of shifting (pioneering) cultivation among the Yąnomamö Indians. In: Ecology in Anthropological and Ethnological Sciences. Man-Culture-Habitat Relationship. VIIIth International Congress of Anthropological and Ethnological Sciences, Tokyo, in press.

———— N. D. Unpublished demographic data.

Fraser, A. S., D. M. Burnell and D. Miller 1967 Simulation of genetic systems. I. Inversion polymorphism. J. Theoret. Biol., in press.

Gershowitz, H., M. Layrisse, J. V. Neel, C. Brewer, N. A. Chagnon and M. Ayres Gene frequencies and microdifferentiation among the Makiritare Indians. I. Eleven blood group systems and the ABH-Le secretor traits. A note on Rh gene frequency determinations. Amer. J. Hum. Genet., in press.

Hajnal, J. 1963 Concepts of random mating and the frequency of consanguineous marriages. Proc. Roy. Soc., B, *159:* 125–177.

Layrisse, M., and J. Wilbert 1966 Indian Societies of Venezuela. Their Blood Group Types. Fundacion LaSalle de Ciencies Naturales, Monograph No. 13. Caracas.

Matson, G. A., H. E. Sutton, E. M. Pessoa, J. Swanson and A. Robinson 1968 Distribution of hereditary blood groups among Indians in South America. V. In northern Brazil. Am. J. Phys. Anthrop., *28:* 303–330.

Neel, J. V. 1967 The genetic structure of primitive human populations. Jap. J. Hum. Genet., *12:* 1–16.

Neel, J. V., and F. M. Salzano 1967 Further studies on the Xavante Indians. X. Some hypothesis-generalizations resulting from these studies. Amer. J. Hum. Genet., *19:* 554–574.

Neel, J. V., and N. A. Chagnon 1968 The demography of two tribes of primitive, relatively unacculturated American Indians. Proc. Nat. Acad. Sci., *59:* 680–689.

Reynolds, P. K. 1927 The Banana: Its History, Cultivation, and Place Among Staple Foods. Houghton Mifflin Co., Boston.

Rose, F. G. G. 1960 Classification of Kin, Age Structure, and Marriage Amongst the Groote Eylandt Aborigines. Akademie-Verlag, Berlin.

Salzano, F. M., J. V. Neel and D. Maybury-Lewis 1967 Further Studies on the Xavante Indians. I. Demographic data on two additional villages; genetic structure of the tribe. Amer. J. Hum. Genet., *19:* 463–489.

Simmonds, N. W. 1959 Bananas. Longmans, Green and Co., Inc., New York.

Weitkamp, L. R., and N. A. Chagnon 1968 Albumin maku: a new variant of human serum albumin. Nature, *217:* 759–760.

Weitkamp, L., and J. V. Neel Gene frequencies and microdifferentiation among the Makiritare Indians. III. Nine erythrocyte enzyme systems. Amer. J. Hum. Genet., in press.

Zerries, O. 1958 Kultur im übergang: die Waika-Indianer des oberen Orinoco—wilbeuter oder pflanzer? Die Umschau in Wissenschaft und Technik, *58:* 177–180.

——— 1964 Waika: Die Kulturgeschichtliche Stellung der Waika-Indianer des Oberen Orinoco im Rahmen der Völkerkunds Südamerikas. Band I. Klaus Renner Verlag, Munich.

Growth and Environment

ALL HUMAN BEINGS BEGIN LIFE AS SINGLE CELLS WHICH would be somewhat difficult to distinguish from one another, despite their genetic differences. As we grow, differences emerge, so, except for some monozygotic twins, no two individuals look alike. Are these differences due to heredity alone? During the nineteenth century, as pointed out earlier, this was the standard assumption among human biologists. The processes of growth were studied from the point of view that they represented only the blossoming out of already fixed traits, including anatomical dimensions. This point of view has now been replaced by a more open-minded one: students of growth seek to find out, by appropriate research, what can be predicted about the future course of a child's growth.

Of course growth involves more than expansion in size and alteration of some proportions. Permanent teeth replace the milk dentition. At pubescence, girls begin to menstruate and boys to become hairy. Studies among peoples of the most diverse origins, and living under the most varied circumstances, have demonstrated that among all peoples the sequence of events during growth is the same. They have also demonstrated the manner in which the environment influences the speed of development. Climate, diet, childhood diseases, and amount of work done by youngsters all have effects, some of which may be permanent during adulthood. Stature is often affected, for instance. Our next selection, "Effect of Ecological and Socio-economic Factors on the Age at Menarche, Body Height and Weight of Rural Girls in Poland" by Dr. Teresa Laska-Mierzejewska, deals with the way in which environment affects growth in a Central European population.

20. Teresa Laska-Mierzejewska

Effect of Ecological and Socio-economic Factors on the Age at Menarche, Body Height and Weight of Rural Girls in Poland

The material for the present report comprises rural girls from eight regions and 5 voivodships of Poland (see Fig. 1). It was collected from November 1966 to September 1968. Studies on the age of menarche embraced 9589 girls. Of these body height was measured in 7427 and body weight in 5973. In six regions a further division into three socio-occupational groups was made: 1. The *agricultural* group: girls of families making their living exclusively on their farms. 2. The *farmer-worker* group, including those whose parents own a farm, but one of them, usually the father, also works outside of agriculture. 3. The *non-agricultural* group, comprising girls living in the countryside, whose parents, however, do not own farms, and make their living exclusively by non-agricultural work.

The percentage of girls in each of these occupational groups differs in each regional group investigated and depends on the size of farms in the given area and on the degree of industrialization of the region.

The material analysed in the present article was not chosen by random sampling. In the various districts, however, schools were chosen both from richer and from poorer villages. In the primary schools chosen all girls 11 to 15 years old were examined. The 15 to 18 year old girls were examined in secondary general education schools, and in vocational and agricultural schools. Only girls from the countryside were examined in these schools.

The material was divided into annual age classes, the 11.5 class including girls aged 11.0 to 11.99 years.

The ages at menarche were obtained by the status-quo method and calculated by probits.

RESULTS AND DISCUSSION

Age at Menarche

The average age at menarche of rural girls from eight regions and 5 voivodships of Poland amounts to 14.04 ± 0.02 with standard deviation of 1.2 years. A good fit to the probit distribution obtained; Chi-square tests being between 0.40 and 12.40

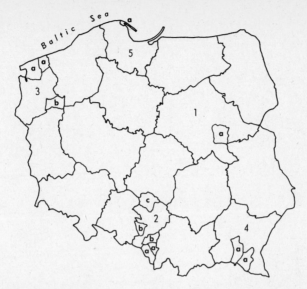

Fig. 1. Regions of Poland investigated. 1. Warsaw voivodship: a. Ostrów Mazowiecka district. 2. Katowice voivodship: a. Bielsko-Biala, Cieszyn districts; b. Gliwice, Pszczyna districts; c. Czestochowa district. 3. Szczecin voivodship: a. Kamień Pomorski, Wolin districts; b. Choszczno district. 4. Rzeszów voivodship: a. Sanok, Krosno districts. 5. Gdansk voivodship: a. Hel peninsula.

at 6 degrees of freedom (the 5% significance limit is 12.6). This is evidence of homogeneity of the material and of the social and regional groups singled out (Table 2).

Girls living in the Hel peninsula (13.78) and the group of Gliwice and Pszczyna (13.88) menstruate the earliest. Girls from the Ostrów Mazowiecka district in the Warsaw voivodship exhibit the latest age at menarche (14.29); the mountain group comes next (14.16). The difference between extreme groups amounts to 0.51 years, and is statistically significant. A statistically significant difference appears also between two groups in the Katowice voivodship; that is between the mountain group (Bielsko-Biała and Cieszyn district), and the lowland group (Gliwice and Pszczyna).

The early age at menarche of girls of the Hel peninsula is probably caused by living conditions differing from those in average villages. All localities of the peninsula are attractive holiday resorts in summer, and this fact is one of the sources of income for the inhabitants. The agricultural population here makes up an insignificant percentage of the population. The children are not burdened with manual work on the farms, as is the case under ordinary rural conditions. It may be that the maritime climate, too, exerts an accelerating effect. The early maturing of girls of Gliwice and Pszczyna is undoubtedly caused by the good economic situation of that region.

No relationship between the age at menarche and the geographic situation of a

TABLE 1

Numbers and percentage of persons in different regions

| Voivodship | District-region | Population | | | | | | Total |
| | | agricultural | | farmer-worker | | non-agricultural | | |
		N	%	N	%	N	%	N
Katowice	Bielsko-Biała and Cieszyn mountainous region	162	15.9	545	53.4	314	30.8	1021
"	Gliwice, Pszczyna lowland region	310	42.0	312	42.2	117	15.8	739
"	Częstochowa	456	20.3	1151	51.3	636	28.4	2243
Szczecin	Kamień Pomorski, Wolin seaside region	549	50.0	216	19.7	332	30.3	1097
"	Choszczno	353	42.5	162	19.5	316	38.0	831
Warsaw	Ostrów Mazowiecka	1092	55.9	411	21.0	452	23.1	1955
Rzeszów	Sanok, Krosno							1134
Gdańsk	Puck [Hel peninsula]							569
Total		2922		2797		2167		9589

TABLE 2

Age of menarche of rural girls in various social and regional groups

Voivodship	Districts, regions	Agricultural group				Farmer-worker group				Non-agricultural group				Entire region (all groups)				Degrees of freedom
		X̄	S.E.	S.D.	χ^2	X̄	S.E.	S.D.	χ^2	X̄	S.E.	S.D.	χ^2	X̄	S.E.	S.D.	χ^2	
Warsaw	Ostrów Mazowiecka Central Poland	14.45	0.06	1.2	12.4	14.27	0.10	1.2	3.0	13.90	0.10	1.1	2.8	14.29	0.04	1.2	10.9	6
Katowice	Bielsko-Biała, Cieszyn mountainous region	14.38	0.19	1.4	5.9	14.14	0.09	1.1	6.2	14.02	0.14	1.2	4.3	14.16	0.07	1.2	4.4	5
"	Gliwice, Pszczyna lowland region	14.16	0.12	1.2	6.0	13.71	0.10	1.1	2.1	13.67	0.19	1.2	5.2	13.88	0.07	1.2	6.4	5
"	Częstochowa	14.37	0.10	1.2	5.8	14.04	0.05	1.1	1.2	13.72	0.09	0.9	1.0	14.03	0.04	1.1	1.7	6
Szczecin	Kamień Pomorski, Wolin seaside region	14.08	0.09	1.4	2.6	13.93	0.13	1.2	4.2	13.64	0.11	1.2	5.8	13.93	0.06	1.3	2.8	5
"	Choszczno	14.21	0.13	1.4	6.0	13.99	0.17	1.2	4.1	13.73	0.14	1.3	0.4	13.98	0.08	1.3	6.9	6
Rzeszów	Sanok, Krosno mountain region													13.94	0.06	1.2	2.3	6
Gdańsk	Puck [only Hel peninsula] seaside region													13.78	0.08	1.1	1.8	7
	Entire material	14.30	0.04	1.3	8.23	14.04	0.04	1.2	1.47	13.77	0.05	1.2	3.49	14.04	0.02	1.2	5.2	

region could be found. In order to follow up such relations, the factor exerting the strongest influence on the rate of physiological development of the body ought to be excluded from the observational material. It is generally considered that living conditions, in particular, nutrition, are this factor.

The division of rural materials into occupational groups, is an attempt at assessing the age at menarche in groups of closely similar living conditions. Such a division was made in six regional groups.

In the three occupational groups girls from families making their living exclusively by work at their farm, menstruate at the latest time (14.08–14.45) and this is valid for all regions under consideration.

Girls whose families own no farms, although they inhabit the countryside, mature the earliest. In all regional groups, the girls of this social group mature before the 14th year of age, the mountain girls excepted (14.02). The girls coming from families with two means of support, that is a farm and a non-agricultural job, show an intermediate age at menarche. The differences between agricultural and non-agricultural groups are statistically significant in every region and, between the other groups significant in two-thirds of the comparisons.

The differentation with respect to age at menarche of various regional groups can not be explained by variations in the proportion of agricultural group in each region. In the mountain group (very late menstruating), the percentage of girls belonging to the agricultural group is the lowest (15.9) as compared with other regions, and—inversely—in the regional groups menstruating at the earliest age, the percentage of girls from agricultural groups amounts to as much as 42–50%.

The differences between the social groups maturing at the earliest age and those maturing at the latest age within each regional group (0.36 to 0.65 years) are greater than the differences between entire regional groups (0.05 to 0.41 years).

The girls who differ so markedly from each other from the point of view of rate of maturing mostly come from the same villages and attended the same schools.

The fact that farmer-worker families have two means of subsistence suggests that they have the best living conditions in the rural environment. However, in all regional materials under consideration here, girls of the farmer-worker group are characterized by intermediate age at menarche as compared with girls of the other two groups. Therefore, there ought to be some factor causing a delay in the maturing of these girls as compared with non-agricultural groups. Manual work is probably this factor. The burdening of maturing children with work occurs in particular in the families in which the adult members of the family work in non-agricultural jobs for several hours daily.

When comparing regional differences within social groups, girls of the agricultural and non-agricultural groups of the Szczecin seaside display the earliest maturing. This fact can not be explained by living conditions (Piskorski, 1966). Girls from the Hel peninsula make up the second earliest menstruating regional groups. Perhaps the maritime climate is the factor that accelerates maturing. Kowalska (1966) by retrospective investigation found that girls living in the Hel peninsula menstruated earlier than girls from central Poland and from mountain regions. Škerlj also suggests an accelerating effect of oceanic climate on the maturing of girls (1932).

When dividing the entire observational material into occupational groups, it was only partially possible to present in a uniform way the living conditions of the girls studied, as there was no analysis of either the size or the quality of farms, the number of family members living at the common farm, dwelling conditions, hygienic and sanitary conditions, the amount of the non-agricultural income and the like. Only in a social group thus singled out would it be possible to follow up more accurately the connections between maturation rate and the geographic situation of the region from which the girls come.

Girls in the countryside of all regions of Poland under consideration mature 1.03 years later than girls in Warsaw (Milicer, Szczotka, 1966).

Height and Weight

Body weight and height was assessed in socio-occupational and regional groups.

Tables 3 and 4 show the results in social groups in the entire material studied, without division into regions of the country.

TABLE 3

Height (cm) of Polish rural girls, regions combined

Age	Agricultural group			Farmer-worker group			Non-agricultural group		
	N	Mean	S. D.	N	Mean	S. D.	N	Mean	S. D.
11.5	290	139.5	6.4	444	140.1	6.6	272	139.9	6.4
12.5	370	145.2	7.0	492	146.2	7.2	286	145.9	7.0
13.5	410	150.4	6.7	521	151.2	7.7	220	151.2	7.0
14.5	350	154.7	6.0	431	154.7	6.2	324	155.6	5.4
15.5	413	156.7	5.8	403	157.7	5.5	474	157.9	5.5
16.5	270	158.1	5.1	259	159.1	4.8	356	158.5	5.2
17.5	216	159.2	6.7	144	160.0	5.8	291	159.8	4.8
18.5	61	159.0	5.1	51	160.7	5.6	73	159.6	6.0

Girls of the agricultural group are of a somewhat smaller stature than girls of the farmer-worker and those of the non-agricultural group. The differences vary from 0.4 to 1.2 cm; in the 18.5 year age class the difference was as much as 1.7 cm. Statistically significant differences occur in the 12.5, 15.5, 16.5 age classes between agricultural and farmer-worker girls; in the 14.5 and 15.5 age classes between agricultural and non-agricultural girls.

No marked and uni-directional differences in the height of rural girls from various regions of Poland were found. The differences between regional groups are small, and their direction changes from one age class to another.

TABLE 4

Weight (kg) of Polish rural girls, regions combined

Age	Agricultural group			Farmer-worker group			Non-agricultural group		
	N	Mean	S.D.	N	Mean	S.D.	N	Mean	S.D.
11.5	188	33.6	5.2	374	34.0	5.3	231	35.4	6.3
12.5	246	38.2	6.6	404	37.9	6.3	221	38.0	6.3
13.5	293	43.0	6.1	429	42.8	6.4	175	43.4	6.3
14.5	217	48.4	6.6	362	47.8	7.1	275	49.6	6.7
15.5	258	51.9	6.7	320	51.7	6.3	368	51.9	6.4
16.5	174	54.5	6.2	235	53.2	6.1	295	53.4	6.3
17.5	129	55.1	5.6	139	55.1	5.4	231	55.3	6.2
18.5	29	56.3	4.9	34	56.8	6.3	60	57.8	6.9

In five age classes the weight of girls of the agricultural group is lower than that of the non-agricultural group. Statistically significant differences are in 11.5 and 14.5 age classes.

Thus height and weight show a considerably smaller environmental and regional differentiation than the age at the first menstruation. Somatic features seem to be less sensitive to the effect of external factors than the age at menarche.

ACKNOWLEDGMENTS

Hereby I should like to express my heartiest gratitude to Stefania Bialas, Wanda Mendyk, Alexandra Rytwińska and Janina Rysińska, for their hard work collecting the materials under discussion, and to Prof. Dr. T. Dzierżykray-Rogalski, head of the Department of Anthropology.

SUMMARY AND ABSTRACT

The age at menarche was assessed by probits, and body height and weight were examined in rural girls from various regions of Poland. The mean values were calculated for the regional groups and in the three occupational groups of the rural environment: I. Agricultural group—families making their living exclusively by farming; II. Farmer-worker group—families obtaining income both from a farm and work outside of agriculture; III. Non-agricultural group—families living in villages, but owning no farms.

The mean age at menarche of countryside girls in Poland amounts to 14.04 ± 0.02 years, standard deviation 1.2. Statistically significant differences of the age at menarche were found between girls of different regional groups. Among occupational groups, girls of the non-agricultural group menstruate earliest; girls of the agricultural group latest; those of the farmer-worker are intermediate. This order is repeated in all regions; the differences are statistically significant. Material conditions and also the burdening of the farm girls with manual work are probably the factors causing this differentiation. Much greater differences in the age of menarche were found between social groups of girls living in the same region than between regional groups.

The girls of the agricultural group are somewhat less tall and less heavy than the girls of the farmer-worker or the non-agricultural group. The differences between the regional groups are small in height and weight; and their direction changed in course of the age period investigated. Height and weight show a smaller sensitivity to the influence of external conditions than the age at the first menstruation.

LITERATURE CITED

KOWALSKA, I. 1966 Wiek i pora roku menarche u kobiet wiejskich i miejskich. Prace i Materiały Naukowe I. M. D., *8*: 69–77.

ŁASKA-MIERZEJEWSKA, T. 1966 Menarche in Cuban girls. Przegląd Antropologiczny, *32*: 29–44.

MILICER, H. AND F. SZCZOTKA 1966 Age at menarche in Warsaw girls. Human Biol. *38*: 199–203.

PISKORSKI, C. 1966 Województwo Szczecińskie, Sport i Turystyka, Warszawa.

ŠKERLJ, B. 1932 Menarche und Klima in Europa. Z. Ethnol. *63*: 413–414.

Heterosis in the Human Species

MENDEL NOTED MORE THAN A CENTURY AGO, WHILE CONducting his breeding experiments with peas, that the offspring of a purebred short vine and a purebred long one grew to be longer than either. Similar phenomena have been noted in many later genetic experiments too. This is known as heterosis or hybrid vigor. After the first generation, it disappears. Each of the parent purebred stocks was homozygous at many loci, so that the reduction of homozygosity which results from cross-breeding seems to release extra energy in the growing offspring. After a single generation, there will be little or no further increase in heterozygosity. But to start with, the increase in vigor may be very considerable indeed.

Plant breeders, if they are careful, can easily control the mating of their plants. Animals are less easy to control. They move about and are likely to have wills of their own. Human beings, although they can be indoctrinated, and are always culturally conditioned, live as long as the experimenter, which makes them very poor subjects for intentional genetic experiments. Of their own volition, to be sure, they are constantly conducting unintentional experiments. Alert anthropologists can observe the results although they cannot control the conditions. So a number of studies have been made seeking for signs of heterosis among the descendants of matings between people of different races. Unfortunately, little is known about the first generation hybrids in almost all cases.

Furthermore, it is obvious that all the races of our species are highly heterozygous anyway. None of them remotely resembles a purebred stock. However, until quite recent times, a high degree of endogamy existed among many groups, such as Alpine villagers or European royalty. Homozygosity at many loci may well exist in some such groups. At present, however, such genetic isolates are breaking down. Dr.

Eugène Schreider, in two brief articles "Body-height and Inbreeding in France" and "Inbreeding, Biological and Mental Variations in France," argues persuasively that by looking in the right places we may find evidence of human heterosis.

21. Eugène Schreider

Body-height and Inbreeding in France

Abstract. Dahlberg's ('43) hypothesis that heterosis is a major component of the secular trend towards increased stature is supported by the significant negative correlation between stature and the coefficient of inbreeding in 70 departments of France. This phenomenon is especially evident after the onset of puberty (r at age $7 = -0.25$ for boys: -0.24 for girls; but r at age $14 = -0.44$ for boys and -0.56 for girls) and is found also in adults.

Secular changes in body-height are considered sometimes as a delusion produced by the acceleration of growth process. It is difficult to deny that the differences between statural averages of men measured successively after a long time interval are largely due to earlier attainment of maximal height in recent generations (Genovés, '66). Nevertheless, there are good reasons to recognize that the "final" adult size is also increasing. Aubenque ('57) has shown that with advancing years of birth, French University students become taller *at all ages,* even when the body-height is already declining. Of course, this "real" increase is less spectacular than the differences between body-height averages of soldiers measured 30 or 40 years apart.

As the genetical component of maximal body-height is far from negligible, Dahlberg ('43) was inclined to explain the secular changes by heterosis. We cannot discard this hypothesis if we realize that, contrary to the "apparent" increase, the "real" body-height increment amounts to millimeters rather than centimeters. But, first of all, we must collect data showing that geographical and secular variations in body-height are related to endogamy or exogamy.

The most impressive evidence concerning heterotic changes in human stature has been published by Hulse ('58) in his work on Swiss villagers and their descendants who emigrated to California. It is now possible to show in a less direct way, but on a country-wide scale, the influence of consanguinity on statural variations in France. Sutter and Goux ('62) have published coefficients of inbreeding (α coefficients of Bernstein) for most French departments (counties) and for seven successive periods between 1926 and 1958. In spite of some sampling difficulties—the consanguinity of spouses is known only for religious marriages—these coefficients represent a very important research tool.

In order to check their value, I tried to find out whether they were related in a genetically meaningful way to the geographical distribution of blood groups: for 71 departments, there is a correlation between the α coefficients and the frequency of O phenotypes: $r = 0.32$ (blood groups data borrowed from Vallois and Marquer, '64). As O is recessive, its frequency should be increased by consanguinity, but the correlation cannot be very high because inbreeding is not the primary determinant of regional blood group frequencies.

Now, there is also a negative correlation between the α coefficients for the period 1936–1940 and statural averages of soldiers born in 63 counties during the years 1939–1940: $r = -0.32$[1]. Again, the correlation is -0.32 with the averages of soldiers born in 1940–1941 (70 counties).

Table 1 shows that there are significant correlations between statural averages of boys and girls and α coefficients calculated for periods corresponding to their years of birth.

TABLE 1

Correlations between statural averages of French children born in 71 counties and the coefficients of inbreeding calculated for the period covering their years of birth

Age	Year of birth	Boys r	Girls r	Period for which α coefficients were calculated
7	1943	-0.25	-0.24	1941–1945
8	1942	-0.21	-0.25	1941–1945
9	1941	-0.17	-0.39	1941–1945
10	1940	-0.23	-0.39	1936–1940
11	1939	-0.35	-0.36	1936–1940
12	1938	-0.44	-0.39	1936–1940
13	1937	-0.36	-0.45	1936–1940
14	1936	-0.44	-0.56	1936–1940

An outstanding fact is that in the youngest age groups, the correlations are very low and practically of the same magnitude in both sexes. They increase rather abruptly in girls at the age of 9 and in boys only at the age of 11. At the age of 14, the correlation rises again in girls. This obviously means that the heterotic effect becomes more evident as the age increases, but there are important sexual differences which are not difficult to understand: the highest correlation is that of girls

---

[1] A previously published figure (Khérumian and Schreider, '63) was a little lower (-0.27) because it was obtained on the largest possible number of departments, some of which were grouped together for the calculation of the coefficients of inbreeding. The elimination of departments, the α coefficients of which are not known with precision, raises the correlation.

who, on the average, have already attained puberty. This might explain why Morton ('58) did not find any sizeable heterotic effect in body-length of new-born Japanese infants. Birth dimensions are largely determined by environmental (maternal) factors. Genetic influences seem to manifest themselves with increasing strength at more advanced ages.

These results are in agreement with the heterosis hypothesis. There is little doubt that the average stature in French departments is influenced by the frequency of consanguineous marriages. This appears to be true for different ages and for both sexes. Moreover, the following results suggest that this is true even for a relatively remote past, for which we do not know either the body-height nor the coefficients of inbreeding!

County averages of body-height are unknown for the first half of the last century. Nevertheless, for most departments and for successive periods, we know the percentages of young men discarded from the army because their body-height was below the minimum requested by the law. Broca (1869) already used these percentages in order to estimate the geographical variations of body-height. The rather surprising fact is that between the percentages of men too short for military service in 1831–1849 and the coefficients of inbreeding calculated for the period of 1926–1930, there is a significant positive correlation: $r = 0.44$ (calculated on 61 departments). There is still a correlation with the percentages of men discarded for their short stature in 1855–1860: $r = 0.45$.

At the first glance, these "retroactive" correlations are meaningless, but this is not so in reality. Percentages of men too short for the army are related to statural averages, as Broca rightly believed. As a matter of fact, between the percentages of 1831–1849 and the recently published statural averages for 1880 (Chamla, '64), there is a negative correlation which is logically sound: $r = -0.56$ (calculated on 83 departments). There is again a negative correlation between the same percentages and the statural averages of French soldiers measured in 1959: $r = -0.27$ (77 departments).

This strongly suggests that despite the secular changes, there is something very "permanent" in increasing adult stature as well as in decreasing consanguinity. After all, in most cases, tallest and shortest people are still inhabiting the same areas as 100 years ago. In spite of sampling differences, between the statural averages of 1880 and those of 1960, the correlation is 0.44. Differences in body-height are obviously related to the frequency of inbreeding which was much more frequent in the past, especially in rural communities. The decline of consanguineous marriages probably favoured heterosis and growth, but the old parallelism of average body-heights and inbreeding frequencies is still perceptible. Like stature, coefficients of inbreeding appear to be *relatively* stable: for the whole country, between 1926 and 1958, they decreased from 86.1 to 32.2 ($\alpha \times 10^5$), but in the general ranking, many departments retain their relative position: in spite of the rapid decrease, the correlation between α coefficients calculated for 1926–1930 and those calculated for 1950–1958 is fairly high: $r = 0.81$. In accordance with some historical facts, we may suppose that in the past the geographical "gradient" of α coefficients was much the same as to-day, even if the numerical value of coefficients was higher. This is the only possible explanation of apparently meaningless "retroactive" correlations.

But we must keep in mind that coefficients of inbreeding, based on the frequency of consanguineous marriages, cannot give a complete estimation of heterozygosity changes. During the first half of the last century, in many rural areas, heterosis was probably dependent on slowly declining family size: the number of relatives among which a marriage partner could be chosen, decreased. Afterwards, the population mobility appeared as a more effective factor: to-day, heterozygosity may increase as a consequence of population displacements even if coefficients of inbreeding based on marriage statistics remain constant, because unrelated marriage partners are genetically more dissimilar than in the past. This perhaps explains why "retroactive" correlations between recent coefficients of inbreeding and the percentages of short men measured more than a hundred years ago, are higher (0.44–0.45) than the correlations between statural averages of adult men measured recently and the coefficients of inbreeding calculated for the years of their birth (−0.32). To-day, the relative weight of consanguineous marriages has been lessened by the growing influence of heterosis induced by population mobility and the increased dissimilarity of unrelated spouses.

LITERATURE CITED

Aubenque, M.   1957   Note documentaire sur la statistique des tailles des étudiants au cours de ces dernières années. Biotypologie, *18:* 202–214.

Broca, P.   1869   Nouvelles recherches sur l'Anthropologie de la France en général et de la Basse Bretagne en particulier — . Mém. Soc. Anthr. Paris, *3:* 147–206 and the appendix added to this article, reproduced in Mémoires d'Anthropologie, t. I, Paris, 1871.

Chamla, M. C.   1964   L'accroissement de la stature en France de 1880 à 1960. Comparaison avec les pays d'Europe occidentale. Bull. Soc. Anthr. Paris, *6:* XI ser., 201–278.

Dahlberg, G.   1943   Arv och Ras, Oslo.

Genovés, S. T.   1966   El supuesto aumento secular de la estatura a partir de circa 1800 d.C. Anales de Antropología, *3:* 67–98.

Hulse, F. S.   1958   Exogamie et hétérosis. Arch. Suisses d'Anthr. Gén., *22:* 103–125.

Khérumian, R., and E. Schreider   1963   Répartition départementale de la stature, du poids et de la circonférence thoracique en France métropolitaine. Biotypologie, *24:* 1–27.

Morton, N. E.   1958   Empirical risks in consanguineous marriages: birth weight, gestation time and measurements of infants. Am. J. Human Genet., *10:* 344–349.

Sutter, J., and J. M. Goux   1962   Evolution de la consanguinité en France de 1926 à 1958 avec des données récentes détaillées. Population, *17:* 683–702.

Vallois, H. V., and P. Marquer   1964   La répartition en France des groupes sanguins ABO. Bull. Soc. Anthro. Paris, *6:* XI serie, 1–200.

22. Eugène Schreider

Inbreeding, Biological and Mental Variations in France

Abstract. Coefficients of inbreeding, known for most French départements, correlate not only with body-height, as previously shown, but also with other anthropometrical, physiological, biochemical and mental characteristics. It does not appear that these correlations were primarily determined by differences in socio-economic or cultural levels.

In a previous work it has been shown that there is a negative correlation between the statural averages of French "départements" and the corresponding average inbreeding coefficients (α–coefficients of Bernstein). In children, this correlation alters with age; in boys it decreases for some years and in both sexes it reaches its highest numerical value towards puberty. Thereafter it reappears in young adult males (no anthropometrical measurements are available for adult females). In spite of some sampling differences, the coefficient of correlation is exactly the same for two successive generations of French soldiers: $r = -0.32$ (Schreider, '67). These results were obtained in a country-wide survey, of from 63 to 81 départements.[1]

More recently, a similar study was undertaken on body weight. In children, correlations between inbreeding coefficients and ponderal averages are distinctly lower than inbreeding/body-height correlations and vanish completely in adult males (Schreider, '68; calculated on 63–72 départements). Therefore, the heterotic effect is much less obvious for body-weight than for stature. Moreover, it appears to be transient.

In this paper, other biological characteristics are studied in the same way. Correlations have been calculated between average coefficients of inbreeding and

---

[1] Until very recently France was divided into 90 "départements" (counties). Five new departements were added by splitting the département of Seine-et-Oise. Our calculations are based on the old list of counties because coefficients of inbreeding of new territorial units are not known.

departmental averages for anthropometrical, physiological, biochemical and mental traits.[2] This work is based on large samples for a few variables, while for several others it is based on a smaller sample, thoroughly studied in the laboratory. The young adult males belonging to the latter were grouped according to their département of birth. Unfortunately, in the Laboratory sample only 25 départements were represented by a number of individuals large enough to make calculations worth while.

From this point of view, the Laboratory sample is not the best obtainable, but nonetheless it should not be neglected. For the time being, it is the only one which can be used as a basis for studying a relatively large number of variables and (at least provisionally) the results are worthy of attention. The 25 départements represented in this sample do not belong to a geographically limited area, but on the contrary, are scattered all over the nation. For some comparable characteristics, such as body height, vital capacity, blood pressure or mental test scores, their averages correlate positively with averages for the same départements which have been calculated on much larger samples. Again, whenever comparison is possible, the correlations of their averages with α–coefficients appear to be similar to the correlations found on a much larger number of départements. Of course, the r's are not identical, but they are always of the same sign, positive or negative. This agreement is an empirical, but not despicable test of significance. Finally, it must be remembered that the Laboratory sample includes about 800 individuals.

Anthropometric Characteristics and Secular Trends

Among the secular trends studied by many authors, the increase of body height is the best known. Our previous results show that in France body height correlates negatively with coefficients of inbreeding. As the latter are much lower than they were at the beginning of the century, the increase in statural averages, very marked during the recent decades, can be, at least partly, explained by the diminution of consanguinity. For the Laboratory sample we find again a negative correlation between body height averages and α–coefficients: $r = -0.22$.

For the Laboratory sample, some other anthropometrical characters are known. There is a *negative* correlation between inbreeding coefficients and head-length and a higher *positive* correlation between inbreeding coefficients and head-breadth. In other words, when consanguinity decreases head-length increases, whereas head-breadth decreases. Therefore, cephalic index must decrease at the same time.

Now, according to recent investigations, in some parts of France body-height increase is paralleled by a decrease in cephalic index and this is due to a lengthening of head-length and a shortening of head-breadth (Giot et al., '56; Olivier, '57; Billy, '66). This double secular trend agrees with our correlations and can probably be related to changes in consanguinity.

---

[2] The coefficients of inbreeding used in this work have been published by Sutter and Goux ('62).

TABLE 1

Correlations between anthropometrical traits and coefficients of inbreeding

Anthropometrical character	r
Laboratory sample (N^1 = 25)	
Body-height	−0.22
Head-length	−0.28
Head-breadth	+0.38
2 Army samples (N^1 = 63 and 70)	
Body-height	−0.32

[1] N = number of départements.

Physiological and Biochemical Variables

No correlation between coefficients of inbreeding and blood proteins was observed in the Laboratory sample. The correlation with blood bilirubin must be considered with caution because it was calculated on the basis of 14 départements only. On the other hand, the very low positive correlation with systolic blood pressure should not be discarded: there is a much higher positive correlation with diastolic pressure. Moreover, on a much larger sample of firemen grouped by département of birth we again find positive correlations with both blood pressures, the correlation with diastolic pressure being once more the highest. In all probability, coefficients of inbreeding correlate positively with blood pressure, but r's exact numerical value remains uncertain.

The low negative inbreeding/vital capacity correlation, found in the Laboratory sample, is confirmed when calculated on a very large army sample (63 départements) by a negative correlation which is twice as high. These results make good sense because the correlation between α–coefficients and body height is also negative and there is a well known positive correlation between vital capacity and stature. The higher negative correlation between coefficients of inbreeding and the strength of the right hand is also consistent with negative correlation between α–coefficients and body height, because muscular strength correlates positively with body size.

There is also a negative correlation between coefficients of inbreeding and fasting blood sugar level, but postprandial glycaemia (30 minutes after sugar ingestion) does not correlate with α–coefficients. Finally, we find an unexpectedly high negative correlation between inbreeding coefficients and département blood cholesterol level averages. Perhaps this may be related to the secular increase in blood cholesterol level, sometimes suspected and usually explained by nutritional changes.

TABLE 2

Correlations between physiological or biochemical traits and coefficients of inbreeding

Physiological or biochemical trait	r
Laboratory sample ($N^1 = 25$)	
Blood proteins	−0.07
Systol. blood pressure	+0.14
Diastol. blood pressure	+0.54
Blood bilirubin	+0.35[2]
Fasting glycaemia	−0.46
Postprandial glycaemia	+0.03
Blood cholesterol	−0.71
Right hand strength	−0.46
Vital capacity	−0.17
Firemen (N = 31)	
Systolic blood pressure	+0.20
Diastolic blood pressure	+0.27
Army sample (N = 63)	
Vital capacity	−0.33

[1] N = number of départements.
[2] Calculated on 14 départements only.

Inbreeding and Twin Births

Many authors have studied the genetic components of twinning which appears more than once in some family lines. The results, even though not conflicting, are not very clear. In this connection, it may be interesting to note that between département percentages of twin births and coefficients of inbreeding there is a fairly high positive correlation: $r = +0.65$; calculated on 73 départements. The percentages used in this calculation do not discriminate between monozygotic and dizygotic twins. As monozygotic twinning is much less frequent, this correlation, calculated on a country-wide scale, suggests involvement of a genetic factor in fraternal twinning.

Inbreeding and Mental Level

Average scores, based on six different mental tests, have been calculated for all French départements (Montmollin, '58). Moreover, separate département averages have been published for some occupational groups, cultural extremes being represented by peasants and clerical workers (Montmollin, '59). Only one test

(Raven's progressive matrices) was used for the Laboratory sample. In all instances correlations between mental scores and coefficients of inbreeding are negative, ranging from −0.31 to −0.52.

TABLE 3

Correlations between département average mental test scores and coefficients of inbreeding

Test	r
Laboratory sample (N^1 = 25)	
Raven's progressive matrices	−0.48
Army sample (N = 61–71)	
Average score for six mental tests	
All occupational groups	−0.52
Peasants	−0.51
Clerical workers	−0.31

[1] N = number of départements.

These results are important, perhaps a little disturbing and not very easy to understand. Montmollin, who published the mental averages for all the départements, did not attempt to explain his findings. Département averages show that the highest scores are obtained by clerical workers, while peasants have the lowest. On an environmental hypothesis alone, this seems to be "logical." Clerical workers are mostly town dwellers. Educational and other inequalities seem to account for differences between these two occupational groups.

However, we find a relatively high positive correlation (0.59) between average test scores achieved by peasants and by clerical workers. Should we say that this correlation is due to environmental dissimilarities which supposedly explain mental differences between the two occupational groups? It may be assumed that this correlaton is due to inbreeding effects which vary from one département to another but affect both occupational groups, in every département, to the same degree. This cannot be true because, as was to be expected, the correlation between test averages and α–coefficient is clearly higher in peasants than in clerical workers: the two occupational groups are not influenced to the same degree by consanguineous marriages. On the other hand, if inbreeding coefficients are held constant, the correlation between occupational groups does not disappear, but falls slightly from 0.59 to 0.53.

Finally, it may be speculated that the correlation between occupational groups is produced by some genetic factors common to the whole population, in every département, whatever the occupation, but such an hypothesis is neither easily substantiated nor very likely. The connection between average test scores and inbreeding is obvious, but the position is not crystal-clear.

Discussion

Insofar as heterotic effect is concerned, we are dealing with a purely biological phenomenon, based on some gene assortment. However, the relative frequency of consanguineous marriages is not a purely biological fact, as it is influenced by economic, demographic and cultural factors. In many instances, coefficients of inbreeding are high in agricultural or mountainous areas, in economically and culturally handicapped départements. This is not a strict rule, but a recognizable tendency. Therefore, one may wonder whether variations correlated with α–coefficients are determined by inbreeding infrequency, rather than by economic and social inequalities.

It is often assumed that body-height differences are largely dependent on nutritional and other environmental factors. Whatever may be the influence of the latter, it is difficult to concede that they are the main cause of the correlations studied in this paper. It is generally recognized, with good reasons, that body-mass is much more responsive than body-height to external conditions. If correlations with inbreeding coefficients were determined by environment, they ought to be higher for body-weight. As a matter of fact, the reverse is true: correlations with body-weight are *lower* in growing children, especially in boys, and *disappear completely* in adult males.

The environmental hypothesis is also inconsistent with the following fact. So far as boys are concerned, there is in successive age groups a regular decrease in inbreeding/body-height correlations, followed by a marked rise. Should we therefore say that youngest boys are the least influenced by environmental factors, favorable or unfavorable?

Finally, on the environmental hypothesis, we should suppose that départements with the highest average statures are among the best endowed economically. Calculated for these départements only, correlations between body-height and α–coefficients should decrease abruptly or disappear completely. In fact, it is not so. We chose 29 départements whose body-height averages were the highest: they fall between 170 and 171.7 cm. These départements are widely scattered between the Seine Valley and the eastern or southeastern borders. They are not among the less economically advanced and in spite of the very restricted range of their statural averages, there is still an inbreeding coefficient/body-height correlation: $r = -0.32$. This value is exactly the same as for the whole country.

If for the same selected and relatively privileged départements the correlation is worked out between α–coefficients and the averages of mental test scores, the result ($r = -0.41$) compares well with figures for the country as a whole (from -0.31 to -0.52) and for the Laboratory sample (-0.48). In other words it seems that these correlations are not essentially determined by economic and cultural differences. This seems to be true for mental test scores as well as for statural averages. Of course, this does not preclude some social influence on both. Heritability of body-height and of "tested intelligence" is rather high, but the non-heritable part of their phenotypic variance is far from negligible.

Unfortunately, we can find no reasonable criterion to enable us to assign to each département a socio-economic or cultural score. Therefore, it is impossible to work out partial correlations or to use some more sophisticated statistical device in order to hold constant the socio-economic or cultural level. For the time being, we can only choose some territorial units, more or less similar from a given point of view, and try to find whether correlations with inbreeding coefficients tend to vanish. As we have shown, they have not disappeared, so far.

LITERATURE CITED

Billy, G.   1966   Nouvelles données sur l'évolution contemporaine des dimensions céphaliques. L'Anthropologie, *70:* 238–308.

Giot, P. R., J. L'Helgouach and J. Briard   1956   Données anthropologiques sur les populations du Nord-Ouest de la France; I. Les variations de l'indice céphalique et de la stature. Bull. et Mém. Soc. Anthrop. Paris, 10ᵉ ser., *7:* 309–315.

Montmollin (de) M.   1958   Le niveau intellectuel des recrues du contingent. Population, *13:* 259–268.

———   1959   Le niveau intellectuel des recrues du contingent. Répartition géographique pour certaines professions. Population, *14:* 231–252.

Olivier, G.   1957   Documents anthropométriques sur les conscrits du Nord de la France. Bull. et Mém. Soc. Anthrop. Paris, 10ᵉ sér., *8:* 47–60.

Schreider, E.   1967   Body height and inbreeding in France. Am. J. Phys. Anthrop., *26:* 1–4.

———   1968   L'influence de l'hétérosis sur les variations staturales. L'Anthropologie (in press).

Sutter, J., and J. M. Goux   1962   Evolution de la consanguinité en France de 1926 à 1958 avec des données récentes détaillées. Population, *17:* 683–702.

23. Frederick S. Hulse

Has Mankind a Future?

Our species, which until recently could have been considered a biological success, has perhaps been too successful for its own good. This of course has been the fate of other species in the past: the palaeontogical record shows that most species have become extinct (Simpson 1949). The sabre-tooth felines are alleged by some authorities to have depleted their food-supply and been left with nothing to eat. Elephants in Kenya are said to be destroying the vegetation upon which they subsist more rapidly than it can grow again. I doubt whether our problems are novel. It is, however, emotionally upsetting to find ourselves in the same sort of predicament which has proved fatal to other species. It disturbs our pride to be told that we are not exempt from the laws which regulate biological phenomena. At the same time, among our biological characteristics are the ability to plan for, and the tendency to worry about, the future—even the long-range future. So there is room for hope. Doubtless we will eventually become extinct, but it should be possible to overcome the present ecological crisis which we have so fecklessly brought upon ourselves.

When I went to school, Economics was called the Dismal Science, and indeed so it seemed to be in the early 1930's. Present circumstances might lead us to believe that Ecology is the Dismal Science of the 1970's. It could be. Like economics, it demonstrates that we don't get something for nothing, that living on one's capital eventually results in disaster. Resources are not infinite, nor is the surface of our planet. Any area, whether a pond, a forest, an ocean, or the entire earth, has a limited carrying capacity. The living creatures in an area are mutually dependent upon one another, whether they like it or not. Creatures at an upper level of the food chain cannot, in toto, comprise more than a small percent of the total bulk of creatures at the next lower level. No population can increase its numbers forever, and a population will remain stable only when the birth rate and the death rate are equal (Ehrlich 1967). And as Malthus (1798) pointed out seven generations ago, populations have the ability to increase in numbers geometrically unless some check is imposed.

This is the source of our problem. There are too many of us. Some obvious remedies are at hand, but I do not care to advocate them. A nuclear holocaust might reduce the population quite drastically, for instance. The use of bacteriological warfare would probably be even more effective, as it was—temporarily—when used against rabbits in Australia. Or males could be sterilized by exposure to radio-activity, as has been done to eliminate the screw worm in a number of places. Widespread famine could do a pretty good job of controlling the human population. In some species, overcrowding appears to reduce both the libido and fertility, but there is as yet no suggestion of this among humans. All of these solutions, like the Nazis' attempted final solution of the Jewish problem, fill us with horror. They are not solutions in human terms. Our trouble is that we realize the need to reduce the population but don't want to cause any deaths. Indeed, we are understandably reluctant to impose any new limitations on the freedom of the individual. This is our dilemma. We can be, as unfortunately we have been, completely ruthless in our dealings with other living creatures, but most cultures train us to treat our own kinfolk with more self-restraint. We think of our own species as unique.

Each species, of course, is unique in its relationship to its environment, and in the totality of adaptations which enable it to occupy a certain habitat. But the special ways in which the human species is unique need to be considered when we are dealing with the problems of human ecology. As I mentioned earlier, we are unique in our ability to think about and to predict the future. We are unique in the extent to which we dominate and control our surroundings. We are unique in our ability to invent, and in our dependence upon the use of what we have invented.

The bases of human behaviour are, naturally, biological. We can learn a great deal from studies of non-human ecological communities, and even more from ethology. But we need to use care and caution in extrapolating from the data derived from studying the behaviour of one species in order to make interpretations of the behaviour of another. Interpreting the behaviour of other animals by attributing human motivations to them has been anathematized as anthropomorphism. Are reverse interpretations any more justifiable? The dramatist Robert Ardrey has, in one book (1961), explained all human behaviour as being due to inherited predatory instincts, and, in another book (1966), explained all human behaviour as being due to inherited territorial instincts. We could manage things better if our problems were as simple as that.

In fact, of course, human behaviour is not at all simple. The urges which we certainly share with other animals are modified, rechannelled, or even repressed by culture, an aspect of behaviour that evolved as our genus evolved, to become the most distinguishing trait setting us apart from all other forms of life. Culture has been termed our ecological niche and also called our mode of adaptation. These statements are not in the least contradictory. Forms of behaviour evolved by any species, such as nest-building or tunnel-digging or child care, or courtship displays or living in social groups, become vital parts of the environment to which the species must adapt. Human culture has simply modified the environment in which we live to an enormously greater extent than have the efforts of other creatures. The inevitable result is that all aspects of human behaviour have had to adapt to the culturally modified environment. The human species and human culture have become mutually dependent upon each other: neither could exist alone.

Our biological requirements and our biological characteristics are those of mammals in general and of primates in particular. We are bisexual, homeothermous, four-limbed, inquisitive, milk producing and so on. Yet modifications have evolved in response to the fact that our mode of exploiting environmental resources differs from that of any other primate. These modifications have led to complexities in human behaviour which are not only academically interesting, but which it is vital to analyze and understand if we are to handle our crisis adequately. We are not just naked Apes, or any other sort of Apes. The term "Naked Ape," which Desmond Morris (1967) uses to describe the human race, is not only naive but has implications which are dangerously misleading. An ape, naked or hairy, has ecological relationships which do not resemble, even remotely, those of a human being. Since it is clear that apes are our closest cousins, this is quite extraordinary, and a clear sign that, as Julian Huxley has said, "Man Stands Alone" (1941).

Our method of exploiting resources, our way of making a living, has led to certain emphases in development which form a unique and highly efficient pattern. We have emphasized predation, for instance, just as Ardrey claims, and need not spend most of our waking hours foraging for vegetation as Gorillas do. We have emphasized vertical bipedal posture, and consequently evolved pelves of a most distorted shape. We have emphasized year-round sexual expression and females need not be in oestrus to arouse and be aroused by males. Here Morris is correct: this condition has had profound effects upon social organization. We have emphasized slow growth, delayed maturity, and survival past the years of reproductive ability. Less than half of a healthy female's life span is devoted to child bearing. All of these features may be considered to be species-specific biological traits.

We have emphasized mental flexibility, learning by observation and precept rather than individual experience. Our learning process has been socialized, and we have thus become capable of intelligent cooperation. We have emphasized moral and esthetic judgements in our dealings with each other and with the world around us, so that we deprecate and appreciate as well as simply act. We have emphasized self-consciousness, awareness of our own bodies and our own mental processes. We have emphasized verbal symbolism, the use of language in the true sense which is the most effective form of precise communication. These emphases are not only species-specific in the biological sense, but are cultural characteristics as well. They are not simply spontaneous urges, awaiting the proper releasing mechanism to be expressed, but depend instead upon growing up in the society of other human beings. Culture is most simply defined as that set of behaviours and attitudes which is learned in, shared by, and transmitted from one generation of a society to the next (Linton 1945). It is what permits human activities to have become so complicated, so diverse, so effective that they have profound ecological consequences.

Many ecological consequences flow from the presence in the world of a species with our biological and cultural characteristics. Let us consider, for a moment, the effects of the purely biological traits of humans upon the ecology of an area which they inhabit. We are predacious creatures, whose ancestors long ago began to hunt game, even large game, with great skill and success. Ferocity and ruthlessness are adaptive in hunters, and no doubt were selected for during tens of thousands of generations. But these behavioural characteristics are useful to the species only up to a certain point. If a predatory species becomes too successful, overkill is possible. When we add the cultural capacity to make and use tools to the biological capacity to kill, this danger is enhanced. There is plenty of evidence that even in palæolithic times a number of species were entirely wiped out by human hunters. The ruthless destruction of forests by slash-and-burn horticulturalists is also well attested. But it is self-deceiving to attribute the ecological dangers which result from these practices to our predaciousness. Whales and shrews are equally predatory. These dangers which have accumulated are the results of our *efficiency* at predation.

The evolution of hunting among our early ancestors, in combination with other human biological characteristics, had other results as well. It is quite common for carnivorous mammals to bring food home to the young. Due to our erect posture and the consequent pelvic rearrangements, childbirth is less easy for human females than for most mammals; and this reduces the efficiency of women as hunters. The division of labour between the sexes, which has made more intense exploitation of resources possible, probably came about because of this. Due to our slow growth, children need to be fed and protected for many years. Food sharing between parent and offspring as well as between male and female is a vital necessity. Mutuality and family affection, taken to be signs of virtue, have long been adaptive among humans, just as much as predation, which is so often condemned as a sign of inborn wickedness. Yet they share a common origin and are capable of producing equally disastrous over-exploitation of natural resources.

The ability to stand erect for a long time and to stride bipedally has enhanced still further the biological efficiency of the human body. Our physical abilities are highly diversified. By standing upright we are able to see far. Alone among the genera of the super-family Hominoidea, we swim easily. Alone among all the families of the order Primates, we are able to kick with force and accuracy: a useful ability in unarmed combat. Since our forelimbs need not be used for support, we can throw with speed, force, and precision. I know of no other animals which can approach our ability in this respect; and among our ancestors it must have had a high survival value. And of course we can manipulate with a superb degree of delicacy and precision. All of these abilities have added to our power from a purely biological point of view and have permitted the loss of features which are most useful to even our closest non-human relatives. We no longer require large canines for agonistic display in social relations, for instance. It may be significant that, whereas in apes and monkeys the permanent canines erupt late, after the individual has almost matured, in the human species they erupt earlier in the sequence. A human adult need not feel threatened when he observes the canines of a youngster.

The fact that the human species lacks a breeding season is of course far from unique, although it is unusual for a species of our order. In all probability all the genera of the Hominoidea are alike in this respect, but Homo is the only genus which lives outside of tropical forests. That we have retained the habit of breeding the year round, and consequently of producing children at any season, is perhaps a symbol of our effectiveness in dealing with all sorts of environmental hazards. At the same time it does tend to promote the stability of social units within our species: food sharing is a constant rather than an intermittent necessity. Males are aware of their masculinity, and females of their femininity at all times, which aids in their habituation to the roles which they play. The habit of cooperation within a band or community is re-enforced. The ecological importance of sexual expression throughout the year is that this is one more factor leading to greater efficiency in the exploitation of resources. Not only do we lack a breeding season, but from the time of pubescence onward, males and females alike are as easily aroused, sexually, on any day of the month as on any other day. Human females do not come into heat only when they are approaching their most fertile period: this is in marked contrast to the situation found among our primate relatives, as well as many if not most other animals. Nor do human males feel the urge to mate only when in the presence of females who give overt signs of being fertile. Consequently the rules and standards concerning sexual behaviour in our species, although they vary enormously from culture to culture, are all based on the assumption that copulation is just as likely on any one day as on any other day of the month. The oestrual cycle which regulates the sexual behaviour of members of other species vanished, in ours, at some time long ago: this, too, has promoted the social cohesion which is one of the main bases of our species' unprecedented degree of power.

However, perhaps the most significant characteristic of the human stock, from the point of view of ecology, is the lengthening of the growth period. This is an evolutionary novelty which has facilitated the ability of human beings to learn. In consequence, we have become more and more dependent upon learning, and less and less upon inborn, spontaneous reactions. With more free (because protected) time at our disposal, the opportunity to learn a great deal is available. The utility of intelligence to members of a species is always a relative thing: other abilities may be more vital. Even among creatures as clever—from the anthropocentric viewpoint—as chimpanzees, large teeth and strong jaw muscles have a greater adaptive significance than big brains do. Since the skull vault serves to encase the brain as well as being the point of origin of the jaw muscles, there is contradiction here during the growth period. Our brains increase in volume, during growth, twice as much as do those of apes: apparently, if we are to learn to behave like human beings, this is a necessary modification. Spending many years in the process of learning has had enough survival value to *homo sapiens* to counteract the troubles which accompany a prolonged growth period. We have become able to engage in constant, intelligently planned cooperative endeavours. We have increased our awareness and comprehension of our surroundings. We have attained the capacity of exploiting our environment with long-range benefits in mind. We have evolved into very efficient animals indeed. This leads us to the point where it is time to consider the ecological consequences that flow from our cultural characteristics.

What is learned by one generation, whether it be true or false, or simply irrelevant, can be transmitted to the next by teaching. What is learned in one part of the world can be taught in another. Intelligent rather than stereotyped cooperation is a characteristic of culture, and provides us with much more flexibility in the face of new situations than any other creature can manage. Conscious self-restraint is a closely allied characteristic. Both of these tend to enhance still further our power to exploit resources efficiently; and to alter our environment according to plan. Beavers, of course, alter the landscape by building dams, digging canals, and cutting down trees. We do far more: we build bridges, irrigate deserts, bore tunnels, and in general rearrange the landscape to suit our fancy. All of these accomplishments require the skilled cooperation of large numbers of people, who are motivated by the anticipation of future rewards. The development of technology, which has given us this power, is an aspect of the development of culture.

An immediate result of greater efficiency—better adaptation if you will—is an increase in population. Since the dawn of recorded history, less than three hundred generations ago, the human population has increased perhaps a hundredfold. The quantity of protoplasm contained in the bodies of human beings exceeds that which is contained in the bodies of the members of any other one species. By now it is at least 150 million tons. This has caused a drastic rearrangement of the ecological balance, and is undoubtedly a drain upon the resources of the planet. It has also, of course, led to total dependence, by the human race, upon the artifacts devised by culture. We have created a new environment for ourselves, and continuing natural selection has begun to lead to adaptations useful for life in this new environment. It is not unreasonable to guess that by now we may have become biologically adapted to the situation in which our ancestors found themselves ten thousand years ago, at about the time that some plants began to be cultivated.

One of the most important aspects of culture is social organization, complete with formalized statuses and roles, obligations and expectations, kinship terms and divisions of labor. This is justified on ethical grounds, not just learned by experience. Casual aggression, whether innate as Lorenz (1966) believes or not, takes place not infrequently between individuals of non-human species. Group aggression within a species, although much less common, is also well documented. Organized warfare, however, is a purely cultural phenomenon, depending upon the existence of formally organized societies, upon ethical justification, and upon intelligent, planned cooperation. Warfare, which plagues us so much today, does not depend upon aggressive instincts as is so widely and understandably believed. The actual physical combats which take place during warfare require the arousal of aggressive feelings which have been taught by societies to their members. But warfare itself is a social institution, a formalized technique for settling disputes. Like other social institutions, it has changed and evolved over the centuries, is understood in different ways by different cultures, and is practiced in accordance with varied ethical standards and for varied purposes, depending upon the beliefs of the peoples concerned. Consequently, like other social institutions, it can be changed or even abolished, and doubtless will be in time if the ecological crisis which we now face has not overwhelmed us first. The waste of resources, the intentional destruction of resources, the neglect of efforts at conservation and prevention of pollution which results from the practice of warfare boggle the imagination. The deep seated suspicion which societies engaged in warfare feel for each other prevent the sorts of international efforts which are vital to avert ecological disaster. Entirely aside from the agony caused by warfare, it is one of the major hazards which we face. It is about as adaptive, today, as were the oversized antlers of the Irish Elk, which became extinct.

Another aspect of culture which is pertinent to the study of ecology is the development of ethical and esthetic standards and judgements. Child-rearing practices in all societies include the teaching of standards and mythology so that the young may learn not only how to behave, but why they ought to behave. The rough and tumble encounters which teach a youthful baboon or chimpanzee his manners are not eliminated from the human experience, but they are supplemented by positive instruction. We constantly judge things, people, and events in terms of good and bad, beautiful and ugly. In all cultures, the feelings which people have about such matters provide the ideological bases for the sort of social structure which they will accept, and the justification for actions which they will undertake. Cultures differ in their judgements to be sure, but judgements are made. Mutual sympathy, human kindness, a sense of duty actually exist, and have influenced the manner in which resources have been exploited. Ecologically, these imponderables have had varied results. Species which in their homeland formed part of a natural ecological community have been introduced, for sentimental reasons, into new areas where they became pests. Land has been over-cultivated and ruined by farmers intent on feeding families. Forest clearings have provided excellent breeding grounds for mosquitoes which spread malaria (Livingstone 1958). The inertia of tradition has prevented the adoption of conservation practices. Sympathy for human suffering has led to the introduction of life-saving drugs, widening the gap between the birth-rate and the death-rate, and thus accelerating the speed of the population explosion. Religious tabus in some areas, a sense of obligation to the family life in others, simple love of babies or innocent pride in virility have inhibited the application of birth control methods. In contrast to these dismal results of kindness and virtue, it must be said that it is possible to appeal for action against pollution, against overcrowding, against destructive practices, on moral and esthetic grounds. People may well respond to such an appeal more readily than to an appeal couched in terms of immediate self-interest, which is likely to sound unconvincing.

The development of self-consciousness has also, interestingly enough, had ecological consequences. Each of us observes himself, his own condition and circumstances in contrast to that of others. Ambition becomes possible, as of course does vanity. Human beings are not content to live like other animals. We have been hearing a great deal, lately, about the "Revolution of Expectations" but this is really nothing new. To desire, and to strive for, greater comfort, greater prosperity, greater beauty or greater distinction is expectable in all cultures. Therefore it is standard practice for human beings to exploit their environment for more than food alone. Bodily ornamentation has been practiced since at least the Upper Palaeolithic, more than a thousand generations ago, as cave paintings demonstrate. Bodily covering, at least to protect against frigid weather, seems to have been in use much earlier, and this required the use of animal skins. Fire was used at least half a million years ago, in the cave at Chou-ko-tien and perhaps on the French Riviera, and this requires fuel—until recently wood much more often than not. All the larger apes make nests in which to sleep: with the advent of human technology, more complicated shelters began to be constructed. These require the use of still more materials obtained from the environment. As the standard of living rises, an even greater drain is made upon irreplaceable resources. Fossil fuels began to come into common use a few generations ago. There is only a limited supply, and the rate of consumption rises constantly. In the meantime, the atmosphere becomes polluted with smog. Indeed, in the opinion of some scientists, the amount of carbon dioxide in the air has already begun to change the climate of the whole world. This might have a great variety of interesing consequences.

A few thousand years ago, the cultivation of crops began. Improvements in the efficiency of agriculture have accumulated ever since, and each improvement has had, as a by-product, some effect upon the balance of nature. Many feet of top soil have been flushed down the drain of the Mississippi River into the Gulf of Mexico. Enormous fields have been planted to a single crop, giving wonderful opportunities for population explosions of species, other than man, which find them good to eat. We call our competitors pests, or varmints, and apply enormous amounts of poisons (often in a most reckless fashion) for the protection of "our" crops. The results have begun to be obviously disastrous, as Rachel Carson (1962) has pointed out. A universal consequence of food-production is the increase of population within the area concerned. People become more crowded together, facilitating the transmission of infectious disease. Human waste becomes a hazard to health, and gastrointestinal disorders become common. Only recently have public sanitation measures become at all adequate to deal with this self-imposed problem. And of course, since sanitation has improved, fewer children die and the crowding becomes accentuated.

Only a couple of hundred years ago, after the invention of the steam-engine, did enough energy become available for the large scale production of all sorts of material goods. Naturally this has led to a still more rapid increase in the crowding of the planet. Not only that, it has led to concentrations of population in urban areas to an unprecedented extent. There are probably more human beings in Tokyo today than there were in the entire world a thousand generations ago.

This is alleged to be convenient for the operation of factories, which does not mean that it is convenient for the human beings involved. Resources are being consumed, the landscape is being rearranged, the ecological balance is being upset, more and more rapidly, drastically and disastrously than ever before.

The final aspect of culture which seems to have profound ecological significance, and which I will mention, is the use of (and the dependence upon the use of) language in human societies. This has many ramifications. In the first place, of course, it permits precise communication between individuals who speak the same language. Information rather than the emotional states can be transmitted. The future as well as the present, the non-existent as well as the actual, can be spoken about. The ability to plan, of which I have already spoken, is enormously facilitated by the use of language. All of these things add to the power of humans in contrast to other animals; it is this power, of course, which is so potentially hazardous to the ecological balance. At the same time, and as an inevitable corollary of the basic characteristics of languages, we are uniquely capable of lying. It is as easy to say "The moon is made of green cheese" as to say "The moon is a globe 2,000 miles in diameter." Many animals may use deceptive movements to fool each other: we can deceive ourselves. Myths, fictions, and flattery are among the most common uses of language. Sometimes these serve as morale boosters, sometimes as outlets from frustrations, sometimes as useful stimulants to the imagination, sometimes as amusing pastimes. But sometimes they lead to catastrophe, to fatal misconceptions about the nature of a situation. This fact can have ecological consequences too: substances labelled "Pesticide" are likely to be used more recklessly than were they labelled "Poison," for instance.

The ability to use and to understand language is an inherited species-specific characteristic. But the actual languages spoken have to be learned—they number in the hundreds, and of course they all change as time goes by. They are of many diverse structures, and guide the thoughts of their users into varied channels. The myth of the Tower of Babel suggests some of the difficulties which are caused by this fact. The difficulties of translation from one language into another are well known, but it is necessary to be reminded of them. Scientists are fooled just as readily as other people by verbal misunderstandings; and international cooperation is often impeded. Even within a given speech-community, the meaning attached to a word or phrase may vary from person to person. My grandmother, for instance, considered the word "leg" to be obscene. Quite irrelevant hostilities are often aroused in consequence, and cooperative endeavours are rendered less effective or totally ineffective. Words are the repositories of tradition, and convey emotion as well as meaning: this often impedes the acceptance of new techniques and makes it more difficult to deal with new hazards and opportunities. All of these things influence the way in which we relate ourselves to our environment, and are therefore an important aspect of human ecology.

The problems involved in studying the human species in its relation to the world which it inhabits are most complex. The solution of the problems which our past activities have brought upon us is bound to prove even more complex. Our power, and the tremendous increase in numbers which has resulted from our power, have forced us into a real dilemma. All past social actions have had unforeseen results. Acts of virtue have led to disaster as frequently as have acts of vice. Inventions which add to our comfort all too often have lethal by-products. Acts which are individually unobjectionable, like driving an automobile, become dangerous in the mass. We will unquestionably have to sacrifice much that we value if we are to solve the ecological crisis. Any measures undertaken to alleviate the situation are bound to meet with suspicion and often violent resistance. No one likes to accept the idea that there are too many people. Proposals to promote birth control are denounced as genocide. Proposals to reduce smog and pollution are denounced as infringements upon our liberty. Proposals to control the over-exploitation of resources are denounced as sentimental.

Yet the cultural history of mankind shows that societies have changed, that people are perfectly capable of learning, that feelings of responsibility to others are among our personality characteristics and can be appealed to with success. It also shows that guidance and persuasion work more smoothly than force. The imposition of drastic measures in an arbitrary manner by "those who know best" may seem to provide quick solutions. But in fact they are quack solutions. They evoke resistance, evasion and subterfuge. Even though the time available to us before catastrophe strikes is short, informed consent is required if measures to avert catastrophe are to be workable. The effort can succeed.

LITERATURE CITED

Ardrey, Robert   1961   African Genesis, Collins, London
———   1966   The Territorial Imperative, Atheneum, New York
Carson, Rachel   1962   Silent Spring, Fawcett, Greenwich
Ehrlich, Paul   1967   The Population Bomb, Ballantine, New York
Huxley, Julian   1941   Man Stands Alone, Harper and Sons, New York
Linton, Ralph   1945   The Cultural Background of Personality, Appleton, Century, New York
Livingstone, Frank B.   1958   Anthropological Implications of Sickle Cell Gene Distribution in West Africa, *American Anthropologist,* Vol. 60, pp. 533–62
Lorenz, Konrad   1966   On Aggression, Methuen, London
Malthus, T. R.   1798   Essay on the Principle of Population, London
Morris, Desmond   1967   The Naked Ape, Cape, London
Simpson, G. G.   1949   The Meaning of Evolution, Yale University Press, New Haven

About the Author

Frederick S. Hulse is Professor of Anthropology at the University of Arizona and a member of the National Academy of Sciences. Extensive field work has taken him to Cuba, England, Finland, Greece, Hawaii, Israel, Japan, Mexico, Spain, and Switzerland. In all his research, he has attempted to uncover the effects of social and cultural aspects of environment upon human physique and gene frequencies.

He has been President of the American Association of Physical Anthropologists, Associate Editor of the *American Anthropologist,* and Editor of the *American Journal of Physical Anthropology*. In addition, he represented the United States as a Vice President of the VIII International Congress of Anthropological and Ethnological Sciences at Tokyo in 1968.

He has frequently contributed articles to the *American Journal of Physical Anthropology,* the *Southwestern Journal of Anthropology, American Anthropologist,* and *Eugenics Quarterly*.